ECOLOGICAL BY DESIGN

ECOLOGICAL BY DESIGN

A HISTORY FROM SCANDINAVIA

KJETIL FALLAN

THE MIT PRESS
CAMBRIDGE, MASSACHUSETTS
LONDON, ENGLAND

© 2022 Massachusetts Institute of Technology

All rights reserved. No part of this book may be reproduced in any form by any electronic or mechanical means (including photocopying, recording, or information storage and retrieval) without permission in writing from the publisher.

The MIT Press would like to thank the anonymous peer reviewers who provided comments on drafts of this book. The generous work of academic experts is essential for establishing the authority and quality of our publications. We acknowledge with gratitude the contributions of these otherwise uncredited readers.

This book was set in Arnhem Pro and Frank New by Westchester Publishing Services. Printed and bound in the United States of America.

Library of Congress Cataloging-in-Publication Data is available.

ISBN: 978-0-262-04713-5

10　9　8　7　6　5　4　3　2　1

CONTENTS

ACKNOWLEDGMENTS   (vii)

INTRODUCTION   (1)

1   DISPOSABLE DESIGN: FROM THROWAWAYISM TO ENVIRONMENTALISM   (25)

2   NORWEGIAN WOOD: MATERIAL SYSTEMS OF THOUGHT   (61)

3   WE ARE THE WORLD: ECOLOGICAL DESIGN FOR DEVELOPMENT   (97)

4   DEMO! THE ECOPOLITICS OF DESIGN ACTIVISM   (143)

5   DEEP GREEN: PHILOSOPHICAL TOOLS   (185)

6   TURBULENT TIMES: ALTERNATIVE ENERGY FROM EXPERIMENT TO ENTERPRISE   (229)

CODA: ASPEN COMES TO SCANDINAVIA   (259)

NOTES   (275)
BIBLIOGRAPHY   (319)
INDEX   (337)

ACKNOWLEDGMENTS

This book grew out of the research project Back to the Sustainable Future: Visions of Sustainability in the History of Design which I directed from 2014 to 2018. Funded by the Research Council of Norway and generously supported by my employer, the University of Oslo, this project provided a highly stimulating environment in which to work on this book and related research. I am particularly indebted to my former PhD students Gabriele Oropallo (died October 2021), Ingrid Halland, Ida K. Lie, and Malin Graesse, who made this project such a unique experience in collective curiosity and lateral learning. Thanks are due also to Peder Valle for providing valuable research assistance in the early phases. I am grateful to the Design History Society for awarding me its Research Publication Grant for 2022.

Substantial parts of this book were written during my sabbatical in the academic year 2018–2019, which I spent as a visiting researcher at the University of California, Davis. Made possible by a Fulbright fellowship and additional funding from RCN and the Career Development Program at the University of Oslo's Faculty of Humanities, the Californian sojourn was greatly enriched by the company of and stimulating conversations with my UC Davis colleagues, especially Christina Cogdell, Simon Sadler, and Jim Housefield.

Taking shape over the course of many years, material making up this book has been presented at a range of events in Giessen, Chicago, Kolding, Helsinki, Stavanger, Oslo, Davis, New York, Newcastle, Mexico City, Milan, Moscow, Basel, and Bologna. I am grateful to the organizers of these events for allowing me to discuss work in progress and to the audiences for valuable feedback. In less formal settings, I have benefited tremendously from exchanges with esteemed colleagues near and far, including Peder Anker, Larry Busbea, Greg Castillo, Mads Nygaard Folkmann, Elena Formia, Maria Göransdotter, Denise Hagströmer, Rebecca Houze, DJ Huppatz, Hans-Christian Jensen, Dolly Jørgensen, Finn Arne Jørgensen, Grace Lees-Maffei, Sarah Lichtman, Tania Messell, Anders Munch, Monica Obniski, Tim Stott, Bobbye Tigerman, Even Smith Wergeland, Christina Zetterlund, Carl Zimring, and many more.

This book could not have been written without access to archival materials and collections at a number of institutions, including the University of Oslo's Humanities and Social Sciences Library, the National Library of Norway, the National Museum's Library and Archive, the National Archives of Norway, Design Museum Denmark, Konstfack College of Arts, Crafts and Design, the Swedish Society of Crafts and Design, Moderna Museet, the University of Brighton Design Archives, San Francisco State University, the Peter J. Shields Library, and the University of California Libraries. Archival material is not always institutionalized, however. Ane Vedel and Karen Vedel kindly allowed me to study Kristian Vedel's personal archive, generously giving of their time and knowledge. The late Ulla Tarras-Wahlberg Bøe trusted me with papers collected by herself and her late husband Alf Bøe. Many time witnesses have shared their recollections of the period and events discussed in this book, including Nils Faarlund, Sultan Somjee, Amrik Kalsi, Eva Trolin, Varis Bokalders, and Maria Benktzon.

Moving from researching and writing the book to publishing it, I would like to thank Victoria Hindley at the MIT Press for believing in and refining the project and Gabriela Bueno Gibbs for shepherding it. The three anonymous reviewers deserve my praise and recognition for their time and effort, as well as for their insightful comments and sage advice. Finally, I owe my most heartfelt gratitude to Miriam Ardiles Fallan, my cherished partner in this complex design project called life, and to our children, Ulrik and Alma, for directing a historian's gaze toward the future—parenthood significantly changed my view of how design matters. This is for you.

INTRODUCTION

How did the two words "ecological design" become entangled? And what do the intrinsically global phenomena of environmental crisis and modern design culture look like from the edge of the earth? These questions form the driving force of this book, which explores the making of ecological design in a globally situated Scandinavia in the late 1960s and 1970s. In so doing, it provides a much-needed historical understanding of what is arguably the most significant development in design culture since the industrial revolution: the quest for a more sustainable future. This imperative permeates all aspects of contemporary design discourse, from research and education to professional practice and popular media—but its historical emergence remains virtually uncharted. *Ecological by Design* addresses this lacuna by examining ecological design in its making during the era of popular environmentalism and what is often referred to as the "crisis" of modernism.

The Scandinavian countries are widely considered pioneering societies in the shift toward a more sustainable future. Scandinavia is also widely acclaimed for its design culture. Rarely, however, have these two understandings been considered together. This book is the first to examine how they are deeply entangled in surprising and significant ways, thus comprising a novel history of the emergence of what is now known as ecological design. Scandinavia's image as a driving force in environmentalism and sustainable development makes an easy target, of course—there are plenty of beams in the eyes of Scandinavian politicians, planners, manufacturers, designers, and consumers—but it isn't entirely unwarranted either. The region proved a fertile soil for political activism, counterculture, and the modern environmental movement, and is home to the world's first Environmental Protection

Agency (Sweden, 1967) as well as the world's first Ministry of Environmental Protection (Norway, 1972; Denmark, 1971/1973). This is not to argue for any sort of regional exceptionalism, but to establish a distinct and productive perspective. The study might set out from a specific geography, but it is by no means isolationist in its outlook. Reflecting the global nature both of the environmental crisis and of modern design culture, this book's case studies are consistently placed in an international context, resulting in a narrative that ventures far beyond the shores of Scandinavia, tracing key connections to continental Europe, Britain, the western United States, Central America, and East Africa.

A second disclaimer of sorts is that this is not a heroic history. If read cynically, it could on the contrary seem a history of fringes and failures. The history of Scandinavian design is no less riddled with unsustainable products, practices, and policies than is any other design history. It remains a (sad) fact that the history of ecological design is not a history of mainstream design, and Scandinavian designers and critics were not necessarily any more environmentally concerned than their brethren elsewhere. It is of vital importance to recognize the "dark side" in order to challenge the prevalent portrayal of design as an intrinsically benevolent force.[1] Just as Melvin Kranzberg declared of technology, design "is neither good nor bad; nor is it neutral."[2] Therefore, environmental histories of design should comprise narratives of unsustainability as well as of sustainability. Within this broader field, histories of ecological design will tend to emphasize actors, institutions, and ideas that sought to align design with environmentalism—but the discourses produced by and around these nodes will still acknowledge the ambivalent position design holds in both making and unmaking the environment.[3]

Brian Eno's notion of the "Big Here" and the "Long Now" might elucidate the broader relevance of focusing on a specific place and time. Contemplating a "Big Here" connects Scandinavia with the rest of the world, and invoking a "Long Now" includes the past (and the future) in the present, thus expanding our sense of empathy, relevance, and responsibility beyond this small region and this short period in time.[4] It is no coincidence, though, that a history of ecological design emphasizes the late 1960s and the 1970s. As Finn Arne Jørgensen and I have argued, this period commands attention because it represents "a moment in time when concerns over environmental destruction went mainstream and the crisis of modernity prompted comprehensive soul-searching by design professionals of all kinds. The centrality of this specific period is thus also evidence of how we are historicizing our contemporary concerns—as every society does—at a time when the environmental crisis seems more urgent than ever before."[5] "There is virtually no theme, practice, or technological advance being addressed today that was not discussed at length at the end of the 1960s and the beginning of the next decade," writes Larry Busbea.[6] Similarly, Daniel Belgrad argues that the period's intellectual climate offered a sense of hope and agency that resonates particularly well with us today: "In the seventies, ecological thinking took on widespread significance because it offered a new way of understanding how to go about changing society for the better."[7] But before delving into the archives, this introduction will pan out and provide a broader context for the historically and geographically grounded narrative that follows, showing how so many of the key issues discussed in this book remain at the forefront of design and environmental discourse even today. Activism, reform movements, social change, consumption, capitalism, biodiversity, natural resources, environmental justice, colonialism, and so on are not particularistic concerns, but deeply entangled both in space and time and of vital importance to any history of ecological design as well as to contemporary design culture.

A QUESTION OF CHANGE

Design changes everything.[8] Or so we are conditioned to believe. From the socialist utopias of nineteenth-century reform movements, via the scientistic "problem-solving" of modernism, to contemporary mirages of sustainable development and "massive change,"[9] the agency instilled in design has often carried a certain hubris. In his critique of this hubristic heritage, Simon Sadler showcases alternative registers of imagining transformation that may be more promising, or at least more sympathetic. But no matter the scale or the agenda, change remains at the heart of the matter: "I propose that design necessarily 'imagines' the situation in which it operates—that in setting out to make things and change things, designers (whether amateur or by vocation, singly or collectively) assume or create mental models of the environment in which they will work."[10] Design's capacity to produce change is of course not necessarily a good thing. Since the industrial revolution, design has done more to harm Earth's ecosystems than to heal them.

Identifying environmental challenges as a particularly important area for historical scholarship, Jo Guldi and David Armitage argue that historical case studies "from the deep or recent past alike can point to alternative traditions in governance, collecting and describing the fringe movements of the past that are bearing useful fruit today."[11] From a design history perspective, their claim chimes exceedingly well with the field's longstanding engagement with precisely such traditions and movements, the full value of which often has been appreciated only significantly later. These types of historical narratives, they continue, "perform an important role: they are energising of new movements; they give scientists and policy-makers on the ground a sense of where to look for possible futures."[12] In this manner, by studying past examples of actors, events, and movements working to—explicitly or implicitly—reduce, mitigate, or revert environmental problems, design history can contribute to the forging of more resilient futures.

Design reform movements have long formed a staple of design historical research, and none more so than the arts and crafts movement. These histories tend to be tales of artists and craftsmen who—revolting against the social, cultural, ethical, and aesthetic corollaries of industrialization—moved from the city to the country to set up collective workshops where life and work would be one, producing quality artistic goods inspired by premodern communal practices and the beauty of nature. As such, established design historical narratives of the arts and crafts movement have largely cast its relationship with nature and the environment as one of creative inspiration and social critique rather than in ecological terms.[13] However, as Anne Massey and Paul Micklethwaite point out, there is much about the arts and crafts movement that could warrant a rereading of its ideological underpinnings in the light of subsequently escalating concerns for design's more troublesome entanglements with nature and the environment.[14] Key figures wrote at length, and with ardor, about their observations of the defilement of nature caused by industrial manufacture and urbanization. John Ruskin did not limit his castigation of industrial society to its pollution of the environment and defilement of natural beauty by way of its end products; he was equally eager to point out the detrimental effects of modern manufacturing processes in terms of the depletion of natural, material, and human resources alike.

Similarly, William Morris took a broad view of the environmental ramifications of industrial society. This is particularly evident in his fiction writing, nowhere as poignantly as in his 1890 novel *News from Nowhere*, a utopian tale of a future (twenty-first-century) society where all the ills of capitalism have been healed and industrialization has been reversed. Often considered an early example of "eco-fiction," the book depicts a pastoral paradise where all labor is of love; profit and private property are unknown concepts; and all pollution, from production and products alike, is a thing of the past, as people live in symbiotic harmony with nature. Rivers, fields, and forests are pristine and opulent, yet considered "gardens" for human recreation and consumption. Industrial cities like Manchester have disappeared without a trace.[15] Morris's aversion to dirty factories, cheap trinkets, speculative capitalism, and other trappings of industrialism is of course well known and also duly noted in design history. Surprisingly, though, design historians have been slow to relate these aspects of arts and crafts ideology explicitly to issues of ecology and environmentalism.

Casting Morris as a proto-environmentalist is not entirely unproblematic, of course. But the "green" strand of arts and crafts ideology has an intriguing legacy also in later episodes in the history of ecological design. In the 1970s, initiatives as different as the Italian Global Tools collective and the British alternative technology movement paid homage to Morris and the arts and crafts movement.[16] Even the broader environmental movement embraced these Victorian design reformers as pioneers and kindred spirits. An evocative example of this infatuation is Nicholas Gould's feature on Morris, chosen as the cover story of the July 1974 issue of *The Ecologist*—the environmental movement's premier periodical. The cover design included both his portrait and one of his characteristic floral patterns. The article claimed that "his voice was one of the first to be raised against the environmental effects of industrialization" and quoted forceful statements by Morris. *The Ecologist* clearly found Morris's environmentalist concerns to be even more pressing in the 1970s than they had been in his own time: "The rape of the English countryside has advanced so far since Morris' day that it comes as a surprise to find how often he echoes our own complaints." Ultimately, though, Morris was to be lauded for practicing what he preached, wrote Gould, finding in his example the proof that it is possible to be a pragmatic idealist.[17]

It was of course his proclivity to imagine design otherwise, to envision a path toward a more symbiotic relationship between humans and nature—to *change*—that made Morris such a fascinating figure to environmentalists and counterculturalists of the 1970s. The timeframe covered by this book saw a rising public awareness of ecological principles along with the rapid expansion of the environmental movement's reach and role in public discourse. This coincided with a development in design culture that profoundly questioned design's integration with capitalism, industrial production, and consumer society, resulting in the emergence of related responses such as anti-design, ecodesign, and design activism. A common denominator for both these trajectories is the broader notion of counterculture, which encompassed a broad spectrum of insurgent ideologies and activities, yet was coherent enough to make up a significant social and political force. Historians of technology, environment, and design alike are taking an interest in this countercultural moment/movement, where established knowledge, structures, and practices were challenged and alternative models were sought.

The caricature of the Californian hippie has become hegemonic in most imaginaries of counterculture, far beyond its US origins. And not without reason. Both the mythical figure and the movement that spawned it have proved enormously influential, also on design historical scholarship. This study is no exception: through travels, networks, and mediations, the makers of Scandinavian ecodesign crossed paths with many familiar figures and collectives emanating from the vibrant communities in the San Francisco Bay Area and beyond. And as we shall see in chapter 4, these transcultural encounters were not always harmonious. The reason was often, as became abundantly clear when countercultural entrepreneur and *Whole Earth Catalog* editor Stewart Brand and the Hog Farm collective descended on the United Nations Conference on the Human Environment in Stockholm in June 1972, that their Scandinavian counterparts were overtly political in their battle to change the world. Young Scandinavian designers eager to make themselves "useful to society" did not buy into the notion that they could save the world one mail-ordered "tool" or makeshift tin-can radio at a time; they believed in grassroots activism, collective responsibility, and political engagement. Their political radicalism reached a zenith at "People and the Environment II" (Menneske og miljø II), the final seminar organized by the short-lived Scandinavian Design Students' Organization (SDO) at the School of Arts and Crafts in Copenhagen in the summer of 1969, where Victor Papanek—designer of the infamous tin-can radio mentioned above—watched to his great frustration as the organization he had followed closely since its inception two years prior "imploded under the yoke of its own radical design activism."[18] Graphic designer Terje Roalkvam and a delegation from Oslo's National College of Applied Art and Craft drove down to Copenhagen to attend the seminar in a van adorned with a billboard designed by Per Kleiva proclaiming that "The revolution has started, come along!"[19] Two years later, Kleiva—a driving force in the radical artist collective GRAS (*grass*)—produced the serial print *American Butterflies* (figure 0.1), a work that castigated the

0.1

Per Kleiva, *American Butterflies*, 1971.
© Per Kleiva/BONO 2021. Photo courtesy of the National Museum of Art, Architecture, and Design.

US ecocide in Vietnam just as vehemently as Sweden's Prime Minister Olof Palme would do from the podium at the UN conference in Stockholm the following year. And five years after the revolution road trip to Copenhagen, Roalkvam designed the *Oil or Fish?* poster depicted in figure 0.3.

Despite Brand's lukewarm Scandinavian welcome, the *Whole Earth Catalog* and what it represented remains a significant reference point. Pointing again to the centrality of change, Sadler observes that "the *Whole Earth Catalog* was one of those rare instances of design's operating environment rendered (somewhat) explicit, allowing its users to debate what in our relationship to nature can and cannot be changed."[20] In its very essence, as revealed by the *Catalog*'s subtitle, the project was about navigating and managing that change by giving people "access to tools"—both intellectual and practical. Andrew Kirk has shown how it conceived and promulgated a brand of environmentalism that was less about conservation of nature, anti-industrialism, or political lobbying, and more about harnessing technology for creative, subversive, sustainable use and living.[21] This type of hands-on attitude can be seen as a variety of design activism in its own right, but Kirk goes further, showing how Brand and his associates were instrumental in propagating the alternative technology movement in the US, as well as in formulating what would soon be known as ecological design. What makes the counterculture of the late 1960s and 1970s, in all its locales and permutations, such fruitful material for design historians looking for an objective—a societal purpose—for their work is the strong expression of discontent, the palpable sense of urgency, and the remarkable capacity for imagining and experimenting with alternative modes of thinking, acting, and organizing. At the risk of stating the obvious, these ideas and values have not diminished in relevance. Studying their history and how they materialized in activist practices of design might serve to revitalize them at a time witnessing the emergence of a new design culture of discontent.

A QUESTION OF RESOURCES

Design is garbage. Or, perhaps more precisely, design generates garbage—inconceivable amounts of garbage. It might take a while before your heirloom silverware or your treasured easy chair ends up on the landfill, but they will eventually. "Waste is every object, plus time."[22] The real impact, however, comes from the vast majority of objects, from plastic cups to cars, which are discarded and replaced at

such a pace and in such quantities that the environmental degradation caused by their production, distribution, consumption, and disposal can only be marginally mitigated by shifting to more benign materials and processes (figure 0.2). As we shall see, especially in chapter 1, these problems began to occupy design professionals and environmentalists a great deal from the mid-1960s on, and continue to do so today. Across all scales and levels of abstraction, design is implicit in the creation of waste. From the nuclear or coal-fired power plants that feed our endless appetite for energy (see chapter 6), via the economic systems and infrastructures that make

0.2

Landfill operation at Jamaica Bay, New York. Photograph by Arthur Tress in May 1973 as part of DOCUMERICA: The Environmental Protection Agency's Program to Photographically Document Subjects of Environmental Concern. U.S. National Archives and Records Administration (NARA record: 1100153).

your new hairbrush cross half the world on an oil-burning ship to reach you, to the communication platforms that mediate our desire for ever more things, design is involved every step of the way. But even though, in the words of Ben Highmore, "it is hard not to see global warming and climate change as a consequence of a variety of design processes, design values and design products,"[23] these problematic aspects of design are rarely made the object of design history.

If design historians have been reluctant to treat design as garbage, this corollary to the usual gospel of design as a beneficial force underpins some interesting developments in the realm of design theory and methodology. But true to the problem-solving ethos of the profession, the focus has largely been to develop models and methods for how design can contribute to leaner production and cleaner consumption. The best-known exponent for this type of thinking, the Cradle to Cradle (C2C) framework developed—and trademarked—by William McDonough and Michael Braungart, is a prime example of the positivistic approach to design as a technofix capable of solving environmental problems caused by conventional manufacturing. Waste and wastefulness can be designed away, they have argued ever since the framework's inception as the Hannover Principles, drafted in 1991: "'Eliminate the concept of waste'—not reduce, minimize, or avoid waste, as environmentalists were then propounding, but eliminate the very concept, by design."[24] According to this logic, in which the waste of one product or process becomes the "food" of another, there are, at least in theory, no limits to growth. One can easily understand the appeal this bright outlook has to industry, especially after C2C also became a certification system providing commercial actors with an economic incentive to distinguish products as "eco-friendly." Recently, however, C2C has been criticized, e.g., for its blind faith in growth and for ignoring key aspects of products' environmental impact, especially during use and transportation.[25]

If there are good reasons for the (utopian) attempts at eliminating waste from (and by) design practice, there are equally good reasons for *not* eliminating waste from design history. First, histories of "dirty design" are needed to balance out the bias toward an understanding of design as intrinsically "good" in most current scholarship.[26] To fully grasp the environmental impact of design—past, present, and future—requires us to acknowledge that the history of design is, perhaps more than anything, a history of waste and wastefulness, of unsustainability.[27] Second, rethinking the history of design in this way will strengthen the knowledge base for the type of redirective initiatives exemplified by C2C, allowing such necessarily flawed attempts to "fail better" in the future. From R. Buckminster Fuller's "comprehensive design science" via the Brundtland Report's definition of "sustainable development" to today's ecomodernism, the belief that "scientific and technological progress will entail environmental benefits through increased resource efficiency" has paired environmental concerns with an emphasis on design for efficient use of resources.[28] Whether waste is considered residual, something unwanted to be reduced or eliminated through clever designs and manufacturing processes, or something of potential intrinsic value that can be reused, repurposed, or recycled, the moral economy of waste constitutes an important, albeit underexplored, topic in the history of design.

The broader public awareness of basic ecological principles and the onset of the environmental movement in the 1960s and 1970s led to a significant change in the perception of waste and garbage, at least in the affluent parts of the world, with large-scale investments in increased and improved recycling systems and containment technologies.[29] Granted, even the most advanced and successful recycling systems today are nowhere near closing the loop of our manufacturing and consumption infrastructures—but that does not mean the efforts are in vain. Although comprehensive, governmentally controlled recycling systems explicitly motivated by environmental concerns are a relatively recent phenomenon, practices of recycling, repurposing, and reuse of course have a much longer history. Recent scholarship in design history and related fields has begun documenting these practices, the relevance of which to contemporary concerns over resource depletion should be evident to any student of design culture.

Practices of waste reduction through reuse and repurposing that are bottom-up rather than top-down in nature are readily seen as having a creative streak, and have thus attracted the interest of scholars of design culture. In such scholarship, these activities become acts of design in themselves, and are often interpreted, explicitly or implicitly, as examples of *bricolage*. David Lucsko shows how even in the most emblematic of all manifestations of rampant consumerism—US car culture—there are strong forces and alternative practices running counter to the throwaway mentality with which it is normally associated. "For if nothing else, gearhead activities like customization, street rodding, and restoration clearly suggest that bricolage, which Douglas Harper, Susan Strasser, and others have lamented is a dying art, is and has been alive and well within the automotive realm."[30] The similar, remarkable creative energy and resource economy that goes into securing old US cars a new lease on life in postrevolutionary Cuba was the focus on Viviana Narotzky's study of this extreme case of make-do-and-mend design culture: "The American *cacharros* require endless tinkering, are held together with chicken wire and mechanical ingenuity. These monumental objects never die in Cuba: they become part of an endless life cycle, a vortex of use, re-use, transformation, appropriation and reconstruction."[31] As these two cases demonstrate, there is a rich and diverse history of product afterlives that is of great value in exploring how use and users matter in constructing understandings and practices of waste(-fullness) and resource (-fullness) in design culture.

As crucial as the practices of use and users are in understanding the design cultures of waste, recycling, and reuse, the latter cannot be fully grasped without also considering their structural traits, which often result from top-down initiatives. The more extreme cases of such governmentally enforced waste reduction and control over resource allocation can be found in wartime manufacturing, as emergency situations justify emergency measures—even in societies normally characterized by a high degree of liberal market dynamics and individual freedom. Perhaps most famously and comprehensively in modern history, World War II saw the proliferation of elaborate systems for rationing of materials and goods as well as direct state intervention in design and production. Since the demand for many, if not most, materials was virtually endless in manufacturing for the war effort, efficient and intelligent use of resources was crucial. This speaks to the centrality of design in these endeavors, but also highlights the extreme attention to frugality in use and post-use—particularly in the form of salvage and recycling of materials of high strategic value for the munitions and supply industry.

In the field of design history, the most well-known example of such governmentally imposed restrictions on resource allocation and design is the Utility Scheme introduced in the UK by the Board of Trade from 1941/1942 regulating the output of "civilian" industries such as clothing, furniture, and ceramics. The objective of the scheme was to secure rational production and fair distribution of essential consumer products and durables without compromising the munitions industry and while preventing profiteering. This was to be achieved "using as little power, labour and material as possible" by imposing strict regulations on which materials and products were to be used and even fixing profit margins and retail prices.[32] Although in the design history literature on the Utility Scheme the focus has often been on how the restrictions put on design resulted in pared-back, unornamented products interpreted as modernism-by-decree, strong arguments have also been made that this episode may hold lessons for the environment today as well. Judy Attfield argues that while "the distinctiveness of the historical period in which the

Utility Scheme arose is quite specific . . . there are nevertheless certain broad parallels that can be drawn with current concerns for an ethical design practice." More specifically, she continues, "the economic management, use and consumption of materials has echoes in current global concerns over the depletion of natural resources expressed in a growing 'green' consciousness."[33] Anne Massey and Paul Micklethwaite emphasize the scheme's strict regulation of resources and its localized nature of both production and consumption as potential lessons for contemporary design challenges: "This model of production and consumption now appeals to us in terms of its efficient materials cycle and low-energy manufacture and distribution."[34]

Despite its renewed relevance, it is important to acknowledge that the Utility Scheme is no panacea of sustainable design. Its legitimacy rested entirely on the command economy of wartime production and reconstruction shortages, and not much love was lost on Utility designs by British consumers or manufacturers. In peacetime, this level of state control over design and production is only paralleled in socialist planned economies. Perhaps the most striking example is the East German Central Institute of Design, which, when subsumed under the German Office for Measurement and Product Testing in 1965, effectively was given veto power over the output of the nation's manufacturing industry. From 1973, its control became total, as all factories now were required by law to let the Central Institute's staff designers do the actual industrial design work for them, rather than simply submit their proposals for approval.[35] Although the German Democratic Republic design community at the time engaged in an elaborate debate over product durability versus planned obsolescence,[36] there is little evidence to suggest that ecological sustainability was a prominent concern in the Central Institute's dictatorial design work. Nevertheless, such totalitarian scenarios could of course be conceived as potentially providing a more efficient strategy for a rapid and wholesale transition to sustainable design practices than do insular practices of profit-driven design in a free market economy—but its political viability seems limited in the current age of neoliberalism, and its undemocratic disposition is decidedly unsavory.

Whether seen through the lens of bottom-up cultural practices or top-down political structures, material ecologies have preoccupied historians of design for some time now. Increasingly, these studies are also focusing specifically on the ecological performance and impact of the materials which make up our designed world, including plastics, aluminum, steel, and wood.[37] Such accounts of the waste and want of materials are of great value in forging a type of design history that improves our understanding of how design practice and design culture shape the use of resources and thus how this can be reshaped for a more sustainable future.

A QUESTION OF JUSTICE

Design divides; design unites. Both practices and studies of design are therefore deeply entangled with discourses of justice. The notion of justice in the context of design culture can of course be explored along a range of vectors, including gender, sexuality, race, class, and ability—as well as what is broadly conceived of as global justice and environmental justice. All these entanglements of design and justice are distinctly diachronic, in that they have both historical and contemporary significance. Some of these discourses have become relatively mature topics in design history literature (gender, sexuality), some are currently receiving greater attention (class/labor, ability, race), whereas others remain underexplored (global justice, environmental justice). It is predominantly these last that weave through the current study.

Hailing from the realms of philosophy and policy, the notion of global justice throws modern design culture into sharp relief. Any conventional understanding of design and its histories conjures up strong connotations of enlightenment epistemology, a colonial (and later postcolonial) world order, industrialized production systems, capitalist economies, consumer societies, etc. Design has been proven integral to imperialist modes of government,[38] portrayed as industry's make-up department,[39] and cast as one of the most harmful professions in the world.[40] It has even been suggested that the very term "design" itself is too mired in these historical and cultural connotations to serve as an analytical category beyond the linguistic culture of its origin, and that it therefore should be replaced with other, local/indigenous words for "prefigurative practices."[41] Heeding this call would quickly become deeply impractical, however. Learning from anthropology, where translinguistic discourse is commonplace, we can instead acknowledge that the "definition is not isomorphic with the practice."[42] In a similar vein, Dipesh Chakrabarty has argued that "European thought is at once both indispensable and inadequate" in making sense of coloniality and its legacy.[43] Rather than debunking design, then, a more viable strategy for conceptually decolonizing design is to update, refine, and expand our understanding and use of the term to embrace a broader and less prejudiced range of practices. But even so, no terminological exercises can change the fact that design is complicit in the creation and maintenance of a world where the distribution of both wealth and health is disturbingly lopsided. What, then, are designers and design scholars across the globe supposed to do when faced with structural inequity and injustice of this magnitude? The sheer scope of the challenge could make it tempting to fall back on Tomás Maldonado's position that design's capacity to bring about substantial change toward a more just and ecologically sound society is severely curtailed by political structures, and that its true potential thus can only be realized following a revolution.[44] But that somehow seems too fatalist. How can individuals and collectives address structural unsustainability? Studying its history is no panacea, but it does offer new insight and it can open paths for new initiatives: "Historical knowledge can feed back into actual practice, strengthen the potential for positive socio-environmental impact, inform policy and more generally foster plurality of voice and agency."[45]

Issues of global justice and environmental justice are intrinsically connected by the specter of colonialism. Recently, scholars such as Arturo Escobar have demonstrated just how critical design is in addressing both sides of the equation: "The contemporary crisis is the result of deeply entrenched ways of being, knowing, and doing. To reclaim design for other world-making purposes requires creating a new, effective awareness of design's embeddedness in this history."[46] This could serve as a mantra for the book as a whole—but it seems particularly pertinent in the context of design for development, a topic explored at length in chapter 3. Globalization and environmentalism intersect also in the discussions of ecoactivism in chapter 4 and ecophilosophy in chapter 5, thus providing additional evidence that the long and winding cultural history of nature constitutes a rich subject for design history. Drawing on Bruno Latour's take on the foundations of the modern world order,[47] Marisol de la Cadena observes that "notwithstanding the differences that sparked liberalism and socialism in the nineteenth century, both groups (in all their variants) continue to converge on the ontological distinction between humanity and nature," which is why it remains so challenging for "moderns" to accommodate or even conceptualize "earth-beings" in their/our ontologies.[48] This might go some way in explaining why there is such a strong correlation between global injustice and environmental injustice, and why ecological design must be in conversation with the quest to decolonize design. As Rob Nixon has pointed out, "We may all be in the Anthropocene but we're not all in it in the same way."[49] And, rather disturbingly, environmental injustice is to a large extent a product of design. Extreme weather events caused by climate change disproportionately affect communities relegated to poorly designed housing in precarious and poorly planned neighborhoods. The health hazards involved in recycling the mountains of discarded electronic products are largely borne by people far removed from their designers and consumers. The war machine's designed destruction of ecosystems and communities alike tends to strike far from the warlords' own abodes. The list goes on.

Environmental justice also has a strong temporal, even futural, dimension. And so does design. Past and present acts of design condition the future. Design is, in Tony Fry's words, a "futuring" and "defuturing" activity—it opens up and closes off potential futures by way of its ecological consequences.[50] This, of course, is the design response to the Brundtland report's warning that "the results of the present profligacy are rapidly closing the options for future generations."[51] When considering the defuturing properties of design in an environmental justice perspective, it is hard to think of a more salient point of convergence than the world's addiction to oil and the petrocultures developed in its wake. From a Norwegian outlook, this issue is particularly vexing. The nation's current and future wealth and welfare are built on its vast oil reserves, as the government has accumulated its share of the revenues in what has grown to become one of the world's largest investment funds currently worth about NOK 11 trillion (USD 1.2 trillion) and owning 1.5 percent of all shares in the world's listed companies. When the country at the same time consistently has cultivated an image as a global leader in environmental protection and sustainable development, the paradox is not lost on anyone. This discrepancy—if not outright hypocrisy—recently reached a symbolic crescendo when the environmentalist organizations Young Friends of the Earth Norway (Natur og ungdom) and Greenpeace sued the government for violation of the Constitution's §112, which states that citizens *now and in the future* are entitled to a clean and healthy environment, following the government's 2016 granting of new oil drilling permits in the ecologically precarious Arctic Ocean. The carefully orchestrated and highly mediatized Climate Lawsuit, as it was dubbed, went all the way to the Supreme Court, which in December 2020 rejected the case, ruling that that the constitutional "right to a clean environment did not bar the government from drilling for offshore oil, and that Norway did not legally carry the responsibility for emissions stemming from oil it has exported."[52] Oil has fueled, fed, and furnished design culture for well over a century, but concerns over its ecological ramifications caught fire following the rise of the modern environmental movement. Following the discovery of oil on the Norwegian continental shelf on December 23, 1969, and the opening of the first field in 1971, it did not take long before ambivalences appeared and conflict lines formed. The international oil crisis of 1973 only carried fuel to the fire, of course. On the occasion of the first Offshore North Sea (ONS) meeting, a major event for the booming oil industry, in Stavanger in September 1974, Young Friends of the Earth Norway and other environmentalist organizations set up a parallel event called Alternative Oil Debate highlighting the problematic aspects of the oil industry. Reflecting the widespread fear that offshore oil extraction would jeopardize marine life, one of the campaign's main slogans was the characteristically confrontational "Oil or Fish?"[53] Terje Roalkvam, who, as mentioned above, had attended the 1969 seminar on design and the environment in Copenhagen, designed a correspondingly binary black-and-white poster for this campaign (figure 0.3).

Roalkvam's poster also serves as a poignant reminder that environmental justice is not limited to human subjects, but pertains also to the more-than-human realm and thus to the burning issue of biodiversity. As I will show in chapter 5, this topic was a key concern for the deep ecology movement long before it became a household term. Again, the Arctic provides a useful setting for thinking about design's impact on nonhuman life as well as on nonbiotic nature. The long history of commercial activity and resource exploitation in volatile Arctic landscapes has upset both biotic nature, geological formations, as well as human settlements, and climate change is rapidly transforming the territories and ecological systems of the far north, rendering their fate uncertain in the face of future speculation.[54]

Fortunately, though, design and environmental justice do not converge *solely* on doom and gloom. Now and again, it is useful to remind ourselves that even if "we've committed some very stupid acts over the course of our history, . . . our stupidity isn't inevitable," as Margaret Atwood puts it. She then goes on to list "three smart things we've managed to do":

First, despite all those fallout shelters built in suburban backyards during the Cold War, we haven't yet blown ourselves up with nuclear bombs. Second, thanks to Rachel Carson's groundbreaking book on pesticides, *Silent Spring*, not all the birds were killed by DDT in the '50s and '60s. And, third, we managed to stop the lethal hole in the protective ozone layer that was being caused by the chlorofluorocarbons in refrigerants and spray cans, thus keeping ourselves from being radiated to death. As we head towards the third decade of the 21st century, it's hopeful to bear in mind that we don't always act in our own worst interests.[55]

What I have tried to show with the examples outlined above is that design history is, or at least can be, a history of both sustainment and unsustainment, and that

this type of knowledge can in fact provide important lessons for the environment. This is not to argue for an instrumentalist understanding of design history. Rather, it is a reminder of the importance of "staying with the trouble," as Donna Haraway insists, of living in the present "not as a vanishing pivot between awful or edenic pasts and apocalyptic or salvific futures," but as an ongoing struggle "in myriad unfinished configurations of places, times, matters, meanings."[56] If the history of design has taught us anything, it is that through present practice the future is in constant dialogue with the past. As David Orr explains, "we have a heritage of ecological design intelligence available to us if we are willing to draw on it."[57] What follows can hopefully serve as a guide to some of that heritage.

HEXAHEDRAL HISTORY

The book is structured thematically rather than chronologically, with each chapter discussing different but interconnected topics and arenas of key importance for the increasing entanglement of ecology and design in this period: consumerism, systems thinking, international development, activism, ecophilosophy, and alternative energy. Taken together, these discussions produce an account that elucidates the underappreciated role that design played in the rise of modern environmentalism and, conversely, the importance of ecological thinking in the profound transformation of design culture in and beyond Scandinavia as the modernist faith in progress and prosperity dwindled. The six chapters that follow are intended as facets of a historical space. As such, they provide different but intersecting viewpoints, angles, and approaches to the multifarious and entangled historical development that is the making of ecological design in Scandinavia. In the abstract, there is of course no limit to the number of facets of the polyhedral prism of historical analysis—but in a world of finite resources and practical constraints, I will posit that this hexahedral model provides a sufficiently rich and nuanced narrative of a little-known

0.3

Oil or Fish? Poster designed by Terje Roalkvam for a campaign by Young Friends of the Earth Norway (Natur og ungdom) in 1974. Photo courtesy of the National Museum of Art, Architecture, and Design.

history. So even if there surely are more than six sides to the story, those presented here should at the very least outline some complementary perspectives for an initial foray into the topic at hand.

The first chapter is set in the arena where most people engage with both design culture and environmental concerns: the sphere of everyday consumption. Sustained and substantial economic growth converged with decades of design reform campaigns to create the contours of a consumer society which, in the course of the 1960s, would shift from promising to problematic. In Sweden, this development is hallmarked by the so-called throwawayism debate at the outset of the decade, in which design critics battled over the merits of disposability versus durability, and by the subsequent rise of the environmental movement spurred by public intellectuals bridging science, politics, activism, and design. This chapter discusses how design professionals sought to negotiate the increasing ambivalence and unease concerning the social and environmental cost of consumption. Running through this discourse are concerns over how to grapple with issues of waste, value, resources, and environmental ethics in a predominantly commercial design culture. Conversely, environmentalists saw both problems and potential in design's ecological entanglements, arguing for a societal shift toward more sustainable modes of production and more conscientious modes of consumption.

The second chapter shifts the attention from the sphere of consumption to the realm of production, taking a close look at how design professionals in ecology—and especially its emphasis on systems thinking—found inspiration to critically reassess and contextualize their own practice and its environmental impact. The growing acknowledgment in the 1960s that the serenity and purity of nature hitherto taken for granted now was under threat, and that design and designers were implicit in this environmental destruction, significantly changed how nature was perceived and invoked in design discourse. This chapter examines some of the earliest Scandinavian efforts to bring an ecologically inspired mode of systems thinking into dialogue with design. Starting from the writings of the first architects, landscape architects, and industrial designers attempting to reform design practice and education according to ecological principles, the chapter moves on to examine the morality of materials in the marked shift from teak to pine as the dominant material in Norwegian furniture design. As a whole, this journey through widespread and dense Norwegian wood(s) aims to show how ecological design grew from many and different roots, and that one of its main characteristics is the dual attention to the local and the global.

Placing global connections front and center, chapter 3 examines the intersection of ecological design and the new paradigm for developmental aid emerging in this period. Design for development was by no means a Scandinavian invention, but, as this chapter shows, the phenomenon has a long history in the region, with a close but little-known relation to ecological design. The case of the Danish designer Kristian Vedel, who in 1968 was deployed to Kenya by the Danish International Development Agency (DANIDA) to develop Africa's very first industrial design program at the University of Nairobi, is here mobilized to probe the paradox that has haunted design for development ever since, and which forever binds it to ecological design: how to design for the improvement of human living conditions in a manner that respects the communities, societies, cultures, economies, environments, and ecosystems intervened in. Following a brief outline of the concept of design for development and of Scandinavian development aid polices, the chapter traces Vedel's professional formation with an emphasis on an extensive study trip to Central America in 1965 which greatly influenced his thinking on the social and ecological aspects of design. The chapter then details his work at the University of Nairobi and its aftermath, before zooming out to place Vedel's ideas and efforts in the broader international discourse on design for development.

If Scandinavian design thus ventured out into the world to engage with global environmental problems, the reverse movement soon followed. Chapter 4 explores design interventions at, and in the wake of, the UN Conference on the Human Environment, which for a hectic week in June 1972 brought the world's political leaders, high-level bureaucrats, environmental scientists, NGOs, activists, and media to Stockholm. Sidestepping the official proceedings of the summit, attention is instead aimed at the environmental-political activism of design students and the design practices of the broader activist movements and events surrounding the conference. The chapter begins by exploring how the UN conference and the associated alternative programs prompted and related to the students' activism. It then delves into one of the most emblematic outlets of this activism, namely the use of graphic design as a practice of public protest. Whereas the chapter thus initially revolves around the notion of demonstration understood as public protest, the latter half of the chapter is concerned with another, but closely related, understanding of demonstration as a practical exhibition and explanation of how something works. By taking a closer look at two exhibitions on so-called "alternative technology" staged in Stockholm in 1972 and 1976, the chapter explores how activists sought to demonstrate key principles of their approach to ecological design and the significance of design to the environmental movement.

Many of the key themes discussed in this book, including degrowth, environmental activism, global justice, systems thinking, etc., are rooted in the new ecophilosophy emerging at the time. Chapter 5 demonstrates the symbiotic relationship between philosophy and design developed around such concepts. From the late 1960s on, a group of Norwegian philosophers, who were also avid mountain climbers, developed a distinctive mode of thinking about the interconnectedness of human and nonhuman nature and of material and nonmaterial culture. Prominent amongst these was Arne Næss, who coined the concepts of "deep ecology" and "ecosophy." Notably, this conceptual development took place in close dialogue with fellow philosophers, climbers, and countercultural ecodesign initiatives in Næss's beloved California. Emerging as it did at a time when the environmental movement had awoken designers, critics, and consumers alike to the ecological entanglements of design, it is easy to understand the appeal and relevance many found in the concept of deep ecology. Conversely, Næss's simple cabin life, his passionate and advanced mountaineering, and his championing of "clean" climbing technologies were part and parcel of his ecophilosophy. At the heart of this mutual movement toward an ecophilosophy of design is a deep fascination with tools, shared by both philosophers and designers.

The sixth and final chapter discusses alternative/renewable energy technologies as an essential element in the emergence of ecological design. The early history of Denmark's pioneering windmill industry provides a highly instructive case study to better understand how the discourse on ecological design is not the sole preserve of anticapitalist ideologies, but also comprises commercial considerations and industrial applications. Drawing on insights both from business history and the history of technology, this account traces the development of this considerable feat of engineering design and energy policy from technical experiments, via countercultural initiatives, to commercial enterprise. Wind power now covers half of Denmark's electricity consumption, and the nation's windmill industry is the undisputed world leader with the lion's share of the international market. From the perspective of ecological design, then, windmills are a far more substantial contribution to Danish modern than is fine furniture. As windmills transitioned from a technical curiosity to a cornerstone of the national economy and energy policy, they have also become cultural heritage and design icons.

The book closes with a coda that brings together many of the major themes and trajectories running through it. Aspen came to Scandinavia in the final week of September 1979. In the history of design, the name of the Colorado town has come to stand for the series of conferences it hosted from 1951 to 2004, the International Design Conference in Aspen (IDCA). Although both the town and the conference are quite place-specific, the latter actually did travel on two occasions—to London in 1978 and to Oslo in 1979. The IDCA is perhaps most famous for the countercultural rebellion at the 1970 conference, Environment by Design—and the ensuing decade is noted for its political activism. But when the kingpins of the US design world descended on Oslo at the end of the decade, the momentum of both counterculture and political activism had waned, and the dynamics of US-Scandinavian design relations were at a turning point. So, when Aspen came to Scandinavia in 1979, it was part of an effort at realigning interests along vectors of professionalism rather than activism, of problem-solving rather than revolution. The polished, corporate professionalism displayed by the US delegation provoked suspicion and criticism in their Scandinavian colleagues. Conversely, the nonconsumerist and socially responsible approach to design that characterized the bulk of the Scandinavian projects presented at the conference did not seem to resonate well with IDCA dignitaries deeply connected in corporate America.

1

DISPOSABLE DESIGN

From Throwawayism to Environmentalism

We watched the tragedy unfold
We did as we were told, bought and sold
It was the greatest show on Earth
But then it was over
. . .
The alien anthropologists
Admitted they were still perplexed
But on eliminating every other reason for our sad demise
They logged the only explanation left
This species has amused itself to death

The design historical equivalent to Roger Water's laconic 1992 song "Amused to Death" appeared 20 years earlier, in the Italian designer Gaetano Pesce's contribution to the "Environments" section of the exhibition *Italy: The New Domestic Landscape* shown at New York's Museum of Modern Art in 1972. His project consisted of a plastic bunker, a subterranean refuge for the last humans on earth during the plasticized period of the late twentieth century, dubbed "The Period of the Great Contaminations" by alien archaeologists who discover the bunker in the year 3072.[1] What these two tales of self-inflicted annihilation and environmental catastrophe have in common, besides the alien eye, is the unequivocal identification of consumption—and, by implication, design—as the root cause. It may seem a commonplace by now that we are consuming ourselves to death, but this dire acknowledgment, so central and evident to contemporary discourse on sustainable design, is the result of historical developments well worth exploring.

Consumption, and its relation to design on the one hand and the environment on the other, became a particularly contested issue in Sweden throughout the 1960s and 1970s. Having assiduously promoted "beauty in the home" and "better things for everyday life" for a century or so,[2] Swedish design professionals were apparently taken somewhat aback by their eventual success and the dawn of what the Canadian-US economist John Kenneth Galbraith termed "the affluent society."[3] No sooner had Sweden's remarkable economic growth materialized in the everyday life of its citizens in the shape of Volvos and villas than concerns arose over the potential social, and increasingly also environmental, ramifications of an economy centered on private consumption and the production that fuels it. The ambivalence over consumerism virtually exploded in what became known as the throwawayism debate, instigated by a heated exchange beginning in 1960 between two of Sweden's most notable design critics, Lena Larsson and Willy Maria Lundberg. This debate and its aftermath became such a defining feature of Swedish society at the time that it even inspired a major hit single in 1966, "Slit och släng," performed by Siw Malmkvist (Swedish lyrics by Christer Jonasson to the melody of "Lucky Lips" made famous by Cliff Richard).

The debate over disposability as against durability was only one aspect of this culture of contradictions, however. In 1967, the Swedish government established the world's first Environmental Protection Agency—the very same year Swedish designers suggested transforming furniture from durables to consumables by employing materials such as cardboard and inflatable PVC. Similarly, the landmark United Nations Conference on the Human Environment taking place in Stockholm in 1972 and the international oil crisis the following year did little or nothing to abate growth of the "gadget society" (*prylsamhället*). The problematic politics of consumption even became the subject of an exhibition at Stockholm's Moderna Museet in 1971, when artist Björn Lövin in response to a marketing campaign by the mighty and seemingly omnipresent Cooperative Union (Kooperativa förbundet, KF) staged the fictive yet eerily realistic home of a "Consumer in Infinity."[4] Conscientious design professionals worked hard to negotiate these complexities and contradictions of life with all the modern conveniences. This chapter charts their efforts to come to terms with their role as both makers and unmakers of the environment. With the rise of the environmental movement the cost of consumption became more and more apparent for all to see, requiring a reappraisal of what to make of waste and value(s), of resources and resourcefulness. A key challenge for designers was to forge an environmental ethics in a commercial design culture, while their brothers in arms in the expanded field were more concerned with fostering conscientious consumption. Recapitulating these contested developments of the 1960s and 1970s, the chairman of the Swedish Society of Crafts and Design (Svenska slöjdföreningen), Sven Thiberg, concluded that the design reform movement he represented "must become an integral part of the unified environmental movement. Not just in theory, but also in practice, we must adjoin our issues of form and function to the mission of the broader environmental movement."[5] In retrospect, Thiberg's moral imperative takes the form less of a prediction of things to come than a culmination of a period of particularly intense deliberations on the role of design and consumption en route from throwawayism to environmentalism.

The contested nature of consumption is integral to any history of design and the environment. In charting how design professionals learned about the environmental costs of consumption, the following account is also an exploration of what David Larsson Heidenblad has termed "the societal circulation of environmental knowledge" which facilitated the rapid rise of the modern environmental movement in Sweden in the late 1960s.[6] This learning process was part of the broader "formation of a global understanding of the environmental crisis,"[7] which in turn became the sine qua non of the very notion of "sustainable development" in general and of all efforts at reconciling an ecological ethic with a commercial design culture.

LOVE IT OR LEAVE IT: THE DEBATE ON THROWAWAYISM

"*Buy—wear out—throw out: that is the motto for the young, affluent public.* . . . It is their slogan against the old-fashioned hardwearing durability."[8] With these words, interior architect and design critic Lena Larsson sought to challenge both the prevailing public notion of thrift as a virtue and the modernist dogma of durability as a moral imperative. Published in the Swedish design magazine *Form* in 1960, her article set off a heated and remarkably public debate across TV, radio, and newspapers on the role of design and the nature of quality in the budding Scandinavian consumer society. In her article, Larsson questioned the received wisdom of durability as an inherently positive characteristic and sought to nuance the predominantly negative reactions amongst her peers to the emerging product culture driven by desire, playfulness, and fashion. She argued that not all types of products should be measured against the same standards. Consumer durables, such as a wristwatch, photo camera, or radio, should be expected to last, because of their high cost and (purportedly) primarily functional nature. But the same expectations could not be applied to the entire gamut of consumer products. Even relatively expensive goods, like a pair of elegant shoes, dance to a completely different tune, Larsson remined her readers. They do not come with an extended warranty, but "we accept that because these and similar things represent a different kind of value dimension: taste, whim, chance."[9]

Appealing to and sanctioning such "irrational" consumer behavior was highly controversial in the context of professional design discourse around 1960. But her appreciation of perishability and ephemerality was not just about embracing hedonism and the logic of fashion. Taking the example of the washing machine—a recent but highly appreciated acquaintance in Scandinavian households at the time—she called upon another key value in defense of disposability: convenience. It was common knowledge, Larsson claimed, that the washing machine was harder on the bed linen than the manual laundry which until recently had been the norm. "But still one now wishes for a washing machine, because one at the same time buys an easier job, saving manual labor. These are values we have discovered in today's society in contrast to that of yesteryear when it was more common to wear oneself out while the stuff lasted. *The consumer good actually shows humane considerations.*"[10] Whether new household appliances like the washing machine in fact *were* labor-saving was later questioned by historians of technology, notably Ruth Schwartz Cowan.[11] Nevertheless, the appeal to convenience and leisure as justifications of disposable design was at the time as compelling as it was controversial.

In contrast to earlier paeans to throwawayism, such as the notion of planned obsolescence, Larsson's concern was not to generate business or stimulate economic growth, but to critique the monolithic modernist moralism of her peers and to call for a less pietistic and philistine policy on consumer advice. Scandinavia has a strong tradition of public consumer research and advice. In the Swedish context, influential and vocal practices developed in and around institutions like the Home Research Institute (Hemmens forskningsinstitut, HFI) established in 1944 and the National Consumer Council (Statens konsumentråd) established in 1957 (figure 1.1).[12] Maria Göransdotter and Johan Redström have even argued that this tradition, and the extensive and systematic research carried out by HFI in particular, constitute an important historical antecedent of what today is known as human-centered design methods.[13] By 1960, however, Lena Larsson believed that this comprehensive consumer information work had taken on a rigid form and dogmatic tone,

1.1

Two women measuring kitchen units, c. 1960—a typical activity at the Home Research Institute as part of their agenda to promote "rational" consumption. Photo courtesy of Nordiska Museet.

especially on the issue durability. Eager to change this, she argued that "consumer information must become more attuned to the psychology of shopping and the ever more independent behavior of the consumer than to that factor callously called the product's 'quality.' It is a fundamental mistake to equate 'quality' with the necessary durability of yore. Our demands for selection and use are now based on entirely different criteria."[14] Finding the exaltation of durability, both in the popular nostalgia for antiques as well as in modernist design ideology, to be powerful but problematic, she argued that in both cases it promoted inertia at the expense of change and development. With change being the order of the day, disposability could in many cases be a more desirable quality than durability.

Larsson's diatribe against durability was provoked by a recently published book by fellow tastemaker and journalist Willy Maria Lundberg. Lundberg praised the longevity and soulfulness of traditional artifacts and dished out her contempt for contemporary consumer culture with its emphasis on novelty, fashion, advertising, attractive commercial spaces, and new shopping practices.[15] Larsson, by contrast, emphasized the empowerment mass consumption brought to an entire generation by providing access to convenience, leisure, and joy on an unprecedented scale. Sveriges Television, Sweden's public service TV network, saw potential in this collision of worldviews, and organized a debate between Larsson and Lundberg on a prime-time show in January 1961. In the TV studio, the two protagonists were flanked by economist Jan Wallander and design critic Arthur Hald—chairman of the Swedish Society of Crafts and Design and former editor of its magazine, *Form*. To illustrate her point that ephemeral products could be superior to durable ones, Larsson demonstrated to the TV audience the revolutionary convenience afforded by disposable nappies. Lundberg retorted by showing how easily she could bend a cheap stainless-steel spoon. What the debate so eminently demonstrated, then, was that if durability is designed, then so is disposability.

The prime-time TV debate ignited a broader public conversation, with extensive coverage in radio, newspapers, and magazines. Surprised by the massive attention, *Form* decided to strike while the iron was hot and put together a special issue devoted to the topic in response to the media frenzy. The issue included contributions from a broad range of writers representing a variety of professional and ideological perspectives. For instance, venturing rather far off the beaten path of design discourse, the editors called on Ingvar Svennilson, professor of economics at Stockholm University. In his response, Svennilson complicated the received knowledge of market development in high-cost, late-industrial economies by pointing to the continued relevance of craft-intensive manufacturing and the importance of price elasticity, arriving at the antideterminist argument that the predicted development toward a throwaway society—which is how many read Larsson's initial provocation—was not a given.[16]

In his contribution to the special issue, Arthur Hald appealed to an enlightened consumer making well-informed, deliberated choices: "The best guarantee in the long run for an appropriately varied market is to be found in consumers' increased sense of quality," he wrote—"not of some fixed, 'inherent' quality, but of different qualities, different longevities, of different combinations of needs, of the shifting interplay between practical, aesthetic, and other values."[17] As chairman of the Swedish Society of Crafts and Design and director of design at Gustavsberg—noted manufacturer of household goods in ceramics and plastics—he made sure to point out, though, that competent designers were absolutely essential in producing those values and qualities in the first place. Representing the latter profession's view was Erik Berglund, a furniture designer who worked for the Swedish Society of Crafts and Design as head of the organization's efforts at developing common standards and quality assessments for the furniture industry. While conceding that neither durability nor other types of quality (utilitarian, ergonomic, aesthetic) were necessarily directly correlated to cost, he made it abundantly clear that furniture design "is obviously not an appropriate field for wear-and-throwaway propaganda."[18] Despite Berglund's distinct disapproval, the Swedish furniture industry was about to witness rather dramatic changes pointing precisely toward more disposable design. IKEA's mass-market breakthrough was just around the corner, and within a few years, designers experimenting with materials such as cardboard and inflatable PVC challenged the very essence of furniture as heirloom pieces.[19] Not surprisingly, Larsson expressed great enthusiasm for the latter development, particularly the work of Stephan Gip and Mikael Björnstjerna (figure 1.2).[20]

One of the more conservative voices in the debate, supporting Lundberg's anticonsumerist agenda, belonged to the seasoned journalist and critic Eva von Zweigbergk. But rather than targeting Larsson, her criticism was aimed at the economists who had chimed in in support of throwawayism—presumably because she saw them as direct exponents for societal power, policy, responsibility, and authority, and therefore as constituting a more apt target than her fellow culture worker. The potential convenience afforded by disposable design—one of Larsson's main points—was not entirely lost on von Zweigbergk either, although she had her misgivings: "I would gladly give up returning beer bottles, had not canned beer been

1.2

Front cover of the design magazine *Form* (1967, no. 9), featuring a veritable epitome of disposable design: Stephan Gip's inflatable PVC chair Blow-Up, manufactured by Hagaplast.

more expensive . . . I would gladly buy milk in cartons if only they had been sensibly designed for the consumer's use, not just the convenience of the vendor"[21] (figure 1.3). By and large, however, she found the tendency toward throwawayism to be faddish, unethical, and uncultured—and she blamed it all on the downfall of the old social structure of the urban bourgeoisie and the landed gentry with its "national economy of thrift."[22] Von Zweigbergk's dim view of the (middle- and working-class) consumer as lacking in taste and cultural capital has of course been a familiar trope

1.3

A particularly successful case of Swedish disposable design is the Tetra Pak milk carton. The original tetrahedron-shaped version from 1951 (left) had some significant usability challenges, though, which were resolved with the now iconic Tetra Rex model introduced in 1965 (right). Photo: Ridde Johansson, courtesy of Nordiska Museet.

DISPOSABLE DESIGN

in consumer criticism and design reform since the mid-nineteenth century—but one emphatically out of step with the experiences of the postwar generation Larsson was addressing.

The *Form* special issue also provided Lena Larsson with the opportunity of responding to the media frenzy set off by her original diatribe. In her brief retort she countered the misconception that her appreciation of throwawayism entailed a preference for shoddiness over quality. Quite the contrary, she claimed, pointing to mechanisms both on the production and the consumption side. Both craft and industrial design are inherently iterative practices—designers will always seek to improve on their previous outputs, thus contributing simultaneously to shorter product lifespans *and* increased quality. As for the consumers, it was all about learning, she quipped: "I wholeheartedly believe in the repeat purchase, because experience is gained primarily through the opportunity to correct oneself, thus producing true consumer knowledge. To me, experience is exactly the 'wear-and-throwaway-procedure.' I want to buy in order to *learn* how to buy. But I will not acknowledge the material power of things."[23] When Larsson refused to acknowledge "the material power of things," it was because she found this prevailing modernist ideal of the one true and lasting design solution to be stifling and oppressive, rife with paternalistic assumptions about people's needs and desires. By refusing to be consumed by durables, she reasoned, one could retrieve the true, *liberating* power of things in their consumption.

Despite their many differences and strong disagreements, there are some notable affinities between Lena Larsson and Willy Maria Lundberg. Both were deeply involved with consumer education efforts, but also rather critical of the rationalist bias of this discourse. As Orsi Husz has perceptively shown, what brings the two critics' otherwise antagonistic arguments together is their attention to emotional appeal. Lundberg waxed lyrical about the pleasure she took in beholding and handling beautiful, well-made old objects, and emphatically expressed her outright hatred of shoddily produced commodities. Conversely, Larsson urged her readers to not only acknowledge but even embrace the practice of consumption as an experience that far exceeds the realm of reason.[24] The debate thus "signalled a rupture in the persistent polarisation by introducing passion, emotions and feelings in a positive way—on *both sides* of the debate. Rather unexpectedly, the controversy on throwawayism justified a passion for commodities."[25] As such, it constitutes a breaking point where the conventional normative polarities in consumer criticism are upended, opening space for new conceptions of and approaches to the ethics of design and consumption.

In light of that shift, the timing of the debate on throwawayism is significant. It erupted on the heels of a decade of massive economic growth and on the verge of a consumer society, but before environmentalism went mainstream. The latter was just around the corner, though, perhaps best symbolized by the 1963 Swedish translation of Rachel Carson's *Silent Spring*, that keynote of the environmental movement, originally published in the US the previous year. Shortly after this pivotal moment, consumerism came under attack in a way previously unimaginable, with arguments centered on issues such as pollution, nature, ecology, and the environment rather than the dichotomies of tradition versus modernity, frugality versus hedonism, and quality versus shoddiness which had dominated the 1960–1961 debate.

OF WASTE, VALUE(S), AND WHOLE SYSTEMS

The only contributor to the 1960–1961 throwawayism debate to broach the subject of environmental ramifications was Eva von Zweigbergk. As mentioned above, she fully understood the potential advantages of disposable products, despite their—in her view—economic, functional, and aesthetic shortcomings. Her most significant objection, however, was not about designing, marketing, shopping for, or using such products, but about their afterlife:

One must also discard the worn-out in a tasteful manner. Where to dispose of everything we throw away? As long as it can be incinerated, fine, unless the smoke itself further degrades our air. How long can the depths of our seas absorb not only all our usual filth, but also all the glass, all the rubbish, before polluted water is a matter of fact everywhere? Our seabeds cannot take any more. It is no small matter if seven million people on a daily basis throw out huge quantities of private waste, not to mention that of industry. Throwing away also has its costs; someone has to collect it. Have the scrap-advocating national economists really taken account even of this cost in their calculations? Those numbers never got a say, it seems.[26]

That these concerns for the natural environment cropped up in the midst of an article that was otherwise distinctly on the traditionalist side of the exchange might at first seem somewhat surprising. But the shared roots of conservationism and conservatism are both etymological and ideological—even if these connections tend to be more palpable in the philosophical realm than in the political.[27] And with the imminent rise of popular environmentalism, some of the conservative/conservation-ist views expressed by von Zweigbergk and Lundberg would soon seem more progressive than the joy and convenience of throwawayism embraced by Larsson.

With the 1967 volume, *Form* introduced a new feature in which certain pages were printed on coarse, green paper in stark contrast to the regular glossy white pages around them. One of the first articles to receive this distinctive design treatment was penned by Finnish designer Kaj Franck. Primarily known for designing remarkably unremarkable tableware, Franck had the previous year publicly decried the growing personality cult following in the wake of the international success of Finnish design and called instead for an ethos of anonymity and social responsibility, earning him a reputation as the "conscience of Finnish design."[28] Symptomatically, then, his message to the readers of *Form* amounted to a quest for conscientious production and consumption, picking up on several of the key issues at stake in the earlier throwawayism debate, but with added environmental concern. In black on green, under the heading "Material and anti-material," Franck opened by firing a broadside: "Humankind is always, whether she is a saver or a squanderer, a hoarder or a scatterer, a terrible producer of waste."[29] His reaction to the ever more prevalent phenomenon of disposable design was that it required a fundamental shift in our understanding, not only of consumption—which had been Larsson's main point—but also of the value of materials, the notion of ownership, and—not least—how we dispose of our stuff. From this new knowledge emerges, he posited, "the idea of nonpossession as necessity—but also as a dream of a lighter and more nimble life."[30] So, five years prior to Superstudio's more ontological musings on "the possibility of life without objects"[31] and John Lennon's political imagining of no possessions, Franck identified object ownership as a major obstacle to reinventing design for environmental sustainability. All the more ironic, then, that Franck's tableware designs some 40 years later, still in production, were converted into covetable commodities as the embodiment of the Iittala brand's strapline "lasting everyday design against throwawayism."

Objects, of course, are only matter in transition. To Franck, design was, at its core, about the management of these material flows, and it was high time for designers to acknowledge their responsibility and reconsider their agency: "As a designer one feels both complicit and powerless facing the accelerating course of events which is gradually degrading the landscape and quickly transforming it into a new material, a conglomerate of cultural debris, 'urbanite,' covering in a thick layer the earth, riverbeds, and ocean floors."[32] Resembling much later accounts of the Anthropocene, he argued that "humankind surely has always sought to transform nature, but her 'slow shaping of daily life' [anonymously quoting from Sigfried Giedion's 'contribution to anonymous history']³³ has now been integrated into an inexorably functioning system of extraction, fabrication, distribution, and consumption, which cannot be disrupted without causing serious malfunctions in the social machinery."³⁴ The human-controlled processes through which materials in massive quantities are distributed and transformed had now taken on "topological dimensions," he warned, and lack "the capacity for self-regeneration which can be found in the cycles of nature."³⁵

In light of this grave situation, Franck reasoned, designers, manufacturers, and consumers alike should aim to escape the "dictatorship of the material." This was particularly pertinent in Scandinavia, he argued, where even the education of designers was still structured by materials and their associated values and properties (figure 1.4). Such a system, which had often been hailed as a hallmark of Scandinavian design and one of the explanations for its international fame, was according to Franck entirely unsuited for the momentous tasks ahead: "We need a new conception of human existence, one not entirely based on material wealth. We also need a new understanding of materials and a revision of our values."³⁶ Disposable design was not ruled out by default; it all came down to the appropriate use and appreciation of materials. Citing a study undertaken by his students at Helsinki's School of Art and Design (Taideteollinen oppilaitos), he suggested that designing for single-use settings should not be confined to devising poor substitutes for better products, but instead should attempt to reimagine the need and its solution. Perhaps more importantly, though, as a step toward ecological design, Franck urged that "materials research must to a much greater degree focus on developing materials which can be reconsumed."³⁷ Even if reusing scrap in the production of new materials and products has a long history, such practices had until this time chiefly been motivated by economic rather than environmental concerns. By contrast, Franck saw a systematic change in this direction as a way of facilitating design for recycling based on an ecological rationale, giving his proposal a distinctly progressive streak.

In the public discourse on design in Sweden in the late 1960s, resource ecology became a matter of concern both upstream and downstream from manufactured objects themselves. In March 1968 Stockholm's National Museum of Science and Technology (Tekniska Museet) showed the exhibition *Environment Tomorrow* (*Miljø i morgon*) in its new science center, Teknorama. The aim of the exhibition was to "showcase just how much the design of our future environment depends on access to energy in forms which do not entail the pillaging of our natural resources or the

DISPOSABLE DESIGN

37

pollution of our surroundings."[38] (See chapter 6 for more on renewable energy.) The museum argued that "a rational application of electric power, soundly produced in a long-term perspective, can in many fields prevent the environmental destruction now threatening."[39] This persuasion clearly stemmed from the fact that the exhibition was organized in collaboration with the Association for Rational Application of Electricity (Föreningen för elektricitetens rationella användning, FERA), which since its founding in 1927 had worked to convince the public of the advantages of electricity. In *Environment Tomorrow* the future ecodesign promises of electricity were exemplified by a series of interior "landscapes"—an open-plan office, a home environment, a factory floor, and a vision for a future classroom—showcasing a

1.4

A student working in the ceramics studio at Konstfack College of Arts, Crafts and Design in Stockholm, 1966. The curriculum at Scandinavian design schools was at this time still very much structured according to traditional materials and crafts. Photo: Studio Gullers, courtesy of Nordiska Museet.

broad range of applications, from telecommunication instruments, kitchen appliances, and lighting fixtures to ventilation, cooling, and heating systems. However, except perhaps for the experimental electric vehicles (an electrified Saab, an electric scooter, and a Renault-based Mars II imported from the United States) also featured in the show—functioning as something of a shorthand for the eco-friendly identity of electric power—it is less clear how the exhibition's gadget-riddled interior environments were supposed to prevent the degradation of the natural environment (figure 1.5). One visitor who did not accept the exhibition's premise that increased

1.5

A Saab 96 (designed by Sixten Sason in 1960) equipped with an electric power train shown at the exhibition *Environment Tomorrow* at Stockholm's National Museum of Science and Technology in March 1968. Photo: Magnus Atterberg, courtesy of Tekniska Museet.

DISPOSABLE DESIGN

electrification would be ecologically sound was Dag Romell, a consultant engineer and inventor and later cofounder of Sweden's Green Party (Miljöpartiet, established 1981). He criticized the exhibition for greenwashing the continued growth imperative inherent in the government's dominant energy policies as expressed through the work, for example, of FERA and the Royal Waterfall Board (Kungliga vattenfallsstyrelsen). These policies, he argued, "have as their main goal to increase as quickly as possible the consumption of electrical power" for financial gain, and the environmentalist rhetoric of the show was just a means to this end.[40]

A further expansion of what Simon Sadler has called "design's ecological operating environments"[41] emerged, in Sweden as in Norway (and elsewhere), through the encounter with "whole systems" thinking (see chapter 2). "Where do I learn," asked architect Mårten J. Larsson, director of the Swedish Society of Crafts and Design (and Lena Larsson's husband), "that the changes to the environment concern me too, whether I flush the toilet, start my car, or have a picnic in the grass?"[42] In light of this overwhelming acknowledgment it was imperative, he proclaimed, that the Society, its journal, and the design community in general make sure that the designer was not perceived as an inconsequential beautifier, but as the de facto constructor of everyday life and thus as responsible for the environment's systemic functioning and operational health.

These questions became ever more prevalent on the—often green—pages of *Form* from 1968 onward. After attending two seminars staged by a new generation of designers and design students (recently united in the Scandinavian Design Students' Organization, SDO) that summer, the first addressing "Industry—Environment—Product Design" at the island of Suomenlinna outside Helsinki and the second on the topic of "Humans and the Environment" at Konstfack College of Arts, Crafts and Design in Stockholm, Gunilla Lundahl, one of the magazine's staff writers, concluded that "designers seek to define their role in new terms, in new contexts."[43] As Ida Kamilla Lie has shown, these seminars functioned as important arenas for the exchange of ideas between young Nordic designers and the invited speakers, which included Bruce Archer, Christopher Alexander, R. Buckminster Fuller, and Victor Papanek,[44] designers and scholars who all—albeit in very different ways—insisted on the necessity of understanding design in fundamentally systemic terms. Lundahl's colleague Marika Hausen reported from her visit to Victor Papanek at Purdue University that she found biomimical processes taught and practiced by him and his students, for example through a basic course in bionics which was intended to teach students to use biological prototypes for the design of artificial systems.

Reflecting on Papanek's close ties to Sweden and Scandinavia, Hausen remarked that "this 'return to nature' is essentially different from the closeness to nature which many Nordic designers have lived in and with."[45] The biologically inspired process-oriented and structural methodologies promoted by Papanek and others had the potential, argued *Form*'s staff writers, to shift the way Nordic designers conceived of the relationship between design and nature more toward a whole-systems approach, and thus to engender more genuinely ecological design practices.

THE COST OF CONSUMPTION

As the 1960s drew to an end, the debate on consumption and disposable design kicked off by Lena Larsson's provocative intervention at the decade's outset had by no means subsided. If anything, the increased attention to environmental degradation and social injustice over the course of the decade had only carried fuel to the fire. It was hardly surprising, then, that when the Swedish Society of Crafts and Design convened its annual conference in 1968, it was under the heading of "Consumption—at what cost?" (Konsumtion—till vilket pris?) Fittingly, the event took place at Vår Gård (Our Estate), an estate comprising a group of late nineteenth-century summer houses in the exclusive seaside resort Saltsjöbaden acquired by the Cooperative Union in 1926 and converted into a convention center and training facility for its staff. Heavily invested in manufacturing (owning Gustavsberg, for instance), a major player in retail (6,000 shops across the country in 1950), and an innovator in corporate identity (launching a comprehensive new design program in 1967 and acquiring Sweden's largest advertising agency), the Cooperative Union was a mighty actor in postwar Swedish society and a valued ally to the governmental bodies at the heart of the consumer education effort.[46] The conference venue thus simultaneously symbolized both the conspicuous consumption of the old elite as well as the purportedly rational consumption practices of the modern social democracy's working and middle classes.

An editorial in *Form* sampled some of the questions that had honed the topic and presaged the conference:

Can the consumer at all influence the goods on offer? Does advertising control our needs? How can an individual influence the design of our common environment? What is it worth, our freedom to choose amongst toothpaste brands and car models? Can we afford our standard of living? Can we change or redirect the excessive consumption to more important social needs? What responsibility do society and manufacturers have toward the consumer? How does an active consumer politics work?[47]

The conference program and list of speakers conform to the pattern of interdisciplinary interest and broad outreach cultivated by the Swedish Society of Crafts and Design. Opening the proceedings were Lund University mathematician and economist Jan Odhnoff, speaking as a consulting expert for *konsumentutredningen*, the forthcoming Swedish government official report (SOU) on consumption, and Per Holmberg, an economist with the Swedish Trade Union Confederation (LO) and secretary for *låginkomstutredningen*, the ongoing SOU on low-income groups. Criticizing the widespread use of the model of *homo economicus* in political and economic planning as overly rationalistic, Odhnoff warned that such simplistic methods had allowed industry to write off environmental destruction as inconsequential "side effects" exogenous to its operations, and that far more complex and holistic methods for assessing needs and satisfaction on a variety of levels (individual, family, society) were needed in order to plan for a more sustainable development.[48] Speaking on behalf of his working-class constituency and from his government mandate as an advocate for the interests of low-income groups, Holmberg fastened on the notion of freedom of choice as an illusory mantra which in reality only served the privileged and the powerful. All the "talk about freedom of choice" amounted to an alibi for irresponsible priorities; a "wretched defense of ruthless environmental destruction, moronic advertising, foolish space exploration, cold-hearted exploitation of developing countries, a growing low-wage proletariat, and much more."[49] The mantra of consumer choice was thus not really rooted in respect for the individual, Holmberg argued, but should instead be seen as an ingenious strategy for individualizing—and thus pulverizing—responsibility for consumer society's many structural problems, such as the environmental crisis (this critique of individualism will reemerge in chapter 4).

The debate on the cost of consumption also brought to the fore the common etymological root of economy and ecology in the Greek word for household, *oikos*, making them both "household sciences" in Bruno Latour's gloss,[50] and therefore converging on design discourse. By the time Victor Papanek published his first book *Miljön och miljonerna: Design som tjänst eller förtjänst?* (The Environment and the Millions: Design as Service or Profit?) in 1970,[51] he already had an established relationship with Scandinavia, and especially Sweden, having visited and taught regularly at design schools and student-led seminars since 1967. When *Form*'s Gunilla

42   CHAPTER 1

Lundahl—who had attended several of these seminars—reviewed the book, she criticized him for becoming "repetitive," for "pushing at open doors," for eclectic sampling and hyperbolic arguments, and for failing to flag his position on key social issues.[52] Of course, when the book subsequently, in 1971, appeared in English as *Design for the Real World*, it quickly became an international bestseller and a rebel yell for socially, ethically, and environmentally responsible design. In a subsequent review of the English edition, Lundahl upheld her criticism, adding that Papanek gravely overestimated the agency of designers in effecting social change and faulted him for being thoroughly apolitical: "Societal change arises from a political struggle which Papanek refuses to touch upon."[53] Significantly, though, the original Swedish edition was published as part of a book series called *Ekonomi och samhälle* (Economy and Society), and when *Form* published an excerpt of the book on the occasion of its publication, the selected text resonated very well with the ongoing debate on disposable design and the cost of consumption. Under the heading "Design as Service or Profit?," the magazine's readers got a taste of Papanek's signature polemical style and his diatribe against corporate greed, planned obsolescence, and the conformity and complacency of designers. Refuting the inevitability of throwawayism, he pointed to the success of tried-and-tested durable designs like the Polaroid camera, the Volkswagen Beetle, the Zippo lighter, and the Chemex coffee maker as proof that a more sensible design culture was possible. Although Papanek did, even in the published excerpt, express concern for how "the pollution of our seas, waterways, and the air above our major cities demand that the men [sic] of design reconsider environmental problems," his main objections to what he considered to be the wastefulness of mainstream design practice was in fact predominantly economically rather than ecologically grounded.[54]

Even if the Swedish Society of Crafts and Design's 1968 conference on the cost of consumption was a response to an ongoing debate, its most significant preamble was Brita Åkerman's book *Makt åt konsumenten* (Power to the Consumer) published earlier that year. Åkerman, who naturally spoke at the conference, was a seasoned and central player in Swedish consumer research, policy, and criticism. A literary scholar by training, she was a cofounder of and long-time manager with the Home Research Institute and had also worked for the Swedish Society of Crafts and Design and the National Consumer Council. Based on the premise that "the consumer is the most important figure in economic life," her book outlined the basis for a new consumer policy focused on targeted action and industry influence rather than general information and education.[55] As part of this more proactive agenda, she recognized the recent rapid rise of the environmental movement and its significance also for consumer policy:

> The public interest in topics not pertaining to individual consumption, but to common goods, has soared astonishingly over the last years. Industrial society's mismanagement of water, air, soil, and vegetation . . . has become a burning issue on all levels. . . . It costs a lot of money to make our common external environment cleaner and less noxious, to conserve nature and culture, to make cities more children-friendly and service-centered. Everyone seems to agree that these costs are necessary, even if much of what would be done now only will benefit future generations. We suddenly have in Sweden a new environmental morality.[56]

In retrospect, Åkerman's description of a popular and political consensus may seem overly optimistic—but her observation on the rapid rise of the environmental movement and the emergence of a new environmental morality is perceptive, and particularly interesting in the context of the debate on the cost of consumption.

RESTRAINT: RESOURCES AND RESOURCEFULNESS

As Åkerman rightfully observed, both popular and political environmentalism were quickly gaining traction in the late 1960s. One of the protagonists of this development in Sweden was the biochemist Hans Palmstierna. Hailing from a family of high nobility, a baron by title, Palmstierna became a passionate socialist and dedicated his life to science and environmental activism. From his base as a researcher at Karolinska Institutet, where he had earned his doctorate in bacteriology, he applied his expertise in a variety of capacities, including serving as an expert on biological warfare with the National Defense Research Institute (Försvarets forskningsanstalt). He had close ties with the governing Social Democratic Party, and helped outline its environmental policy program in 1968. That same year he also drafted the proposal which four years later brought the first international conference on environmental policy to Stockholm, the 1972 United Nations Conference on the Human Environment (discussed in chapter 4).[57] When the Swedish government in 1967 established the world's first Environmental Protection Agency, he was soon (in 1968) recruited as its research liaison, an affiliation he kept until his premature death in 1975, only 49 years old.

Palmstierna's position as a public intellectual and environmentalist was established in earnest with the publication of *Plundring, svält, förgiftning* (Plundering, Hunger, Poisoning) in October 1967, a call to arms that sold 60,000 copies and received massive media attention. Along with most of the other books discussed in this chapter, it was thus a prime example of what Johan Östling has identified as a key "new arena of knowledge that was typical for the 1960s and 1970s": the widely circulated paperbacks written by socially and politically engaged academics (figure 1.6).[58] The book was a key part of what has been called a "turning point" in the history of environmentalism in Sweden, when for "the first time . . . a choir of scientists argued aloud that the environmental issue was not just a series of local inconveniences," but "a pressing global question of survival."[59] Appearing a year prior to Paul Ehrlich's influential *The Population Bomb*,[60] and inspired by Georg Borgström's writings on the finite nature of the earth's resources,[61] Palmstierna's book shared these authors' neo-Malthusian worries over the world's limited carrying capacity. The human species had simply become too successful, he argued, both in procreation and in consumption. Without some form of internationally coordinated "planned housekeeping" to curb this success, we would consume ourselves to death. In one of many biological analogies, he claimed that "in nature every animal and plant species develops its capacities in absurdum unless curtailed by its environment and forced to adapt to its setting. The same is true of human industrial development."[62]

In a subsequent book, *Besinning* (Restraint), Palmstierna singled out industry as the main cause of environmental destruction and urged an ethos of reason and restraint to combat the widespread sentiments of either paralyzing pessimism or ignorant/opportunistic optimism.[63] It is worth noting here that both his books were published by Rabén & Sjögren, a publishing house owned by the Cooperative Union, a consistent promoter of rationality and restraint in consumer culture and a pioneer in corporate social responsibility, as mentioned above. In a direct reference to the throwawayism debate instigated by Lena Larsson, Palmstierna embraced durability in combination with designing for recycling. The considerable environmental footprint all manufacturing entails means that "there is every reason to make [materials] as durable as possible. This is in direct conflict with the current capitalistic buy-wear-out-throw-out-mentality (which in reality only the wealthy can 'afford')."[64] Extending the serviceable lifetime of consumer durables such as cars would not only greatly reduce the energy consumption in mining, smelting, and metallurgic industry, but at the same time conserve nonrenewable resources.[65] When (durable)

products eventually wear out, he proposed, "their constituent materials can be processed for recycling, reuse in new guises." This could be applied to anything "from buildings and machines to the smallest articles of daily use such as glass bottles."[66] Recycling of materials, and particularly of metals, would become the rule rather than the exception as resources for virgin production grow scarcer, he argued—and this change would profoundly implicate design, because "it requires that cars, airplanes, machines and much else be constructed in such a way that it will be easy to scrap them when they are decommissioned," e.g. by "not mixing the metals in the constructions in a way that prohibits their separation upon scrapping."[67] Four years later, this logic had made its way into Swedish design education, as evidenced by a Konstfack student project on paper recycling where "not mixing materials which complicate recycling," such as paper and plastics, was upheld as a key design input.[68] The principle outlined here, *avant la lettre*, is, of course, what we now know as "Design for Disassembly." Despite his acknowledgment of the role of design in developing more environmentally sustainable manufacturing systems, Palmstierna cautioned that resource depletion could not be designed away—recycling and its facilitating design practices would only ever be part of the solution, albeit a crucial one. He thus clearly understood that, as Finn Arne Jørgensen has put it, "recycling is a last resort."[69]

As a charismatic and radical public intellectual, Palmstierna found fertile ground for his environmental activism among designers and design students. He was invited to lecture at the seminar "Industry—Environment—Product Design" (Industri—miljö—produktdesign) organized by design students at the island of Suomenlinna outside Helsinki in the summer of 1968 alongside such figures as Papanek, Fuller, and Alexander (figure 1.7), and excerpts of his writings were included in the catalog accompanying the traveling exhibition *And after Us . . . (Än sen då . . . / Og etter oss . . .*) organized by teachers and students at Chalmers Institute

1.6

Cover of *Framtiden kräver: Energi, arbete, miljö* from 1974—one of the widely circulated paperbacks by Hans Palmstierna and fellow politically engaged academics which boosted public discourse on environmentalism. Courtesy of Nordstedts Förlag.

of Technology and the Oslo School of Architecture in 1968/1969 (see chapter 2). Palmstierna's work caught the attention of the professional design community beyond Scandinavia as well. Notably, he was among the speakers at the sixth congress of the International Council of Societies of Industrial Design (ICSID) organized in London in 1969 under the heading "Design, Society and the Future."

In his first book, Palmstierna was particularly concerned with the uneven distribution of resources between the global North and South and the unjustness of

1.7

Hans Palmstierna (center, seated) and Victor Papanek (front, left) in a group discussion with Scandinavian design students during the "Industry—Environment—Product Design" seminar on the island of Suomenlinna outside Helsinki in July 1968. Photo: Kristian Runeberg 1968/The Finnish Museum of Photography.

world trade. He was convinced that "if our Western way of managing the Earth's resources becomes dominant across the world, then there is no significant hope that the human species will survive."[70] Another key trope was the problem of industrial pollution and waste, condensed in his petition that "*societies must transform garbage into products which again can be utilized in production*."[71] Both of these trajectories resonated deeply with design professionals in search of socially and ecologically sustainable approaches, and soon intersected also on the pages of *Form*. In 1971, under the heading "They don't throw away the garbage," Lund University art and architectural historian Sten Åke Nilsson reported on a particular type of "upcycling" he had encountered on his travels in East Africa: a highly organized, skilled, and inventive use of empty tin cans in the design and manufacture of new, useful products such as cooking stoves, oil lamps, coffee pots, etc. "Stewardship of this waste has actually been systematized, and the reuse has developed into an industry," Nilsson explained. "This industry has come about entirely by itself and exists to fill basic needs. . . . It is quite advanced and specialized, and shows evidence, in my view, of sophisticated design."[72] Later that same year, at a congress in Ibiza, Spain, in October 1971, ICSID hosted the first meeting of its newly established working group on design in developing countries (see chapter 3). One of the speakers at this event was the Swedish industrial designer Liv Berg, who had done field work in Tanzania and ran a research group called "Alternative Design" at Chalmers Institute of Technology in Gothenburg.[73] The following year, deliberately timed to coincide with the UN Conference on the Human Environment, Berg teamed up with Indonesian-Swedish architect Krisno Nimpuno to publish the booklet *Recycling: Från skräp till nytta* (Recycling: From Trash to Use)—a compendium of products of what they termed the "waste industry" in East Africa and Indonesia (figure 1.8). Like Nilsson, Berg and Nimpuno were deeply fascinated by this phenomenon, and considered it an object lesson for a more environmentally sound design practice in the global North. Crucially, though, their appraisal was a critical one: examples included both ingeniously designed, expertly executed objects, but also less successful ones.[74] On a similar note, Nilsson concluded that the appreciation of this kind of creative resourcefulness should not excuse or gloss over the many social and environmental problems caused by the Western industrial and trade system which necessitates and facilitates such practices—but that it rather should inspire change in approaches to design as well as to disposal also in wealthy nations. If recycling and reuse could be motivated not by economic necessity but by ecological responsibility, it would introduce an entirely new understanding of disposable design in

LIV BERG – KRISNO NIMPUNO

RECYCLING
från skräp till nytta

which disposability evokes upcyclability rather than throwawayism, carefulness rather than carelessness.

The concept of reuse certainly proved alluring on the authors' home turf. So much so, in fact, that the Cooperative Union (KF)—arguably the single most influential shaper of Swedish consumer culture—devoted an issue of its wide-circulation weekly magazine, *Vi* (Us), to the topic in June 1972. The special issue was inspired by, and published to coincide with, the landmark UN Conference on the Human Environment.[75] As if responding to Nilsson's recent reportage in *Form* on African upcycling, *Vi* reminded its readers of the environmental geopolitics of design: "the Earth's resources are not infinite, we cannot continue the destruction of the environment, we in the West are the main cause of this situation, we must learn from these facts." More surprisingly, perhaps, given the collectivist ideals of the cooperative movement, is the magazine's association of reuse with individual action, as "something which each and every one can handle in their daily life" and as something requiring "trust in the individual's common sense."[76] This approach can probably be attributed to the fact that *Vi*, despite the exceptional context of the UN conference, was a publication intended for a readership of private consumer-citizens rather than for politicians and bureaucrats. But KF took recycling seriously also at the corporate level. In response to increased expectations that corporations show greater social and environmental responsibility, KF had announced in 1970 an environmental protection program, promising that they would "avoid or reduce the build-up of waste in production and in the natural environment and seek to return whatever waste is still generated to the cycle of nature."[77] Two years later they had of course not yet delivered completely on this highly ambitious promise, but, *Vi*'s writer reported, work had begun. Several KF-owned companies including the cardboard packaging manufacturer Fiskeby, the wood-processing plant Karlholms-bruk, and the plastics company Celloplast (which, ironically, had introduced the world to the plastic grocery bag in 1960) had already made the recycling of waste from their own production part of their manufacturing processes (figure 1.9).[78] Irrespective of the scope and merit of these measures, the report reveals how, from

1.8

Front cover of Liv Berg and Krisno Nimpuno's 1972 booklet on recycling design in the global South.

DISPOSABLE DESIGN

1.9

Plastic bag featuring the Cooperative Union's infinity-symbol logo designed by Paul Persson and introduced in 1967. The bag was manufactured by KF-owned Celloplast AB, inventor of the plastic bag. Photo: Ulf Berger, courtesy of Nordiska Museet.

a business perspective, recycling and reuse quickly became a question of resources and resourcefulness, thus again underlining the joint etymological root of ecology and economy.

The reuse issue of *Vi* also provided Lena Larsson with an opportunity to revisit her position on throwawayism, twelve years after she had sparked the infamous debate, and in the wake of the subsequent rise of popular and political environmentalism. These latter developments had of course by no means passed her by. For instance, in her capacity as lecturer at Stockholm's Konstfack College of Arts, Crafts and Design for decades, including the transformative period of the late 1960s, she witnessed Scandinavia's most radical design student protests from within. Acknowledging how radically the intellectual landscape had changed over the course of the preceding decade, she asked her readers to "note that this was long before today's discussion about environmental values, about the problems regarding developing countries, about toxic pollution, about littering, about the wasting of resources."[79] But she was not apologetic: "I have not changed my mind. Not really. Not regarding ownership. Because this was—and is—the heart of the matter."[80] Echoing Kaj Franck's earlier idea of "nonpossession as necessity," discussed above, Larsson reasoned that a material culture based on ownership was problematic because it prioritized symbolic value over use value in the name of social aspiration and status. In a world where you are what you own, she asserted, "buying disposable cups is a political action."[81] Larsson envisioned a consumer culture that was genuinely social, collective rather than conspicuous: "I believe in the collective effort, wearing out stuff collectively, together. . . . More commons for all. Rational discussions about resources."[82] Having worked both with industry and in retail, she had become disillusioned with profit-maximizing cynicism and realized that "users and manufacturers have such diametrically opposed interests in the thing-product."[83] By 1974 she was disillusioned even with the counterculture's failure to fundamentally change the dominating pattern of consumption, and longed for a new organization of social and productive life "which amounts to living rather than consuming."[84] The emancipatory potential and the anti-fetishization she originally had seen in the ideological and material lightness promised by throwawayism thus now seemed more likely to be realized through a material culture which emphasized collectivism and performance rather than competition and possession. It is perhaps only an apparent paradox, then, that the most outspoken champion of throwawayism now had become an advocate of reuse. In fact, according to *Vi*'s editor, it was Larsson who had suggested they adopt the term *reuse* rather than the more established *recycling*—possibly to highlight the active and creative aspects of consumption over the economic and technical aspects of production.[85] Larsson's take on reuse thus introduces yet another understanding of disposable design, where what is to be disposed of is not so much the designed objects, but the very activity of design itself in its conventional conception as purveyor of consumer goods.

ENJOY RESPONSIBLY: ENVIRONMENTAL ETHICS IN A COMMERCIAL DESIGN CULTURE

In a 1975 *Form* editorial, Monica Boman expressed some of the same disillusionment which Lena Larsson had arrived at regarding the economy of design and the cost of consumption: "Where do designers stand today, when the enthusiasm of the 1960s has been quenched in the pensiveness of the 1970s? With their unrealized visions and their bad conscience? Because the role of the designer in the consumption and disposal society is just as marginal as ever before." The designer remains, she lamented, "a small cog, tightly squeezed between production and commerce in a political and economic system which ever more obviously results in injustice, wastefulness, resource depletion and environmental damage."[86] Cut down to size, what was a mere designer to do in the face of impotence and impending doom? Pessimism, Boman argued, "can lead to resignation and paralysis. Or to an opportunistic acceptance of the situation, garnished by uncritical design-PR and market-oriented *esprit de corps*. But there is also a third alternative: to rekindle the debate."[87] Boman, a philosopher by training, was here quite literally taking a page out of Palmstierna's book. Her belief in a "third way" built around rational activism and empathetic professionalism as an antidote to pessimism and cynicism alike bears a striking resemblance to his call for reason and restraint: "Restraint is active reflection. Restraint facing the unknown that is the future entails an element of hope for the future. Restraint is the prerequisite for rational action. It stands in opposition to the paralysis caused by resignation."[88] Conscience and restraint prompted action, Boman reasoned: "The energy crisis has shaken us. The waste cannot continue. The gadget society does not make us happy." Therefore, she insisted, "Ever more people will demand **that** private consumption shall be reduced; **that** the stuff we own shall be long-lasting; **that** the products that are made do not harm those who make them or the environment."[89]

As part of this agenda, she instigated a debate on the design profession's code of ethics, seeking to map out the "moral and political assessments underpinning design practice."[90] Most of the responding designers felt that these issues regrettably were above their paygrade, resulting in the kind of resignation Boman and Palmstierna warned against. Hans Sjöholm, for instance, asked rhetorically if "Volvo's designers should refuse to work on new car models because it is a waste of natural resources, because automobilism costs society dearly, etc.—would the cars currently roaming our roads then be the last of their kind?"[91] Others were less bogged down by fatalism, though. Henrik Wahlforss, founder of Ergonomidesign—a consultancy which pioneered design for disability—and a speaker at the 1968 Suomenlinna seminar alongside Papanek, Fuller, and Palmstierna, argued that "designers, if properly educated, could be amongst those who set the course [toward a sustainable future], as Hans Palmstierna says about researchers."[92] In a more pragmatic reflection, Sven-Eric Juhlin, a designer with Gustavsberg's plastics division (yet another KF-owned company) and a collaborator of Wahlforss, asked if it was realistic to practice environmentally sustainable design "without necessarily ending up in an imperious planned economy?" Juhlin answered his own question in the positive, albeit with some qualifications. While acknowledging his responsibility to design commercially viable products for his employer, he argued that designers were in a position to steer product development in the right direction by avoiding unnecessary products and toxic materials, minimizing waste and energy consumption, and designing for longevity and ease of disassembly and recycling. Recycling of plastics was challenging, he admitted, but emphasized that they were hard at work increasing the use of scrap plastics in their production and that they were seeing promising results in the case of thermoplastics.[93]

Plastics, of course, were readily and repeatedly singled out as the very epitome of the consumer society and an environmental hazard. Designers who had more or less built their careers on developing plastic products, such as Juhlin as well as Tom Ahlström and Hans Ehrich of A&E Design (established 1968), contested this reputation by stressing that the environmental performance of thermoplastics like ABS, SAN, or polystyrene was a far cry from the toxic PVC, and that designing "valid" products (useful, high-quality, long-lasting) in such materials represented responsible practice, even in ecological terms (figure 1.10).[94] For most concerned critics, though, plastics remained an efficient, if not always very nuanced, shorthand for ecological destruction by design. In a debate on "environmental cosmetics" in May

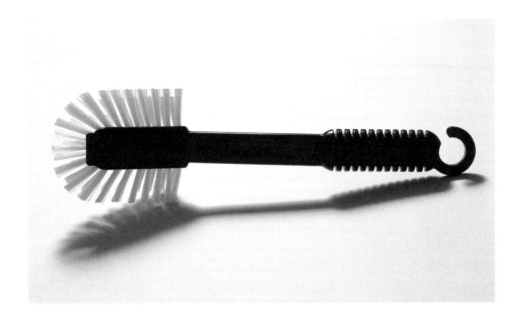

1976, organized by the Swedish Society of Crafts and Design and hosted by the Cooperative Union, the author and environmentalist Marit Paulsen asked: "Can anyone tell me why we, in forested Sweden, use PVC plastic e.g. in cupboard interiors? Plastic is not more practical, it is not more beautiful, it is made from an unrenewable resource, it is very dangerous to dispose of, it never gets entirely clean, it is very dangerous if it burns, and it is very difficult to refurbish."[95] Paulsen's denunciation of plastics represents a prominent trajectory in the quest for an environmental ethics of design, where modern materials and industrial processes were questioned by looking to traditional alternatives: glass could replace plastics, paper, and aluminum in packaging design;[96] local waste recycling could replace large-scale, wasteful

1.10

A durable yet disposable design emblematic of the paradox of plastics: the Jordan 1230 dishwashing brush designed by A&E Design AB, Tom Ahlström/Hans Ehrich, in 1974; 67 million have been sold. Photo courtesy of Nationalmuseum.

renovation systems;[97] durable, domestically sourced and manufactured clothing could replace imported "fast fashion" made from cotton.[98] These attempts at operationalizing what David Orr has called "a heritage of ecological design intelligence"[99] collectively illustrate a crucial conceptual convergence mentioned above, and with which Paulsen concluded her diatribe: "It is said again and again that it is economically impossible to change the course of development. But economy and ecology are the same word—it means housekeeping."[100] Reuniting these two meanings of that word, then, was at the very heart of the search for an environmental ethics which could be applicable in a commercial design culture.

CONCLUSION: CONSCIENTIOUS CONSUMPTION

Despite the fatalism and powerlessness expressed by some designers, there was scant faith amongst environmentalists and design professionals alike in the ability of a free-market economy to foster a socially responsible and environmentally sustainable design culture. In the pamphlet *Framtiden kräver* (The Future Demands), Hans Palmstierna teamed up with his artist wife Lena Palmstierna, Marit Paulsen, Jan Odhnoff, and others to warn against the effects of market liberalism, suggesting that the "frugal society" that the future demanded could only be achieved through the same kind of solidarity and community which had underpinned the Swedish labor movement's considerable successes in curbing the exploitative tendencies they believed to be inherent to capitalism.[101] In the same vein, the chairman of the Swedish Society of Crafts and Design, Royal Institute of Technology professor of architecture Sven Thiberg, argued—in full coherence with key characteristics of what has become known as the "Nordic model" of governance—that market forces had to be complemented and curtailed by legislation, regulations, professional codes of ethics, free and informed journalism, and collective opinion-forming efforts through organizations such as his own.[102] Heeding his own call, Thiberg and the Society organized an exhibition on the ethics of consumption shown at Stockholm's House of Culture (Kulturhuset) in the spring of 1978, under the guidance of *Form* editor Boman. The title of the exhibition, *Vara och undvara*, amounts to an untranslatable wordplay: *vara* is a verb meaning both "to be" and "to endure," but also a noun meaning "commodity," "existence," or "care"; adding the prefix *und-* ("away") turns it into *undvara*, meaning to "manage without." How to be, and how to care? What to have, and what to do without? Bundled up in just two words, then,

DISPOSABLE DESIGN

were a whole host of existential issues relating to design and life in the consumer society, with a clear bent toward its limits.

The exhibition, which subsequently traveled to Malmö, Västerås, Umeå, and Gothenburg, consisted of four interiors conceptualized as "symbolic images of contemporary views of life, stylized tendencies in 1970s Sweden." The first showcased what the organizers considered to be the worst of the current mainstream market, replete with a "luxurious, pastel-colored velveteen corner sofa, the marble table on gleaming legs, the dark and heavy bookcase," a veritable chamber of horrors symbolizing "the new bourgeoisie's . . . withdrawal from societal problems to the private realm, to the world of things."[103] By contrast, the remaining three interiors suggested possible paths toward a more just and sustainable society. The second one was furnished entirely with recycled, repurposed, or reused objects, suggesting that the time-honored virtue of thriftiness itself should be reclaimed, but for ecological rather than economic purposes. Its (hand-written) wall text called for "Reuse as lifestyle, not as fashion. Reuse as creativity, not as stagnation. Reuse as housekeeping, not as romanticism."[104] The third interior was by far the most conventional, in that it featured exactly the type of objects organizations like the Swedish Society of Crafts and Design had been promoting for a century already: contemporary furniture that was "practical, sturdy, beautiful, easy to clean and to move about." The "voluntary simplicity" associated with this kind of by then time-honored modern design remained laudable, Boman argued—with the caveat that it "must not become snobbery," because "we cannot change consumption toward simpler, more durable, beautiful, and less resource-demanding products unless we simultaneously change the conditions under which people live." This insistence on the co-dependency of social and environmental change motivated the fourth and final interior of the show: a design for a community center, suggesting that prioritizing communal spaces and collective solutions could help reduce both the economic and the ecological costs of individual consumption.[105] The ideal of collectivism was expanded upon in the catalog. Gunilla Lundahl argued that the profound changes in social organization and consumption patterns which were required to create a better future could not be achieved by individual action, but by "recreating the lost everyday collectives," taking inspiration from historical examples such as housing associations, consumer cooperatives, labor unions, and so on.[106] Local communities could thus develop "secondary economies" around local production for their own basic needs. Employing "alternative" or "soft" technologies and local resources, this system would not only benefit the environment but also regenerate social bonds, increase the quality of life, and foster individual creativity and joy of work.[107]

Whereas Tomás Maldonado at the outset of the 1970s had argued that the hope in design as an agent of positive change rested on the primacy of politics,[108] Thiberg was more hopeful that the type of design culture envisioned in the exhibition could turn the tide, as it were. But eliciting such a development would require "solidarity and collective efforts which change not only the opinions and actions of individual people, but also the basic political structure."[109] Whatever the place of politics and the potential for political revolution, it remains that Swedish design professionals in the course of the 1970s converged on the imperative of collective responsibility and the need to combine environmental ethics and conscientious consumption. Because despite key moments of contemplation, such as the European Conservation Year and the institution of Earth Day in 1970, the 1972 United Nations Conference on the Human Environment, and the international oil crisis of 1973, what was derogatorily referred to as "the gadget society" (*prylsamhället*) showed no signs of abating. This might help explain why the *Vara and undvara* exhibition catalog included a brief essay by Willy Maria Lundberg in which she reiterated the main points of the gospel of quality and durability she had elaborated in her book *Ting och tycken* (Things and Thoughts) 18 years earlier and which had provoked Lena Larsson to speak up for throwawayism.[110] By 1978, then, Lundberg's ideals of a material culture characterized by functional and emotional durability, which may have appeared somewhat quixotic in 1960, had themselves proved more durable than Larsson's paean to ephemerality. In a sense, this closed the loop on the throwawayism debate, but in doing so, the dramatic developments of the intervening years, most notably the rise of the environmental movement, had shifted the ground under the notion of disposable design. If disposability had once signified the convenience and emancipation promised by modern mass culture, the new ecological awareness commanded attention to the responsible disposal of the products of design through recycling and reuse—and ultimately perhaps also to the disposal of design itself.

2

NORWEGIAN WOOD

Material Systems of Thought

It is inconceivable to me that a culture that was at home with wood and comfortable with it, would ever feel any need to discuss wood at this high intellectual level. . . . For, let us face it, we are not considering the structural, operational, and visual exploitations of a mere natural resource, a raw material like any other. We are considering a material that is loaded with meanings, a material which inspires strong feelings in most of us.[1]
—Reyner Banham (1967)

Made famous by the Beatles' 1965 hit song, and subsequently catalyzed by Haruki Murakami's 1987 novel, the term "Norwegian wood" has taken on a mythical allure in international popular culture.[2] Its commercial appropriations today include a rock festival, a best-selling book about firewood, a craft beer, as well as a purportedly ethical and sustainable fashion and homewares brand—all favoring the phrase for its allusions to something genuine, wholesome, and natural. While the appropriateness of many of these appropriations certainly could be questioned, the term's universal familiarity and distinct connotations make it an apt point of departure for an examination of the foundations of ecological design in Norway, converging on the role of materials and systems thinking. Just like the song and the novel, this emerging discourse on ecological design bridged the local and the global, inserting the national in the international—and vice versa. The rise of popular environmentalism and the migration of basic ecological ideas from the life sciences to general and professional media in the latter half of the 1960s helped change the meaning of internationalization in design discourse. If this previously had revolved around the local export of exquisite objects and the rising fame of national design heroes, it now came to imply a new concern for how local communities were affected by the border-defying nature of environmental problems and a growing awareness of the global connections underpinning our material culture and natural ecosystem alike.

This chapter traces the origins of this new understanding of the environmental entanglements of design in Norwegian professional discourse in the 1960s and 1970s. Although Nordic design in general tends to be associated with nature and the natural, at least when mediated internationally, the trope of "nature" has been particularly pronounced in Norway. During the heyday of "Scandinavian design" in the 1950s, nature was portrayed as a sublime presence, a majestic force—a source both of material resources and creative inspiration. The growing acknowledgment that the serenity and purity of nature hitherto taken for granted now were under threat, and that design and designers were implicit in this environmental destruction, significantly changed how nature was perceived and invoked in design discourse. The concept of ecology, at this very time spilling over into the public realm from the narrower confines of the life sciences, quickly became a favored tool for thinking man-nature relations anew amongst design professionals. This chapter analyzes the first efforts to bring an ecological, or ecologically informed, critique to bear on design, its practices and ideologies. I start out by following the pioneering and persistent endeavors of Canadian-Norwegian architect Robert Esdaile, who made it his life's mission to reform design practice and education according to ecological principles. I then briefly consider the institutional convergence of ecology and landscape architecture in Norway before exploring the key discussion on "spaceship Earth" and the notion of (ecological) design as instrumental to its safe navigation. The last sections of the chapter turn more closely to design practice and to Norwegian wood in the literal sense. First, I discuss the dystopian writings of architect Bjørn Simonnæs and compare these to his more optimistic practice, as represented specifically by a small, rural hotel now considered a landmark in the development of ecological architecture. Finally, I examine the morality of materials in the marked shift from teak to pine as the dominant material in Norwegian furniture design. As a whole, this journey through widespread and dense Norwegian wood(s) aims to show how ecological design grew from many and different roots, and that one of its main characteristics is the dual attention to the local and the global.

FINDING ECOLOGY

At the same time as the Beatles released "Norwegian Wood," in December 1965, Canadian-Norwegian architect Robert Esdaile launched a targeted and comprehensive criticism of designers' lack of concern for environmental problems, on the pages of the architectural magazine *Arkitektnytt*. His acutely titled essay "The Environmental Crisis" was published in five installments from 1965 to 1967, setting the tone for the budding debate on ecology and design. The Canadian-born Esdaile had trained at McGill University in Montreal and at the University of Cambridge. After marrying Norwegian Elin Høst he moved to Norway in 1948, where he first worked as a planner before setting up an architectural practice in 1955. Collaborating with key figures such as Odd Brochmann, Dag Rognlien, and Christian Norberg-Schulz, Esdaile remained a steadfast modernist, a member of CIAM to the very end, and a key promoter of Le Corbusier's ideas in Norway (figure 2.1). From 1964, initially filling in for Sverre Fehn, he taught at the Oslo School of Architecture; in 1971 he was appointed professor at the Norwegian Institute of Technology (Norges tekniske høgskole). Esdaile was as radical a citizen as he was a design theorist and educator. After he attended the seventh congress of the International Union of Architects (IUA) in Havana, Cuba in 1963, where both Fidel Castro and Ernesto "Che" Guevara addressed the delegates, he took to signing private letters "*Venceremos*" and "*Hasta la victoria siempre*." Deeply inspired by his experience in Cuba, he would later cite Castro's and Guevara's IUA talks in his teaching as a way of convincing his students that they and their profession could make a difference in—and to—the world.[3]

With a background in planning, in his essay on the environmental crisis Esdaile homed in on perhaps the most obvious target: the car and its implications for the organization of transport systems and settlement patterns. Esdaile argued that this quintessential symbol of modern society and personal liberation had become a massive paradox, paralyzed by its own success: "The dream of 'living freely' murders the freedom of living."[4] The car was both a societal and an environmental problem: "the privately owned automobile . . . creates chaos, pollution, an alarming number of deathes [sic] and wounded. It distorts civic life and will in time congest and pollute the most exquisite countryside, our last reserve of inspiration and human dignity. This is not a fantasy, but a pure statement of facts."[5] He did not oppose the car as such, but believed that its production, distribution, and use had to be brought under strict regulation in order to keep it from suffocating our airways and highways alike.

    The car was just a convenient example, though, and Esdaile cast the entire human history as "a career which gradually freed him [Man] from the inhibiting discipline of nature. The acquired knowledge of this last millenni[um] of his existence on earth is like a bulldozer out of control. All the 'signs' and warnings which nature gently confronts us with are being trodden upon in a gigantic stampede. This planless stampede leaves behind it an environmental crisis."[6] Stopping the bulldozer required coordinated planning and a holistic, or at least systemic, approach to design.

2.1

Robert Esdaile, apartment building at Bjørnekollen, Oslo, 1956. Photo: Bjørn Winsnæs (1959). Courtesy of the National Museum of Art, Architecture, and Design.

Overspecialization resulted in tunnel vision and the pulverization of responsibility, he argued. However, it is in Esdaile's prescription for curing this illness that his intervention becomes particularly perceptive. Addressing the environmental crisis, he suggests, requires design to engage with "ecological issues, because this exact and beautifully broad science coordinates mans [sic] behaviour with the laws and habits of nature."[7] Esdaile's trumpeting of ecology in a mainstream design context stands out, three years before the arrival of Buckminster Fuller's *Operating Manual for Spaceship Earth*[8] and the first *Whole Earth Catalog*—publications that were key in popularizing ecology and promoting the idea of "whole systems" thinking in design discourse.[9] Although ecological thought has a long history, there is wide consensus that as a distinct discipline ecology emerged in the early twentieth century. It was only in the 1960s that it gained public prominence, as a consequence of increased concern for the state of the environment.

Esdaile was an architect, not a biologist, and there is nothing in his article that indicates any profound scientific knowledge of ecology. His interest in the concept seems to have been as an inspiration or tool with which designers could learn to think more holistically about their interventions in the world and the environmental impact of their practice. Designers and architects needed not aspire to *become* ecologists, he explained—but their "designs and actions must be imbued with an intention stemming from ecology."[10] The time was ripe, he claimed, for the human species to put its creative capacities to better use: "The success of people to adapt themselves has been at times astonishing and admirable, at other times they have wasted the land depleting both their energies and reserves. Never before has the power of man to waste and ravage been so decisive. Final destruction lies in his own hands."[11] This latter observation on the prospect of human-originated obliteration is clearly colored by the Cold War climate in the wake of the Cuban missile crisis. In an environmentalist context, Esdaile's comment recalls a tagline later made instantly famous: "We have met the enemy and he is us," which cartoonist Walt Kelly originally applied to a poster he created for the first Earth Day in 1970.[12] In a design context, it preempts a very similar remark by György Kepes in the context of the vastly ambitious "Universitas Project" at the Museum of Modern Art in 1972: "At this historical junction, the real beasts are man-created: we face ourselves as the enemy."[13] Kepes, an artist, designer, and scholar teaching at MIT, went on to say that this new awareness of our precarious situation had made us begin "to see that our extended body, our social and man-transformed environment must develop its own self-regulating mechanisms to eliminate the poisons injected into it and to recycle useful matter. Environmental homeostasis on a global scale is now necessary to survival."[14]

Like Kepes, Esdaile saw in ecology a conceptual model for thinking across scales and along relations. Only by adapting an ecological mindset, he argued, could designers help to reinstate the equilibrium they had contributed to upset. To pull back from the brink of Armageddon and set spaceship earth on a more sustainable course, Esdaile reasoned, we needed an entirely new approach to planning the human environment. What he suggested reads rather like an outline of the principles of what would later become known as ecological design:

What resources can we now call upon to face this new situation? Certainly not new weapons; certainly not a new invention. No, a conscientious ability to see with microscopic clarity and macroscopic breadth the interwoven and complex unity of man and nature. The science is called ECOLOGY. If we could apply it in its generous wholeness which is its supreme justification, we might have time to regain a balance. But the application of Ecology demands a changed state of mind: an *I-Thou* relationship instead of an *I-it* relationship. This has nothing to do with the sentimentality of a "back to nature" attitude which is the prestige of the well-to-do urban dweller. It embodies rather humility and collaboration, expressing the balance in biological sciences. Most important to the architect, it gives a very clear picture of environmental factors and their interplay.[15]

SHOWCASING DOOM AND GLOOM

"The Environmental Crisis" was just the beginning of Esdaile's passionate and long-lasting efforts in the name of ecological design. While he channeled these efforts mostly through his teaching and campaigns for educational reform, he also used the medium of exhibitions. Marking the occasion of the move in 1968 by his employer, the Oslo School of Architecture, out of the premises of its parent institution, the National College of Applied Art and Craft, he organized an exhibition about urban environmental problems. He viewed this event as the "precursor" to another exhibition shown in Oslo "on [his] initiative" the following spring, called *And after Us . . . (Og etter oss . . .).*[16] This claim is slightly misleading, though, as the latter exhibition was a local adaptation of a concept developed by architecture students at Chalmers Institute of Technology in Gothenburg and shown at a dozen venues in Sweden since May 1968, generating considerable media coverage and public attention. A delegation from the Oslo School of Architecture, led by Esdaile, along with representatives from the Norwegian Society for the Conservation of Nature (Norges naturvernforbund) and the United Nations Association of Norway (FN-sambandet) met with the curators of the Swedish exhibition, among them Ivar Fernemo, in December 1968 to plan a Norwegian version of the show.[17] The basic message of the exhibition—that the future of the world and of humanity alike was threatened by our own maltreatment of the environment—was carried over from the Swedish version, including excerpts of research by leading Swedish environmentalist-scholars underpinning this view, such as Georg Borgström and Hans Palmstierna (see chapter 1). As agreed, though, Esdaile added Norwegian material, sampling from zoology professor Rolf Vik's popular writings on the environmental crisis, a Rachel Carson-derived exposé of DDT by zoology professor Ragnhild Sundby, historian Tore Linné Eriksen's work on developmental aid, and Esdaile's own crusade against the private car.[18]

Through the medium of a pop-up exhibition structure designed for ease of assembly and transport accompanied by a comparatively comprehensive catalog, Esdaile and his architecture students—assisted also by design students from the National College of Applied Art and Craft—organized and presented a broad swath of scholarship by means of visually striking infographics and photomontages accompanied by succinct texts (figure 2.2).[19] The catalog cover featured an ultrasound image of a six-week-old fetus rendered in red superimposed on a black-and-white image of Earth seen from space (figure 2.3), an extreme example of the trope of "children as emotional emblems of the future" identified by Finis Dunaway as a key strategy for visualizing environmental threats which are largely invisible.[20] Paired with the distressing title, this illustration, a forceful symbol of Mother Earth, efficiently communicated the exhibition's sense of fragility and urgency. And the message hit home. According to Lars Saabye Christensen's period novel *Beatles*, the exhibition, which was "thick with people," made the visitors feel that "we lived on a time-bomb. We lived in a sewer. We shat in our own food. We dug our own graves." The juxtaposition of images and text was perceived as particularly efficient: "The photographs burned a stronger pessimism into my eyes than what the optimistic text tried to convey. It said we could still do something about the situation, about the crisis. It was all a political question, a question of economy, distribution, power, profit, of solidarity."[21] Not only was the exhibition met with great public interest, drawing 80,000 visitors in Oslo alone before moving on to Bergen, Trondheim, and other venues,[22] but it pushed back at the academic community, becoming "important in

2.2

Spread from the exhibition catalog for *And after us . . .* illustrating "today" (left) and "tomorrow?" (right).

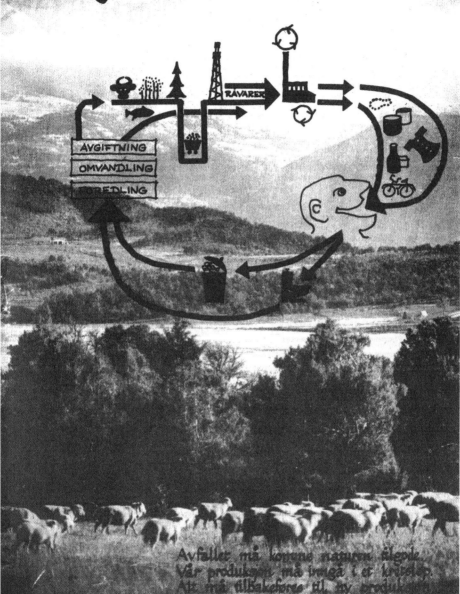

og etter oss...

triggering a call to action amongst the environmentally concerned at the University [of Oslo]," especially for the emerging ecophilosophers.[23] Sigmund Kvaløy, a graduate student and research assistant to professor Arne Næss and prime mover in the formation of the Ecophilosophy Group, "was greatly impressed by the exhibition, and invited the architects to join hands with students of ecology, philosophers, and technical climbers from the Alpine Club, to create a Co-working Group for the Protection of Nature and the Environment at the University."[24] Three of the architecture students who organized the exhibition—Turid Horgen, Dag Norling, and Snorre Skaugen—promptly accepted the invitation. Their subsequent correspondence reveals that Esdaile was flattered and motivated by Kvaløy's gesture, as it meant bringing design discourse to the epicenter of environmental scholarship and activism (Næss, Kvaløy, and their Ecophilosophy Group are discussed in chapter 5).[25]

DECENTRALIZING DESIGN

In June 1966, Esdaile wrote to the rector of the National College of Applied Art and Craft regarding an exhibition planned for the institution's 150th anniversary two years later. At this point, at least until its relocation two years later, the Oslo School of Architecture had a rather symbiotic relationship with the National College of Applied Art and Craft, from which it had spawned in 1962. Exactly what his role was in these plans seems unclear, but Esdaile's involvement is testimony to his commitment to the reform of design in general, across professional specializations. Turning again to ecology, he advised that the exhibition should showcase "a new attitude towards the idea of dwelling, showing that it is possible to make a fundamental improvement in the urban structure, in the dwelling structure, or an integration of both which would combine to solve a large number of pressing ecological problems."[26] Furthermore—and perhaps somewhat surprisingly, coming

2.3

Front cover of the exhibition catalog for *And after us . . .* featuring an image of a fetus superimposed on a "blue marble" photo of the earth.

from a Canadian immigrant—he lamented the fact that our material culture was being transformed through "a steadily increasing number of mass-production articles of foreign design and origin," making it all the more "imperative that Norway makes an effort to express the material and regional quality of its products—especially those products which form our own environment."[27] It is not unlikely that Esdaile's interest in design's local context and environment was informed by his collaborator and colleague Christian Norberg-Schulz, who at this time had just begun developing his theories of place in architecture which later would become massively influential. Crucially, though, Esdaile's interest in locally distinct design solutions was paired with his appreciation of the global perspective fostered by ecological thinking in response to the environmental crisis. This juxtaposition of scales inspired by ecology and regionalism effectively anticipated the idiom "think globally, act locally," which some years later would become the slogan of the Friends of the Earth (established 1969) and emblematic of the environmental movement in general.

This insistence on acting locally for the greater (global) good would become a staple in Esdaile's teaching practice and his steadfast drive for educational reform. Not long after he started teaching at the Oslo School of Architecture he wrote to the head of the school, professor Knut Knutsen, complaining that "two scientific subjects that concern relations between humans and nature, ecology and ethnology . . . are utterly neglected in the school's curriculum."[28] Knutsen was known for his renewal of Norwegian timber architecture and his gentle treatment of the natural surroundings, especially following his cabin in Portør (1949), so Esdaile presumably expected his superior to take favorably to his ideas for teaching ecological design. Writing again to the school's management in April 1968, he presented a "draft program for socio-ecological studies." The purpose was to increase the students' knowledge about the most pressing of "current problems," emphasizing the consequences of the environmental crisis for the design professions.[29] "Failing to address these questions," he claimed, "is tantamount to denying our descendants the right to live, or to accepting the aggravation of the misery of the world."[30] His proposed reading list included works by scholars represented also in *And after Us . . .* such as Borgström, Palmstierna, and Vik.[31]

To Esdaile, though, introducing courses on ecology and related topics would only go some way toward the required educational reform. Dismissing what he dubbed "the 98% adoption of a technical scientific approach to Ecology for training of architects," Esdaile argued that "for architects the important thing is to UNDERSTAND, see, smell, feel and diagnose in this way, respecting with an almost religious awe the beautiful synthesis of all nature from the cosmic to microcosmic."[32] Therefore, merely revamping the curriculum would not do—the very structure of architectural education had to change, from large, centrally located, academic institutions to small, geographically dispersed nodes of practical learning. This type of distributed learning was required because "students need more intimate working knowledge of environmental issues, and it is questionable if this can be achieved from an institutional mileau [sic]."[33] What he suggested was that a "mother-school" could serve as a central hub for, say, 60 "outposts" located in small communities around the country. Each outpost would consist of a dozen or so students conducting locally specific, real-life projects supervised by one or a few teachers. The local context was crucial to the new type of design and planning expertise he envisaged: "Here the group is confronted with the people, the resources, the traditions, and the future prospects of the place. Here is the architect's laboratory."[34] Moving to a new outpost every semester, interspersed by brief visits to the mother-school for theoretical teaching components as well as project presentations and appraisals, the students would thus in the course of the program receive solid yet varied hands-on and *in situ* experience with planning and design work. "An outpost," he explained, "is perhaps best likened to F. L. Wright's Taliesin, but the purpose is entirely different. We are to serve society's needs under its organic development, not a subjective formalism."[35]

Writing to an acquaintance he hoped could help set up such an outpost, Esdaile was confident that "in a very near future we could count on creating a miniature school of architecture in Alta [a small town in the far north of Norway], a school complete with an ecologist, sociologist, and an architect-planner."[36] Not surprisingly, Esdaile's radical proposal proved hard to realize. Hoping to secure broader academic support for the idea, he wrote to Sigmund Kvaløy suggesting they could discuss the matter in the Co-working Group for the Protection of Nature and the Environment at the University of Oslo.[37] Even though the latter had little to offer beyond moral support, they kept in touch—also with their "godfather," Arne Næss.[38] His own institution's management was not entirely dismissive of the decentralization idea, agreeing to establish a committee tasked with exploring its feasibility.[39] Except for a couple of ad hoc trial projects more akin to summer excursions, though, the scheme would remain at the proposal stage. That did not deter Esdaile from persistently promoting the idea, even long after he moved to Trondheim in 1971 to take up a professorship at the Norwegian Institute of Technology. His new institution was no more enthusiastic about it than was the Oslo school, but as late as 1975 he described the scheme as "a new educational response to our environmental crisis."[40] He also sought to publish the idea internationally, writing to *Architectural Design* magazine, "We can't count on initial Govm't support nor on students who primarily want qualifying semesters. We have to count on the appeal that the idea has for the few and the appeal of Norways [sic] dramatic landscape."[41]

Norway's dramatic landscape clearly held significant appeal for Esdaile himself. For the cover of its first issue of 1976, the architectural magazine *Byggekunst* chose an image of Esdaile's own DIY cabin—a repurposed coastal artillery emplacement on top of a cliff above the Jøssingfjord in southwestern Norway (figure 2.4). The simple and unintrusive structure consisted of a low, wooden roof raised on top of the artillery emplacement built in 1942 as part of Hitler's Atlantic Wall. Reclaiming a remote, spectacular site from the destructive forces of military technology and, by the smallest means possible, turning it into a sanctuary for the appreciation of the natural landscape, the project constitutes a highly symbolic gesture—a three-dimensional manifesto of ecological design. The location of the site made the project doubly symbolic, as the Jøssingfjord featured prominently in environmentalist discourse at the time, due to the heavy pollution of the fjord caused by waste from the Titania company's ilmenite mines nearby (the world's largest source of that mineral). As a concerned citizen Esdaile contributed to this attention by complaining to the newly established (1974) Norwegian Pollution Control Authority (Statens forurensningstilsyn), accusing it of being too lenient toward the company's practices.[42] The power of the double symbolism inherent in his cabin project was naturally not lost on Esdaile, who presented it to the readers of *Byggekunst* explicitly as a commentary on the combined ills of society and an intervention in the name of more sustainable modes of interaction with nature.[43]

A NEW INTELLECTUAL LANDSCAPE

As might be expected, one of the first design disciplines to take an interest in environmental issues and to explore the potential of ecology as a component of design theory was landscape architecture. In Norway, this disposition was underscored by the fact that the institutional base for education and research in landscape architecture was not a design school, but the Norwegian College of Agriculture (Norges landbrukshøgskole). This institution's strong research communities in various fields of life sciences and geosciences made it a natural home for work in ecology. Ecology was a new discipline in Norway at this time, with zoologists Arne

2.4

Front cover of *Byggekunst* (1976, no. 1) featuring Robert Esdaile's DIY cabin on top of a cliff above the Jøssingfjord in southwestern Norway. Courtesy of Arkitektur N.

Semb-Johansson and Eivind Østbye setting up a course at the University of Oslo in 1962 and botanist Eilif Dahl lecturing on the topic at the Norwegian College of Agriculture from 1963. These early courses were inspired by the work of American ecologist Eugene P. Odum on ecosystems and energy circulations in nature.[44] As Peder Anker has shown, there were significant interchanges in the late 1960s between these scientists and Arne Næss and his students in the philosophy department at the University of Oslo in the formative phase of what would become known as deep ecology, or "ecosophy"—and both of these groups again heavily influenced the environmental movement and environmental policies in the 1970s (see chapter 5).[45] But these early proponents of ecology were not far removed from the realm of design either. Dahl, for instance, also taught ecology at the Oslo School of Architecture, and published a booklet titled *Økologi for ingeniører og arkitekter* (Ecology for Engineers and Architects) in 1969. In this text he made it abundantly clear that design professions who "intervene in nature need knowledge about how our interventions impact the nature that surrounds us."[46]

Following committee work beginning in 1963, the Norwegian College of Agriculture established a new degree program in the field of nature management in 1972. Dahl explained the choice of terminology thus: "Many of nature's values that we wish to preserve are partly the result of longstanding cultural interventions. The cultural landscape, too, has values that should be preserved, which requires management. Nature conservation thus becomes nature management."[47] The program was motivated by the increased public awareness of environmental issues and the recognition of a market for specialists in the field for work in new branches of government and organizations. Working from "the ethical basis of managing natural resources according to ecological principles," the curriculum included topics like systems ecology, resource economy, pollution, and environmental protection as specializations following basic training in relevant aspects of biology, economy, planning, law, etc.[48] This new intellectual landscape of nature management and environmental preservation cast a much wider net than had the conventional conservationist approach, and thus appeared relevant to a much broader constituency. The health condition of the natural environment was no longer the preserve of a select group of scientists and avid nature lovers, but became a matter of concern for a wide range of actors and groups, from political activists and governmental organizations to apprehensive consumers and design professionals.

Witnessing these seismic shifts in the intellectual landscape of environmentalism both on campus and off, landscape architects were among the first designers to convene on the topic. In 1968, the Association of Norwegian Landscape Architects organized a conference at the Norwegian College of Agriculture on the topic of "Pollutions—Nature—Human." *Arkitektnytt* covered the event by printing a lecture by Johan Lyche, chief agricultural officer of Østfold County, indicating its relevance to a wider design constituency. Lyche assumed the by-then-familiar position of techno-criticism, but with a perceptive, nuancing coda: "It is primarily modern technology that has made the pollution problems such a current topic. This technology is created in the interplay of techno-scientific development and the economic aims of the welfare society. This is why in some countries one has been discussing what is known as alternative technology."[49] By "alternative technology," Lyche is referring to the emerging discourse on how to use leaner/softer/smaller-scale technologies as an alternative to the conventional technologies of industrial society—a movement which in more formalized terms became better known as "appropriate technology." Lyche's remark, albeit cursory, is intriguing because the alternative/appropriate technology movement would, in the 1970s, become a key component in shaping the new field of ecological design (see chapters 3 and 4). Much of its appeal to designers rested on its pragmatism, providing a bridge between the politics and activism of the environmental movement and the problem-solving ethos of the design professions. Lyche ended his contribution with another keen comment, questioning the inherent anthropocentrism of the conference theme: "We have chosen to put humankind in the spotlight. That might be a strength as well as a weakness. The strength is that we, after all, consider ourselves nature's master, and that we therefore should have both the right to, and the responsibility for, exploiting the earth's resources."[50] The logic of custodianship underpinning this argument suggests that because environmental problems are created by human design, they also need to be addressed by human design.

If landscape architects were the first to explicitly relate ecology to design in an educational context, the neighboring professions soon followed suit. In April 1973, the National College of Applied Art and Craft organized a "Resource Seminar" with the aim of increasing the attention paid to environmental issues in teaching and practice across all programs.[51] Three years later, describing the industrial design curriculum at the school to Nordic colleagues at a seminar, Roar Høyland explained how it emphasized "the societal responsibility regarding the consumption/reuse of natural resources and the responsibility for any damages to humans and their environment caused by the product or its manufacture."[52] Most of these initiatives relied on external ecological expertise, however, so dedicated theories and methods

NORWEGIAN WOOD

of ecological design remained underdeveloped at the National College of Applied Art and Craft, as they did at most similar schools throughout Scandinavia in this period (see chapter 4).

PUTTING THE ARK IN ARCHITECTURE

Under the editorship of the theoretically oriented Christian Norberg-Schulz, *Byggekunst* regularly published writers from other fields offering contextual or perspective views on issues of concern for readers from the design professions. In 1968, as the student revolts surged across Europe, sociology graduate student Ragnvald Kalleberg—who would later become a professor at the University of Oslo—was given ample space to reflect on the social and environmental ramifications of the consumer society and the potential role of architects in correcting the current course. Heavily influenced by the radical Canadian-American economist John Kenneth Galbraith, especially his 1958 book *The Affluent Society*, Kalleberg lashed out against consumption-stimulating strategies such as planned obsolescence and the mushrooming "production of socially superfluous products." One of Galbraith's most significant and controversial arguments was that private wealth came at the expense of public poverty—a point his young Norwegian follower took to heart: "Why can we not afford to improve healthcare, invest more in social medical research, clean the Oslo Fjord, etc., when we can afford to waste billions in the cosmetics and fashion industry alone?"[53] Through statements like these Kalleberg highlighted both the responsibility and the potential of designers. Singling out the most ostentatious of all design-intensive industries was probably smart, especially since architects, interior designers, and industrial designers—*Byggekunst*'s core readership—often themselves ridiculed the cosmetics and fashion industry in an effort to assume the identity of problem-solvers rather than beauticians. By appealing to that professional ethos, Kalleberg sought to convince his readers that the design professions should apply their expertise toward solving the most pressing problems of the time, namely the mismanagement of resources and the environment.

The Galbraith-inspired criticism of consumer society is important here, but Kalleberg offered a far more intriguing—albeit ostensibly opaque—reference as well: "The Earth can be seen as a confined spaceship, staffed as of 1968 with 3.5 billion people. The limited nature of the spaceship's resources in terms of soil, forests, air, and water is becoming ever more evident."[54] What is remarkable about this conception of the earth as a spaceship is the timing and the venue. In design and architecture circles, the concept is widely attributed to Buckminster Fuller, who integrated the term in lectures from the mid-1960s.[55] However, it was only with the publication of his *Operating Manual for Spaceship Earth* in 1968 that he moved the analogy beyond lecture theaters.[56] So, at the time Kalleberg addressed Norwegian architects and designers, the concept was by no means familiar to them. Since Kalleberg did not cite any source for his spaceship metaphor, it is difficult to ascertain where he culled it from—but given the contemporaneity it is unlikely that he was familiar with Fuller's version. Although the term in a design context is inseparable from Fuller, he is not its originator. The exact genesis is somewhat contested, but an influential place of use was no doubt the British economist Barbara Ward's book *Spaceship Earth* from 1966. Both because of its earlier date and because Kalleberg was a social scientist, this is a much more plausible source of his inspiration.

The main point of the spaceship earth metaphor for Kalleberg, as for Fuller and for Ward, was that the world must be understood as a whole, as one delicately balanced, integrated system. This fostered increased attention to the importance of interactions on geographical scales, in conceptual realms, and in professional domains not normally considered immediate. One pertinent example of this sense of profound relationality and immense interconnectedness was the acknowledgment that pollution knows no borders. Kalleberg here referred to recent research revealing that the surging levels of acid rain in Scandinavia were caused by air pollution from heavy industry in Central Europe. Just as environmental problems exposed new transnational connections and pinpointed the need for transnational collaborations, Kalleberg found that they also exposed transprofessional connections and pinpointed the need for transprofessional collaborations. Like Esdaile, Kalleberg worried that "the increasing degree of specialization within ever more professions means that each expert is more poorly equipped to understand and influence the whole."[57]

The design professions were key in these endeavors, Kalleberg argued, but he warned that "the architects and other professions are faced with a development where it is difficult to separate cause and effect."[58] Designers and architects, with their relatively low degree of specialization and a high level of general planning expertise, might have been the closest to his ideal form of education by which students would "get a full understanding of our situation, and not just an image of the world of the day before yesterday. . . . It is fundamentally important that every discipline seeks to see itself in a total context."[59] The aim should be, he maintained, to educate "professionals, not specialists," citing Norberg-Schulz's recently published *Intentions in Architecture* as corroborating evidence for his claim that every professional must see their domain as part of a universal whole—perhaps not a coincidental reference, as Norberg-Schulz was, as mentioned above, the editor of *Byggekunst* at the time. Kalleberg's emphasis on whole-systems thinking and comprehensive planning, and the designer's reimagined role in this brave, new world, are entirely in line with Fuller's ideas. Styling himself a "comprehensive anticipatory design scientist," Fuller considered himself—and by implication, any designer worth their salt—a "nonspecialist" whose true expertise was to generate visionary yet practical responses to highly complex problems by thinking in "'comprehensive' or universal terms."[60] Casting design expertise as comprehensive in scale and scientific in nature could also be seen as a strategic advantage in terms of the design professions' standing in society. This conception was a far cry from the notion of design as some sort of applied art or as industry's make-up department—derogatory perceptions all too common in the preceding midcentury modern period that did little to further the public image of design. With the rise of the comprehensive or ecological designer, however, such charges would be groundless. On the contrary; designers and architects would, according to Fuller, eventually "take over and successfully operate SPACESHIP EARTH."[61]

Two years later, in 1970, Fuller's appeal for a new type of designer characterized by expertise in "comprehensive thinking" was more elaborately and explicitly presented to the Norwegian design community. In an essay titled "Resources and Methods," architect Edvard Hiorthøy recapitulated one of Fuller's most ambitious and unconventional publications, the six-volume *World Design Science Decade 1965–75* coauthored and edited by his research assistant John McHale and published between 1963 and 1967. Fuller conceived of this document as the basis for a profound reorientation of design and architectural education in line with his ideal of the comprehensive planner. This provenance of the publication takes on added significance in our context because Hiorthøy soon after, in 1972, embarked on a long teaching career at the Norwegian Institute of Technology, alongside, amongst others, Robert Esdaile. In his essay, Hiorthøy picked up on the question of world resources and efficiency in design, to which Fuller and McHale devoted much attention. Whereas Kalleberg took a rather dim view of the prospects of improved resource distribution and environmental health, Hiorthøy found inspiration in Fuller's characteristically optimistic approach, which saw science and innovation as having the potential to solve these challenges if properly harnessed by comprehensive planners.[62]

Just like Kalleberg, Esdaile, and Fuller and McHale, Hiorthøy cited Georg Borgström's research on the world's population and resource crisis. The Swedish botanist and professor of food science and economic geography at Michigan State University was a key contributor to the neo-Malthusian discourse picking up momentum in the latter half of the 1960s and reaching its zenith with the Club of Rome report *Limits to Growth* in 1972. In books such as *The Hungry Planet* (1965) and *Too Many* (1969),[63] Borgström warned against the West's unsustainable exploitation of the world's resources and ensuing ecological disasters, thus contributing to an ideological foundation for a new environmental criticism. In the late 1960s, Borgström advanced "from prophet to superstar" status in Norway.[64] His explicit influence on the exhibition *And after Us . . .* , discussed above, is a case in point. Ecologically minded designers and architects of a more techno-optimistic bent, like Fuller and Hiorthøy, took such warnings as a challenge and an opportunity to rewrite the role of design in society. Channeling Fuller, Hiorthøy observed that designers still chiefly worked on narrowly defined projects of limited significance, defined by others, and sought to "solve" them in a largely superficial manner by producing static objects, "rather than consciously developing basic prototypes as means to integrate dynamic processes within an ecosystem. The architect-planner-designer is nevertheless the best qualified to do this, given his traditional role as integrative force amongst specialists."[65] Through comprehensive planning, based on scientific methods and technological innovations, the designers of the future would not only solve the resource crisis and environmental problems, they would also free the world of the stubborn socioeconomic entanglements of material culture. In such a new world order,

Resources, and the products into which an automated industry can transform them, will lose their traditional meaning as carriers of *value*, and instead represent stages in a continuous cycle of production, use, and reuse. These circulations of material and energy would be integrable as parts within the total circulation—the earth's ecosystem. "Consumption" will be replaced by "use," and "things" will become temporary configurations without any significance beyond the given need; easily available as *means*, they will cease to be *ends*.[66]

In the abstract, this new, distinctly ecological vision of what design is and does lends itself to biological metaphors. Resembling Kepes's later notion of the environment as "our extended body," discussed above, Hiorthøy thus concluded that the task of designers was ultimately "to improve the possibilities for humankind's 'external metabolism' in the widest sense to run as automatically and painlessly as in the organism's internal organs."[67]

In the end, both metaphors—the earth as spaceship and design as metabolism—are intrinsically linked. They both speak of comprehensive self-containment, of complex and precarious systems which needed to be reconfigured from within. The sobering realization that we are all in the same boat was crucial to the notion of a new role for designers to control the course of the spaceship and the health of our material metabolism. Both Kalleberg and Hiorthøy thus envisioned designers as comprehensive planners whose expertise should be directed toward saving the earth, like latter-day Noahs—thus putting the ark in architecture.

AN APOCALYPTIC ARCHITECT

We evolve from architects to ecologists, because we want to hide our sins and our shame. We see an ecological idea. Entirely clear. With the help of a new SCIENTIFIC mechanism we dream of cleansing the world of all the filth we and science have dispersed. But we turn away. Close our eyes and our mind. To that which we sense is there all the time. (Not just subconsciously.) The ecological idea's poisonous excrements.[68]

The architect Bjørn Simonnæs was no less concerned about the environmental destruction caused by modern industrial technology than were his colleagues—but contrary to Esdaile and other aspiring ecodesigners, Simonnæs did not find salvation in the emerging science of ecology. At least not initially. His objection to the notion of ecology as a panacea capable of "cleansing the world" seems to have been grounded in the logic that you can't fight fire with fire. If, as he believed, science was to blame for our destruction of the environment, science could not be the solution—not even the "greenest" science of all. Understood as science, he reasoned, ecology was underpinned by the very same basic structures and principles as any other science, including those most culpable for the current crisis.

This distrust even in science-based ecology as a way forward is what set Simonnæs apart from other anti-growth proponents, preindustrial romantics, and back-to-the-land activists that populated the environmental movement at the time. Another intriguing aspect of his rather pessimistic outlook, which aligned better with other streaks of anti-growth thinking, is his view on energy consumption. Based on the notion of the earth as a steady-state energy system, he argued in a

1974 essay that the exponential growth in energy consumption in the twentieth century would be our road to perdition: "Here in Norway, Director General Vidkunn Hveding [of the Norwegian Water Resources and Energy Administration] fables of doubling Norwegians' consumption in only 15 years."[69] Such technocratic visions spelled disaster to Simonnæs, who claimed that "Any power plant implies the loss of lives on an immeasurable scale. The life-giving water in creeks and rivers dries up between dam and turbine. The temperature changes, the climate changes, plants die, insects die, fish die. Only so that technologists can produce even more useless and harmful aluminum."[70] That Simonnæs deemed even the production of aluminum, normally considered the most environmentally friendly metal due to its high potential for efficient recycling,[71] by means of hydroelectric power—as opposed to, say, coal-fired power—unacceptable, is highly revealing of his dim view of industrial society. This criticism must also be understood in the context of the spate of highly mediatized environmental activism starting with the sit-in demonstrations against the hydroelectrical power development of the Mardøla River in the summer of 1970 (see chapter 5). Naturally, though, Simonnæs reserved his most intense aversion for the short-sighted exploitation of fossil fuels: "Nature has stored this enormous amount of energy for millions, billions of years. And now it is burned up on a gigantic bonfire in the course of a few decades." Long before global warming became a household phrase, the apocalyptic architect laconically noted that "the temperature is about to rise in the greenhouse Tellus." The "privileged technologists" would not stop, he continued, until they have surpassed "the Creator himself" and succeeded in tapping energy from the earth's glowing core and, ultimately, in "creating artificial life." Beyond this final frontier, "nature may just as well succumb completely" only to be "resurrected artificially in reservoirs, zoos and electronic greenhouses."[72]

Amidst all his bleak prognostications, Simonnæs eventually acknowledged that there were counterforces at work—but that these efforts made up a classic case of too little, too late. The "privileged conqueror human" was facing resistance "from a new type of humans" who respected life, and not just human life.[73] Based on the same neo-Malthusian view regarding the challenges of the exponential increase in the world's population that underpinned the Club of Rome report *Limits to Growth* published two years earlier—coauthored by Norwegian climatologist Jørgen Randers—Simonnæs sought to overturn the image of the "privileged conqueror human" in favor of an understanding of humans as "unprivileged," as one life form amongst many—a key tenet also of Næss's ecophilosophy, examined in chapter 5. In other words, the reigning anthropocentric worldview was untenable, challenged by an increased ecological awareness. By now his view of ecology had taken a turn for the better, five years after he had dismissed it as integral to the technofix ethos of "big science": "Ecology—the science of balance—has provided the unprivileged human with a great challenge. The greatest of all challenges. To stop the insane crusade. To stop the plunder of energy. To stop the murder of nature."[74]

The only hope he saw was in grassroots activism. Self-identifying unprivileged humans should get together and stage revolts against plunder. "For example through active participation in the new people's movement: 'The Future in Our Hands.'"[75] This organization, discussed in chapter 5, had been founded just a few months earlier by former advertising consultant Erik Dammann, based on the remarkable success of his eponymous book published in 1972.[76] Dammann and his organization, which grew rapidly to include more than 25,000 members and wielded considerable political influence, pushed for significant reductions in the production and consumption of goods and for a global redistribution of resources.[77] Simonnæs hoped that initiatives such as Dammann's could inspire people to "consume less, earn less, and pay less taxes." A particularly promising area in this respect, he believed, was agriculture. Norway was riddled with small plots of land left idle in the wake of the mechanization of farming. These, he argued, could be utilized by turning the entire population into "finger farmers": "No tractor. No oil. No electricity. Soon we will be completely self-supporting."[78] To Simonnæs, this prospect was no mere ideological construct or daydream. In 1972 he bought and moved to a small, abandoned nineteenth-century farmstead in a remote and roadless location north of Bergen, with the intention of giving up his architectural practice and living off the land.[79] Fully aware that this sounded exactly like the oft-ridiculed back-to-the-land romanticism, he hurried to mention that well-reputed, politically recognized organizations like the Norwegian Society for the Conservation of Nature (later known also as Friends of the Earth Norway) and the Norwegian College of Agriculture currently were planning seminars to teach people how to live off of nature's nonfarmed food. In the end, however, these hopes were just a momentary lapse of his pessimism, because "the energy technologists have all the power" and would not listen to any protests. The recent oil crisis had, paradoxically enough, only made matters worse, he argued, as it had made their quest even more relentless. Simonnæs thus ended on a gloomier note than ever: "There is no hope. We must accept that the world will end with a tremendous bang."[80]

Despite the fatalistic flavor of his prose, Simonnæs did try to practice what he preached. He was actively engaged in heritage preservation and nature conservation

projects, and styled himself a "nester." The most remarkable "nest" he designed, with his office partner Jacob Myklebust, was Brekkestranda Fjordhotell (1966–1980) (figure 2.5). This small hotel overlooking the Sognefjord, an hour's drive north of Bergen, represented a new type of ecological design and can be seen as a manifestation of Simonnæs's radical ideology. "Brekkestranda hotel is to grow out of nature," he proclaimed.[81] The bulk of the buildings is broken down into irregular volumes adapted to the natural topology of the site, so that the comparably large structure becomes subordinate to the landscape. The foundation walls are made from natural stone, the roof is turfed, and both interior and exterior wall cladding is of rough, untreated pine flitch—the edge of the log, a material that is normally considered

2.5

Brekkestranda Fjordhotel, designed by Bjørn Simonnæs and Jacob Myklebust (1966–1980). Photo courtesy of the National Museum of Art, Architecture, and Design.

residual, suitable only for low-grade constructions such as fences or ground to chip. Simonnæs also designed much of the furniture for the hotel, relying on craft production and local materials.[82] These contemporary explorations of traditional techniques, materials, and methods were intended to demonstrate that a low-tech approach could be a sound alternative, both ecologically and economically, to the high-tech strategies of mainstream modernist architecture. Brekkestranda Fjordhotell can be seen as a total work of ecodesign in which every aspect of the project is planned to work *with* nature rather than against it.

If the built result is remarkable in its carefulness, so is the design process. Firstly, the project was planned and developed in close collaboration with the owners of the hotel, the local Brekke family. Given the family business context and the small-scale economy involved, the project did not lend itself to a conventional top-down design process dictated by the architect as a sovereign, heroic figure. Instead, it called for a genuine dialogue capable of converging the clients' concerns and the architects' visions.[83] This dovetailing of ecological and socioeconomic considerations on the one hand and the rethinking of the design process on the other makes Brekkestranda Fjordhotell a good example of how, as Ida K. Lie has shown, the rise of socially responsible design as a key concern in Scandinavia at this time went hand in hand with the emergence of participatory design as methodology.[84] Secondly, the design and construction process was deliberately slow. The little hotel was constructed in six stages over a period of 14 years, with the first part opening in 1970, four years into the process. This prolonged process was a willed method fostering—and fostered by—an ethics of engagement and attentiveness. The planning and development of Brekkestranda Fjordhotell thus revealed an understanding of design in terms of consequential and long-term thinking, making it tempting in retrospect to cast it as a case of "slow design" *avant la lettre*. Sognefjord might be a long way from Yosemite, but the roots of the "combination of design thinking and practice with activism and environmental concerns" that characterizes slow design can be found in the careful design of a low-impact hotel in western Norway just as it can in the careful design of low-impact climbing gear in the western United States, as studied by Michelle Labrague (and discussed in chapter 5).[85]

Simonnæs was clearly more hesitant than some in embracing the scientific discipline of ecology as a panacea for design. Not because he was not convinced of the gravity of the environmental problems or that radical changes were required, but because of a deep distrust in the structures and institutions of big science. He might also have doubted that even the most radical versions of ecological design held the potential of arresting the looming apocalypse. But his humble hotel project reveals a hope that slow design could perhaps help slow down what he saw as our frantic race toward the inevitable end. Like many ideologically motivated architects and designers, Simonnæs brought his views to bear on education as well, lecturing for design students at the Bergen School of Craft and Design from 1979.[86] A few years later, he and fellow travelers in Bergen's countercultural architecture circles institutionalized their dedication to societal and environmental issues, slow design, and ecological principles with the establishment in 1986 of the Bergen School of Architecture—a small, private institution motivated by the desire for an alternative to the educational principles and priorities of established programs.

PINING FOR MORAL MATERIALS

What's in a chair? The rise of the environmental movement and the emerging ecological sensitivity of design professionals discussed in this chapter coincided with a marked shift in furniture design: the sudden abandon of tropical woods in favor of indigenous ones. The Norwegian furniture industry had enjoyed considerable commercial success and critical acclaim from the mid-1950s as part of the wider international interest in Scandinavian design. Paradoxically, though, this furniture, which to international audiences apparently expressed something inherently Scandinavian, was predominantly made from woods nowhere to be found in the region, but which had to be imported from far corners of the globe—most notably teak, but also mahogany, rosewood, and others. Always fearing a fad, design critics grew skeptical of the fashion for tropical woods in the 1960s, but their arguments soon moved beyond the usual warnings against herd mentality and lack of originality. First of all, there is of course a colonial history to this seemingly paradoxical design practice which grew less savory as the quest for increased global justice picked up pace (see chapter 3). In fact, it was the Danish East Asiatic Company which introduced teak wood from Siam to European markets at the turn of the twentieth century.[87] But issues of cultural identity and environmental concern were equally prominent in the turn to local alternatives. The tropical materials that had contributed to the international fame of Scandinavian design were now cast as alien, false, and extravagant; as inappropriate for Norwegian furniture. Alf Midtbust, director of the National Federation of Furniture Manufacturers, put it succinctly: "The Danes conquered the world with teak from Siam. . . . We Norwegians have the opportunity to conquer the world using pine and birch."[88] In stark contrast to Denmark, Norway (and Sweden) has vast forests ripe with resources readily available to local designers and manufacturers, and utilizing these rather than tropical imports became a moral imperative.

The design magazine *Bonytt* led the way, advocating quite intensely for the use of indigenous woods, especially birch and pine, in the name of functional appropriateness, national traits, ethics, and resource management alike (figure 2.6). Leisure cabins became a steppingstone in this campaign, on the assumption that these spaces required furniture which was simpler, sturdier, and cheaper than in permanent homes—and pine, especially, was considered optimally suited for such designs.[89] This approach to pushing pine was no coincidence, of course. The combined and rapid expansion of the welfare state and the consumer society had resulted in significant increases in both leisure time and disposable income for large proportions of the population. One of the consequences was an unprecedented boom in leisure cabin construction and ownership (figure 2.7). In a society dominated by a temperate social democratic ideology and still marked by a puritanical heritage, conspicuous consumption was a delicate issue. One way to circumvent such anxieties was to direct consumption toward the material cultures of skiing, hiking, hunting, camping, etc.—in short, toward traditional leisure activities undertaken in intimate interaction with nature and perceived as healthy, wholesome pursuits.[90] The leisure cabin and its accoutrements were at the heart of these new practices, which might be said to make up something of an environmental consumer culture. The cabin boom of the 1960s did stir environmental concerns regarding its impact on fragile landscapes and ecosystems, but design reformers preferred to see it as a welcome opportunity to argue for a shift to a more "honest," "local," and "natural" approach to furniture design—especially the widespread adoption of pine as a morally superior material. What was initially pitched as cabin furniture soon migrated into the (pine-clad) houses of suburbia, functioning also as an indoor reflection of the surrounding woods so symbolically significant to many Norwegians.

2.6

Cover of *Bonytt* (1966, no. 5), emphasizing the acute attention to the character of wood as material. Courtesy of Egmont Publishing.

«Design for Living»
26. årgang 1966
Nr. 5/kr. 4.-

Nye norske møbler
Finsk dristighet
Møbler for gamle
Norske kontormøbler
Svenske møbler

Felt møbler
Tekstiler for møbler
Rullende bord
BONYTT intervju -
fantasi og dristighet

bonytt

In 1965, a spate of design competitions organized by the National Federation of Furniture Manufacturers, the Norwegian Home Craft Association, and the Furniture Industry Trade Council resulted in a wide range of innovative furniture, much of which was made from pine. The same year, the Norwegian Furniture Fair in Stavanger dedicated a designated exhibition to new designs in pine, which generated considerable attention. At the fair, *Bonytt* editor Arne Remlov interviewed designer and manufacturer Gunnar Sørlie, asking his opinion on the shifting trend

2.7

Ålhytta, a modular, prefabricated cabin model intended to blend in with the surrounding landscape. Designed by Jon Haug of the architectural office Lund & Slaatto in 1966. Photo: Dag Andre Ivarsøy, courtesy of the National Museum of Art, Architecture, and Design.

in materials. Sørlie's response is revealing of the morality of materials: "I hope that pine and the other blond woods can tell us and the world something good about Scandinavian design aptitude. Few countries have such extensive leisure-, cabin-, and weekend life as we do. Herein lies an inspiration for furniture designers to create."[91] The young designer couple Elsa and Nordahl Solheim took part in all these competitions, as well as the exhibition, specializing in pine furniture of a rustic yet modern design, developed for production by small, local, craft-intensive manufacturers. The leading furniture design offices Bruksbo and Rastad & Relling also explored the potential of pine, but for larger-scale production. An early example is the comprehensive Biri line designed by Torbjørn Afdal, Harry Moen, Rolf Hesland, and Gunleik Svartdal of Bruksbo and manufactured by Konrad Steinstads Snekkerverksted from 1961. The competing practice Rastad & Relling introduced its similarly comprehensive Futurum line in 1965 (figure 2.8). Designed by Adolf Relling, Rolf Gabrielsen, Bibben Løken, and Torbjørn Bekken, it was produced by two manufacturers, Karl Sørlie & Sønner and Mysen Møbelindustri, but was marketed and sold through the design office's own retail operation Futurum AS. Futurum is particularly interesting in that its design idiom represented a marked departure from the sculpted shapes of earlier teak furniture, developing instead a rectilinear expression more appropriate to the material characteristics of pine and to the line's structural logic of using modular components for rational production.

Pine, of course, has many applications other than furniture, and was the basis for many small businesses and industries in small towns and rural districts across the country. Designing furniture in pine to be manufactured by such enterprises rather than by traditional cabinetmakers or furniture factories had a double effect: Firstly, it allowed these enterprises to move into the production of finished goods with a higher profit margin, thus potentially generating economic growth in local communities threatened by depopulation. Secondly, designing for simple, rational production without relying on specialized craft expertise, and using an inexpensive and abundantly available material, resulted in affordable products. Such design projects could thus also contribute to social sustainability, a feature considered inseparable from design for environmental sustainability by key thinkers from William Morris to Arne Næss (see chapter 5), and intricately intertwined also in other, contemporary efforts to revitalize local communities by means of design.[92] This duality also serves as a poignant reminder of the shared roots, both etymological and conceptual, of the terms economy and ecology—"a valuable message that comes

out of a historical examination" of cultural practices in which design and issues of sustainability intersect.[93]

The work of designer Edvin Helseth becomes particularly interesting in this context. Throughout the 1960s he developed several furniture systems—all in pine—for small, local industries based in the heavily forested regions around Norway's largest lake, Mjøsa. In 1961 Helseth designed the modular storage system 5-15 for Systemtre A/L (figure 2.9) in Hamar (the town was also home to Helseth's design practice) and redesigned the flexible bookshelf system BBB for the rake manufacturer Eidsvoll Rivefabrikk. None of these companies had any experience with furniture production but extensive knowledge about wood processing, so the choice of material, the unconventional know-how, and the constraints and affordances of the production

2.8

Rastad & Relling's Futurum line shown at a foreign furniture fair in 1966. Photo courtesy of Rastad & Relling Arkitektkontor.

2.9

The modular storage system 5-15 designed by Edvin Helseth in 1961, manufactured by Systemtre A/L. Photo courtesy of DOGA—Design and Architecture Norway.

process were key factors in the design process. Helseth brought these experiences to the table when he designed the furniture series Trybo, launched in 1965. Manufactured by the local sawmill Stange Bruk, the various pieces in the series were designed using pine in standard dimensions, assembled in right angles and straight lines, requiring as little finishing as possible. The joints used pine plugs rather than nails or screws.[94] To be assembled by the customer (or retailer), the furniture was shipped flat-packed for more economical (and thus also more environmentally friendly) transport—a concept later made world-famous by IKEA on an entirely different (and correspondingly less sustainable) scale. Trybo was favorably received in design circles, and it was precisely its social design ambitions and attention to resource use that were highlighted. Awarding it the Norwegian Design Award in 1967 (figure 2.10), the jury hailed it as "an exceptionally good example of product development based on strictly limited raw materials and production facilities."[95]

As mentioned above, whole-system thinking was essential in formulating theories of ecological design. Helseth's design practice can be seen as a real-world manifestation of this mode of thinking. His systemic approach to design made apparent—and thus consequential—the many material, social, economic, and ecological connections extending from his pine furniture. Fully in line with his systemic design philosophy, the Trybo furniture was originally developed as an integral part of a new, modular, prefabricated leisure cabin model, the Trysil cabin, commissioned by Trysil Municipal Forest District. When the project was presented in the British Council of Industrial Design's *Design* magazine, it was again as an example of environmentally sensible social design: "[the cabin] was designed in response to two needs. The first was to create more work in an area of depopulation. The other was to produce a holiday house which was easy to erect and would fit into the landscape, as part of a plan to develop tourism in the region."[96] The cabin itself, naturally also made from pine, was designed by Helseth's colleague in the architectural office Arkitim, Hans Østerhaug. Their partner in Arkitim, Are Vesterlid, was appointed professor at the Oslo School of Architecture in 1967, and soon joined Robert Esdaile's initiative for the decentralization of architectural education, discussed earlier in this chapter.[97] This affiliation tied the Trybo project to the broader, more ideologically driven emphasis on regionalism and ecology in design discourse. Trybo was thus part of the new, morally acceptable material culture of leisure, but also a paradigmatic example both of the systemic thinking and the attention to regional specificities integral to the development of ecological design.

2.10

Designer Edvin Helseth (left) and the general manager of Trysil Municipal Forest Administration, Jostein Bjørnersen (right), demonstrate a Trybo chair for the minister of industry, Sverre Walter Rostoft, on the occasion of receiving the Norwegian Design Award in 1967. Photo courtesy of DOGA—Design and Architecture Norway.

CONCLUSION: ISN'T IT GOOD?

Just as the Beatles established "Norwegian Wood" as an instant enigma in popular culture, from the mid-1960s Norwegian wood took on a new meaning in design culture—both literally and figuratively. The growing awareness of and attention to the precarious state of the natural environment and the harm inflicted on it by industry and consumer society made designers and architects recalibrate their professional ethics. Inspired by models and ideals culled from the life sciences, and particularly from ecology, radically minded and eloquent educators and practitioners called for new approaches to design, manufacture, and consumption—ultimately, to life itself. Conceptually and ideologically, Norwegian wood represented a reaction both to the refined but elitist niceties of 1950s Scandinavian design and to the rampant consumerism symbolized by jukeboxes and Juicy Fruit. Simultaneously a model ecosystem, a material and economic resource, and a setting for a natural and healthy leisure life, Norwegian wood is a shorthand for the broad scope of professional and societal changes deemed necessary to design a more sustainable future.

"Isn't it good / Norwegian wood?"

3

WE ARE THE WORLD

Ecological Design for Development

Ecological design begins with the intimate knowledge of a particular place. Therefore, it is small-scale and direct, responsive to both local conditions and local people.[1]
—Sim Van der Ryn and Stuart Cowan (1996)

The world became smaller in the 1960s. The omnipresence of television news broadcasting connected the farthest corners of the world; commercial long-haul flights made intercontinental travel much more accessible; new transport technologies such as the shipping container made even the most trivial product a global commodity; international free-trade agreements accelerated and exposed the far-flung economic entanglements of the industrial society; the popularization of ecology explained that environmental problems know no borders; the "mutual assured destruction" promised by the looming threat of nuclear war made it abundantly clear that we only have one world; space exploration meant that the inhabitants of Earth for the first time in history could view their home planet from without, as a single entity; and the dramatic increase in and attention to development aid both highlighted and sought to remedy the vast global injustices created by colonialism. These broader developments greatly affected how Scandinavian design interacted with the world at large. Internationalization was no longer primarily an exercise in cultural diplomacy and export ambitions, but as much driven by concerns for social and environmental justice. "Environmentalism," too, explain Marco Armiero and Lise Sedrez, "exists in this delicate balance between local and global. It must be local and global at the same time."[2] For design professionals exploring the intersection of ecological design and the new paradigm for developmental aid, then, globalizing design and localizing design became two sides of the same coin.

Design for development was by no means a Nordic invention, but as I will show in this chapter, the phenomenon has a long—albeit little-known—history in the region, with a lasting legacy. From the mid-1960s, Nordic design professionals, their organizations, as well as governmental agencies became increasingly concerned that design should "do no harm"—or, expressed more emphatically, that it should "do good." Faced with a rapidly shrinking world marred by jarring global injustices, one favored strategy shared amongst these heterogeneous realms for making design "do good" was to enroll design expertise in the policies and practices of development aid alongside other, related professions including architecture and engineering. The initiatives came both from design organizations and from development aid agencies. As an example of the first, the Finnish Society of Crafts and Design funded glass artist and scientist Mikko Merikallio's project the Harambee Village Glass Industry in Kenya in the mid-1970s to foster local social and economic growth in the region.[3] Exemplifying the converse lead, the Norwegian Agency for Development Cooperation (NORAD), in the early 1980s, commissioned designer Bjørn A. Larsen to develop school furniture intended for production in Tanzania.[4] The lasting legacy of these initiatives is manifest in the Design without Borders program established in 2001 by the Norwegian Foundation for Design and Architecture and designer Peter Opsvik to run projects in developing countries using design competence to solve challenges and improve living conditions.

Western (or global North) designers' interest in, and intervention into, non-Western (or global South) societies and cultures have a much longer history, of course—and even when limited to the context of design for development, they stretch further back than the case study to be discussed in this chapter. Of particular note here is the so-called *Eames Report*, or *India Report*, written by Charles and Ray Eames in 1958 for the government of India with funding from the Ford Foundation, because it so distinctly highlighted the conflict between development through large-scale industrialization based on the transfer of Western technology and development through small-scale manufacture based on the cultivation of local craft skills, a conflict which in an Indian context often is pinned to the different strategies favored by the recently independent nation's two most formidable political leaders, Jawaharlal Nehru and Mohandas K. Gandhi, respectively.[5] Herein lies the germ of the paradox which has haunted design for development ever since, and which forever binds it to ecological design: how to design for the improvement of human living conditions in a manner which respects the communities, societies, cultures, economies, environments, and ecosystems intervened in. Ashoke Chatterjee has argued that history might help us better understand this conundrum, because "document[ing] key experiences in design for development from the past" can substantiate present advocacy for "the regeneration of crafts, the protection of fragile ecosystems and environments, the conservation of scarce materials," and other elements of ecologically sustainable design for development.[6] Therefore, in the words of Alison Clarke, "it has never been more timely for historians to turn their attention to the historiography and objects born of the specifics of a design and development discourse."[7] Heeding these calls, this chapter will examine the work of Danish designer Kristian Vedel, who in 1968 was deployed to Kenya by the Danish International Development Agency (DANIDA) to develop Africa's very first industrial design program at the University of Nairobi.

All the Scandinavian governmental development aid agencies established in the early 1960s soon homed in on East Africa as a prioritized region for their strategically coordinated effort, reflecting "a certain urgency in the competition for the hearts and minds of the newly independent peoples."[8] The new organizational infrastructure of Scandinavian aid policy coincided with the decolonization of the region, whose newly independent nations under the banner of "African socialism" needed to build crucial infrastructure and institutions for health, education, transport, industry, and government—tasks which the Scandinavian countries found to be particularly interesting targets for their new and largely concerted foreign aid policies. Deploying professional expertise quickly became an integral aspect of Scandinavian development aid strategy, with agronomists, veterinarians, teachers, medical personnel, planners, engineers, architects—and designers—sent to employ their trade skills to help build the new nation-states and improve the living conditions of their populations. Denmark spent between 12 and 17 percent of its total bilateral development aid budget in the latter half of the 1960s on sending experts, deploying more and more toward the end of the decade.[9] To make sense of how Danish design expertise was enrolled in the humanitarian and geopolitical realm of international development aid, however, its foray into East Africa needs to be contextualized. This chapter will therefore first trace Kristian Vedel's prior professional formation, with an emphasis on a study trip to Central America in 1965 which greatly influenced his thinking on the social and ecological aspects of design. The main part of the chapter then details his work at the University of Nairobi and its aftermath, before zooming out to place Vedel's ideas and efforts in the broader international discourse on design for development.

AN EXPANDED VIEW OF DESIGN IN THE WORLD

In 1961, his stackable plastic bowls were acquired by New York's Metropolitan Museum of Art. A decade later, he moved to an old farmstead in rural Jutland to breed sheep and tend the landscape. Whatever prompted this dramatic development in the life and work of industrial designer Kristian Vedel? His career began in a very conventional manner. Like many Danish designers of his generation, he had first trained as a cabinetmaker before attending the School of Arts and Crafts (Kunsthåndværkerskolen) in Copenhagen in the mid-1940s, following a stint as a guest student of Kaare Klint, professor of furniture design at the Royal Danish Academy of Fine Arts. He then worked as an assistant for several established architects, while showing his prototypes at the Copenhagen Cabinetmakers' Guild's annual exhibitions and teaching at the School of Arts and Crafts. However, when Vedel established his own practice in 1954, he veered off the beaten path which had led Danish design to international fame, working instead on children's furniture and modular furnishings and interiors for schools, shops, etc., and experimenting with the formal potentials of aluminum and melamine.[10]

Vedel may have chosen his own path, but in the early 1960s he was still very much part of the Danish design establishment. A good indication of this is the fact that he received the prestigious Nordic design award the Lunning Prize in 1962 (figure 3.1), previous Danish recipients of which included Hans J. Wegner, Henning Koppel, and Poul Kjærholm. If he received the award for his potential to renew the Danish design tradition from within, proven through his melamine bowls and his modular furniture, his career would soon take a different and more dramatic turn. Looking back at Vedel's by then somewhat less obvious place in this pantheon on the occasion of an exhibition about the award in 1986, the catalog explains,

An evaluation of Kristian Vedel's significance as a designer might well elicit the conclusion that this importance derives, at least in part, from a different sphere from that for which he received the Lunning Prize in 1962—and that, moreover, it is not the design sphere in the traditional sense. If being a designer means not only the realization of specific product concepts, but also—and perhaps especially—the formulation of an ethic for the form-world surrounding us and an analysis of the rules of its creation, then Kristian Vedel's achievements merit any number of awards.[11]

The prize came in the form of a travel grant for a longer period of study abroad to stimulate professional development. Fully in line with the above description of Vedel as an unconventional grantee, for his study trip he decided on a road less traveled, certainly by Scandinavian designers of his generation: Central America. He did not arrive at this decision by himself, however. It was in large part influenced by the experiences of his wife, Ane Vedel. She had worked as an interior designer for the promotional exhibition building Den Permanente and the department store Illums

3.1

Kristian Vedel reading the announcement
from the Lunning Prize committee
to his family. Photo: Kristian Vedel's
personal archive.

Bolighus, and in this capacity she had been sent to Venezuela in the late 1950s on a one-year contract to help set up an exhibition of Danish design. This had left her with both fond memories and relevant contacts, which she was eager to share with her new husband—they were married in 1961—when opportunity came knocking in the shape of the Lunning Prize.[12] The award was 17,000 Danish kroner (DKK), the equivalent of about DKK 200,000 or USD 32,000 today, which was a substantial amount—but making it last for a five-month journey required careful planning and careful spending. The couple therefore relied heavily on Ane's existing network for accommodation and travel.

The Vedels were heading for a region in rapid albeit uneven development, where the more economically advanced countries including Venezuela and Mexico had adopted the doctrine of developmentalism. This policy entailed state-sponsored industrial development and import substitution strategies which generated unprecedented opportunities for local design of a modernist conviction, but with strong ties to the nations' own histories, traditions, and cultures. Even if this brand of Latin American modernism, at least in its private domain incarnation, was predominantly catering to cosmopolitan elites, it testifies to the existence of a vibrant professional community which sought to cultivate modern design based on distinctly local conditions.[13] And it was precisely this complexity, embracing and interweaving the modern and the ancient, the cosmopolitan and the rural, the international and the indigenous, the industrial and the artisanal, the cultural and the natural, that attracted the Danish designers. Writing to an acquaintance they would meet up with both in Costa Rica and in Mexico, the US chemist and coffee plant developer Joe K. Trauerman, Kristian Vedel explained the purpose of their trip: "We hope the journey will give us a true feeling and knowledge of the countries, their background, and their problems of industrializing in a human way. Naturally we will look at the old art, but we are not there to study monuments."[14] Rather, the Vedels went to Central America to expand their view of design in the world.

OVER THE BLUE, INTO THE GREEN

After careful preparations, including "studying in our Ethnological Museum [and] reading several books about Central America," the couple embarked on their adventure in February 1965.[15] Already in the first letter Kristian Vedel wrote to his family back home, we get a clear sense of what a transformative experience this journey would be in staking out a career path far removed from the fetish of exquisite objects which had propelled Danish design to international fame, but rather pursuing "an ethic for the form-world surrounding us." Writing from Antwerp, where they had boarded the cargo ship M/S *Hornland* bound for Venezuela via Barbados and Trinidad, he noted that "the string of German industrial towns" they had traveled through "seemed, if possible, more depressing than ever before." "It can't be humankind's intention," he contemplated, "to spread this kind of life throughout the globe."[16] The nightly train ride through this landscape lined with "endless ferroconcrete halls, sawtooth roofs, breast walls, glazed surfaces dimly reflecting the moonlight, factory sheds in all shapes and sizes, the silhouettes of junk and debris, discarded machines, shredded car wrecks, warped cranes, broken and crumbled buildings" functioned like "a magnifying glass between me and this 'wirkshaftswunder' [sic]" and left him wondering "what has made [people] suddenly, like lemmings, march toward their own doom."[17] These few lines written at the outset of the voyage reveal that the dual concern for the environment and for global justice, and its relevance for his role as a designer, were present even at this stage: "It is so exciting whether this trip will help me work more wisely. I think it will."[18]

Despite his love of the ocean and the lessons it held, getting back on dry land allowed the Vedels to experience a rich and unfamiliar material culture which also proved distinctly inspirational. Arriving in Caracas, Venezuela, they stayed with a friend of Ane's whom she had met during her previous visit and kept in touch with: the architect Daniel Fernández-Shaw. He had even visited Copenhagen, in 1961–1962, working in the architectural studio of professor Viggo Møller-Jensen and Tyge Arnfred (the brother of Vedel's first wife, Birgit Arnfred). Back in Caracas, Fernández-Shaw taught both at the Universidad Central de Venezuela's school of architecture and at the newly established Instituto del Diseño Neumann, and had arranged for Kristian to give lectures at both institutions.[19] In his lectures, Vedel showed slides of traditional and modern Danish houses, before moving on to his own work and how it sought to address what he identified as the major challenges of the design profession. One of the main problems, he believed, was that design and design education suffered from an intellectual and structural inertia which implied that "the ideals we subscribe to today impact development, not just tomorrow, but far into the future."[20] Western designers were such prisoners of their own traditions, he submitted to his Venezuelan audience, that non-Europeans were better qualified "to critically analyze the intentions and consequences of what we have brought about and based on the ensuing experiences plot a more humane course for future work."[21] Despite the specific context of this reflection, it suggests that the Danish designer had come to Central America to learn, not to lecture.

After an adventurous 1,300-kilometer drive across the Andes and around Lake Maracaibo, marveling at the landscape's extreme contrasts, the Vedels rejoined the German cargo ship, which took them along the coast of Colombia and across the Caribbean Ocean to Puerto Limón, Costa Rica, where they disembarked.[22] The train ride inland, uphill to the capital city of San José, revealed rampant economic, social, and ethnic injustice, "giving us the impression that *Uncle Tom's Cabin* is only about to be written."[23] In San José they visited museums and private collections of pre-Colombian art, which made a deep impression. "The pre-Colombian mythology," he wrote, "is deeply marked by the fact that nature has been both friend and foe."[24] Vedel reasoned that the "cultural treasures" the indigenous population had left behind were testament to a peaceful hunting people, not warriors. "They have left behind an unbelievable richness of objects of use made from clay, volcanic rock, jade, and gold." To Vedel, the indigenous design culture he found in Costa Rica bore witness of the tragedy of colonization: "These treasures are found everywhere; one cries thinking of the human abilities which have been lost with the advance of the Spaniards."[25] He worried deeply about the longstanding and continued Western influence on Central America, and especially how it materialized in the ramifications of the region's industrialization.[26]

Vedel was hardly the first, and certainly not the last, to be confronted with his own earlier attitudes in the wake of increased ecological awareness. One of the main pragmatic purposes of the Costa Rica leg of the trip was "to study species of wood which could potentially be utilized in Denmark."[27] To this end, the entourage headed for the rainforest-covered Peninsula de Osa on the southern Pacific coast, spending several days gathering samples accompanied by representatives of a logging company and guided by a young indigenous man, Augusto, whose knowledge of the forest greatly impressed Vedel. Even if Vedel arrived in the rainforest with a distinctly instrumental intent, the experience clearly taught him to appreciate its complex and delicate ecosystem: "The forest is so overwhelming, an adventure, hard to describe because of its diversity," he wrote.[28] A decade after Vedel's visit, the Costa Rican government realized that this ecosystem was under threat from industrial exploitation and created the Corcovado National Park and the Gulfo Dulce Forest Reserve to protect the region from illegal mining and logging.

THE MAYAN TIE-IN

After three weeks in Costa Rica, the Vedels' journey continued via Nicaragua and El Salvador to their main destinations, Guatemala and Mexico. They planned to stay for a month in each of these countries, citing as a main reason that the indigenous peoples here made up about half the population—a factor they assumed would facilitate encounters with more "genuine" cultural expressions,[29] even if their general impression was one of decline and deterioration.[30] In Guatemala they traveled—partly by jeep, partly by horse—the rural areas of the mountainous region of Huehuetenango, attentively studying ways of life and material culture, including trading, transport, work patterns, infrastructure, construction materials, housing, tools, furniture, ceramics, cooking utensils, etc.—but with particular attention to weaving practices, textiles, and clothes (figures 3.2, 3.3). Awed by the dramatic nature and the rich cultural heritage, and deeply captivated by the living traditions, they were also disheartened by the widespread poverty and related social and health problems they witnessed everywhere they went.[31]

The Vedels' sense of desolation lifted considerably when they arrived in Mexico, where they were impressed by "the progress made in the country over the last 15 years" and felt that "one has a firm grip on the tasks at hand—both social and humanitarian."[32] This characterization of the state of the nation was based on a 2,000-kilometer road trip looping through much of central Mexico from Mexico City via Morelia, then north and east through Querétaro, Ixmiquilpan, Zacatlán, Puebla, and Xalapa to Veracruz and Tlacotalpan on the Atlantic coast, before heading south, ending up in Oaxaca. But despite the allure of "progress" and the familiar comfort of modern conveniences, they were again drawn to the extraordinary experiences of natures and cultures found in more remote regions. Heading to the southern town of San Cristóbal de las Casas, the Vedels spent about a week at Casa Na Bolom, a nineteenth-century monastery converted in the 1950s by the Danish explorer and archaeologist Frans Blom and his wife, the Swiss journalist and photographer Gertrude Duby Blom, into their home, doubling as a hotel and cultural center dedicated to the support of the Lacandón Maya people and the preservation of the Chiapas rain forest.[33] Frans Blom, hailing from a Copenhagen family of antique merchants, had emigrated from Denmark in the wake of World War I. He found work in the oil industry in Mexico, traveling to remote regions of the country and developing an interest in Maya ruins. This led him to study archaeology at Harvard University, followed in 1925 by a position as associate professor of Maya

archaeology at Tulane University, New Orleans. In 1943 he left his job and moved to Mexico, where he met Gertrude Duby, with whom he established Casa Na Bolom as a hub for their shared dedication to the people and nature of the southern Mexican jungle.[34] By the time the Vedels visited, Gertrude had been a widow for two years. Her concern for the Lacandón Maya was now taking a distinctly ecological turn, in response to new practices of industrial-scale logging, slash-and-burn farming, and cattle ranching threatening the indigenous culture and nature alike.[35] During their stay Gertrude took them around to a number of villages, leaving the visitors infatuated and infuriated in equal measure.[36] Returning to Oaxaca and Mexico City, Vedel lamented having "left the beautiful Indian villages" and a way of life "which within a few years will be devoured by our culture, which in many respects seems

3.2

Ane Vedel on horseback in Guatemala. Photo: Kristian Vedel's personal archive.

3.3

Studying weaving in Guatemala. Photo: Kristian Vedel's personal archive.

poorer, less humane. We need many of the qualities these societies, now in rapid decline, have."[37] What the Danish designers encountered in the Mexican rainforest, then, was an eye-opening experience of the profound destructive power wielded by the twin forces of colonialization and industrialization, and of the urgent need for environmental activism and ecological justice in the quest for countermeasures.

Back in Mexico City, toward the end of their monthlong stay in the country, Kristian Vedel gave a guest lecture at the recently established Escuela de Diseño y Artesanías.[38] Here he met one of the school's founders, the architect Jorge Stepanenko Trejo, who worked also for the newly inaugurated Museo Nacional de Antropología, the Instituto Nacional Indigenista, and the Museo de Artes e Industrias Populares, and was thus exceptionally well placed to discuss Vedel's interest in bridging modern/Western design and pre-Columbian/indigenous craft (figure 3.4).[39] In mid-June 1965 the Danish designers' Central American adventure was drawing to an end, and they left for their final destination, New York City. Sitting in a small, dark apartment in noisy Manhattan, Kristian Vedel laconically concluded that "the colorful part of the journey is over."[40] Here more prosaic activities awaited, and his introduction to the metropole's design elite became something of an anticlimax. He enjoyed their meetings with Edgar Kaufmann Jr., who had encouraged the Metropolitan Museum of Art to acquire Vedel's melamine bowls four years prior, "so it wasn't all entirely an exercise in futility."[41] Ultimately, the adventurous designer found that the highlands and rainforests of Costa Rica, Guatemala, and Mexico held deeper lessons for design practices better attuned to social justice and ecological responsibility than did the modernist metropolis. On July 16 Ane and Kristian Vedel got on a plane bound for Copenhagen, almost five months after they had left home.

RELUCTANT INTERVENTION

Once back in Denmark, Kristian Vedel settled back into his role as a leading professional figure. His work was shown at the Danish Museum of Decorative Art (Det

3.4

Kristian Vedel's photo of a cradle exhibited at the newly inaugurated Museo Nacional de Antropología, Mexico City. Photo: Kristian Vedel's personal archive.

danske Kunstindustrimuseum),[42] and in 1966 he cofounded Industrial Designers in Denmark and served as the organization's first chairman. On the home front, the Vedels embarked on the restoration and renovation of their home and studio, an old smithery in the fishing village of Humlebæk, north of Copenhagen (figure 3.5). Five months after their return, one of Denmark's leading newspapers paid them a visit to query what the designers had learned on their study trip and reported that Vedel was "planning industry for developing countries."[43] The headline seems somewhat misguided, as he was hardly harboring any ambition of becoming an imperial industrialist—but it does call attention to the fact that their Central American journey had resulted in a sustained interest in what is now variously termed design for development, design aid, or humanitarian design. The reporter wrote

3.5

Kristian Vedel in his studio in Humlebæk, north of Copenhagen. Photo: © Steen Jacobsen/Nf Ritzau Scanpix/NTB.

that "Kristian Vedel has received requests from several developing countries to assist in the planning of furniture industry and the production of kitchen utensils." Crucially, though, this could not be done simply by expanding the export markets of existing Danish products: "Developing countries require something special and in a very different price range than that of Danish export products," the newspaper rather naively explained.[44]

If the general media was curious about what a Danish designer had learned in Central America, so were his peers. In a lecture for the Danish Society of Arts and Crafts and Industrial Design (Landsforeningen Dansk kunsthaandværk og kunstindustri), Vedel shared his thoughts on the complexities and paradoxes at the heart of the very concept of design for development. While he remained convinced that the professional ethos of design was capable of producing positive change, witnessing the ramifications of colonialism and lingering coloniality firsthand had led him to believe that foreign intervention could also do more harm than good. The basic premise for design, he emphasized, was to understand the situation into which one would intervene—and this was clearly a major challenge if "Western" designers were to operate in what was called developing countries based on a "have expertise, will travel" logic. The material culture of the region, he argued, contained much that "appears remote to us, that is not possible for us to familiarize ourselves with, let alone expand upon,"[45] so any foreign design intervention would have to be made with the utmost care. Its justification was *not* given: "In order to understand to what extent such countries had a genuine need for foreign cooperation, it was necessary to observe and understand the degree to which people could be served by their own staff of technicians and artists. That is why we visited academies and design schools."[46]

Education, then, was absolutely key to the ideal of cultural specificity and self-governance, according to Vedel: "why should these new countries commit the same mistakes which we have made in Europe and which they inevitably will make if people down there exclusively send their children to our schools and settle for copying our ideals?"[47] In this manner, colonialism had had a detrimental and enduring effect on education, including design education: "even at the best schools in these countries they educate people based on a European pattern. . . . Architects were trained . . . conspicuously in support of the wealthy."[48] Vedel's description certainly corroborates Silvia Fernández's argument that the Latin American design education emerging in the 1960s was profoundly influenced by European models.[49] Vedel's experience also illustrates what Danah Abdulla has dubbed the "Westernized university" which is characterized by "promot[ing] or diffus[ing] Eurocentric knowledge to produce Westernized elites in the so-called non-West that act as intermediaries between the West and the so-called non-West. Within Westernized universities . . . knowledge is abstract from lived realities and histories."[50] This pitfall, then, was patently clear to Kristian Vedel when he soon—reluctantly—accepted the challenge of designing a design education in Nairobi, Kenya.

DESIGN EDUCATION "IN AND BY AND FOR EAST AFRICA"

The University of Nairobi approached the Danish Ministry of Foreign Affairs in October 1967 with a request for the deployment of a Danish professor of furniture design and interior architecture to join the Faculty of Architecture, Design and Development's Department of Design.[51] Given that Kristian Vedel already had an established rapport with the Ministry in connection with the study trip to Central America, combined with his publicly declared interest in design for development in the wake of that journey, it is not surprising that he was tapped for the task.

Design education at the University of Nairobi began in 1965, with a full-fledged Bachelor of Arts in Design degree course in operation by 1967—the first of its kind in Africa. It soon saw some radical changes to the syllabus, with "more emphasis . . . placed on the study of the African traditional society and environment."[52] Key to this endeavor was the South African artist and educator Selby Mvusi, who established and ran the program until his premature death in a car accident in December 1967, at only 38 years old. Mvusi embarked on the arduous task of setting up a design program at the University of Nairobi after he, as the sole delegate from the global South, had attended a seminar on design education organized by the International Council of Societies of Industrial Design (ICSID) in collaboration with UNESCO in Bruges in March 1964. The conference became an eye-opener for Mvusi, as he saw in design a source of hope following his realization "that art was not going to promote real progress."[53] Spurred by support from the international (Western) design establishment, Mvusi soon relocated to Nairobi and secured funding from the Rockefeller Foundation to transform the university's struggling fine art department into a new and unique Department of Design.[54]

To Mvusi, the nurturing of genuinely African industrial design expertise was a decolonial project, a seamless extension of political independence. Without African industrial design, he mused, "the form of this century will continue to be defined and determined by non-African people."[55] Mvusi detested primitivism, and insisted that African design must be just as conversant with modern technology and industry as Western design. Crucially, though, he envisioned an ethical custodianship of those tools and methods that would bypass the deeply disturbing social, economic, and ecological ramifications they had produced in the hands of the West.[56] Mvusi had no small visions for his adopted field. Design was not about developing useful and well-functioning products; "design was about remaking nature, in its totality."[57] Indicative of his approach, the culmination of the foundation course he codirected with Derek Morgan of the architecture program was a series of projects under the banner of "man/environ interaction" in the spring of 1967, where students were tasked with exploring design as a situated, networked, and subjective activity embedded in a built and natural environment, and to appreciate that they were being taught "in and by and for East Africa."[58] The days of the experimental and exploratory foundation course were numbered, however. The (British) managers of the architecture program believed Mvusi and Morgan's approach to design was much too abstract and theoretical, and closed the course to make room for more training in practical skills.[59]

When Kristian Vedel first arrived in Nairobi in May 1968, the Danish architecture studio Poul Kjærgaard & Partners were at work designing a new building for the recently renamed Faculty of Architecture, Design and Development, partly funded by the Danish government (completed in 1972—the university's science building, designed by Norwegian architect Karl Henrik Nøstvik, was completed the following year). There were also several other Danish architects, planners, and engineers already working at the University of Nairobi, so Vedel's deployment was part of a broader pattern of conceptualizing academic expertise as aid through the Danish International Development Agency (DANIDA)—the Ministry of Foreign Affairs' bilateral development assistance program for developing countries (established 1962). Vedel's initial assignment was to familiarize himself with the existing program, in part by acting as an external examiner, and to draft a report for the Ministry assessing the viability of the suggested scheme. Vedel's report was negative in the sense that he recommended that the Danish government should not send a professor of furniture design and interior architecture, but rather a professor of industrial design—on the condition that the university would establish a designated Department of Industrial Design as well as a Design Research and Development Unit.[60]

In his report, Vedel concluded that "the establishment of a chair of industrial design will—if this education is organized and implemented with careful attention to East African conditions—enable the States to improve their conditions for reasonable and effective industrialisation."[61] Focusing on furniture design and interior architecture would be misguided, he argued, as Scandinavian traditions and expertise in this field were too culturally specific and made little sense outside the region's economy. "It would be misleading," he claimed, "to transfer education on that basis to countries which do not have the same conditions."[62] Expertise in industrial design would travel far better, as it could be calibrated to a much higher degree to local resources and needs. The Ministry heeded his advice and decided to support the Kenyan request, on the conditions Vedel had laid out, appointing him to the proposed industrial design professorship. Vedel, along with Ane and his children, then moved to Nairobi in September 1968. The new administrative structure he had requested was formally operational from July 1969: The extant Department of Design was divided into a Department of Industrial Design (which also included graphic design) and a Department of Fine Art, followed by the establishment of the Design Research and Development Unit under Vedel's direction.[63]

Vedel had the utmost respect for his predecessor Selby Mvusi, whom he described as a "gifted theorist and educationalist," and lamented the deferral of the foundation course which Mvusi and Morgan had established.[64] As if anticipating the situation Vedel now found himself in, Mvusi had written that "The promotion of industrial design education in low-income countries is not an 'aid programme'. It is consistent with long-term self-interest in strict economic and political terms."[65] Fully in line with this view, in his plan for the new Department of Industrial Design, Vedel boldly claimed that graduates of the program would "be prepared to work as planners of functional, identity-creating local products suitable for East African requirements, to replace import."[66] In this regard, he was obviously inspired by the promising symbiosis of new design education and import substitution policies he had witnessed in Latin America, hoping to create a similar potential on his new adopted home turf. Both "to avoid wastage of foreign exchange" and to stimulate "trade and turn-over," a new generation of Kenyan designers would generate "improved world market competitive products, for markets in- and outside East Africa."[67] This ambition was accentuated in connection with other Scandinavian development aid projects as well, for instance in the Muguga Green housing complex for Nordic experts and Kenyan clerks built in Nairobi in 1967, funded by the Norwegian Agency for Development Cooperation (NORAD). The architect, Karl Henrik Nøstvik, shared Vedel's interest in locally manufactured products, but quickly ran into availability problems and had to resort to shipping refrigerators, stoves, kitchen units, and bathroom appliances from Norway—a paradoxical situation he hoped would soon be resolved through the design of locally manufactured products.[68] At no point, however, did Nøstvik stop to ask whether these totems of a distinctly Western lifestyle would be of any relevance to an indigenously conceived design practice.

The future graduates of the Nairobi industrial design program were not solely—not even chiefly—envisioned as catalysts for the national economy, however. In Vedel's vision, they would become experts on local material culture, improve public services, and generally function "as an aid for [the] welfare of the population."[69] One of his first students later wrote that Vedel's aim for the University of Nairobi design program was to foster graduates with the capability "to design and make functionally sound, aesthetically pleasant, ergonomically appropriate, economically viable, environmentally friendly, easy to manufacture, safe, secure and sustainable products."[70] It was challenging, though, to piece together a consistent and comprehensive curriculum for such an ambitious program, especially given the small staff and the limited resources at his disposal (figure 3.6). The new first-year students received training in topics ranging from drawing, photography, and printing and communication technology, via construction methods and materials, computer technology, and ergonomics, to design theory, sociology, and cultural studies.[71] Vedel even sent them to take ecology classes, which students found to be a surprising and innovative part of the curriculum, providing them with "an awareness base to understand how humans and nature are connected."[72]

In addition to the more conventional skills and basic contextual knowledge, Vedel wanted his students to become experts in "the relationship between man and his environment."[73] A key component in this strategy would be to prepare designers to plan for "labour-intensive production to increase employment."[74] This, of course, is diametrically opposite the dogma of Western industrial design education, where planning for efficient (mechanized, automated) manufacturing is king. Instead, Vedel's plan had many affinities with the notion of "appropriate" or "intermediate technology" promoted by the UK-based NGO Intermediate Technology Development Group (ITDG) founded in 1966 by economist E. F. Schumacher, and subsequently more widely disseminated in his influential book *Small Is Beautiful*.[75] Transposing Western-style capital-, technology-, and energy-intensive manufacturing systems to non- or low-industrialized societies would be socially, economically, and environmentally detrimental, according to Schumacher. In communities short on such prerequisites but rich in manpower, it made more sense to prioritize labor-intensive, smaller-scale production based on "appropriate" technology. However,

ITDG tended to favor an approach in which products were designed *for* rather than *in* developing countries—whether through their 1967 mail order catalog *Tools for Progress* featuring British goods deemed "appropriate" for use in decolonizing nations or through their later bespoke projects designed in the UK and shipped off to South Asia, Latin America, or Africa. This strategy can be seen as derived from distinctly binary conception of North-South relations and a teleological view of linear progress, with paternalistic and neocolonialist overtones.[76]

By contrast, and despite the fact that the concept had not yet become part of official Danish development aid policy,[77] Vedel insisted that Kenya had to train its own designers to become conversant with the notion of appropriate technology as part of their domestically developed expertise. The appropriate technology movement was already in full swing in Kenya,[78] so Vedel's approach can be seen as an attempt to resist its becoming yet another form of foreign control over the

3.6

Kristian Vedel teaching at the University of Nairobi. From left: Flemming Jørgensen (fellow Dane expat who taught urban planning), students Diana Lee-Smith and Gamaliel Mugumbya, lecturer Amrik Kalsi, professor Kristian Vedel, and students Sultan Somjee, Stine Johansen, and Davinder Lamba. The remaining three persons are unidentified. Photo: Kristian Vedel's personal archive.

country's design culture. The ambition to educate designers to implement labor-intensive production and alternative technology did not necessarily translate effortlessly from strategy documents to seminars and studios, however. For instance, J. P. Odoch Pido, who began his design studies at the University of Nairobi in 1968, has no recollection of Vedel's alternative technology approach informing teaching—quite the opposite: "Design educators of that time did not think of low-technology industrial design because the post-independence euphoric thought of the time was that Kenya would leap from an artisanal production model to a 'smoke stack' model of large factory industrialization without intermediate steps."[79] Vedel certainly did not favor "the 'smoke stack' model." His consistent use of the term "industrial design" reflected methodological concerns, not a commitment to specific manufacturing systems: "The term industrial, I take, as standing for 'methodic work.'"[80] In this he was attuned to Mvusi, who "came to see 'industrial' as something more fundamental than either mechanization or industry. For Mvusi, industrial processes were social forms engaged in the organization of matter and materials."[81] If Vedel's penchant for a domestically developed alternative technology approach has not registered in his former student Pido's recollections, it was because Vedel, in order to focus his work on the Design Research and Development Unit, soon left the daily responsibility of running the undergraduate program to a newly hired colleague with different priorities: Nathan Shapira.[82]

Shapira was an associate professor of industrial design at the University of California, Los Angeles. He had been active in ICSID ever since its founding in 1957 and had met Mvusi at a UNESCO conference on US-Africa relations in Boston in 1961, while Mvusi was finishing his MFA at Boston University. Based on this connection, it was Shapira who had suggested inviting Mvusi to the design education seminar in Bruges in 1964, which in turn led Mvusi to Nairobi.[83] Even after Vedel had arrived in the wake of Mvusi's death, the program was still short on staff. Given Shapira's relation to Mvusi, he was considered a prospective addition. Following a visit to the University of Nairobi in the summer on 1969, he was invited to join the design department as a visiting professor, funded by the Rockefeller Foundation.[84] He took leave from his position at UCLA and arrived in Nairobi in September 1969, a year after Vedel. Although he greatly admired Mvusi, Shapira represented an entirely different outlook on design, applying the South African's theories "only in an attenuated way," as Daniel Magaziner has phrased it.[85] Mvusi's biographer, Elza Miles, likewise argues that Shapira "had not grasped Mvusi's all-encompassing approach to design and was still arguing from the first world's 'developed' viewpoint."[86]

Whereas Mvusi had envisioned an African design expertise capable of challenging and even changing social structures, Shapira was convinced that "if design was going to succeed in Kenya, it needed to serve the niche offered to it by capitalist society."[87] He primarily conceived of the various branches of design practice as "useful instruments in increasing the volume of sales."[88] As it turned out, his views differed considerably also from those of Vedel, including on the issue of appropriate technology. Whereas Vedel advocated local empowerment through appropriation of this strategy, Shapira saw it as an unfortunate but necessary transitional stage: "Developing countries must often rely on an 'intermediary' technology where labour and semi-mechanised processes are used."[89] This corresponds well with their student J. P. Odoch Pido's later characterization: "Nathan Shapira felt that design can accelerate development; though his thought was motivating, we did not know how to implement it, and neither did he. Shapira's understanding and views were different from ours, and we never closed the gap."[90] Pido has also described Shapira's understanding of "African design" as restricted to "the picture of it, how it look[ed], more than what it meant to people who used it."[91] It quickly became clear that Shapira and Vedel did not see eye to eye.

THE DESIGN RESEARCH AND DEVELOPMENT UNIT

Vedel's rationale for establishing the Design Research and Development Unit was to provide the basic research required to run a design program that would be built on scholarly inquiry and systematic methods rather than on tacit knowledge or artistic intuition. This was particularly crucial in Kenya, he argued, given the absence of established academic or professional expertise in the field. Vedel further emphasized that "the Unit's role should be seen as one of major importance in the feasible implementation of the design discipline as an aid to development, and as an important tool for africanization."[92] It was to undertake independent investigations, liaise with governmental organizations, and act in an advisory capacity to public and private enterprises. He suggested early-phase priorities would include studies of rural and urban material culture, economic systems, social structures, public health, and environmental conditions—all in order to build a solid foundation for a design expertise better attuned to local conditions and to develop broader strategies for design in developing countries. One of the main focus areas should be "design for effective use of natural resources,"[93] and a potential practical exploration of this could be through "design for cottage industries" of "articles made from: hide, clay, stone, wood, fibres, metals."[94] This prioritization of locally available natural materials and low-impact manufacturing systems in Vedel's design-for-development strategies points to a profound interconnectedness of humanitarian design and ecological design: designing to improve human living conditions should not be done at the expense of nonhuman living conditions.

When staffing the Unit, Vedel sought to enlist the contribution of a recent graduate of the design program, Amrik Kalsi, who in 1969 had just returned from continuing studies at the California Institute of the Arts and begun lecturing at his alma mater. Together, the two traveled extensively to Kenyan national parks and rural villages to study their material culture (figure 3.7).[95] Vedel considered Kalsi "the only qualified Kenyan citizen" for the position as the Unit's Research Fellow.[96] The admiration was mutual: Kalsi considered Vedel his close friend and mentor, keeping in touch long after Vedel's return to Denmark and even visiting his new home in Jutland.[97] Kalsi started his own design office in Nairobi called Systems Design and would go on to work extensively on issues of development and sustainability with various UN organizations, eventually earning a PhD in development studies and serving as director of sustainabilityAFRICA, an institute promoting locally situated, ecologically sound design and development projects in rural communities. Kalsi's later career development should of course not be attributed to Vedel's early support, but he confirms that Vedel's "thinking and mentorship had significant effect on my thinking and development."[98] The professor's insistence on this particular student's expertise, as well as their continued contact and mutual admiration, is thus indicative of their shared visions for design in Africa as ecological and humanitarian in equal measures.

Getting the Unit fully operational proved a sluggish affair, and it would never function entirely according to Vedel's intentions. The closest he got was a series of projects on issues including housing, transportation, energy, water, and health for rural development. One of these projects, called "Media of Transportation by Use of Human Forces on or by the Body," was conducted over five months in the spring term of 1971 as a joint venture between the Unit and seven second-year product design students from Vedel's class on design and environment (figure 3.8). The project sought to map how the Kikuyu people (chiefly the women) in the rural Kiriaini (hilly) and Maragua (flat) areas of Kenya's Central Province carried water, fuel, and crops on their bodies, in order to identify any problems or undesirable effects of current practice/equipment and suggest possible improvements. Their

3.7

Kristian Vedel (right) and his assistant, Amrik Kalsi, doing field studies. Photo: Kristian Vedel's personal archive.

3.8

Illustration from the project "Media of Transportation by Use of Human Forces on or by the Body" carried out by Vedel and his students at the University of Nairobi in the spring of 1971. Photo: Kristian Vedel's personal archive.

investigations found that these women spent three to five hours a day carrying loads of about 30 kilograms over distances typically ranging from two to four kilometers using the "head to back" technique in which water vessels (mostly repurposed, modified oil drums), woven baskets (for crops), and jute or sisal sacks (for pots, fuel, and manure) are suspended by headbands and rest against the back. Headaches and backpains were very common complaints from the interviewees, and public health records showed that skull deformation—readily observed on the majority of the informants—was much more prevalent with the Kikuyu than with the population in general. When asked about desired improvements, the women emphasized issues such as capacity, durability, comfort, and weight.[99]

Vedel did not expect his second-year students to produce finalized designs, "but it was hoped that, by the end of the project, they would have identified ways and means by which the development of the material culture could be assisted by Designers."[100] The students' proposed conceptual design solutions ranged from wider headbands for improved load distribution; pads fitted to the head, shoulders, or back for increased comfort; an ergonomically designed multipurpose carrying device; a stabilizing frame for improved weight balance; canvas bags to be worn on hips or waist; and a modular, wheeled device capable of negotiating steep terrain and uneven surfaces. The concepts might not seem particularly remarkable, but the main significance of the project lies in its highly systematized methodology in combination with its underpinning ethos of empathy and respect for the community and environment. For instance, the 100-page project report features a section documenting the areas' natural environments, from the macro scale of landscape topography to the micro scale of surface vegetation.[101] Furthermore, even at the level of rudimentary concept, all the suggested design solutions favored the use of locally available, natural materials, which made a lot of sense both in economic and in ecological terms. The manual transportation project was distinctly tentative in tone and reflects the emergent and precarious nature of the design program at the University of Nairobi, but it also testifies to the self-evident place of environmental concerns in Vedel's take on design for development.

Despite the shared etymological roots of the two terms, economy and ecology have often proven difficult to reconcile in design for development. The industrial design program at the University of Nairobi encountered this predicament time and again. One of Vedel's last students in Nairobi, Lorna Schofield, wrote a paper for her third-year exhibition design class about "Design in Kenya for the Tourist Industry and Local People" after having attended the ICSID-sponsored Interdesign

1972 workshop "Design for Tourism" at Kilkenny Design Workshops, Ireland, and a "Seminar on Tourism and Vocational Training" in Nairobi the same year. In her paper she perceptively noted the paradox inherent to the country's booming tourism, which pitted "economic growth" against "despoiling of the environment." Faced with this challenge, she argued, "the designer must try to emphasize the positive and mitigate the negative aspects."[102] She identified waste in its myriad forms as an environmental problem of particular relevance for design: "This means not only the effective collection and disposal of rubbish but also how other forms of waste can be reduced, i.e. industrial waste, land waste, pollution of the air and waters and even the study of noise."[103] Schofield also cited Victor Papanek on the potential design lessons to be learned "from studying the basic principles of nature, or how nature makes things happen," and returned to the issue of appropriate manufacturing systems which was so important also to Vedel: "It may be decided that a wide range of objects produced by craftmanship is more rewarding than Industrial Design. There is a lot in favour of this argument. Large scale factories and mass production are dehumanising and Kenyans are more used to and prefer face-to-face relationships."[104] This example shows that the "smoke stack" capitalist paradigm of design for development attributed to Shapira was by no means representative of the program as a whole, and that, on the contrary, environmental concerns were integral to the strategies Vedel devised for design education at the University of Nairobi.

OUT OF AFRICA

Despite the enthusiasm and support of students and key colleagues, Vedel found it increasingly difficult to navigate institutional bureaucracy and politics. Time and again he felt his initiatives were stifled and obstructed, preventing him from realizing his plans for the program. Two months before his contract ended at the end of June 1971, he therefore wrote a confidential letter to the vice-chancellor declaring that "I have decided not to accept any further period of appointment which may be offered to me."[105] Explaining his decision, Vedel wrote that he had lost his initial confidence that he could "contribute considerably" to the development of a design program attuned to the specific needs of East Africa: "I have had to realise that I could not operate with the efficiency necessary for the success of my aims."[106] It was particularly the struggle to secure adequate support for the Design Research and Development Unit that caused his grievances: "Despite the formal establishment of the Research Unit, it has remained virtually devoid of funds and staff. Under these conditions, it is unlikely that a second two- or three-year period would allow me to rectify the situation."[107] But the straw that broke the camel's back was staffing issues. In his original plans, and as a requirement for taking the job, he had stipulated that "expatriate staff should have consisted of experienced professional designers with a deep interest in the everyday life of the population, and with the capacity and dedication to scientific research into the overall and specific material needs of the population."[108] This was of utmost importance, since "only the activities and presence of such a staff would have ensured sound and fast Africanisation."[109] The problem of the expat teachers' insufficient investment in local conditions was exasperated by the institution's insufficient investment in the Unit, since the research-based knowledge he envisioned resulting from that enterprise "could have established the basic outline for the efficient training and occupation of coming African academic staff."[110]

A few days after Vedel had informed the vice-chancellor of his decision, he wrote to his family back in Denmark to notify them and explain the situation, this time in a much less composed tone. What in the official letter was anonymized as "expat staff," and generalized as insufficient investment in local conditions, he now spelled out: "It is sad to see a project I have initiated derailed by forces I had believed would contribute to its realization."[111] The saboteur was none other than "Nathan Shapira, whom with my contribution and on my recommendation, was tapped to direct the department's daily operation." Vedel clearly felt betrayed by Shapira, declaring that "the purpose of his presence here is purely careerist—clever and empty. His behavior is met with general disgust."[112] It was not just a personality issue. Vedel found Shapira's way of running the department to be reckless, cunning, and damaging. He "has, as far as I can see cemented the department's dissolution. . . . He has been able to, without consulting me, hire unqualified but obedient acolytes, from Romania and Israel, to join the staff. . . . Young Africans devoid of design experience are made to teach and treated completely irresponsibly by him."[113] Moreover, Vedel felt that Shapira was downright conspiring against him to take control of the department.[114] There is a certain Shakespearian *et tu, Brute?* sentiment to the end of Vedel's tenure at the University of Nairobi. He had taken on the challenge hoping to consolidate and develop Africa's first and only industrial design program to genuinely serve Kenyan and East African conditions and requirements, thus honoring the legacy of Selby Mvusi, only to have his work sabotaged by a fellow expat professor who more than anyone else portrayed himself as Mvusi's heir. Whereas Vedel's ecological approach to design for development could be seen as akin to Mvusi's ambition that design should be able to "make rain,"[115] Shapira's "smoke stack" approach represented a distinct departure from it. According to Daniel Magaziner, colleagues found that "although Shapira meant well, his theories about design's utility in building brands and cultivating an Africanist corporate culture did not adequately capture the scope of what the previous instructors of the design program had hoped it might yield."[116] In light of this, it is not particularly surprising that Shapira's own departure from the University of Nairobi two years later has been described as "controversy-shrouded."[117]

Vedel may have been disappointed, but he was not bitter. He believed that he had made a mark on the institution, and felt privileged to have been allowed to devote his time to his "profession's possible societal significance."[118] He believed the experiences he had made urgently needed to be incorporated into Danish development aid policy.[119] Upon his repatriation he therefore presented the work done under the auspices of the Nairobi design program to development aid officials such as the recently established Danish Center for Development Research, pitching the manual transport project as "an exercise by which East Africans would qualify as design advisors."[120] Similarly, he sought to dismantle common prejudices against African culture amongst his peers in the design community. In a lecture for the Association for Applied Art and Industrial Design (Foreningen Brugskunst og Industriel Design), for instance, he recited an excerpt from the Ugandan poet Okot p'Bitek's 1966 postcolonial epic poem *Song of Lawino* to argue against mindless Westernization and demonstrate instead "that development can take place as a continuation of existing culture," relating it to the manual transport project.[121] Based on his years in Kenya, Vedel had come to conclude that Western development aid in its current form "contributes considerably to the division of the societies we claim to be helping" by creating local economic elites, which intensifies the consumerist aspirations of the broader population. Rather that reproducing Western class distinctions and consumer culture, Vedel championed an approach to design for development where "the most efficient form of design is not to design for factory production, but rather to design revised and new types of tools and their manufacture, which is then introduced in the community, either by letting people themselves implement these improvements, or by training craftsmen to make them."[122] This is why the curriculum he devised—based on Selby Mvusi's plans—for the Nairobi design program placed so much emphasis on incorporating insights from sociology, cultural studies, archaeology, anthropology, environmental studies, geology, biology, and ecology.[123]

Though Vedel moved back to Denmark in the summer of 1971 after three years in Nairobi, Kenya would stay with him and continue to influence his work. As we have seen in the case of Amrik Kalsi, he also kept in touch with friends and colleagues from his time there. As part of this same gravitation, two of the students participating in the manual transportation project discussed above, Sultan Somjee and Gamaliel Mugumbya, followed Vedel to Denmark to continue their studies, earning postgraduate degrees from the Royal Danish Academy of Fine Arts' Department of Industrial Design.[124] The two even stayed with the Vedels for several weeks before commencing their studies.[125] Their studies were to further develop the main themes from the manual transportation project, refining the ecological design-for-development approach they had helped outline with Vedel in Nairobi. Key factors in their work included implications of land use, climatic conditions, materials extraction, and energy consumption. The research was to be undertaken in collaboration with the Danish Center for Development Research and under the guidance of Vedel—even if at this stage he had no official institutional affiliation—and Erik Herløw, professor of industrial design at the Academy.[126]

Ultimately, though, the importance of their postgraduate training in Denmark was less about the project in itself than about their formation as professionals with a pioneering expertise in ecological design for development. Shortly after he left Copenhagen and Scandinavia for good, Victor Papanek—with a not-so-subtle nod to what he considered the overly politicized student environments in Scandinavia—expressed his concern that students from "'developing' countries" studying in "'developed' countries" tend to "become embroiled in fractionalized 'political' student games that have no bearing on the political or social realities of their mother country."[127] Judging by the cases of Mugumbya and Somjee, Papanek was decidedly off the mark. Mugumbya, who describes Vedel as "a humane, culturally and environmentally conscious industrial designer" and considered him to be his "mentor who took care of me like a father,"[128] returned to Kenya and later to his native Uganda to build a career in textile design, and is currently a professor in Kampala University's School of Industrial Art and Design. Somjee also returned to Kenya where he "continued to research along Vedel's path and making design models for carts and school furniture for the poor rural population" under the auspices of the Kenya Industrial Estate, a DANIDA-sponsored enterprise supporting small-scale industries.[129] Somjee even attributes his turn to ethnography to Vedel, who, he says, "set a compass for my career" also by encouraging research into indigenous material culture as the only viable basis for new design work.[130] This began as individual studies in the ethnographical collections of the National Museum of Denmark, and continued as he developed a material culture teaching collection at the University of Nairobi's Institute of African Studies and wrote a book on Kenyan material culture.[131] Somjee later obtained a PhD from McGill University with a thesis on art and design education in Kenya.[132]

THE GREEN SHEEP OF THE (DESIGN) FAMILY

Even before the family set foot in Denmark, Kristian Vedel had bought an old, run-down farmstead on Thyholm, a small island in the Limfjord in western Jutland, and had begun designing a new house to be built there. The building's exterior was typologically virtually indistinguishable from the vernacular architecture of the region—but its interior was utterly modern and unconventional, featuring a 200-square-meter open, doorless ground floor. Just as it was after their return from the Central America journey, the media was eager to learn about their adventure and portray their new lifestyle. Discussing their new house, the modern consumer society they had withdrawn from, and the nature of design, Vedel explained to a visiting journalist how he more than anything was "concerned with the way in which humankind creates its material existence—not least considering all our environmental problems." The main problem, he argued, was that "we have gotten used to believing that our material standard of living should forever grow, and that it will be provided by means of technological development."[133] What he had learned in Nairobi was that design had to generate a positive relation to the people, the community, and the environment with which it interacts—and that this was as true in Denmark as in Kenya.

Incidentally, the Vedel family's new home, sheep farm, and design studio were geographically not far from the epicenter of Danish counterculture. The New Society, an anarchist offshoot of the Copenhagen student association, had established an experimental community in the summer of 1970 at Thylejren (the Thy Camp), a mere 70 kilometers further north on the Thy peninsula—a region which would later be designated Denmark's first national park. Attracting some 25,000 participants, the Thy Camp was by far the most spectacular manifestation of the countercultural movement in Denmark.[134] Here, supported by funding from the Danish National Bank's Jubilee Fund, the design/art/architecture practice of Susanne Ussing and Carsten Hoff built a series of experimental modular, temporary structures.[135] This makeshift, participatory building experiment became emblematic of the mythical commune and of Danish counterculture's responses to the rigidity and conformity of modern design and architecture.[136] Ane and Kristian Vedel were hardly hippies, though they did share some of the nearby countercultural community's concerns about the unsustainable development of mainstream Western society, as well as their desire to rethink the role and responsibility of design in this context.

The move to Thyholm did not come entirely out of the blue—or in a sense, that is exactly where it came from: In one of his letters from their voyage across the Atlantic in 1965, Vedel wrote that "During our journey we have often, in our fascination with the ocean, looked at each other and said that we should move to Nissum Bredning" (the large basin in the outlet of the Limfjord southwest of Thyholm).[137] Despite his use of the plural form here, this dream of moving to Jutland and Thyholm was very much *his* idea, partly because he hailed from the region. Ane agreed only reluctantly to the move and the radically different lifestyle it entailed.[138] Here, at a safe distance from the hustle and bustle of urban life, they would reestablish themselves in a combined home, design studio, and sheep farm. Their reason for keeping sheep was twofold. First, letting sheep graze helped restore the cultural landscape and its biodiversity. The small plots of land and uneven terrain were unsuitable for modern, industrialized agriculture, leaving it uncultivated. Also affecting the land use was the widespread development of summer houses along the coast. The reintroduction of grazing sheep resulted in natural fertilization of the soil, which attracted insects, which in turn attracted birds. As the Vedels boldly proclaimed: "sheep is the best environmental protection."[139] Second, their plan was to utilize the products of the sheep—wool, hide, etc.—as raw materials for their design practice, turning them into yarn, woven textiles, knitted garments, and leather goods.[140] They chose Shropshire sheep for the excellent quality and properties of that breed's wool, as well as for their capacity to tend the land (figure 3.9). Deeply inspired by what they had learned both in Central America, particularly about textile design, and in Kenya, for example about designing for appropriate manufacturing techniques and sociocultural contexts, their ambition was to establish a design practice that was both economically and ecologically viable.[141] The Vedels thus used their design expertise in the combined management of their household (economy) and of nature (ecology). The enterprise could therefore be seen as the epitome of ecological design. Eventually the economic viability of this design practice would prove rather limited. But it was not primarily a business venture—it was an experiment in ecological design, which they hoped would inspire others to embark on

similar paths. Underlining the noncommercial aspect of the project, the Vedels' sheep-based ecodesign experiment received financial support from the Danish National Bank's Jubilee Fund,[142] just as Ussing and Hoff's nearby countercultural building experiment did.

The Vedels' sheep farm design studio combination was not just an eccentric ecodesign experiment—it was also an effort to demonstrate that an approach developed in the global South could be equally beneficial in the global North. Visitors came from Kenya, Venezuela, and Japan to discuss design for development, "so that the African can learn from the Indian—or from the Dane, or vice versa."[143] The international network stretching out from Thyholm intensified as Kristian Vedel

3.9

Ane Vedel and their Shropshire sheep at Thyholm. Photo: Kristian Vedel's personal archive.

threw himself into organizational work, primarily in the context of the International Council of Societies of Industrial Design.

ICSID WORKING GROUP IV DEVELOPING COUNTRIES

As the founding chairman of the professional body Industrial Designers in Denmark and later vice-president of the Association for Applied Art and Industrial Design, Kristian Vedel was an obvious Danish delegate to ICSID—but he didn't assume that role until after his repatriation. In 1970 ICSID was reorganizing to better structure its efforts in various areas, establishing a series of thematically defined Working Groups to replace their earlier Commissions. One of these was Working Group IV, devoted to design in developing countries.[144] This unit is of particular interest in the current context for several reasons: first because it is closely related to persons and ideas connected to the University of Nairobi's design program, and second because it became a point of convergence for policies on design for development and ecological design. As Tania Messell has observed: "Whilst concerns for the environment remained peripheral to the organization's activities in Western industrialized countries throughout the 1970s, the promotion of ecologically sound practices and technology constituted a corner stone of ICSID's polices towards developing countries."[145] As we shall see, Working Group IV functioned as ICSID's conceptual laboratory for ecological design for development, but in the end it would have a limited impact on official policy, which to a greater degree was shaped by ICSID's collaboration with organizations in the UN system.

Despite some earlier ideas for ICSID initiatives on design for development, concrete steps toward establishing Working Group IV first began in 1970. Tasked with planning and coordinating the working group was none other than Nathan Shapira—but only after Gui Bonsiepe had turned the assignment down.[146] Following the closure of the Hochschule für Gestaltung in Ulm, Germany, where he had studied and subsequently taught, Bonsiepe left for Chile in October 1968, just a few months after Vedel had moved to Kenya. Bonsiepe had been invited by Chile's Christian Democratic government and at the behest of the International Labor Organization (ILO) to work on the development of small- and medium-sized enterprises.[147] He turned down the role as coordinator of Working Group IV due to insufficient administrative support in his new job at the Pontificia Universidad Católica de Chile, but agreed to become a member of the group.[148] It first convened at ICSID's

130   CHAPTER 3

seventh congress in Ibiza, Spain, October 14–16, 1971, where members gathered for an open seminar followed by an exploratory meeting. For the seminar, Shapira convened a panel discussing the general topics of design promotion, education, research, and practice in developing countries. Speakers included representatives from Hong Kong, Canada, Sweden, Thailand, India, Brazil, and the Philippines, in addition to ICSID Secretary General Josine des Cressonières and N. K. Grigoriev, Director of the United Nations Industrial Development Organization's (UNIDO's) Industrial Technology Division. UNIDO's presence was key, as this encounter was seen as "the starting point of the biggest deed ICSID might ever undertake!"[149] The aim was that Working Group IV would become an "advisory body to UNIDO for all matters of industrial design."[150] Although not included in the panel of presenters, Kristian Vedel was present and took part in the discussions, both at the seminar and the exploratory meeting.[151] After the event, ICSID president Henri Viénot wrote to Shapira suggesting Vedel as an additional member of Working Group IV. Unsurprisingly, given the uneasy relationship between the two, Shapira would have nothing of it, proposing instead Vedel's candidacy for another working group: no. V, on natural disasters.[152] So, whereas ICSID's president found Vedel's expertise on design for development to be of great interest to the organization,[153] Shapira managed to delay—but not prevent—Vedel's appointment to Working Group IV.

Shapira's tenure as coordinator of Working Group IV became contested, and the group never really sprang into action following the Ibiza seminar. The inertia led one of the appointed members, Finnish industrial designer Barbro Kulvik-Siltavuori, to ask ICSID president Henri Viénot flat out: "Is the Working Group only a hoax without real importance?"[154] Learning of Shapira's new appointment as coordinator of the group and the event at the Ibiza congress, some of his colleagues and students back in Nairobi—including Vedel's close collaborators Sultan Somjee and Amrik Kalsi—perceived this as Shapira being considered as officially representing Kenya in international design circles. This provocation catalyzed a general dismay in this grouping with his work and behavior, resulting in protests and even an open letter from the impromptu-established Design Society of Kenya to ICSID and several of its member organizations, accusing Shapira of misconduct and demanding his dismissal as coordinator of Working Group IV.[155] This all transpired around the time he left Nairobi in the summer or fall of 1972 and moved back to Los Angeles. The accusations were never formally corroborated, and he was never reprimanded, but it became a very unpleasant affair not only for Shapira himself but also for ICSID. The investigations were conducted in the run-up to a meeting ICSID was working hard to set up between Working Group IV and UNIDO, and after much deliberation and strong pressure from UNIDO, ICSID therefore decided it was best he stepped down as coordinator of Working Group IV.[156] That meeting, first envisioned at the Ibiza seminar and eventually taking place in Vienna in June 1973, would be led, in Shapira's absence, by another member of Working Group IV, Paul Hogan. Hogan, design manager with the Irish Export Board, would officially take over as coordinator of the group following the end of Shapira's tenure in October 1973.[157] By then, Hogan had already complained to Shapira that the group "at present exists only on paper or, perhaps more accurately, on your person."[158] Given the Nairobi connections, it is worth mentioning here that Hogan had met Selby Mvusi at the fourth ICSID congress in Vienna in 1965, and was greatly impressed with his decolonial critique of Western industrial design, to the extent that it inspired Hogan's subsequent involvement in ICSID's design-for-development initiatives.[159]

Because of these tumultuous beginnings, Working Group IV more or less had to start over with the UNIDO meeting, almost three years after its establishment. As Viénot wrote to Hogan after that event, "WG 4 was more or less WORDS before the meeting. Now it looks like an operational body."[160] The aim of the meeting was "to evaluate the importance of industrial design in relation to the developing countries and to discuss the means by which the contribution of industrial design can be maximised."[161] With Shapira sidelined, the preparation of a working paper requested by UNIDO and intended to serve as a basis for the Vienna meeting was reassigned to Gui Bonsiepe. Imploring Bonsiepe to take on the task of drafting it, Cressonnières emphasized that "it is terribly important, because we are in a process of developing a very close and active cooperation with UNIDO."[162] Bonsiepe accepted, and his working paper "Development through Design" was tabled at the much-awaited Vienna meeting with UNIDO in June 1973. In it, he wrote that "the ecological crisis caused by technology of 'developed' countries raises the question whether it is justified to call these technologies 'developed.' . . . Countries not yet industrialized still have the possibility, at least theoretically, to opt for a different pattern of industrialization which pays attention to ecological compatibility and which contains built-in preventive measures against environmental sell-out."[163] Following the meeting, the document was revised into a "consensus report," or policy paper, now titled "Design for Industrialization." Intriguingly, in this version, design for development was much more explicitly tasked with mitigating environmental problems:

Industrialization and urbanization have in numerous cases over-charged the absorption and resilience capacity of the biotical frame and have caused alarming disequilibrium in the ecosphere. To alleviate the pressures on atmosphere, hydrosphere and geosphere, industrial design can contribute by focusing on the application of re-use materials and re-use products and taking into account pollution. In this way it may even stimulate the development of alternative environmentally compatible technologies.[164]

There is a certain paradox to this emphasis on ecological sustainability in Bonsiepe's report, given that UNIDO's mandate was industrial development. In its collaboration with UNIDO, then, and not without a certain level of frustration, "Working Group IV has only concerned itself with industrial design as a tool of industrial development in the Third World and has ignored the relationships which industrial design has with many arts and sciences and the educational, social and cultural implications of industrial design"—and the environmental implications, one might add.[165] The positivistic, progressivist approach to design for development advocated by UNIDO was only partially and reluctantly accepted by Working Group IV, and this tension goes some way toward explaining why ICSID's relationship with UNIDO would prove so precarious and ambivalent.

As soon as Hogan officially took over as coordinator of Working Group IV, he nominated Jörg Glasenapp, Victor Papanek, Kristian Vedel, and Knut Yran as members.[166] Of these, only Glasenapp had been part of the previous constellation. He was a recently repatriated German industrial designer who had been working in Taiwan and Thailand since 1965 as a consultant to their governments, on an assignment from ILO. With the exception of Glasenapp, all the members of the group had strong ties to Scandinavia. Hogan had studied at the Royal Danish Academy of Fine Arts in the 1950s and was involved in the planning of the Scandinavian-inspired Kilkenny Design Workshops (established 1963).[167] Yran, a Norwegian national, served as Director of Industrial Design for the Dutch electronics company Philips, and would later be elected to ICSID's executive board.[168] Papanek was at this point teaching at Manchester Polytechnic, following his sabbatical in Denmark during which he had become good friends with Vedel.[169] This time Vedel's candidacy was recommended by outgoing member Gui Bonsiepe, who had been appointed to the ICSID board and acted as its liaison with Working Group IV.[170] Hogan's iteration of the group conceived its mission to be "working at the centre of a network of expertise" aiming "to become an international forum for ideas and experience, needs and problems" and "to encourage an arduously self-critical understanding of industrial design's contribution to developing countries."[171] This self-criticality was essential to the group's understanding of what design for development should entail. At his first Working Group IV meeting, Vedel went on record stressing that "the people who knew best the needs were those in the developing countries" and that "the Working Group at all times must go to these authentic sources for information and guidance and avoid the danger of academic or Western oriented solutions."[172]

To increase global reach and thus improve its credibility, Working Group IV was soon expanded to include representatives from Asia, Africa, and South America. One of the new members was Amrik Kalsi, Vedel's former student and mentee.[173] The two friends met again when Vedel visited Nairobi in the summer of 1975, and they subsequently proposed holding a Working Group IV meeting there the following year.[174] The latter idea never transpired, but it speaks to an interesting University of Nairobi continuity in ICSID's design-for-development efforts. There is a trajectory running from Selby Mvusi's contributions to the early ICSID congresses and conferences, via Nathan Shapira's key but controversial role in the first phase of Working Group IV, to Vedel's continuation of the strategies developed on site in Kenya in his subsequent organizational work, and, finally, to Kalsi's close collaboration with other international organizations such as the International Council of Graphic Design Associations and various UN agencies. And the ecological sensibility to design for development, carried on from Vedel to Kalsi, was noticed in this context: upon Kalsi's appointment to Working Group IV, ICSID president Carl Auböck wrote to him exclaiming how he was "extremely impressed by the splendid and interesting work which has been done in Nairobi concerning environmental problems" and emphasizing that "ICSID attaches more and more importance to environmental problems with special consideration in developing countries."[175] Fully in line with this, one of Kalsi's first contributions to Working Group IV was a report on the activities of the United Nations Environment Programme (UNEP), assessing its relevance for ICSID. UNEP had been established in the wake of the 1972 UN Conference on the Human Environment in Stockholm (discussed in chapter 4), and set up its headquarters the following year in Nairobi,[176] in the newly opened Kenyatta International Convention Centre. (The building was designed by Norwegian architect Karl Henrik Nøstvik under the administration of the Norwegian Agency for Development Cooperation, NORAD.) Kalsi argued that since ICSID was "mainly concerned with design activities related to Man and his Environment," it "is important to be involved with UNEP to try to solve some of the environment problems."[177] Despite Kalsi's strong engagement with the ecological aspects of design for development, however, ICSID's main partner in the UN system would be UNIDO, not UNEP.[178]

ICSID had high hopes for the collaboration with UNIDO, and Working Group IV was from its inception the main conduit for these ambitions. Even after the meeting in Vienna finally took place in June 1973, it remained a precarious relationship. For instance, the working group agreed that the revisions UNIDO required Bonsiepe to make to his working paper discussed at the meeting amounted to a "progressive emasculation"[179] resulting in a "bowdlerized version" and "that ICSID's association with this was undesirable."[180] Hogan complained that UNIDO didn't even acknowledge the many proposals the working group had prepared for them, and in the summer of 1975 the group "regretfully concluded that the contact with UNIDO had broken down."[181] Like ICSID in general, Working Group IV was extremely poorly funded. In fact, it had no budget at all, and the members even paid their own travel expenses. The initiation and implementation of projects in the field was therefore beyond its means—its role could only ever be advisory. In a moment of sanguinity, "It was agreed with humility that the possibility of the Working Group making any significant impact in relation to the problems of developing countries was remote."[182] Nevertheless, to stave off resignation, Papanek reminded his colleagues "that the Working Group had shown itself an effective instrument of ICSID and had real achievements to its credit in terms of the policies which had been and would be proposed to the ICSID board."[183] These policies stipulated that design for development should be "based on an approach that integrates economical, social and ecological dimensions" and characterized by the "utilisation of natural and human resources for the satisfaction of the basic needs of a population in order to ensure an improvement in the quality of life of present and future generations."[184] On behalf of ICSID, then, Working Group IV devised policies on design for development which were ecologically rather progressive, but which at the same time proved challenging to reconcile with UNIDO's doctrine of industrial development and economic growth.

ICSID's most ardent proponents of ecological design for development therefore pursued alternative outlets for their ideas. One notable venue was *Design for Need*, an exhibition and symposium at London's Royal College of Art in April 1976, where designers, scholars, and educators convened to discuss how "design for need" related to resources, environment, aid, and development. The event was co-organized by Frank Height, who had been involved in the initial planning of

Working Group IV, and featured contributions by several past and present members, including Gui Bonsiepe, Sudhakar Nadkarni, and Victor Papanek.[185] Another alternative outlet, described as one of "the main achievements of the Working Group,"[186] was the ICSID Philips Award for design-for-development-focused projects. Launched at the ninth ICSID congress in Moscow in 1975, and first awarded the following year, the scheme was brokered by Knut Yran securing his employer's patronage and funding.[187]

No sooner had *Design for Need* opened and the first ICSID Philips Award been announced than Working Group IV folded. At the last meeting of its term of appointment, in April 1976, the group recommended its own discontinuation to the ICSID board and upcoming General Assembly, arguing that in its place, the nimbler system of the "DC/DIG [Developing Countries/Design Information Group] scheme should be the main instrument of future ICSID involvement [with developing countries]."[188] The DC/DIG was launched as "an effort to establish an international person to person communications network devoted to the design problems of developing countries."[189] The former Working Group IV would initially function as a coordinating committee for the DC/DIG, which from the start counted some 40 members from across the world.[190] Put simply, the DC/DIG scheme offered a "boots on the ground" approach, since its dispersed structure and larger, geographically much broader membership would be able to "articulate the real needs as seen by them."[191]

Despite these noble intentions of moving toward a more peer-to-peer-based system enabling local empowerment, the legacy of Working Group IV and of ICSID's work on design for development in general would nonetheless primarily be tied to the protracted and precarious collaboration with UNIDO. In April 1977, six years in the making, ICSID finally signed a memorandum of understanding with UNIDO. The agreement formalized the "already existing cooperation between the two organisations and permitted the inclusion of industrial design activities in the yearly UNIDO programme and country programmes in developing countries."[192] This, in turn, led to what must be considered the apex of ICSID's collaboration with UNIDO as well as of formalized, international policies of design for development: the Ahmedabad Declaration on Industrial Design for Development. Signed during a seminar on the same topic at the Indian Institute of Design in January 1979, the declaration aimed "to accelerate . . . industrial design activities in developing countries" through a series of recommendations for policies, promotion, government action, action by industry, information, education, and international cooperation.[193] In preparation for this seminal agreement, ICSID's past president Carl

Auböck, who was instrumental in the negotiations with UNIDO (partly because he lived in Vienna where UNIDO was headquartered), started out by calling attention to the ecological crisis, "a situation comparable, but more dramatic than any eve of revolution in the history of mankind." Design for development could not be thought of solely in terms of economic or technological progress, he concluded, because "the future of design and the environment, good or bad, will be the direct result of planning efforts and capabilities of today."[194]

These concerns did partially influence the wording of the declaration, at least in the points (duly highlighted in Kristian Vedel's copy of the document) declaring that "design in the developing world must be committed to a search for local answers to local needs, utilising indigenous skills, materials and traditions" and that "designers in every part of the world must work to evolve a new value system which dissolves the disastrous divisions between the worlds of waste and want."[195] Despite these sincere and important nods to the ecological conditions of design for development, the main thrust of the Ahmedabad Declaration did little to promote the more radical ideas bounced around in Working Group IV by the likes of Glasenapp, Papanek, Vedel, and Kalsi, but rather reflected UNIDO's emphasis on industrial development and economic progress. In this optic, design in developing countries should absorb "the extraordinary power that science and technology can make available to it," with the designer cast as "an agent of progress." Cultural traditions were reduced to a resource to be "utilised to current advantage."[196] But a nonbinding policy document can only be so efficient.[197] Ultimately, then, as several scholars have pointed out, the Ahmedabad Declaration had limited impact.[198] Just two months earlier, in November 1978, ICSID-UNIDO had the opportunity to showcase how their joint policy could be turned into practice when the eighth installation of the Interdesign workshop series was organized in Cuetzalan, Mexico on the topic of "Alternative Energy Sources: Wind and Solar Energy for Use in Rural Areas in Mexico." Directly opposed to the repeat warnings of the final iteration of Working Group IV, who time and again had emphasized the importance of designing from on-site specificities and indigenous knowledge, the event was dominated by US and European experts helicoptered in to propose solutions to local challenges. The majority of the many Latin American participants were highly critical of this top-down approach, pointing out its patronizing and neocolonialist overtones and arguing that local design solutions should be pursued without the intervention of international design organizations.[199] As such, Interdesign '78 placed ecological design at the heart of one of the thorniest issues of the day: the legacy of a colonialist world order.

DECOLONIAL CRITIQUE OF DESIGN FOR DEVELOPMENT

The very notion of development aid is a contested one. At least since Teresa Hayter provocatively framed "aid as imperialism"[200] in 1971—the same year Vedel returned from Kenya—the question of what genuinely motivates development aid and who actually benefits the most from it has haunted the discourse. Arturo Escobar has claimed that "the entire project of development . . . was an immense design project," thus emphatically implicating design in this critique of how development was conceived of as a process of modernization teleologically modeled on Western industrialized societies.[201] But even when design purportedly tries its best to "do good," it is criticized for being politically blind, naïve, or self-complacent: "humanitarian design interventions help the public and the design community to imagine themselves and their practice as essentially good, positive, and sympathetic; thereby disguising the privileges and inherent historical violence embedded in designing."[202]

Whereas there are forms of development aid in general, and Danish development aid in particular, which "may indicate a strain of social and mental imperialism, an eagerness to project own methods, norms, values, conceptions and even ways of life onto others,"[203] it is difficult to see how Vedel's work at the University of Nairobi could be characterized as such. Vedel's student and colleague at the University of Nairobi, Amrik Kalsi, recalls how

Kristian Vedel encouraged the students to question the colonial oriented design education and practice and to research for a new identity in the context of the developing world's needs. . . . By prioritising the development needs, the academic curriculum firmly established a more humanistic role of design and thus demonstrated its effectiveness and relevance to a newly developing country. This approach also ensured that products would remain close to local cultural practices and thrive on the diversity. Some of his efforts continued, in some ways for some time, but the emphasis and enthusiasm tapered, after his departure in 1971 from Kenya.[204]

Even Victor Papanek, whose own activities at this time were deeply entangled in the geopolitics of development aid and the United States' Cold War agenda to institute alignments strongly resembling "a neocolonial form of dependency,"[205] acquitted Vedel and his Danish colleagues of any such tarnishes. Looking back on the phenomenon in 1986, Papanek wrote that "Industrial Design attempting to work with

Third World countries . . . began as colonialism ended, frequently it ended up as a conscious or unconscious tool for neo-colonialism and exploitation."[206] But not everyone and everywhere: "Christian [sic] Vedel of Denmark worked in Kenya to good effect,"[207] he proclaimed, having long since singled out the Danish approach to design for development as particularly progressive: "They do not anymore set out as missionaries to the developing countries to spread the gospel of the late-capitalist consumer society, *they have also learned to learn*."[208] This notion of an inverted knowledge transfer came to expression also in the context of ICSID's Working Group IV, when "Mr Vedel and Mr Papanek both agreed that design in the Third World could give the lead to design in the developed world," where "design in a large measure had lost its way."[209] Design itself had to be redesigned. The founder of the Nairobi design program, Selby Mvusi, wrote in 1964—in an unpublished paper which Vedel kept in his files for the rest of his life—that "we cannot divorce design for development from design development."[210] To Vedel, this meant that design for development should not imply helicoptering in Western solutions or models. For design to foster development, design itself—as an activity, a methodology, a practice, a profession—had to be developed, refined, improved, in order to produce results more appropriate to the given context. This line of thought was his very rationale for establishing the Design Research and Development Unit: only by starting from a solid knowledge base about local conditions and needs could design and design education in Kenya and East Africa be developed to become a catalyst for (positive) development. From his journey through Central America, via his tenure in Nairobi, to his sheep farm design studio at Thyholm, Vedel's approach to design sought to move the discipline beyond its deeply flawed high-modernist iteration to a mode more sensitive to local conditions, social justice, and environmental implications—in short: ecological design for development.

As recent initiatives to decolonize design have argued, however, good intentions are not necessarily enough. A poignant critique of much contemporary "do-good design" is that it proffers "technological remedies for problems rooted in imperial histories" and operates in a neoliberalist context where "the global poor are construed as objects of elite benevolence and non-profit largesse, rather than as historical subjects possessing their own unique worldviews, interests, and passions."[211] But even seemingly neutral mainstays of design methods, such as "problem-solving" and participatory processes, come with inherent biases. When Knut Yran of Working Group IV opined in a 1975 interview in *Design* magazine that "we should not provide the solutions, but the methodology, the systematic approach to the problem-solving part of design,"[212] he naively assumed, as Jamer Hunt has recently written about participatory design, that the methodology was "an untroubled practice, that it doesn't also bring with it a risk of paternalism and even cultural violence."[213] Similarly, Mahmoud Keshavarz points out that "the Western notion of design as a task of 'problem-solving' . . . assumes a universal truth in addressing the complexity of the world as a series of problems to be solved. Moreover, it assumes the position of center for itself as given, and approaches other epistemologies from that given center, trying at best to collaborate with or at worst to assimilate them."[214]

It is hard to see how anyone could steer completely clear of such a categorical critique of the most fundamental epistemological underpinnings of practice. Efforts to establish internationally recognized educational programs certainly cannot, as such institutions and initiatives assume at least a certain degree of intellectual universalism, or at least compatibility. "These ideas and methods, disguised as 'universal' have traveled, carrying with them the structures of Western thinking," writes Danah Abdulla, "and continuing to reproduce the cycle where the Westernized universities are reliant on knowledge produced elsewhere."[215] As discussed above, Kristian Vedel was very much aware of this problem, and found design schools in Central America to be prime examples of such Westernized institutions.[216] He also believed that the establishing of design schools in Africa "enables us to see, and avoid, the more or less obvious mistakes in [Western] schools." Chief amongst the latter was "the failure of western designers to create on the basis of the real needs of society," working instead "according to the demands and requirements of individual companies—to maximise profits, which in itself is a very narrow goal, not essentially productive or efficient in terms of society as a whole, and in fact potentially dangerous."[217] Vedel's later colleague in Working Group IV, Paul Hogan, shared this same sense of danger. In his address to the general assembly in connection with the eighth ICSID congress in Japan in 1973, with Vedel in the audience, Hogan reported that it "is the working group's view that the solutions to problems of industrial design in the developing countries must be found within those countries themselves. What we mean here is that the transfer of design know-how from the industrialized countries, whether in the form of hardware or software, is dangerous and can even be counter productive."[218] This applied to education as much as to practice and policy, Hogan continued, stressing that it therefore also was "clear to the Working Group that any such design school in a developing country should not be modelled on the schools of the industrialized countries but should reflect the special characteristics of the region."[219]

Shortly after Vedel's repatriation, a group of Danish students publicly accused Danish experts (designers, architects, planners, engineers) deployed to East Africa by DANIDA of neocolonialism. Vedel and his peers promptly replied that the students should have informed themselves better about the conditions on the ground and the nature of their work before making such allegations.[220] This episode clearly illustrates that the ideological realm of politics does not always align with the pragmatic realm of practice. The very notion of development aid inevitably implies inequities of power which cannot be ignored. But empathy, ethics, and expertise are key in mitigating this bias, and ethnographically grounded approaches such as those explored by Vedel and his students at the University of Nairobi are still to this day being championed as key routes to decolonizing design.[221] As Arturo Escobar has argued, "a decolonial perspective on development is . . . essential for approaching codesign with subaltern groups in ways that strengthen, rather than undermine, their collective autonomy."[222] As we have seen in this chapter, this is exactly what Vedel was trying to achieve in Kenya. He was keenly aware of his status as an outsider, and that Western expertise could not "solve" the problems of the global South, but rather should aim to empower subaltern groups in the quest for greater autonomy in their locally situated design work.

CONCLUSION: . . . AND JUSTICE FOR ALL

The growing awareness from the mid-1960s on that environmental problems were both local and global, as well as deeply entangled in social and economic structures, profoundly influenced how Scandinavian design professionals conceived of their role in the world. Tracing the unusual but emblematic career journey of Kristian Vedel, this chapter has discussed how humanitarian design and ecological design came together in the project of design for development. Emerging from his pilgrimage through Central America's precious but precarious cultures and natures, Vedel's approach for an ecological design for development then matured during his years in Kenya, shaped on the anvil of everyday practice, and subsequently informed his work both back home on the sheep farm design studio and in ICSID's Working Group IV Developing Countries. Running through it all is the growing acknowledgment that design for development must not be a euphemism for "Westernization" or "modernization." Herein lies a close connection to the work of the Norwegian deep ecologists discussed in chapter 5, who were highly critical of what they saw as a myopic, even egotistical streak in mainstream Western environmentalism, and keenly emphasized how profoundly entangled the quest for ecological sustainability is with the aim of global social justice. Philosopher Arne Næss explicitly warned that mainstream environmentalism was perceived as neocolonialism in the global South, and that deep ecology therefore also must promote global social justice.[223] In his characteristically polemic style, Hartvig Sætra wrote, "The central theme in ecopolitics is neither river conservation, energy saving, nor biodynamic vegetables. *It is imperialism.*"[224] In a less confrontational take on the topic, Erik Dammann, ex-advertising designer and founder of The Future in Our Hands, put it succinctly: "The problem of environmental protection/aid to developing countries is not a question of either/or, but of both."[225] Sigmund Kvaløy certainly tried to combine the two when he taught at the Oslo School of Architecture and brought students with him to Nepal's Rolwaling Valley, and subsequently applied to the Norwegian Agency for Development Cooperation (NORAD) for funding for a design-for-development project.[226] In many respects, then, Vedel's work can be seen as a kind of deep ecological design for development, more aligned with bio- and socio-egalitarian philosophies than with ICSID's and UNIDO's "smoke stack" model. His former student in Nairobi, Sultan Somjee, recalls that "Vedel had some profound ideas about 'design for development'. They were far beyond what Papanek and others wrote [on the topic]. Vedel's design approach contained social, environmental, cultural and economic considerations."[227] Whether or not this is a fair assessment of the two friends' and colleagues' relative merit is ultimately less important. But Somjee's remark does emphasize the main conclusion of this chapter: that when Scandinavian design in the late 1960 was enrolled in development aid programs, the ecological aspects were inseparable from the humanitarian ones.

4

DEMO! THE ECOPOLITICS OF DESIGN ACTIVISM

It is true that particular people remain wedded to particular priorities—to family planning, to model cities, to the wilderness, to threatened whales. But the gross misunderstandings, the total lack of common interest between middle-class groups caring about trees and bald eagles and urban reformers bent on getting lead poisoning out of slum children is surely less divisive and counterproductive today than it was even fifty years ago.[1]
—Barbara Ward and René Dubos (1972)

"In 1972 there was still grass . . ."[2] Thus read the tag line of a protest poster made on the occasion of the United Nations Conference on the Human Environment, which took place in Stockholm in June 1972 (figure 4.1). Part of a series of posters made by a group of students at Konstfack College of Arts, Crafts and Design and illicitly put up across the city, this poster envisions a rather depressing, post-ecocidal future. Designed by Eva Trolin, the poster features a simple drawing of a man with a young child on his arm standing in a bleak, barren landscape sometime in the near future and gesturing toward a conjured-up image of an airplane spreading pesticides over a field of green grass back in 1972.[3] The motif and the dramatic rhetoric are emblematic of both the radical environmentalism and the activist design practices of the period. What makes it remarkable is the fact that this poster was designed as an act of protest *against* by far the most comprehensive political effort of the time to address the world's environmental problems.

The UN conference, described by *Newsweek* as "a complex cross between a scientific convention, a summit conference and a rock festival,"[4] resulted from a

proposal put forth by the Swedish government in 1968, the year after it had established the world's first Environmental Protection Agency. The conference has been credited with laying the foundation for global political cooperation on environmental issues, as it served to "legitimate and introduce to a much wider public these various ideas and practices that had begun to be carried out in the name of environmentalism."[5] The main outcomes of the conference were the Declaration on the Human Environment and the establishment of the United Nations Environment Programme (UNEP) under the directorship of the conference's secretary-general Maurice Strong. UNEP was tasked with following up the Stockholm declaration and taking a global lead in environmental governance. As with any such intergovernmental initiatives, both the declaration and the agency would have to adhere to the logic of the lowest common denominator, but it did nonetheless pave the way for significant subsequent achievements and events, including the organization of the Intergovernmental Panel on Climate Change (IPCC) in 1988 and the Rio Earth Summit in 1992. Nevertheless, the legacy of the UN conference is contested, as the heavily publicized mega-event made it abundantly clear that saving the world by committee would be a protracted undertaking riddled with conflicting interests, power biases, and compromises. This became apparent to local activists already in the lead-up to the conference, sparking a spate of unsanctioned activities in response to the official program. As Trolin's poster illustrates, design and designers were absolutely integral to these acts and artifacts of environmental activism. Moreover, demonstrations are themselves acts and products of design. The 1972 UN conference in Stockholm thus became a point of convergence for design and politics, for activism and governance, for radical and reformist approaches to environmentalism, as well as for local and global actor networks. Despite—or perhaps because of—its contested character and legacy, the conference wielded

4.1

1972 fanns det fortfarande gräs . . . (In 1972 There Was Still Grass . . .) Poster designed by Konstfack-student Eva Trolin on the occasion of the United Nations Conference on the Human Environment, organized in Stockholm in June 1972. © Eva Trolin/BONO 2021. Photo courtesy of Håkan Agnsäter.

considerable influence not only on future political decision making, but also on the development of environmental thinking and ecologically informed design ideology in Scandinavia.

This chapter will explore design interventions at, and in the wake of, the UN Conference on the Human Environment, focusing on the environmental-political activism of design students and the design practices of the broader activist movements and events. The first part of the chapter will explore how the UN conference and the associated alternative programs prompted and related to the students' activism. It will then delve into one of the most emblematic outlets of this activism, namely the use of graphic design as a practice of public protest. Whereas the chapter thus initially revolves around the notion of demonstration understood as "a public meeting or march protesting against something or expressing views on a political issue," the latter half of the chapter is concerned with another, but closely related, understanding of demonstration as "a practical exhibition and explanation of how something works or is performed."[6] By taking a closer look at two exhibitions on so-called "alternative technology," the chapter explores how activists sought to demonstrate key principles of their approach to ecological design and the significance of design to the environmental movement. The first of these exhibitions, *For a Technology in the Service of the People!* (*För en teknik i folkets tjänst!*), was organized as an integral part of the broader activist responses to the UN conference. The second show, *ARARAT*, took place four years later, in 1976, but should be read in connection with its predecessor due to a considerable overlap in topics addressed and actors involved. Even if both exhibitions were organized under the auspices of Sweden's premier museum of contemporary art, Moderna Museeet, they were anything but static displays of elitism and (cultural) capital. On the contrary, they were dynamic works in progress in their own right, actively encouraging visitors to take part in shaping the show and interacting with the exhibits. The strong emphasis on interdisciplinarity and didactic programming was further intended to inspire designers and architects as well as the general public to live more in balance with nature, and to demonstrate that an ecological lifestyle was possible. These two exhibitions were key in the development of a broader ecological consciousness in Sweden, as they used design to convert environmental issues from something ostensibly abstract and theoretical to something manifestly tangible and practical. And as we shall see, designers, design students, and design educators were deeply involved in all these events in several ways.

Whether understood as protests in the streets or as exhibitions in museum galleries, the demonstrations discussed in this chapter are all defined by an activist attitude. The actors we encounter clearly conform to Alastair Fuad-Luke's definition of a design activist as "a person who uses the power of design for the greater good for humankind *and* nature."[7] Through their various modes of demonstrations, they in turn helped define the activist politics that became such a prominent feature of the emerging ecological design practices throughout Scandinavia.

THE PROTEST ENVIRONMENT

In his analysis of activism in Sweden in the late 1960s and early 1970s, Kjell Östberg suggests that the student movement in general played a less significant role than it did elsewhere, because the democratization of higher education was already on its way in Sweden (and the other Scandinavian countries).[8] The students still demanded increased co-determination and influence, but by the early 1970s Scandinavian institutions of higher education had to a large degree accommodated these requests. Consequently, the student protests were directed less at the structure of the educational system itself, taking instead a more societal turn. With the partial exception of the Danish institutions, where students did fight for radical organizational changes including the introduction of direct democracy and the abolishment of exams,[9] in general student activism at Scandinavian design schools took on a Janus-faced character united by a quest for social purpose: internally, they addressed the *content* of the education; externally, they addressed the societal challenges of the day. Through initiatives such as the Scandinavian Design Students Organization's (SDO) summer seminars and other outlets, the students called for an education more in line with what they perceived to be society's true needs. Key social concerns included environmental degradation, design for developing countries, and design for people with disabilities, children, and other previously neglected groups.[10] This resonated very well with the interests of the many activist groups that operated in the broader civic sphere at this time. The student protests in Scandinavian design schools were thus more a response and contribution to the broader social movements and activist practices, and an attempt to foster closer and more reciprocal relations between these and their education, than a revolt against institutional structures and politics.

A key group in the propagation of activism in Stockholm in the years leading up to the UN conference was Alternative City (Alternativ stad), which managed to mobilize surprisingly broad popular support for their fight against the human, social, and environmental degradation caused by the city's rampant urban development projects. Alternative City was inspired by another initiative, Alternative Christmas (Alternativ jul). When the alternative Christmas celebration was organized for the first time in 1968, one of the venues was Konstfack College of Arts, Crafts and Design, and many of the school's students were involved in the event. It was primarily aimed at the homeless and the lonely, but open to everyone who wanted a noncommercial celebration.[11] Alternative City was established in the wake of Alternative Christmas, in February 1969, focusing on issues concerning the urban environment. It was a motley crew that rallied to its cause, including students, political activists, homeless people, senior citizens, housewives, as well as environmental activists. The group's public recognition soared with the since-legendary Battle of the Elms (*Almstriden*) in May 1971, a year before the UN conference. Here, thousands of activists led by Alternative City formed a human shield around a cluster of old elm trees in the public park Kungsträdgården in central Stockholm, which were scheduled for felling in connection with the construction of a new metro station (figure 4.2).[12] Eventually crowned with victory, the Battle of the Elms boosted the activists' confidence and standing, and helped increase public acceptance for activism and cultivate a healthy protest environment in the city.[13]

An issue particularly prevalent to many of those involved in the protests and alternative platforms during the UN conference, and in the Scandinavian public debate of the time in general, was the increasingly controversial US warfare in Indochina. Just a few days before the conference opened, the organizing committee announced that the issue would not be addressed during the conference, a decision that naturally caused resentment in the highly vocal Swedish Vietnam movement.[14] Despite the organizers' effort to skirt the issue, it did strongly color the debates,

4.2

Activists from the Alternative City group protecting the trees scheduled for clearing by inhabiting them during the Battle of the Elms in Stockholm, May 1971. Photo courtesy of Centerpartiet.

even in the official program. In his speech at the conference's first plenary session, Swedish Prime Minister Olof Palme may have refrained from explicitly mentioning the ongoing US military campaign, but nevertheless pinned it to the conference theme by harshly condemning the "ecocide" caused by the environmentally destructive use of machinery and chemicals in contemporary warfare, and chiding the UN's unwillingness to discuss the topic.[15] Palme's remarkable speech must be seen in light of the fact that just a few days prior, Stockholm had hosted the International Commission of Enquiry into US Crimes in Indochina, which detailed the many ways in which US armed forces wrought ecological havoc in Vietnam: using herbicides and defoliants to kill plants providing cover, food crops, and construction materials; mowing down houses, farms, and forests using bulldozers with a purposed-designed plough; carpet bombing to destroy villages and farmland, etc.[16] Needless to say, Palme's statement was not at all well received by the American delegation, who considered it "a gratuitous politicizing of our environmental discussions"[17] and insisted that the topic was inappropriate and extrinsic to the conference.[18] Palme's speech is nevertheless illustrative of the political climate in Sweden at the time, and it serves as an important backdrop to the remarkably broad support the activist campaigns of the early 1970s received in the general public. The origin, organization, and object of these campaigns and the arenas that facilitated them are both entangled and complex. A basic understanding of the different factions and the landscape they operated in is nevertheless essential to grasp the context of further developments, both regarding the design students' interventions in the conference as well as the planning of the alternative technology exhibitions.

A PLETHORA OF FORA

Ever since the idea of the UN Conference on the Human Environment was first conceived, Sweden had played a key role. In a 1968 proposal to the UN's Economic and Social Council, the Swedish representatives stressed the urgent need for intensified action on an international level to limit, and possibly eliminate, the impairment of the human environment.[19] A key figure in this preparatory work was Hans Palmstierna, the biochemist and research liaison of the Swedish Environmental Protection Agency whose role as a public intellectual was discussed in chapter 1.[20] The proposal ultimately led to the realization of the conference in Stockholm four years later, with representatives from 113 invited states, in addition to over 1,500 representatives from the press and a large number of international and nongovernmental organizations.[21] Amongst these was the International Council of Societies of Industrial Design (ICSID), whose former board members, industrial designer Sigvard Bernadotte and design critic Ulf Hård af Segerstad—both esteemed design professionals and both hailing from the Swedish nobility—served as observers to the conference.[22] The conference was of course an elaborately designed event in its own right, symbolized by its insistent and inclusive slogan "Only One Earth" and the accompanying logo, designed by UN staff designer Roy Perrot as a variation on the UN emblem (designed by Donal McLaughlin in 1946) in which the map of the globe is replaced with a stylized human figure with open arms.[23] Another intriguing albeit very different design presence at the official conference was an environmentally friendly transport service. A fleet of specially commissioned Monark Petit mini-bicycles was made available to delegates for local transport (figure 4.3). According to *Time* magazine's correspondent, "even Maurice Strong, the conference's secretary-general, took one out for a spin."[24] The UN conference Petits were stark white, inspired by the activist stunt pulled by the anarchist Provo group in Amsterdam in 1965, where they painted used bicycles white and placed them throughout the city for free use by the public. This well-intended nod to that pioneering countercultural design activism backfired, however, because unlike the Provo bikes in Amsterdam, the white UN bikes in Stockholm were locked when not in use, and keys were reserved for conference delegates. Unsurprisingly, critics interpreted this as yet another instance of exclusion and privilege: "So it was that the wise Technocrats again did as they always have done, and created an Elite who Had Things, and Others Who Did Not."[25]

Just as interesting as the official conference, though, are the counterconferences and alternative platforms interacting with and running parallel to the main conference. Of various affiliations, the common rationale behind these initiatives was to supplement and question the aims and methods of the UN summit. And even if their initial goal might have been the same as that of the official conference, to end the exploitation of the human environment, the many NGOs, social movements, and grassroots initiatives shared a distrust of the UN's ability to reach these goals. "People say that if the UN cannot protect us from the known horrors of war, it has little chance of protecting us from the largely unknown horrors of pollution, resource depletion, and overpopulation," as the recently established Friends of the Earth put it—before nonetheless expressing hope in the organization's and the conference's ability "to make people talk to each other."[26] Others were more

4.3
The Crescent Mini, the identical "brand twin" of the Monark Petit mini-bicycle made available to official delegates to the UN Conference on the Human Environment in Stockholm in June 1972. Photo: Truls Nord, courtesy of Tekniska Museet.

confrontational. The Californian poet and deep ecologist Gary Snyder (who will reappear in chapter 5) responded in verse in the poem "Mother Earth: Her Whales," written in Stockholm shortly after the conference: "How can the head-heavy power-hungry politic scientist/Government two-world Capitalist-Imperialist/Third-world Communist paper-shuffling male/non-farmer jet-set bureaucrats/Speak for the green of the leaf? Speak for the soil?"[27] Local activists were no more lenient. At a press conference ahead of the summit, a group called PowWow took issue with the UN's approach to global justice, claiming that its policies and relief efforts reflected the rich countries' own interests. The claim was exemplified by the fact that the United States, which made up 6 percent of the world's population, consumed 42 percent of the world's resources.[28] The example was not arbitrary, as "it was clear from the beginning that the United Nations Conference on the Human Environment was going to be an American show."[29]

Of the several alternative platforms, the Environment Forum (Miljöforum) was the one most closely related to the conference proper, as an officially sanctioned side program. The rationale for this initiative was, according to the conference's Senior Information Advisor Peter Stone, that "the UN had to find some way to tap the enormous reservoir of informed enthusiasm" represented by the many and diverse environmentalist communities and NGOs. "Indeed to shut these people out by narrowly interpreting the definition of the Conference as an exclusively intergovernmental one," he explained, "would be a certain way of lining up thousands of vociferous potential critics to say—'UN fails again.' . . . So the Environment Forum was invented."[30] As pointed out in its own daily newspaper, the Environment Forum positioned itself somewhere between the UN conference and alternative groupings such as the People's Forum (Folkets forum). Organized by the Swedish UN Association and the National Council of Swedish Youth (Sveriges ungdomsorganisationers landsråd), the Environment Forum was initiated to provide a platform for the voice of international NGOs, groups, and individuals, thus extending debate beyond the confines of the official conference, which was limited to official delegates.[31] As one delegate remarked, the initiative "partly functioned as such, partly as a lightning rod for youthful political activity."[32] Significantly for the present context, the events organized by the Environment Forum took place on the premises of Sweden's premier design school, Konstfack (and at the Film House). Moreover, *Forum: Environment Is Politics*, the daily newsletter produced by Environment Forum throughout the conference, was headquartered at Konstfack.[33] As such, the environmental discourse the Forum represented was arguably by default considered integral to design discourse. The program consisted of daily workshops followed by lectures and debates in Konstfack's main hall, known as the "White Sea" (*Vita havet*). The topics debated ranged from population growth and urban planning, via environmental pollution, to "third world" development and warfare. The list of speakers included names such as Barry Commoner, Paul Ehrlich, Paolo Soleri, and Margaret Mead, many of whom also would participate in the more independent initiative, the People's Forum.[34]

Well before the conference, *Science* reported that "it is feared that the [Environment Forum] might become a 'sideshow,' detracting attention from the conference itself."[35] But even if the Environment Forum eventually became far more politicized than its initiators had envisioned,[36] its character as a "sideshow" was outshone by its entirely unofficial parallel. Whereas the Environment Forum functioned as an extension of the official conference, the People's Forum emerged as a direct response to it, as a bottom-up initiative. This counterconference consisted primarily of a series of events at the headquarters of the Workers' Educational Association (Arbetarnas bildningsförbund, ABF). Initiated by the activist group PowWow, it served as a common platform for a whole range of environmentalist and (leftist) political groups, which, for all their diversity, joined forces in criticizing the establishment nature of the official conference.[37] In a press release sent out before the conference, they proclaimed:

It is becoming increasingly evident that the UN conference will not strike at the root of the environmental problems. Decisive economic and political issues will be concealed or suppressed. To realize this does <u>not</u> mean that one is against the UN itself. [But] more and more people perceive the UN Conference as <u>deficient</u> and want to do something.[38]

To provide an arena for discussions of issues that they surmised would be too controversial for the official program, then, the People's Forum organized working groups, debates, demonstrations, and other activities related to topics such as the war in Indochina, economic growth in the Western world, and the relation between industrialized countries and developing countries.[39] One afternoon's program featured the screening of a documentary film about the sit-in demonstrations in the summer of 1970 to save the Mardøla river and waterfalls from hydroelectrical development,[40] which, as discussed in chapter 5, had been such a defining moment for Norwegian environmentalism and ecophilosophy. Describing the Environment Forum as an "alibi conference" and a "tail" to the main conference, the People's

Forum emphasized their independence from political and financial actors.[41] This became particularly evident when the People's Forum refused an offer of economic support from and possible cooperation with another semiofficial side program, the Life Forum, which was funded by Stewart Brand's Point Foundation and the Kaplan Foundation.[42]

The Life Forum was definitely one of the most peculiar features of the Stockholm conference. Orchestrated by a chief strategist of the Californian counterculture, *Whole Earth Catalog* editor Stewart Brand, the Life Forum was comprised of what activist and reporter Barry Weisberg scornfully described as "a wide collection of Young Americans of the counterculture, including the sixty-odd people and three buses comprising the Hog Farm, . . . and a wide variety of other free-lance pranksters, ecologists, and friends."[43] In the Swedish press Brand and the Hog Farmers were described as "proper organizers" as they had been in charge of much of the infrastructure during the Woodstock Festival.[44] Brand envisioned taking a similar role in Stockholm, hoping to "provide a living reality-model of people taking care of each other."[45] Convincing the Swedish police that tens of thousands of youths would descend on Stockholm for the event, Brand and his crew secured permission to set up camp at the old airfield Skarpnäck on the outskirts of town, purportedly to manage (or deflect) the crowds.[46] They invited supporters as well as the media and the public to shows, discussions, demonstrations, and performances, turning the abandoned airfield into a veritable "Woodstockholm."[47] Even if the Life Forum was a compound group, the Hog Farmers definitely stole the thunder, both in the international and the Swedish press. Their alternative lifestyle sparked wonder and amazement. As a Swedish newspaper quoted one Hog Farmer: "I am not American, I am an Earthman. I acknowledge no flag but the rainbow and the sky. Maybe we actually are the same person. Let us then shake hands with ourselves."[48] But their outlandish if not outright alien appearance and behavior also provoked anxiety and anger, particularly because of their liberal attitudes toward drugs. This made the groups in the People's Forum disassociate themselves from the Hog Farmers and banned all cooperation.[49]

As argued by Andrew Kirk, Brand and his followers considered themselves consistently apolitical, at least in the traditional sense.[50] Refusing to take any political stand, particularly in the vexed question of the Vietnam War, the American counterculturalists thus differed dramatically from the Swedish groupings, which believed the conference should be an arena to educate people on the connection between ecology and politics.[51] According to one contemporary observer, the Skarpnäck village symbolized the dominant American approach to the environmental crisis in all its apolitical, naively romantic, transcendental glory. While European youths concerned themselves with the gloomy political questions that lay behind the economic disparities between rich and poor nations, with colonialism and economic imperialism and with capitalism-versus-socialism, trying to clarify the relations of all these issues to the threat to the environment, the young Americans involved themselves more with symptomology, with resource depletion and wildlife conservation.[52]

By adopting such a "politics no, environment yes" approach, Brand and his motley crew were remarkably consistent with the official US delegation's strategy to steer attention away from the American ecocide in Vietnam, to "safer" subjects such as whaling and overpopulation.[53] This was like adding fuel to the fire for Swedish environmentalists who suspected the Life Forum of being in bed with the CIA.[54] To many members of the People's Forum, the fact that the semiofficial Environment Forum on several instances defended and commended the Life Forum[55] probably exacerbated the suspicions that the Life Forum cooperated with the UN and the police in keeping the city center free from youths and protesters.[56]

THE GRAPHIC LANGUAGE OF PROTEST

Stockholm's activist community would not be diverted or silenced, however. A key tactic in this display of dissent was the production of protest posters such as the one discussed at the outset of this chapter. Students from Konstfack College of Arts, Crafts and Design, and particularly from its Department of Decorative Painting, were at the heart of this activity, making good use of the school's printing press to churn out protest posters against the UN conference. This was a student-initiated project and not part of the curriculum, but it nevertheless became so central to the school's activities that year as to warrant mention in the annual report.[57] These posters were designed and produced under tight restrictions in terms of time, technology, and economy, and their visual traits reflect this situation. Printed using the silkscreen printing technique, the posters feature a very basic color scheme, with one or two colors in addition to black and white, giving the posters a striking expression. The imagery is simple, based on quickly executed drawings of easily recognizable elements juxtaposed for rhetoric effect.

The messages the design students' posters were conveying were largely in line with the positions of PowWow and the rest of the People's Forum, discussed above. Some of them questioned the legitimacy of the UN conference and the intentions of the delegates, others painted industry and industrialists as the root of all environmental evils. Combining these two motifs, a poster designed by Åke Carlsson shows two conspiring men wearing top hats and masks against a backdrop of belching smokestacks cloaked in thick, black smoke on which is printed: "'FN miljövårdskonferens'—en rökridå" ("'The UN Environmental Preservation Conference'—a smokescreen"). Reflecting the deeply anticapitalistic attitude found in the activities of the People's Forum, another example, designed by Eva Lindström, features the tagline "Håll naturen ren från kapitalism" ("Keep nature clean from capitalism") over a drawing of rats eating from overflowing garbage cans.[58] The arresting iconology of industrial pollution, greed, and death is prevalent in this body of work, including in Ulf Frödin's depiction of the globe in the shape of a death's head adorned with smokestacks, sewer pipes, high-rise buildings, a top hat, and a banner across its mouth reading "Håll naturen ren" ("Keep nature clean") (figure 4.4).[59] In another example, designed by Barbro Flygare, an industrialist is lying in a hammock emblazoned with "$100000" strapped between two smokestacks and exclaiming: "I actually can't afford to think about the environment."[60] The figure of the child is also a recurring motif, as seen in Eva Trolin's poster with which this chapter opened (and also in some of her other posters). Trolin herself has explained this work in light of her fear of the future sparked by the debate at the time about the herbicide Hormoslyr, which wasn't banned in Sweden until 1977: "I was worried about my then three-year old son's future. Maybe he is the grown-up [in the poster], carrying my grandson in his arms?"[61] This use of the child as a metaphor for innocence and the future is entirely in line with Finis Dunaway's argument that in the visual culture of environmentalism, "children's bodies provide a way to visualize the largely invisible threats of radiation, toxicity, and other environmental dangers."[62] The vulnerable child is a recurring theme also in the work of Kerstin Abram-Nilsson, which will be discussed below.

During the conference, the students would put up their posters on the walls of buildings in the central parts of Stockholm. In the morning, however, the posters were painted over by the "cleaning patrol," leaving only a series of gray rectangles where the posters had been.[63] The authorities' zero tolerance of demonstrations and visual expressions of protests during the conference had been announced in

advance. The National Transport Office had been tasked with keeping the city clean and orderly, and contracted a renovation company called Lundblads Miljövård AB (*miljövård* translates roughly to environmental preservation) to do the patrolling and cleaning.[64] Not surprisingly, this hardline policy was a bright red flag in the face of the activists, who considered it a blatant attempt to stifle their freedom of expression: "What kind of waste is it that is to be removed—beer cans? Single-use cups? No. It is posters and scribbling on the walls. This is not a question of environmental preservation, but of censorship."[65] The provocation was only exacerbated by the massive police presence in a city not used to such a brazen show of governmental force. In response to alarmist warnings from the FBI that thousands of protesters from the US and elsewhere might turn up ready to engage in direct confrontations, the police braced themselves and mustered 5,000 officers prepared to prevent possible riots.[66] The feared invasion and riots turned out to be greatly exaggerated, however, and the excessive show of police force thus worked to agitate rather than to quiet the activists. This sentiment is evident also in the motifs in several of the Konstfack students' posters. A cleverly subversive example, designed by Ulf Frödin, shows a malign-looking, obese policeman with the following message written across his chest: "5000 poliser har dragits saman för att skydda dej från FN-konferensens delegater" ("5000 police officers have been convened to protect you from the UN conference delegates") (figure 4.5).[67]

As discussed above, the frantic activism in connection with the UN conference must be understood against the backdrop of the emergence in the late 1960s of an impressive array of leftist political groups in Sweden. Even if the causes promoted by these various groupings differed considerably, ranging from international solidarity via environmental protection to consumer criticism, they were nevertheless surprisingly uniform in terms of their organization, actions, and methods. They all favored a nonauthoritarian organization with a more direct democratic approach,

4.4

Håll naturen ren (Keep Nature Clean). Poster designed by Konstfack-student Ulf Frödin on the occasion of the United Nations Conference on the Human Environment organized in Stockholm in June 1972. Photo courtesy of Håkan Agnsäter.

rather than traditional forms of representational, hierarchical structures. This was an organizational form designed for action, and posters, demonstrations, magazines, leaflets, and teach-ins were consequently crucial tools in getting their message across.[68] This context is key in understanding the activists' sentiments toward the UN conference, and the resulting design interventions. The general distrust of the establishment and apparent gap between the opinion of the people and the authorities was transferred directly onto the UN conference and its delegates, as they were representatives of this very system. And nowhere is this feeling of distrust and despair more palpable than in the graphic language of the design students' protest posters.

The dwindling trust in representative democracy and its institutions is reflected also in the work of one of their lecturers, Kerstin Abram-Nilsson, who started teaching at Konstfack in 1971 and coordinated the students' protest posters project. From 1968 to 1974, Abram-Nilsson ran a joint project with fellow artists Boï Edberg and Anna Sjödahl called Images in the City—Alternatives to Advertising (Bilder på stan—Alternativ till reklam). For this project, they rented designated advertising space in Stockholm, where they put up huge self-produced posters that called attention to issues such as abuse of power, nuclear energy, and the depletion of natural resources.[69] In a TV interview from 1971, Abram-Nilsson expresses her concern for the latter topic, while the camera shows posters with messages such as "The children will not forgive the authorities' experimentation with our nature" ("Barnen kommer inte förlåta maktens experiment med vår natur"). She then goes on to criticize the lack of public places for people to express their opinions:

People have very few possibilities of being heard. What kind of alternatives are there? Well, one can write to the editor of *Aftonbladet* [one of Sweden's biggest newspapers] and

4.5

5000 poliser har dragits saman för att skydda dej från FN-konferensens delegater (5000 Police Officers Have Been Convened to Protect You from the UN Conference Delegates). Poster designed by Konstfack-student Ulf Frödin on the occasion of the United Nations Conference on the Human Environment organized in Stockholm in June 1972. Photo courtesy of Håkan Agnsäter.

possibly be published there. But what other options do we have? The lack of possibilities is what made us do this [project]. The powerlessness one feels when one cannot comment on what is happening . . . I think people should be free, there should be spaces simply to speak.[70]

Abram-Nilsson exemplifies the central role assumed by a new generation of intellectuals, such as writers, artists, and young academics, in the period's debate climate, both as contributors to public discourse in conventional fora and as agitators and activists.[71] This activist, public-facing role of the artist emerged as part of the intense politicization of the Scandinavian art scene in general. Many artists and critics strongly believed that art should not only be the privilege of the bourgeoisie, and therefore had to break out of elite institutions and be made available to everyone. Amongst the proponents of such a view was a group of radical young artists who in 1968 formed the People's Atelier (Folkets Ateljé), inspired by the Parisian Atelier Populaire. The same year they published a manifesto-like article in the Marxist-Leninist magazine *Clarté*: "Our purpose is deliberately propagandistic. The artist must leave the galleries. He [sic] must change his technique and adjust it to what he is working for. The oil painting is dead, long live the poster!"[72] Blurring the lines between art and design, the poster thus became a favored medium of expression, as it was a readily available format, relatively inexpensive to produce, conductive to public display, and an efficient conduit for politically charged messages.[73] Somewhat paradoxically, since artists embraced the poster format partly to escape the narrow confines of the institutionalized art world, Moderna Museet quickly pulled them back in with the exhibition *The Language of the Revolution—Communist Posters from All over the World* in the spring of 1968.[74]

According to Eva Trolin, Kerstin Abram-Nilsson and her politically charged and socially engaged activist practice were a great inspiration for her Konstfack students. Not only did she stimulate their interest in issues such as environmental protection, nuclear energy, and international solidarity, but she also had a remarkable ability to involve the students in various projects. Trolin further recalls how Abram-Nilsson convinced the students that they had to "do something" and demonstrated by way of her own example that by recasting their professional identity from the elitism-ridden notion of the artist to the far more proletarian-sounding "image worker," they would be much better placed to engage the social purpose of art.[75] The design students and educators took their environmental activism seriously. Gearing up for their protest poster project, Konstfack's Department of Decorative Painting collaborated with the recently established Environment Centre (Miljöcentrum), which quickly became an important voice in Swedish public discourse on topics ranging from nuclear energy to food additives and pollution. Its collaboration with Konstfack included a guest lecture by its founder, biogeneticist Björn Gillberg, followed by student exercises that resulted in a poster exhibition.[76]

The growing attention to social purpose and environmental issues was by no means restricted to the Department of Decorative Painting, but surged throughout the school. Already in 1968, a group of students in the Department of Graphic Design revolted against the customary commercial assignments and instead developed their own in collaboration with the Environmental Protection Agency (Statens naturvårdsverk), aiming to put the tricks of the advertising trade to better use.[77] The same year, fellow students from the Department of Textile Design organized a comprehensive seminar scrutinizing the social and environmental implications of the fashion industry.[78] So, when the Department of Ceramics and Glass with Industrial Design reported in 1972 of a continued expansion of the scope of the department's remit, it was part of an established trend amongst the students: "A striking feature is an increased interest in more open exercises concerning the public environment at the expense of interest in mass-produced industrial products."[79] The following year, the Department of Furniture and Interiors hosted guest lectures on environmental history (by Claes Tollin) and wind energy (by Arne Bergström).[80] And in 1975, the new academic year was kicked off with a school-wide theme week dedicated to human ecology.[81] But the best indication of the school's broader response to increased environmental awareness was the appointment of a lecturer in environmental studies in 1972. The purpose of the position was to introduce environmental thinking into the education across all the school's departments, which in turn boosted students' extracurricular activism. The first two persons to hold this position, Per Janse and Varis Bokalders (from 1975), were both young architects active in Alternative City and PowWow, and were deeply involved with the exhibition *For a Technology in the Service of the People!* (*För en teknik i folkets tjänst!*) on the occasion of the UN conference.[82]

FOR A TECHNOLOGY IN THE SERVICE OF THE PEOPLE!

Of the nearly 30 groups contributing to the People's Forum, PowWow and Alternative City most emphatically embodied the activist politics of ecological design.

True to their core concern for the (local) urban environment, Alternative City organized alternative sightseeing tours for international delegates and journalists daily throughout the conference. Since commercial and official tours would only showcase the sunny side of the city, they argued, an alternative was needed to demonstrate the real and more troubling sides of urban development. The alternative tours would "take interested visitors around to the new nightmare suburbs and to natural areas about to be raped for the sake of what the city planners call 'progress.' And they will have the joy of travelling on the exhaust-filled, congested spaghetti highways."[83] Appropriately enough, Alternative City's tours departed from the site of the previous year's Battle of the Elms.[84] In a true spirit of activist ecodesign, tours were offered on foot, on old, repaired bicycles—and on a 1940s bus converted to run on methane gas produced from chicken and horse droppings sourced at Skeppsholmen. Not surprisingly, perhaps, the press thus immediately dubbed it the "Shit Bus" (*Skitbussen*).[85] Its redesign was overseen by one of the group's architect members, Varis Bokalders (who was also a key contributor to PowWow's activities); and Eva Karin Svedberg, an interior design student at Konstfack, was responsible for its decoration (figure 4.6).[86]

Alternative City's bike restoration and distribution scheme predated the UN conference.[87] Earlier that year, a subcommittee originally engaged in bicycle demonstrations had begun to "repair old bikes we get from Stockholmers and paint them white and green and lend them out free of charge."[88] So when the fleet of official UN bicycles discussed above hit the streets, Alternative City had mixed feelings about it, and put pen to paper:

We are glad to see they are used today, the glittering new UN-bikes. But even better for the environment had been to recycle old ones instead of encourage [sic] production of new ones and by that also encouraging more waste. A funny rumour says that UN chose those mini-bikes because they fit so well to the trunks o [sic] Volvos and Saabs—what about that?[89]

In another act of transport design activism during the conference, Alternative City borrowed a decommissioned trolleybus from the Tramway Society (Spårvägssällskapet). They used the bus as the centerpiece of an exhibit at Sergels torg—the main square of the new, modernist city center they so despised—designed to demonstrate the political folly of divesting from already established public transport systems such as trolleybuses and trams whose environmental performance clearly outshone that of the automobile, around which so much current planning revolved.[90] Finally,

and further consolidating the close relations between environmental activism and design discourse, Alternative City organized an exhibition at the Architecture Museum on the history of the Swedish environmental movement.[91]

Whereas Alternative City focused on the urban environment and city planning, PowWow sought to put alternative technology in service of the people in other ways. Assuming the Native American (Narragansett Eastern Algonquian) word for council as its name, PowWow was formed in late 1970 to discuss the upcoming UN conference and plan possible parallel activities.[92] PowWow had no faith that the consensus-reliant, intergovernmental approach endemic to the UN could solve the

4.6

Alternative City's converted methane-powered bus used for alternative sightseeing tours during the United Nations Conference on the Human Environment organized in Stockholm in June 1972. Photo: Björn Gustafsson.

DEMO! THE ECOPOLITICS OF DESIGN ACTIVISM 165

environmental crisis. And who could blame them? Even the preparatory report commissioned by the secretary-general of the conference, penned by British economist Barbara Ward and French-American biologist René Dubos, concluded that the "whole variety of United Nations agencies whose duty it is to elaborate worldwide strategies" was as yet largely a product of "lip service," because "the idea of authority and energy and resources to support their policies seems strange, visionary, and Utopian at present, simply because world institutions are not backed by any sense of planetary community and commitment."[93] Sharing this skepticism, PowWow identified three broad categories of environmental problems and corresponding strategies for solutions, none of which the UN was adequately equipped to address, in their view: (1) those that require technological fixes; (2) those that require changes in consumption patterns and production methods; (3) those that require fundamental changes in lifestyles, the organization of production, and political structures.[94] Not surprisingly, PowWow considered techno-fixes to be woefully inadequate, mere "bandage solutions," and also beyond the scope of the UN's toolkit. But even changing production methods and consumption patterns would only buy time, and "cannot be dealt with as a serious issue by the UN Conference because of the strong resistance of governments and powerful corporations with too much at stake in the status quo." Finally, the problems in category (3) were considered the most vexed ones because they "originate deep within our way of living and within the political-economic power structure." Problems such as the centralization of power, the relentless quest for economic growth, and the plundering of natural resources could not be solved "by the UN conference or by governments as we know them today," argued PowWow: "Instead, they would be found by the broad masses of the people creating a new way of life."[95] In their belief that ad hoc and piecemeal efforts were of little help and that the way forward had to be found in profound structural changes and self-motivated lifestyle changes in the broader population, PowWow's views shared many of the basic tenets of the deep ecology movement discussed in chapter 5. In particular, they resonate strongly with the distinction between "shallow" and "deep" modes of ecological thought which Arne Næss—who was present in Stockholm during the UN conference—was developing at this time.[96]

PowWow's call to arms culminated in the formation of the People's Forum in January 1972.[97] Having instigated this broader collaborative arena, PowPow's own efforts would chiefly be focused on the exhibition *For a Technology in the Service of the People!* The exhibition was shown at Moderna Museet's short-lived project

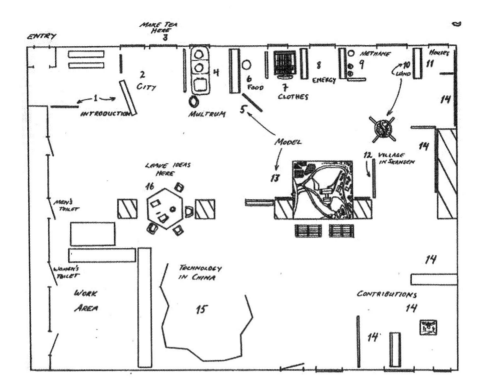

space Filialen ("The Branch"), and curated in collaboration with Filialen's director, Pär Stolpe. Filialen was conceived in 1971 as a vehicle for the museum to explore new exhibition policies and experiment with new forms of visual communication.[98] Through a range of media including wall texts, image panels, collages, posters, interactive installations, and models, *For a Technology in the Service of the People!* demonstrated alternative technologies for clean energy sources, food production for one's own sustenance, and alternative forms of shelter (figure 4.7).[99] In retrospect,

4.7

Draft floor plan for PowWow's exhibition *For a Technology in the Service of the People!* shown at Moderna Museet's project space Filialen during and after the UN conference in 1972. Courtesy of Peter Harper.

one of the organizers, Peter Harper, has suggested that the exhibition might have overestimated the universal potential of small-scale, craft-based manufacturing:

We were fascinated by household, local and regional self-sufficiency, meeting our own needs from the materials at hand. But this quickly proved impossible in practice. You could "make" a simple thermosiphon solar water-heater, and we did. But you had to get the copper tubing, and the joints, and the solder, and the black paint, and the wood for the box, and the glass, and so on. Although that is not very high tech, it is still industrial. And that does presuppose that there are copper mines somewhere, and there are people making tubes. Could we have made our own tubes, panes of glass? Surely not.[100]

Somehow foreshadowing this realization, one of the exhibits was a foot-high model of the Gedser Experimental Mill from 1957, which would soon serve as the archetype design for the Danish windmill industry when it moved from experiment to enterprise in the late 1970s (see chapter 6).[101] Nevertheless, the basic ideas that PowWow wanted to convey with this event were that the production of goods and services should be a collective concern rooted in local communities where everyone, not just experts, could contribute to the making and mending of things, and that manufacturing should be based on local and recycled/recyclable materials and renewable energy.[102] The exhibition opened on June 6, the day after the official opening of the UN conference, and ran through the summer, closing on August 27. PowWow went to great lengths to make the event a more dynamic and participatory experience than a conventional exhibition usually is. In fact, for the first month after the opening, the show remained a work-in-progress, gradually modified and expanded, partially in dialogue with visitors.[103] Exhibits explained topics including closed-chamber composting, soilless horticulture, renewable energy production, low-energy housing, waste reclamation and recycling, and the continued relevance of natural materials and traditional manufacturing methods.

The point of all this was not to inspire a sort of DIY tinkering for off-the-grid living, but to critique the seemingly inescapable path of global modernization laid out by multinational corporations and capital-intensive industry, and to identify instead potential trajectories toward greater political autonomy and socioeconomic freedom.[104] In PowWow's own words, the ambition was to explore

technological changes that could promote the following goals: workers' control over production, fulfilment through creative work, cooperation, independent economic development, low degree of specialization, low energy consumption, local self-sufficiency, resource conservation, environmental quality, recovery from industrial collapse, low risk of major technological disasters, efforts which may help bring down the capitalist system.[105]

By taking such an explicitly political stance, PowWow clearly distinguished their project from the apolitical attitude of Hog Farm and Life Forum. PowWow unmistakably aligned their environmentalist activism and ecodesign proposals with a general anticapitalistic critique, calling for structural changes in the modes and methods of production.[106] As Felicity Scott has pointed out, PowWow "did not seek alternatives to political action, but alternative tools for it."[107] The radical politics of their project must be understood in light of the fact that PowWow belonged to (indeed, initiated) the People's Forum, which had gathered over 20 groupings around the common cause of anticapitalism. This particular bent was shared also by many of the organizations and speakers participating in the Environment Forum, despite its semiofficial character. This massive ideological divide between PowWow and People's Forum on the one side and Hog Farm and Life Forum on the other is thus indicative of a more fundamental difference between the Swedish and the American groups when it came to the role of politics in the struggle against environmental devastation.

PowWow was conceived primarily as an environmentalist action group, but they consistently made use of designerly modes of expression and counted several design professionals amongst their core members, including the engineer Björn Eriksson and architects Varis Bokalders and Per Janse—all of whom were involved with the exhibition. *For a Technology in the Service of the People!* is therefore appropriately read as a piece of ecocritical design activism in its own right. Alternative/ appropriate technology was not an entirely novel concept in 1972, but PowWow's marshaling of it as a critique of the UN Conference on the Human Environment nevertheless marks the onset of a brief period of frantic activity and at times surprisingly enthusiastic governmental support for such strategies, hitherto largely considered subversive or ludicrous, depending on one's point of view. Even if PowWow and the exhibition were local initiatives, the group was significantly reinforced by British alternative technology enthusiasts from the circle forming around the recently established magazine *Undercurrents*, including biologist Peter Harper, engineer Godfrey Boyle, designer Chris Ryan, and architect Ian Hogan. As such, the exhibition in Stockholm became an important testing ground also for subsequent developments in the alternative technology movement in the UK, perhaps most notably expressed in Harper and Boyle's book *Radical Technology* published in 1976, which featured many of the designs and ideas first showcased at the exhibition.[108]

THINKING LIKE A MOUNTAIN

The most direct legacy of PowWow's explorations and demonstrations of alternative technology, at least in terms of its influence on the development of ecological design in Scandinavia, came in the shape of a second exhibition in Stockholm four years later which carried over many of the topics, concepts, approaches, and actors from *For a Technology in the Service of the People!* The institutional partner was also the same, Moderna Museet. But the Filialen project space was no longer operational, so this time around the venue would be the museum's main campus. Also, whereas the 1972 exhibition was planned in a hurry and produced on a shoestring budget, the 1976 event enjoyed the funding and lead time of a more conventional museum show—even if there was nothing conventional about the content of the exhibition. *ARARAT* (Alternative Research in Architecture, Resources, Art and Technology) was the museum's most comprehensive project to date when it opened on April 1, 1976. The venue might have been an art museum, but this exhibition surely pushed the envelope of such a setting.[109] *ARARAT* did not exhibit artworks; it sought to explore alternative ways of creating a society more in harmony with nature. "The main question posed by the exhibition is the uneven distribution characterizing the world as a whole and the fact that everything flows in the wrong direction," proclaimed the organizing group: "It deals with the future, the possibilities we have of building a society that functions in balance with nature and gets its energy from the inexhaustible sources offered by the ecological systems—the sun, wind, water and growth."[110] Even if presented as a clever acronym, the exhibition title's biblical connotation was of course both intentional and essential in communicating the urgency and gravity of the message—but also its essential notion of hope. If Mount Ararat put dry land under Noah's ark and thus provided humanity (and the animal kingdom) with a new beginning, *ARARAT* emphasized the necessity of rethinking the Western way of life. Suggesting that alternative technology and ecological design offered the only safe haven for a civilization currently lost at sea, cast adrift by a flood of overconsumption, pollution, and overexploitation of natural resources, was a powerful rhetorical device—albeit one not entirely devoid of hubris. These somewhat lofty connotations also connect the project both to prominent tropes in ecophilosophy at the time (see chapter 5) as well as to more recent scholarship on "pluriversal" world-making and knowing.[111]

Like its predecessor, *ARARAT* was a distinctly collective undertaking. It was initiated, planned, and coordinated by a core group of architects, designers, and engineers, but the process was deliberately set up to involve many more in developing and executing the plans. According to the catalog, the total number of official contributors in the end exceeded one hundred, and many more were involved in less formal capacities, making it a remarkable experiment in participatory action. A large part of these volunteer contributors were students from the design and architecture programs where members of the core group were teaching, including Konstfack and its sister school in Gothenburg, the School of Design and Crafts (Högskolan för design och konsthantverk, HDK).[112] One of these educators, architect Hans Nordenström, was key to the project's genesis. In 1972, while based at Lund Institute of Technology (he would be appointed professor at Chalmers Institute of Technology in 1975), Nordenström unsuccessfully applied for a grant from the Swedish Council for Building Research (Statens råd för byggnadsforskning) to explore ecological building technology. Even if that particular effort stranded, his interest in this topic resonated with like-minded acquaintants, resulting in something of a taskforce coalescing.[113] This emerging network included familiar figures such as Varis Bokalders, who had been involved with Alternative City, PowWow, and *For a Technology in the Service of the People!*, as well as his Konstfack colleague Kerstin Abram-Nilsson, who had masterminded the protest poster student project discussed above. According to Bokalders, other members of the *ARARAT* group had also been involved in the alternative conferences during the UN Conference in 1972. The two events were thus closely connected, also because that prior experience was a key catalyst for their interest in alternative technology.[114] Others who got involved included design critic Gunilla Lundahl, architects Olof Antell and Axel Valdemar Axelsson, and scenographers Lennart Mörk and Jan Öqvist.[115] Intriguingly, the latter had studied ecophilosophy with Arne Næss at the University of Oslo prior to his career in design.[116] In early 1974 the group established contact with the museum with a view to developing their interest in alternative technology and ecological design in the format of an exhibition.[117]

As part of the planning process, members of the group made two study trips abroad to learn about, and from, pioneering projects, persons, and organizations. The first trip, in the spring of 1974, went to the UK, whose alternative technology community they already knew quite well from the collaborations on *For a Technology in the Service of the People!* The *Undercurrents* community remained an important source of inspiration also for the new exhibition project, but so was Street Farmers, a London-based collective growing out of the Architectural Association School of Architecture (AA).[118] These "guerrilla architects" envisioned "urban revolutionaries humanizing the landscape by ploughing the streets"; in their loose-leaf magazine they published "surreal images of buildings being gradually eaten away and replaced by vegetation" as well as instructions for making a tree house and plans for an ecological house.[119] Their quest for an uncompromisingly ecological way of building, based on anarchist philosophy and a radical vision of urbanism, was exemplified in a version of the latter: the Street Farm House, designed by Graham Caine and Bruce Haggart while they were still students at the AA, and which Bokalders identifies as a key inspiration in the planning of *ARARAT*.[120] Constructed as an experimental, temporary structure in Eltham, southeast London, the Street Farm House was a self-sustaining home for a small family, providing shelter, heat, food, water, cooking facilities, and an ecologically sound waste disposal system.[121] It was exactly this type of mundane technological-environmental challenge that became the essence of *ARARAT*.

A year later, in March-April of 1975, a delegation embarked on a second and more adventurous three-week journey to the United States, primarily to study solar power and other alternative energy technologies.[122] The group of twelve persons traveled from San Francisco to Boston through 13 states, making over 60 visits to universities, research institutes, consulting companies, manufacturers, political authorities, funding bodies, individual researchers, as well as a number of projects focusing on alternative energy support systems aiming for improved ecological balance.[123] Their itinerary featured many staples of the countercultural ecodesign scene in the western US—most of which will reappear in chapter 5—including UC Berkeley's College of Environmental Design (where they were welcomed by fellow Swede Lars Lerup, an associate professor in the architecture department); Sim Van der Ryn's Farallones Institute in Occidental; the Portola Institute in Menlo Park (publisher of the *Whole Earth Catalog*); the New Alchemy Institute in Pescadero; Paolo Soleri's Phoenix office and the site of his experimental desert town Arcosanti; and Steve Baer's alternative energy company Zomeworks and his newly built off-the-grid home in Albuquerque.[124] The New Alchemy Institute, which Andrew Kirk has described as "one of the most celebrated efforts in A[lternative] T[echnology] and ecological design of the 1970s," sought to counter the doom and gloom characterizing much of the environmental movement by exploring positive and proactive responses to environmental problems, focusing in particular on systems for biologically based waste recycling and energy production.[125] As mentioned above, Soleri participated in the Environment Forum during the UN conference; as discussed in chapter 5, he would later become closely involved with the Californian deep ecologists. By 1975, Baer had established a solid reputation as a pioneer of experimental building design and of passive solar energy.[126] He also had impeccable credentials in the countercultural community, partly due to his involvement in the construction of domes at the iconic commune Drop City in Trinidad, Colorado and to publications like the *Dome Cookbook* (1967) and the *Zome Primer* (1970) which became inspirational manuals for experimental ecodesign. By visiting these and other venues, the Swedish group gained firsthand knowledge of the many and varied ecological design experiments percolating throughout the American West and its counterculture. When work on designing and constructing the exhibition commenced in full in the summer of 1975, the organizers had rich impressions from the US trip fresh in mind.

ARARAT: DEMONSTRATING ECOLOGICAL DESIGN

The study trips, the network building, the preparatory research, the participatory planning, the collaborative construction, and the evolutionary design process resulted in an ambitious, comprehensive, genre-defying manifestation. With an indoor and an outdoor section, the exhibition occupied the entire museum. The outdoor section was staged in the museum's courtyard, where three full-scale buildings were erected as didactic examples of ecological architecture: the Straw Bale House (Halmhuset), the Sun Wing (Solhuslängan), and the Recycling House (Återbrukshuset). The Straw Bale House was a curiously humble structure, no more than a single, round room demarcated by walls of stacked, frameless straw bales clad with chicken wire and plaster and covered by a sheet metal roof. The point of this structure, designed by architect Klas Anshelm, was to demonstrate the viability of designing a building using only the bare minimum of resources. The Sun Wing was a technologically far more sophisticated building intended as a testing station for various uses of passive and active solar energy in housing, heavily influenced by the US study trip. Divided into five compartments, each demonstrating different heat storage systems using either air- or water-based solar collectors, the project sought to show how combinations of existing technologies could go a long way in the quest

for more sustainable energy systems in housing design (figure 4.8). Finally, the Recycling House, designed and built by a collective headed by furniture designer Lars Engman (who had just started working for IKEA and would later become the company's global design manager) and populated by architecture students from the Royal Institute of Technology, took yet another approach to resource efficiency. Made entirely from materials and components salvaged from the many recently demolished houses around Stockholm, it was a tall, narrow wooden structure with a distinct bricolage aesthetic clearly communicating its material essence.[127]

4.8

View of the Sun Wing building in the exterior section of the *ARARAT* exhibition shown at Moderna Museet in the spring of 1976. Photo: Hans Thorwid/Moderna Museet/Stockholm.

From the courtyard, visitors entered the museum building through an entrance temporarily redesigned in the shape of Mount Ararat. Inside, the exhibition consisted of three sections. Following immediately after the entrance, the Contemporary Gallery was intended to elucidate the main challenges of the present day, such as the ecological crisis, food shortages, the threat of nuclear war, the environmental ills of consumer society, and global socioeconomic injustice. Reflecting a didactic mode reminiscent of the compare-and-contrast rhetoric characterizing much of the activist responses to the UN conference discussed above, the image of crisis and despair painted in the Contemporary Gallery was mirrored in a corresponding image of hope and possibilities rendered in the Future Gallery, located by the exit. Here, before leaving, visitors were presented with the takeaway message that a more sustainable future is possible, and that the knowledge and inspiration needed to chart that path might be found beyond the trajectories of continued capitalist-industrial expansion—particularly if we look to current experimental practices, living traditions in non-Western cultures, and preindustrial technology.

Sandwiched between the Contemporary Gallery by the entrance and the Future Gallery by the exit was the great hall, which housed the main section of the indoor exhibition. The four walls of the gallery were dedicated to each of the four elements sustaining life on our planet: sun, earth, wind, and water, with exhibits and illustrations explaining nature's circulation systems and energy flows. The large space circumscribed by the wall-mounted exhibits was dominated by an extensive, continuous, multilevel installation made up of mechanical contraptions, designed objects, and artworks, all intended to demonstrate how our lives and practices rely on, and intervene in, nature's circulation systems and energy flows (figure 4.9). It included a kitchen where food waste was composted to produce methane gas which in turn was used to fuel an AGA stove (designed by Gustaf Dalén in 1922) and power an Electrolux gas absorption refrigerator (designed by Baltzar von Platen and Carl Munters in 1925), selected as examples of energy-efficient products long extant in the history of Swedish design. These hands-on, didactic demonstrations were intended to make visitors realize how design practices, manufacturing systems, and consumption patterns are intrinsically intertwined with delicate ecosystems on every scale, and thus to inspire positive change.

In addition to the exhibits, the programming included a series of seminars and lectures organized by Pär Stolpe (who, as director of Filialen, had been deeply involved also in *For a Technology in the Service of the People!*) as well as the Ecothèque (Ekotektet), an information central featuring books, magazines, images,

DEMO! THE ECOPOLITICS OF DESIGN ACTIVISM

and other material on alternative technology and ecological design, including a series of eight booklets produced by the curators and their collaborators.[128] There was also a workshop where visitors could try their hands at traditional building techniques, alternative energy sources, composting methods, and making objects from reclaimed materials and could witness the damaging effect of toxic substances on plants and animals (figure 4.10).[129] Two of the initiators of the workshop, interior designer Bengt Carling and industrial designer Michael Crisp, had worked with schoolchildren as part of the preparations, helping them design and build—using reclaimed materials only—devices and vehicles utilizing renewable energy sources.

4.9

View of the central installation in the main gallery of the *ARARAT* exhibition at Moderna Museet in the spring of 1976. Photo: Hans Thorwid/Moderna Museet/Stockholm.

The results, among them a wind turbine made from old bicycle parts, a solar-heated stove, a "sail car," and a pedal-powered "bus," were all shown in the workshop space at the exhibition.[130]

As mentioned above, several of the key organizers of *ARARAT* were design educators and made sure to involve their students in the exhibition and to incorporate the exhibition in their curricula. In his new role as lecturer in environmental studies at Konstfack, Varis Bokalders perfected this strategy. For instance, he worked with ceramics students on developing tools for alternative methods of cooking and

4.10

A boy learning to forge in the workshop section of the *ARARAT* exhibition at Moderna Museet in the spring of 1976. Photo: Hans Thorwid/Moderna Museet/Stockholm.

preserving food. Based on the premise that nutrients are considerably better preserved if the food is fermented rather than canned, Bokalders and the students developed ceramic containers with water seals to simplify this process. These digesters and other kitchen utensils were then included in the exhibition's model ecological kitchen discussed above.[131] Furthermore, some of Kerstin Abram-Nilsson's graphic design students made environmentalism-themed children's books which were sold at the exhibition.[132]

The most comprehensive of Konstfack's many contributions to *ARARAT*, however, came from the textile designers. The literally largest contribution was a 3-by-11-meter rag rug, made jointly by the textile department's 30 students. Its massive size was made possible by borrowing Sweden's largest loom, which required a crew of three persons to operate.[133] The rag rug technique was chosen because of its associations with thriftiness and reuse, features which in this version were emphasized though exaggeration *in absurdum*. As tradition prescribed, the rug was made of worn-out clothes and other discarded textiles shredded into strips and woven into the warp. But as the work progressed, the students gradually cut wider and wider strips of fabric, with the inevitable result that at the end of the rug entire garments protruded from the warp.[134] This remarkable project was an homage to a humble but venerable design practice, but also a critique of its fashionability at the time. In its traditional form, when the raw materials are garments worn to the last thread and made entirely of natural fibers and natural dyes, the rag rug could be considered a good example of upcycling. But the trendy, modern variety often undermined these qualities by using artificial dyes and materials that had been discarded prematurely. The Konstfack students' giant rag rug was inspired by the school's theme week on human ecology which opened the fall 1975 term and came about as a response to a subsequent visit to textile factories in Borås where the students were horrified by the frantic fashion cycle, the hurried pace of manufacturing, and the widespread use of synthetic fabrics. To mitigate such wasteful practices, they argued, designers and manufacturers should stive to make garments of higher technical quality made from natural materials and with greater care and attention, resulting in products with greater physical and emotional durability.[135]

Another, more specific response to this issue, also resulting in objects shown at the exhibition, was a line of basic clothing made by the textile students in cooperation with the clothing brand Mah-Jong.[136] Established in 1966 by three former Konstfack students—Helena Henschen, Veronica Nygren, and Kristina Torsson (daughter of Lena Larsson, protagonist of the throwawayism debate discussed in chapter 1)—the company became a distinctly political project, combining explicit support for independence movements in Vietnam, Palestine, Mozambique, and Angola with a nonhierarchical business designing locally manufactured, long-lasting garments in natural materials and vivid colors.[137] "Designers want to develop environments shaped by people's real needs, not artificial ones," they proclaimed.[138] Ever the ardent design activists, Mah-Jong continuously fought for precarious Swedish textile industry jobs, filled their advertising billboards at Stockholm's metro stations with pro-National Liberation Front messages during the Hanoi bombings of Christmas 1972 (a strategy not dissimilar from Kerstin Abram-Nilsson's contemporary Images in the City project, mentioned above), and produced a slideshow explaining the ecological aspects of their manufacturing process called *From Plant to Garment* that was screened in their own retail space.[139] The collaboration with Mah-Jong thus gave the Konstfack students a certain cachet and credibility as politically and environmentally alert designers contributing to the exhibition. The final and arguably most original of the textile students' *ARARAT* contributions was not exhibited in the main gallery, but mounted as an integral feature of the Sun Wing. This exhibit comprised a set of curtains designed to absorb and store solar heat energy throughout the day, which would then be released into the building's interior as the temperature decreased at night. Birgitta Eriksson, Ritva Hansson, and Ann-Britt Brånby designed the curtains using a double layer of fabric enclosing triangular, quadrangular, or hexagonal cavities or cells, based on the structure of a beehive. The size and placing of the cavities was determined by a mathematical system developed in collaboration with students from the Royal Institute of Technology, exemplifying an interdisciplinary approach to ecological design that very much characterized *ARARAT* as a whole.[140]

Not surprisingly, given its highly unconventional nature, its participatory spirit, and the sheer magnitude of the undertaking, *ARARAT* received much public attention and was widely covered in the daily press. It attracted a total of 110,000 visitors, more than any previous show at Moderna Museet.[141] Despite the general fascination with the endeavor, however, the exhibition also received its share of criticism. The more salient misgivings revolved around notions of scale and the relation between individual and collective solutions. As one reporter remarked, the vast majority of the alternative technology on show operated on a scale so small that it was difficult to see how it could contribute to the broader societal change needed to mitigate substantial environmental problems.[142] Fully in line with the democratic spirit of the project, the organizers met this criticism with an invitation to

DEMO! THE ECOPOLITICS OF DESIGN ACTIVISM

dialogue, setting up a public seminar at the museum to discuss the matter. A panel composed of Scandinavian scholars from a broad range of fields, from criminology to oncology, were asked to reflect on the exhibition's "connection to society" and whether it was the case, as some critics had claimed, that the quirky demonstration of ecodesign was "so charming that it might result in a depoliticization rather than an activation" of the public. Stockholm University media sociologist Jan Ekecrantz felt the criticism was justified, and feared that *ARARAT* easily could become a dead end, as the exhibition failed to convincingly articulate how the suggested solutions related to societal structures and how they could be implemented on a broad scale. Not everyone shared the view that the exhibition inevitably shouldered such a responsibility, though. Niels Christie, professor of criminology at the University of Oslo, commended the nonauthoritative pedagogy and argued that the absence of explicit prescriptions could inspire a wider range of responses.[143]

The most poignant and paradoxical concern raised at the seminar, however, was the observation made by several of the panelists that the ecological design portrayed at *ARARAT* so clearly emphasized individual over common efforts and solutions. Social psychologist Lars Dencik from Roskilde University and architect Jan Strömdahl both lamented that the design solutions demonstrated at the exhibition compartmentalized environmental problems and placed the responsibility for creating change on the individual. What was needed, they insisted, was a call for common efforts rather than a demonstration of how to build "quirky single-family houses in various ways."[144] This criticism is particularly intriguing because of the close connections between *ARARAT* and the design activism discussed earlier in this chapter, which was so emphatically rooted in a sense of community, fellowship, and social responsibility. Add to this how vehemently the protagonists of the People's Forum had opposed the apolitical individualism they found so blatantly displayed at "Woodstockholm." This time around, however, the ecodesign experiments produced by the very same US counterculture they had vilified during the UN conference had become their most significant source of inspiration. There is a certain irony at play here, then: in 1972 the Swedish ecodesign activists had castigated Stewart Brand and Hog Farm for fetishizing individual action, responding in part by making their own highly political sense of community manifest in *For a Technology in the Service of the People!* Four years later, they fell prey to the exact same criticism when *ARARAT* was perceived as promoting design solutions that were too individualized both in scale and in responsibility to provide a politically feasible path to a more sustainable future.

CONCLUSION: DISOBEDIENT DESIGN

If this chapter has primarily treated ecodesign activism as a discursive object, its materiality nevertheless remains essential. "Protesters . . . are designers of our moral futures," claims James Jasper, but hastens to add that "we should not let this metaphor of design distract us from the other—more literal—connections between protest and the world of objects."[145] In assessing "the critical role of artefacts in design activism," Alastair Fuad-Luke distinguishes between "protest artefacts" and "demonstration artefacts," describing "a *protest artefact* as being deliberately confrontational in order to prompt reflection on the morality of the status quo," whereas a "*demonstration artefact* reveals positive alternatives that are superior to the status quo."[146] Alternative City's sightseeing tours, PowWow's flyers, and the Konstfack students' posters featured in the first part of this chapter neatly fit this definition of protest artifacts, while the exhibits shown at the two museum exhibitions discussed in the latter part clearly aspired to be demonstration artifacts. The exhibition *Disobedient Objects* shown at London's Victoria and Albert Museum in 2014 represents another attempt at conceptualizing the material culture of demonstrations, protests, and social movements. A salient feature of disobedient objects is, according to its curators, that they "are full of . . . the empowering and terrifying idea that our own actions (and inaction) could make a difference."[147] There is hope in disobedience, they argue, suggesting something of a disobedient object lesson: "These objects disclose hidden moments in which, even if only in brief flashes, we find the possibility that things might be otherwise: that, in fact, the world may also be made from below, by collective, organized disobedience against the world as it is."[148] Even if this potential, this hope, was perhaps manifested most emphatically in protest artifacts such as the Konstfack students' posters, it was equally fundamental to the demonstration artifacts exhibited at Moderna Museet.

When PowWow organized *For a Technology in the Service of the People!* as part of the concerted activist responses to the United Nations Conference on the Human Environment, alternative technology had yet to enter the public and political mainstream. The exhibition thus dovetailed nicely with the accompanying activities, and the practical demonstrations of ecological design took on the role of materializing the protests against what the activists perceived as the unacceptably slow, piecemeal, and insufficient responses to environmental problems by governments and industry. Four years later, despite the far more ambitious scope of *ARARAT*, the alternative technology approach to ecological design appeared in a different political light. At least to some critics, its focus on small-scale, individual, off-the-grid solutions seemed more backward than edgy. One might question the validity of such objections, though, as this kind of design activism is best understood as providing prototypes and explorations, not ready-made universal solutions: "Conceived to produce change rather than merely demand it," Jilly Traganou writes, "most prefigurative projects are difficult or impossible to scale up, and do not manage—or even attempt—to achieve wider political change in the immediate future."[149] Nevertheless, this criticism resonates with what Gabriele Oropallo has described as a general tendency at the time, in which the discourse of both design and environmentalism "progressively placed most of the responsibility for the blight of nature on the individual, making individual choice the main arena for solution-seeking debates."[150] Arguably, however, it is precisely its lack of uniqueness that makes *ARARAT* significant. Its close relations to like-minded actors and initiatives throughout Scandinavia as well as in the UK and US places *ARARAT* and its organizers among what Andrew Jamison has described as the many "loosely organised activist networks [that] tried to put into practice the vision of an ecological or 'green' city as an intrinsic part of the larger movement protesting environmental degradation and opposing nuclear energy."[151] What makes these exhibitions so interesting in a design-historical perspective, though, is threefold: Firstly, they functioned as design *studios*, where experimental ecodesign ideas were developed, tested, and implemented, all in a distinctly collaborative and participatory spirit. Secondly, they functioned as design *galleries*, where experimental ecodesign ideas were demonstrated to the public. Finally, these events and spaces functioned as *trading grounds* between activists and established design institutions, most prominently the design and architecture schools. This last factor is also a poignant reminder of how design activism by no means is independent from mainstream design culture.[152] Taken together, then, these institutionally sanctioned creative experiments with, and display of, alternative technology contributed significantly to the circulation of a practice-based knowledge of ecological design grounded in an activist attitude.

This chapter set out from the apparent paradox that environmentalists demonstrated against the most comprehensive political effort to date to address the world's environmental problems, the UN Conference on the Human Environment. Why they felt compelled to do so should have become more evident by now. British science journalist Peter Stone, who acted as the conference's senior information advisor, believed that despite the many disagreements, the NGO delegates and other participants in the alternative forums had had "an extremely valuable experience" in the end. "They learned not to scoff at the government delegates fighting over the wordings of recommendations," he reasoned—"they began to understand what international agreements require in the way of preparatory work, they found that they themselves ran up against the same sort of barriers to action as bureaucrats and politicians."[153] Whereas the activists doubtless learned a thing or two about the challenges of collaboration and compromise, the experience certainly did not have the palliative and disciplinary effect Stone somewhat patronizingly suggested. The impatience with conventional politics and practices did not disappear. In fact, many of the key concerns and strategies of the demonstrators we have encountered in this chapter can be found also in the work of the ecophilosophers and ecodesigners populating the next chapter, several of whom were present in Stockholm. Most significantly, they all shared a predilection for direct action, and the conviction that the profound societal change needed to create a more sustainable future could only be brought about through a cultural imperative for a communal transformation of worldview and lifestyle—not through reports and resolutions.[154]

5

DEEP GREEN

Philosophical Tools

From high mountains and academe a disposition can be cultivated which to a greater degree than production figures makes Norwegians worthy of their harsh paradise—of a land that in today's cold eyes is nothing but a refractory resource.[1]
—Peter Wessel Zapffe (1955)

Mountain climbing and philosophy are somewhat strange yet significant bedfellows in the history of ecological design. From the late 1960s on, a group of Norwegian philosophers, who were also avid climbers, developed a distinctive mode of thinking about the interconnectedness of human and nonhuman nature and of material and nonmaterial culture. Prominent amongst these was Arne Næss, who coined the concepts of "deep ecology" and "ecosophy," denoting, respectively, a broader ideological movement and a philosophy of ecological harmony. These have since traveled far and wide, both politically and academically. Rarely, however, has their relevance for design been examined. By revisiting what Næss referred to as ecosophy T (for Tvergastein, his beloved mountain cabin) with a view to articulating an ecosophy D (for design), this chapter aims to show that the leap from deep ecology to deep design is hidden in plain sight and more relevant than ever before. The aim here is not to prove the validity of ecosophy as a philosophical program or of the deep ecology movement more broadly, but to demonstrate the historical significance of these concepts and these phenomena and their relevance to Scandinavian design discourse of the period.

Even if deep ecology is no ready-made ecophilosophy of design and Næss himself was no design theorist, he crossed paths with designers and architects throughout his career, and in these contexts brought his own philosophical work to bear on the relations between the built and the natural environment. During the Second World War, in 1943–1944, he taught the psychology of aesthetics at the National College of Applied Art and Craft. His assignments for the design students included asking them to contemplate the expressive capacities of trees and plants—an experience he found highly beneficial when he later developed his ecophilosophy.[2] His renown as an ecophilosopher would in turn attract significant interest in design circles. In 1982 he gave a keynote lecture on "ecosophy, future, and visions" at a seminar for students from all the Swedish design schools held at Stockholm's Konstfack College of Arts, Crafts and Design.[3] Around the same time, he lectured regularly on the ecological foundations of urban planning at the Oslo School of Architecture, where his cousin, the architect Wenche Selmer, by then was a key pedagogical authority. A decade prior, around the time Næss developed his concepts of ecosophy and deep ecology, which Selmer took great interest in,[4] she gained international prominence for her sensitively designed wooden houses and cabins that blended harmoniously into their natural environments. Næss got to experience his cousin's environmentally thoughtful architecture firsthand when his second marriage was failing and she designed a pair of twin houses, built in 1976 in the garden of his own house, as a new home for his ex-wife.[5]

The intellectual roots of the deep ecology movement provide fertile ground for exploring this interface between ecophilosophy and ecodesign. As Pauline Madge has noted, the distinction between "deep" and "shallow" introduced by Næss was subsequently reflected in the realms of politics and design, where "light green" approaches were contrasted with "dark green" ones, with "the deeper shades of green being the more radical."[6] "Deep green" thus becomes an apt heading for the design history of ecosophy and the deep ecology movement. It is easy to understand the appeal and relevance many found in the concept of deep ecology, emerging as it did at a time when the environmental movement had awoken designers, critics, and consumers alike to the ecological entanglements of design. Næss stressed that its principles were not logically derived from the science of ecology, but *inspired* by the latter's insights and the perspectives of its practitioners, and were thus *ecophilosophical* rather than ecological. Furthermore, he underlined that, unlike ecology, ecophilosophy is descriptive as well as prescriptive and explicitly emphasized the principles' *normative* nature as expressions of a value priority system. By virtue of this normative character and activist mode, deep ecology resonated well with design professionals eager to employ their skills and knowledge in pursuit of social as well as environmental betterment. Conversely, Næss's simple cabin life, his passionate and advanced mountaineering, and his championing of "clean" climbing technologies were part and parcel of his ecophilosophy, to the extent that it can be argued that Næss de facto developed a basis for an ecosophy D.

CLIMBING HIGH TO DIVE DEEP

Though his love of nature and the simple life came to characterize his life and legacy, Arne Næss was a cultured city boy by upbringing. Nevertheless, his fascination with nature began at an early stage. Born to a wealthy shipping family in Oslo in 1912, he spent most of his summers at a family property by the Hardanger fjord south of Bergen and much time at their cabin at Ustaoset in the midst of the mountain massifs of southern Norway. It was from this vantage point, looking up toward the mighty mountain ridge Hallingskarvet, that young Næss found the perfect spot for his own cabin, Tvergastein, which would become an essential feature of his life and work. Designed by Næss himself and built by local farmers in 1937,[7] the basic shelter, perched high up in the steep terrain at 1,505 meters above sea level, became his preferred material interface with the natural world (figure 5.1). He spent as much time as he possibly could at his cabin, which also became "a crucial tool in his self-fashioning as a sage."[8] To Næss, the cabin was a deeply personal realm, but also part of an important culture: "Clearly the cabin tradition is one of the ecosophically most potent sources of permanent alertness towards the destructive misbehaviours of modern life."[9] If the simple, secluded, contemplative cabin life was one cornerstone of his lifelong communion with mountains, advanced and ambitious climbing was the other. Bouldering and rock-climbing from an early age, the 17-year-old Næss met the philosopher Peter Wessel Zapffe at one such session with a friend at Kolsåstoppen outside Oslo. Zapffe, twelve years his senior, would become a friend, colleague, and climbing partner for life.[10]

Næss was serious about climbing. By the tender age of 18 he had already climbed the 106 highest peaks in Norway.[11] The meteoric start to his career as a professional philosopher—he was appointed (full) professor at the University of Oslo in 1939, at the age of 27—provided him with the freedom to pursue his other passion. He became a leading figure in the Norwegian Alpine Club (Norsk tindeklub), and in 1950 led the first ever ascent of the main peak of Tirich Mir (7,708 meters) in Pakistan, followed by a second expedition in 1964 to climb the even more challenging

eastern peak (7,690 meters). Even though he wrote books about both of these expeditions,[12] it was only toward the end of the 1960s that his professional and personal interests converged into a philosophy of the environment. This in turn informed his climbing practice. When Næss in 1971 returned to Himalaya with his friends Sigmund Kvaløy and Nils Faarlund to climb Tseringma/Gauri Shankar (7,105 meters) in Nepal, they made a point of deliberately stopping 1,000 meters short of the summit out of respect for the mountain's sacred status to the local population and as an expression of their conclusion that mountains should be experienced but not "conquered." After the event, Næss even wrote a letter to the king of Nepal asking that the peak should be protected.[13] According to Andrew Brennan, "It was during

5.1

Tvergastein, Arne Næss's cabin, viewed against the mighty Hallingskarvet. Photo: Thomas Tveit Rosenlund.

this trip that Næss experienced the 'breakthrough' that enabled him to complete the sketch of a new environmental philosophy, or 'ecosophy,' Kvaløy formulated an ecopolitics of a 'life necessities society' (as opposed to the dominant 'industrial growth society'), and Faarlund was inspired to continue his work promoting *friluftsliv* [outdoor life] as a wider approach to outdoor education."[14]

The paradox of mountain climbing is that its fundamental value—the sublime aesthetics of and full immersion in nature—rests on preserving the precarious environment that affords it, and on the relative exclusiveness of the activity. Writing in the British Alpine Club's journal in 1968, Næss contemplated this paradox and other issues pertaining to the ethics of mountaineering. He argued that there were intrinsic values to the "deep and personal experiences" of nature in general and mountains in particular, and as they "belong to the last remains of nature not completely subjugated by man," their conservation was of utmost importance. This, of course, imbued mountaineers with a distinct moral obligation: in order to curtail ecological footprints, a mountaineer "should limit as much as possible the amount of gear and rubbish left behind during climbs and while camping, and even have it in his [sic] mind to minimise scars made on the rock surfaces." To Næss, this ethos of treading lightly extended to "the related ideal of minimising the use of 'artificial aid,'" i.e., designed objects and services (figure 5.2).[15] Two years later, he published a short essay in another British climbing magazine, *Mountain*, making a case against the "chauvinist impulses" which had come to dominate the sport, evident in a terminology in which mountains are "conquered" and subjected to "assaults."[16] He detested such "climbing pornography."[17] "A salutary reaction has set in against the desecration of mountains by garbage (pitons, equipment, etc.)," he observed, "but there is still little protest against this worthless form of 'summitry.'" While acknowledging the diversity of motives for and methods of climbing, Næss maintained that what he called the "achievement attitude" was "massively destructive in nature" (and *to* nature), and that therefore a change in the philosophy and practice of climbing was needed. Following the rapidly growing support of the environmental movement over the preceding years, he believed that "such a shift might today be possible, in the new atmosphere of ecological awareness brought about by technology's overstepping of vital limits."[18] Even if these remarks from a mountaineer author to a mountaineer readership may seem very context-specific, they nonetheless express a broader concern for the consequences of human activities for the natural environment and a budding awareness of the role of design therein.

Looking back at the work of the early days of the alpine club at the Norwegian Institute of Technology in the 1960s, one of its founders, Nils Faarlund, claimed that mountaineering introduced their fellow engineering students "to a different way of feeling the mountains—by climbing them instead of drilling them full of hydropower tunnels," and that these experiences in turn shaped their work: "Though some of them went on to become dam builders with the government, their exposure to mountaineering colored (some have admitted) their designs and dampened their

5.2

Arne Næss in his office at the University of Oslo in 1964, with climbing equipment in his hands. Photo: © NTB.

enthusiasm for these symbols of Norwegian national strength."[19] Mountaineering could thus be a step toward an ecosophy of design by instilling in its practitioners a sense of respect and modesty. To Næss, this "modesty in man's relationships with mountains in particular and nature in general" arose from the acknowledgment that "the smaller we come to feel ourselves compared to the mountain, the nearer we come to participating in its greatness."[20]

Mountains loom large in the deep ecology movement. Many of its proponents were themselves passionate mountaineers; but as a powerful symbol of deep time, panoramic vistas, profound interconnectedness, precarious nature, and majestic experiences, the mountain as figure transcends the personal realm. The prevailing presence of this trope is evident from how Aldo Leopold's phrase "thinking like a mountain," coined in 1949 to promote a holistic view of ecological interdependency, became something of a mantra for the deep ecology movement.[21] Inspired both by nature writers such as Leopold and by Eastern philosophy, the figure of the mountain became for the deep ecologists a central aid in shifting their worldview away from anthropocentrism. The phrase eventually even became the title of a book by Næss and colleagues in which they envisioned "a council of all beings" as a way to foster a deeper identification with nonhuman nature.[22] This ecological imperative to think like a mountain naturally invokes all of humankind, and thus also designers of all denominations. What if designers started designing like a mountain? Can we envision a type of "deep design" understood as a radical expansion of the conventional interpretation of participatory design where the notion of stakeholders is extended beyond users and other "relevant social groups"[23] to include "a council of all beings"? If so, it could become an efficient antidote to the many (and largely unintended) adverse ecological consequences of the habitually anthropocentric bias of design.

DESIGNING ECOSOPHY

Ecosophy was, at least in part, designed by the foot of a mountain. In the summer of 1966, four young men from the alpine club at the Norwegian Institute of Technology—biochemistry engineer Nils Faarlund, architecture student Jon Bruskeland, and mechanical engineering students Knut Støren and Jon Voll—decided to climb the impressive Stetind mountain west of Narvik in northern Norway, an obelisk-shaped peak rising 1,392 meters straight out of a fjord (figure 5.3).

5.3

Stetind in Fog, painting by Peder Balke, 1864.
Photo: Frode Larsen, courtesy of the National
Museum of Art, Architecture, and Design.

Faarlund had recently procured some highly innovative climbing gear from the new US manufacturer Chouinard Equipment (discussed later in this chapter) which he believed would enable new ascents of the mountain, and invited Arne Næss—who by then had climbed Stetind regularly for 30 years—along for the trip.[24] Næss brought with him his psychologist wife Siri and their ten-year-old daughter, and his graduate student and research assistant Sigmund Kvaløy. The two weeks this motley crew spent at the foot of the mountain trying to cobble together ecology and philosophy in between climbs have become known as the "Stetind seminar," and are widely considered the genesis of ecosophy.[25]

Next to Næss, Kvaløy was key in chiseling out the main features of deep ecology. After finishing his graduate studies in philosophy in 1966, Kvaløy received a scholarship to study the aesthetics of electronic music at Columbia University. His New York sojourn was as short as it was momentous, however. Arriving in the city at a time that is generally regarded as the low point in its modern social and environmental history, he found life in the metropolis stifling and hostile, the very epitome of human alienation from nature and of what he would call the "industrial growth society."[26] Renouncing the scholarship and his place at Columbia, he returned to Oslo and a research fellowship at the University of Oslo's Department of Zoology, where ecological science was on the rise. He continued his collaboration with Næss and organized the interdisciplinary seminar series "Human and Nature," which became a central arena for the development of their ecophilosophy. Integral to this development was the view that a viable ecophilosophy could not be a strictly theoretical project; it had to inform practice and action. The aim was to develop a "unique philosophy that transforms the cultural practices in its own discourse."[27] For Kvaløy in particular, this meant deliberately blurring the boundaries between philosophy and politics.[28] This emphasis on applicability naturally made it very appealing to the emerging (largely leftist) ecopolitical movement,[29] but it also opened a door to the relevance of design, which became apparent at an early stage. Kvaløy looked to architecture to analyze the relationship between nature and culture, between landscape and structure.[30] He approvingly cited Ian McHarg's pioneering work on ecological design, and was deeply fascinated by Buckminster Fuller's resource-efficient principles of geodesic design—even if he did not share the latter's techno-optimism.[31] Kvaløy's appreciation of the interconnectedness of design and ecology eventually led to a fellowship at the Oslo School of Architecture (1976–1980), which culminated in his bringing architecture students with him on one of his many journeys to Nepal's Rolwaling Valley, and a collaboration with teachers and students at the school with the aim of establishing a design aid project for the same region focusing on small-scale structures for healthcare and education.[32]

A highly competent illustrator himself, Kvaløy consistently enriched his texts with his own drawings of built and natural environments, keenly aware of the communicative power of design. This might in part explain why he was so taken by the exhibition *And after us . . . (Og etter oss . . .*), a vigorous illustration of the doom and gloom of environmental destruction organized by architecture and design students at the Oslo School of Architecture and the National College of Applied Art and Craft in the summer of 1969 (discussed in chapter 2).[33] So much so, in fact, that he promptly invited the organizers to join his new initiative, the "collaborative working groups on nature conservation and environmental protection [*samarbeidsgruppene for natur-og miljøvern*]," with the Ecophilosophy Group functioning as a subset.[34] Kvaløy thus enrolled ecologically minded designers in the emerging ecophilosophy network, but he also actively cultivated the reciprocity of the relation between ecophilosophy and ecodesign, e.g., by reporting on the group's work on the pages of the architectural magazine *Byggekunst*, at the time edited by Christian Norberg-Schulz.[35]

Providing fruitful discussions and stimulating feedback for Kvaløy while he was drafting his book on ecophilosophy and ecopolitics,[36] the collaborative working groups also immediately became a hub for environmental activism in Norway. Inspired by Gandhian nonviolence (Næss had published two books on Gandhi), in the summer of 1970 they staged a sit-in demonstration against the hydroelectrical power development threatening to subjugate the Mardøla River and its mighty waterfalls. Even if the five hundred activists failed to stop the construction of the dam, this act of civil disobedience, culminating with Kvaløy and Næss being carried away by the police to full media coverage, became emblematic of a new kind of environmental activism (figure 5.4).[37] It was at this tumultuous time that Næss made the remarkable decision to resign his professorship, citing as his main reasons that modern university work with its increasing administrative duties and required urban residence was no longer compatible with his desire to live freely in harmony with nature and to dedicate more time to environmentalism.[38] He did not leave academic life, however, and it was during the Ecophilosophy Group's seminars that he began formulating his concept of "ecosophy," first introduced in a couple of lectures in 1971,[39] and subsequently in "preliminary" versions of what would eventually become his main treatise on the topic.[40]

In the meantime, though, an opportunity arose to present his notions of "ecosophy" and "deep ecology" in an international setting. Næss's former student, now

colleague, Johan Galtung had in 1967 initiated the World Future Studies Federation and hosted its inaugural conference in Oslo. On the occasion of the organization's third conference in Bucharest in September 1972, the two friends packed their bags and manuscripts and headed south. Since its publication in March of the same year, the Club of Rome report *The Limits to Growth* had dominated the public and political discourse on environmental policy, informing also the landmark United Nations Conference on the Human Environment taking place in Stockholm in June (where Club of Rome founder Aurelio Peccei concluded the Distinguished Lecture Series).[41] Both Galtung and Næss were deeply disturbed by the technocratic worldview presented in

5.4

Sigmund Kvaløy being removed by the police during the Mardøla sit-in protest.
Photo: © NTB.

the "doomsday document" through a rhetoric "peppered with graphs and models,"[42] concerned that it diverted attention from the political, social, and moral entanglements of the ecological crisis.[43] In related but distinct ways, then, the two Norwegian scholars and ideologues used their Bucharest lectures to rebuke the kind of "shallow" thinking they believed the report represented. Galtung criticized the report for its Western and middle-class bias, pointing out its blindness to class politics and global injustice.[44] Echoing his friend's view of the technocratic analysis and problem-solving attitude as catering to the concerns of the wealthy, industrialized world, Næss went on to present his vision for a radical alternative. The key idea in his lecture, "The Shallow and the Deep Ecology Movement," was that nature was not just an "environment" for humankind, and that this acknowledgment required a shift in perspective from an anthropocentric (or, rather capitalocentric) to an ecocentric outlook.[45]

After the Bucharest conference, Næss published "a summary" of his lecture in *Inquiry*, an interdisciplinary journal of philosophy and the social sciences he had founded in 1958, offering the first English-language publication on the topic.[46] This brief outline focused on distinguishing the deep ecology movement from what he characterized as the "shallow" variety. The latter, Næss argued, had become the dominant response to the rise of the environmental movement and the "emergence of ecologists from their former relative obscurity," but represented only a half-hearted, myopic, and fundamentally flawed strategy for addressing the ecological crisis. Its scope limited to the "fight against pollution and resource depletion," he criticized it for serving only "the health and affluence of people in the developed countries."[47] What Næss termed the "shallow" ecology movement, then, strongly resembles what today is known as ecomodernism and its emphasis on "green growth" through technofixes. By contrast, the "deep" ecology movement he identified (with) advocated a far more comprehensive conception of the crisis, with fundamental ontological, epistemological, and ethical implications. Setting out seven key principles, Næss explained how the deep ecology movement implied

(1) Rejection of the man-in-environment image in favour of *the relational, total-field image.* Organisms as knots in the biospherical net or field of intrinsic relations . . .

(2) *Biospherical egalitarianism*—in principle. . . . Its restriction to humans is an anthropocentrism with detrimental effects upon the life quality of humans themselves . . .

(3) *Principles of diversity and of symbiosis.* . . . Ecologically inspired attitudes therefore favour diversity of human ways of life, of cultures, of occupations, of economies . . .

(4) *Anti-class posture.* Diversity of human ways of life is in part due to (intended or unintended) exploitation and suppression on the part of certain groups.... The principle of diversity does not cover differences due merely to certain attitudes or behaviours forcibly blocked or restrained . . .

(5) Fight against *pollution and resource depletion.* In this fight ecologists have found powerful supporters, but sometimes to the detriment of their total stand . . .

(6) *Complexity, not complication . . .* Applied to humans, the complexity-not-complication principle favours division of labour, *not fragmentation of labour.* It favours integrated actions in which the whole person is active, not mere reactions. It favours complex economies, an integrated variety of means of living.

(7) *Local autonomy and decentralization.* The vulnerability of a form of life is roughly proportional to the weight of influences from afar, from outside the local region in which that form has obtained an ecological equilibrium. This lends support to our efforts to strengthen local self-government and material and mental self-sufficiency.[48]

Even if these are very general formulations, their relevance for design practice and design culture is fairly evident. Næss stressed that the principles were not logically derived from the science of ecology, but *inspired* by its insights and the perspectives of its practitioners, and thus *ecophilosophical* rather than ecological. Furthermore, he underlined that, unlike ecology, ecophilosophy is "descriptive as well as prescriptive" and explicitly emphasized the principles' *normative* nature as expressions of "a value priority system."[49] Suffice it to say that if designers, manufacturers, consumers, and other key actors had subscribed to these norms and prescriptions, contemporary design culture would be very different from what it is. The first principle postulates that ontological qualities reside in the intrinsic relations between entities (both beings and things), thus prescribing a profoundly *relational* attitude to the design and use of products and services. The second principle—arguably the most radical of the set—eradicates anthropocentrism and demands that any design intervention respect the quality of life of all beings. The third principle prescribes designing for diversity and symbiosis in a way that supports "the fight against economic and cultural, as much as military, invasion and domination."[50] The fourth principle extends the socialist notion of class struggle to a question of global justice, deeply implicating design in the exploitative systems of colonialism and corporate greed. The fifth principle, ordaining the fight against pollution and resource depletion, dovetails with the most conventional approach to ecological design—but cautions that such practices must be calibrated against the other principles to avoid remaining "shallow," i.e., what we today would call greenwashing. The sixth principle, calling for complexity rather than complication, reflects a crucial distinction Næss gleaned from Kvaløy (nature is complex; a machine may be complicated, but never complex),[51] warning against mechanistic understandings of nature and technocratic social organization. As a countermeasure, it promotes "soft technique" in design solutions and favors "combinations of industrial and agricultural activity, of intellectual and manual work, of specialized and non-specialized occupations, of urban and non-urban activity," and "more sensitivity towards continuity and live traditions."[52] The seventh and final principle, of local autonomy and decentralization, flies in the face of the liberal order of world trade, supporting instead ecologically sounder, smaller-scale geographical patterns of design, manufacturing, and consumption—much in line with E. F. Schumacher's main arguments in *Small Is Beautiful* published the same year.[53] These key principles presented in Næss's Bucharest lecture would subsequently be elaborated and incorporated in his further writings on ecosophy, eventually approximating the status of a manifesto of the deep ecology movement.

Næss was no design theorist, and ecosophy was not formulated explicitly for design—even if, as discussed above, design and designers lurked in the background. However, an early reading list he compiled on relevant foundational research includes Jane Jacobs's *The Death and Life of Great American Cities*,[54] and the bibliography of his Bucharest paper included Ian McHarg's *Design with Nature*—a book he elsewhere described as "excellent," "engaging," and "of particular relevance for planners of all sorts."[55] If ecophilosophy was influenced by ecodesign, the converse was also true. At a time when the environmental movement had awoken designers, critics, and consumers alike to the ecological entanglements of design, it is easy to understand the appeal and relevance many found in the deep ecology movement. Its normative character and activist mode resonated well with design professionals eager to employ their skills and knowledge in pursuit of social as well as environmental betterment.

ECOSOPHY D

Whereas Næss devised the term "deep ecology" to denote the broader philosophical, political, and activist movement, and "ecosophy" to signify "a philosophy of ecological harmony or equilibrium"[56] (as distinct from "ecophilosophy," or the philosophy of ecology in a more academic sense), he referred to his own take on the latter as "ecosophy N" (for Næss) or "ecosophy T," where T stood for Tvergastein, his beloved cabin. He explicitly encouraged others to articulate their own variations on this theme, so as to generate a range of ecosophies "A, B, C . . ."[57] and X, Y, or Z.[58] In response to this schema, Siri Næss has suggested "ecosophy F" as a label for a feminist ecosophy.[59] It follows, then, that we might articulate an ecosophy of design as ecosophy D.[60]

Without mentioning the word, Næss implicates design's role in "the environmental challenge" already on page one of the first published edition (still labeled "preliminary") of his book on ecosophy, released in 1972, attributing the environmental crisis to "the aggregation of exponentially increasing, effectively or entirely irreversible environmental deprecations or destructions caused by a deeply rooted material production and consumption ideology."[61] Despite his personal predilection for the simple life and low-tech material culture, Næss did not endorse the off-the-grid, back-to-the-land movement as the only way forward. "In a certain sense," he mused, "we need better and more technology than ever before: to solve the environmental problems, for the decentralization tasks, for the battle against overpopulation."[62] What he did unequivocally condemn, was "the cult of GNP"[63] and the growth imperative intrinsic to modern social economic theory, arguing that ecologically sound policies should aim for increased well-being and welfare rather than wealth, gauge needs rather than desires, and focus on use and users rather than consumption and consumers: "It is the user, not the consumer, who shows the way to ecological harmony."[64] These aspects of Næss's ecophilosophy have a lot in common with what today is known as "transitional design," which "highlights interconnectedness and envisions the decoupling of well-being from growth and consumption, and the cultivation of new values (e.g. solidarity, ethics, community, meaning)."[65] Drawing on the work of his University of Oslo colleague, professor of economy (and later Nobel Prize recipient) Trygve Haavelmo,[66] Næss suggested that economic theories about circular flow of resources needed to be expanded to include all biospheric transactions, thus accounting for environmental values as well as pecuniary ones.[67] Only such a "biospheric turn" in mainstream economy could mitigate the myopic attention to financial chains and quantifiable values by rendering the invisible visible, the intangible tangible, the irrelevant relevant. Without such an extended perspective, both on what "counts" in economic and environmental terms as well as on the place of humans as merely fragments in an inconceivably diverse nature and an infinite universe, "the growth conditions for an ecologically sound politics are meager."[68] Still, Næss was not a pessimist, and did not—despite the claims of some critics—categorically refuse economic growth or technological advances. On the contrary, economic growth and technological advances could be an integral part of a new paradigm of ecological design: "The environmental crisis could inspire a new renaissance: new social forms for coexistence together with a high level of culturally integrated technology, economic progress . . . , and a less restricted experience of life."[69]

Næss quite insightfully criticized the universalizing tendencies of the then recently popularized "spaceship earth" metaphor and its ensuing pulverizing of responsibility (a criticism echoed in current debates on the concept of the Anthropocene): "The maxims that *we* are all in the same boat (or spaceship), that *humankind* must get its act together, are used to suppress the fact that it is today primarily the industrialized nations' politics . . . that are ecopolitically irresponsible."[70] It was obvious to Næss that "we are *not* 'all in the same boat,'" because the developing countries (his term) have been exploited and subjugated, and therefore relegated to a separate boat towed toward ecological catastrophe by a more powerful one populated by the West. No wonder, then, he claimed, that some leaders in developing countries understood the shallow ecology movement "as part of the West's attempt to dominate the poor countries, that is, as part of neocolonialism."[71] It is therefore essential, according to Næss, that the deep ecology movement take heed also of social and economic injustice in a global perspective rather than offer "shallow" solutions such as introducing environmental restrictions or imposing isolated technofixes. His call for a deep ecology approach to sustainable development in what today is more commonly referred to as the global South seems particularly prescient given that it was uttered at a time when design aid, or design as development aid, was gaining substantial traction, before it ran into accusations of neocolonialism (see chapter 3). A major challenge for an ecosophy D, then, would be to devise courses of action which steer clear of such pitfalls—a challenge that ever since has proven notoriously difficult for many a benevolently planned design aid program.[72]

If the "spaceship earth" metaphor and the maxim that "we are all in the same boat" to Næss represented the false egalitarianism of the shallow ecology movement, another and far more radical type of egalitarianism is central to his ecosophy and a hallmark of the deep ecology movement: biospheric egalitarianism, or the principle of equal rights for all living beings, and even for abiotic nature. In this view, humans are but *fragments* of nature. Building on (often non-Western) philosophical traditions proclaiming the "ultimate unity of all life" and its "profound interdependence," he added that "identification is not limited to life, but envelops the mineral world as well, making us conceive ourselves as genuine surface fragments of our planet, fragments capable of somehow experiencing the existence of all other fragments. A microcosm in macrocosm."[73] The only sense of exceptionalism Næss, somewhat reluctantly, is willing to attribute to humans is that of self-reflection: "Within the biosphere we are in the unique position of *understanding* that we are not in all regards in a unique position!"[74] With this human understanding of the interdependence of biospheric life and the ability to identify with other lifeforms comes great responsibility for human actions and behavior. A key tenet of ecosophy D, then, is to rid design of its anthropocentrism and safeguard the value of biospheric life: "It is easy to agree upon the intrinsic value of the richness and diversity of life on planet Earth. What is needed is a methodology of persistently connecting basic value judgements and imperative premises with decisions in concrete situations of interference or noninterference in nature."[75] Although Næss is here addressing conservation biology, he could just as well have been speaking about design—for what is design if not "concrete situations of interference or noninterference in nature"? Whereas Victor Papanek half-jokingly proposed that the best thing designers could do was *"to stop working entirely,"*[76] Næss offered a more sanguine outlook on the question of design as interference: "Less interference does not imply that humans should not modify some ecosystems as do other species. Humans have modified the Earth and will continue to do so. At issue is the nature and extent of such interference."[77] An ecosophy of design rests on the imperative that "you must know what will occur upon intervention in nature. If you don't know the consequences, don't intervene."[78] In practice, though, only a very limited knowledge can be established about the infinite potential consequences of a planned intervention, so the applied ethics of ecological design must always be to proceed with the greatest caution. Næss argues that "the greater our comprehension of our togetherness with other beings, the greater the identification, and the greater care we will take."[79]

According to Herbert Simon's oft-cited 1969 definition, design should be understood as "devis[ing] courses of action aimed at changing existing situations into preferred ones."[80] This is, of course, a distinctly normative understanding of design, and ecosophy D provides an essential probing of the ethics of design's preferences. What is a "preferred" situation? And whose preferences are implied here? As a guide to such deliberations, Næss introduces the concept of "Self-realisation" as the ultimate norm. Based on a colloquial understanding of the term, it might seem counterintuitive. However, the upper-case Self is not the ego but "the universal self" formed by a deep identification with all life forms and the Earth at large. This identification is a "non-rational, but not irrational, process through which *the interest or interests of another being are reacted to as our own interest or interests*."[81] Self-realization, then, cannot be achieved at the expense of other entities, only in striving for symbiosis and a sense of *"ecospheric belonging*."[82] It follows that an ecosophical analysis of Simon's "preferred" situations would have to consider a vast array of factors and actors whose preferences invariably will be in conflict. To stick with an example near and dear to the deep ecology movement: Designing a hydroelectric dam might result in a preferred situation for the government and for energy-intensive industry, whereas the mussels, salmon, and fly fishers would prefer to let the river run free. A vast wall of concrete containing the river might not be preferable for local ecosystems and contemporary populations, but increased supply of renewable energy might be preferable for the global ecosystem and future generations. In short, an ecosophy D transposes design, to use Kvaløy's terminology, from the realm of complicated, mechanistic procedures of "problem-solving" to the realm of complex, organic systems of ecological ethics.[83]

DEEP ECOLOGY GOES WEST

Deep ecology may have its roots firmly planted in Norwegian soil,[84] but its branches soon reached across borders, oceans, and continents. Of particular interest here are its reciprocal relations to the American West, and most notably to California. By the time Næss began working on ecophilosophy, he already had a longstanding connection to California. Courtesy of a Rockefeller Fellowship, he first came to the University of California (UC), Berkeley in 1938, and would return many times for extended periods, forging strong bonds to both the nature and the culture of the region. It was during a sabbatical at Berkeley in 1955 he married his second wife, Siri, then a student there, and in 1961 he returned, this time bringing Sigmund Kvaløy with him, the two spending much time climbing in Yosemite. His many and long visits to California resulted in an extensive network of collaborations which would be highly significant for the development and dissemination both of his own work and of the deep ecology movement.

One of his Berkeley sabbaticals is especially intriguing by virtue of its date: the spring term of 1968. Since his last sojourn a few years earlier, the campus had been completely transformed by the free speech movement, and Berkeley, San Francisco, and the wider Bay Area had become the epicenter of the countercultural movement. Clearly, Næss did not belong to the core demographics of the countercultural movement. Both his sociocultural background and his age (he was 56 years old in 1968) made him an outsider. Nevertheless, he was acutely aware of and keenly interested in the ongoing developments, even to the point of letting his students convince him to try marijuana and LSD between his lectures on Heidegger and existentialism.[85] Following a pilgrimage by car (!) to the Gandhi Institute in Varanasi, India, with Kvaløy and Galtung, and an intermezzo trying to deal with uprisings amongst his own students in Oslo, Næss returned to Berkeley in May 1969 at the height of the battle over People's Park. He arrived in town from a desert excursion with his UC Berkeley colleague Paul Feyerabend, and the two maverick philosophers threw themselves into the frantic protests on Telegraph Avenue.[86] What they fought to protect was a DIY environmental design project—an ad hoc community park built on a vacant city block owned by the university—which "aligned countercultural and environmentalist interests in access to public green space."[87] The project was crushed those very days as the police opened fire, Governor Ronald Reagan summoned the National Guard, and a military helicopter gassed the campus, thus efficiently ending the counterculture's days of innocence (figure 5.5).[88]

Just like his Californian colleagues, Næss keenly read Theodore Roszak, who coined the term counterculture and perhaps more than any other contemporary commentator observed its entanglements with the (deep) environmental movement.[89] Despite his outsider status, Næss sympathized with and found ideological allies amongst the young rebels: "the opposition to technocracy is strengthened by research started or instigated by individuals belonging to one of the counter cultures"[90]—research that could be designerly as much as scientific in nature. Even if he remained an observer, he inadvertently found himself in the midst of a veritable seedbed of countercultural approaches to ecological design. Some of the most important initiatives were already going on full steam in his immediate surroundings on campus. Within the university's College of Environmental Design, enthusiastic educators such as Sim Van der Ryn, Simon Nicholson, and Claire Cooper Marcus provided some of the first sustained efforts at a formal education in ecodesign.[91] Within the urban environment of Berkeley, the activist group Ecology Action,

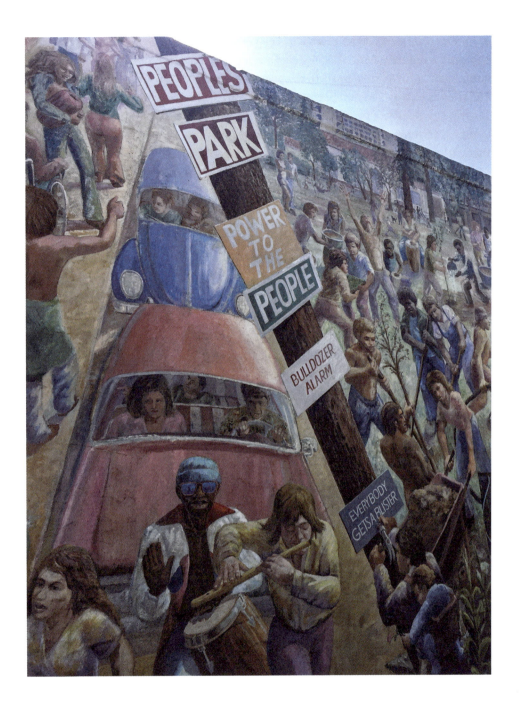

founded in 1968 by archaeology student Cliff Humphrey, immediately became a notable presence. The group promoted and pioneered ecologically motivated recycling and reuse, based on an ideology which dovetailed with many of the key tenets of Næss's deep ecology.[92] Across the Bay, in San Francisco, the design, architecture, and media art collective Ant Farm was also founded in 1968. Their early environmental design installations and performances included the *50 x 50' Pillow* at Point Reyes and *Clean Air Pod* at the UC Berkeley campus.[93] Also in San Francisco in 1968, landscape architects Michael Doyle and Andy Butler established the Environment Workshop to promote urban design that would respect the unique natural features of the city.[94] Meanwhile, Stewart Brand was driving around the West on his "commune road trip," preparing the *Whole Earth Catalog* published later that year out of his Portola office.[95] (Four years later, Næss and Brand both—alongside another important figure in Californian counterculture and the deep ecology movement, mountaineer, poet, and UC Davis English professor Gary Snyder—would convene in Stockholm for the United Nations Conference on the Human Environment.)[96] In addition to these examples making 1968 something of an *annus mirabilis* for countercultural ecodesign centered on Berkeley and the Bay Area, several other notable nodes in this network emerged shortly thereafter, including the Whole Earth Festival at UC Davis, People's Architecture and the Ecology Center in Berkeley, and the Farallones Institute in Occidental.[97] Taken together, these various groupings constituted, in the words of Greg Castillo, "an avant-garde galvanized by the radical mission of inventing environmentalism's everyday material culture."[98] So when Næss in 1968 transplanted his budding thoughts on ecophilosophy to Berkeley, they sprouted in an environment densely populated by pioneering ecodesign initiatives.

Næss repeatedly referred to his experiences in California in his writings on deep ecology, ranging from worries over the disciplinary effects of the academic-industrial complex following the 1969 Santa Barbara oil spill, via sympathies with the animalistic mythology of Native American hunting practices and despair over

5.5

Detail of the mural *A People's History of Telegraph Avenue* (1976/1999) in Berkeley, California, commemorating the battle over People's Park. Designed by Osha Neumann and painted by O'Brien Thiele, Janet Kranzberg, Naniel Galvez, et al. Photo: author.

DEEP GREEN

the clear-felling of Californian forests, to applauding the positive environmental effects of stricter parking policies at UC Santa Cruz.[99] Conversely, his work was noticed, disseminated, and elaborated upon by Californian colleagues and students. One of them, George Sessions, bonded with Næss to the extent that he named his dog Arne.[100] In a later account of their initial contact, Sessions traces Næss's influence on deep ecology in California back to his 1968 sojourn in Berkeley:

In 1973 I had heard about Arne from Joseph Meeker [a pioneer of ecocriticism and friend of Næss]. Several years earlier, I had heard from a UC Berkeley student in Yosemite about a Norwegian philosopher who was teaching a course there strongly emphasizing ecology and Nature, and using poetry from Robinson Jeffers. About 1975, I was wandering around an academic hall at the University of the Pacific, named for my late grandfather, George Colliver, who founded the religious studies department there, when I by chance came across an announcement on a bulletin board calling for graduate students to study Spinoza and ecology with Arne Naess in Norway under the New Philosophy of Nature program. My interest in Arne perked up considerably at this point and we began to correspond and exchange papers. When I finally met Arne at UC Santa Cruz in 1978, I remember going out to a beach to the north, and Arne taking up with a pack of dogs, running gleefully back-and-forth in the surf playing tug-of-war with long strands of kelp.[101]

An avid climber and Yosemite veteran, Sessions had a lot in common with his Norwegian mentor, both privately and professionally. He was a professor of philosophy at Sierra College in Rocklin, a small town in the western foothills of the Sierra Nevada, and fellow scholar of Spinoza's ethics of nature. Through his teaching, scholarship, network, and initiatives such as the *Ecophilosophy Newletter*, which he edited from 1976 to 1984, Sessions was pivotal in the emergence of the deep ecology movement in North America, and in the dissemination of Næss's work.[102] Næss and Sessions became both friends and collaborators. During a camping trip in Death Valley during Easter 1984, they jointly drafted a set of "basic principles," or a "platform," of deep ecology (largely a revised version of the principles devised by Næss in Bucharest twelve years earlier).[103]

Sessions teamed up with another northern Californian environmentalist-scholar, Bill Devall, to write the first English-language monograph on deep ecology, titled *Deep Ecology: Living as if Nature Mattered*.[104] Devall, who had studied leadership practices in the Sierra Club for his PhD (1970), was a professor of sociology teaching courses on forest culture, wilderness, and nuclear waste at Humboldt State

University in Arcata, a countercultural outpost on California's far north coast.[105] By the mid-1970s, both Devall and Sessions had discovered Næss's work and began writing about deep ecology.[106] According to *Rolling Stone* magazine, "the idea caught on like a gas-soaked bonfire."[107] As Warwick Fox later wrote, "Devall's and Sessions' work effectively lifted Naess's distinction [between shallow and deep ecology] out of relative obscurity and put it on the ecophilosophical map in the period 1979–80."[108] Shot through with explicit and implicit references to Næss, their book is an intellectual history of deep ecology—but from a distinctly Californian perspective, tracing also a local genealogy of the movement from the writings of pioneering conservationist John Muir and nature writer Mary Austin to the work of Friends of the Earth founder David Brower and eco-poets Robinson Jeffers and Gary Snyder.

Devall and Sessions's book was key in presenting deep ecology to a wider English-speaking audience, alongside another volume also titled *Deep Ecology*, edited by yet another Californian mountaineer-environmentalist-scholar, Michael Tobias.[109] Tobias completed his doctoral studies in the history of consciousness at UC Santa Cruz in the late 1970s, when Næss was a visiting scholar there. UCSC had opened as recently as 1965 and quickly became a progressive institution facilitating unconventional conversations between liberal arts, ecology, activism, environmental design, and modern architecture. Upon graduation, Tobias coedited the volume *The Mountain Spirit*, to which Næss contributed an essay called "Modesty and the Conquest of Mountains."[110] Santa Cruz was also home to the experimental Pacific High School, where ecodesign pioneer J. Baldwin taught and *Domebook* author Lloyd Kahn tested his ideas and design principles by building dome housing for 60 on-campus residents in collaboration with students.[111] This local exposure to ecodesign initiatives might go some way in explaining why Tobias's *Deep Ecology* anthology included contributions not only by ecophilosophers like Næss, Sessions, and Dolores LaChapelle and ecologists such as Garret Hardin and Paul Shepard, but also a lengthy interview with Paolo Soleri, the Italian architect who since 1970 had been building the ecotopian community Arcosanti in the Arizona desert. Soleri's ecodesign experiments, realized by a workforce consisting largely of architecture students and counterculture dropouts, had been on the ecophilosophers' radar for some time, though.[112] When Joseph Meeker, assisted by Næss, Kvaløy, LaChapelle, Shepard, and others, established a new graduate program called New Natural Philosophy at International College in Los Angeles in 1978, Soleri attended their meetings.[113] Næss might also have encountered Soleri in Stockholm during the 1972 United Nations Conference on the Human Environment, where the architect lectured as part of the side programs.[114]

Furthermore, Soleri's own account of Arcosanti was published alongside Tobias's *Deep Ecology* in the same year and by the same publisher.[115]

Citing Næss's insistence on the synthesis of theory and practice, Tobias conceived of deep ecology as offering "philosophical frameworks, tools by which to integrate thought and action, desire, and design."[116] In this context, then, ecophilosophy and ecodesign were seen as complementary endeavors, mutually beneficial forces, and Soleri was cast as a prime exponent of their convergence. As if a professional-conceptual Venn diagram, Næss's philosophy and Soleri's architecture converged on ecology, neatly exemplified by the fact that each of them, around 1970, coined each an interdisciplinary portmanteau to describe his ideas and practices. While Næss contracted ecology and philosophy to create "ecosophy," Soleri combined architecture and ecology to form "arcology," where "architecture as the materialization of the human environment" is merged with "ecology as the physical, biological, and psychological balance of conditions that account for the specific site and its participation in the whole."[117]

In light of both Næss's and Soleri's prior involvement with the New Natural Philosophy program, their contributions to the *Deep Ecology* anthology reveal some significant similarities in thought. For instance, the crucial distinction between complexity and complication, which Kvaløy had articulated and Næss adopted, clearly appealed to Soleri as well. Explaining how he thought of "negative complexity" as "*complication* more than complexity," Soleri, echoing Kvaløy, went on to elaborate on how technology, no matter how complicated, always represents a simplification with respect to the complex systems of nature: "One thing that technology clearly does is simplify, break down the complex and then come out with complicated devices which are very effective in a very narrow range."[118] Furthermore, just like Næss, Soleri believed that human intervention in nature and modification of ecosystems is inevitable, and not necessarily negative per se. A categorical refusal to intervene—to design—would ultimately lead to self-annihilation. In contrast, Næss's ultimate norm was that of Self-realization through identification with other elements of the ecosphere, a process which would emphasize consequences of interventions and foster caution in design.[119] Similarly, Soleri favored the principle of "lesser intervention" and spoke of the "prudent" designer.[120] Naturally, there were divergent views as well. Unlike Næss, Soleri had no time for Asian philosophy, and he remained profoundly anthropocentric, even in his view of material culture as "neonature." But they agreed on the importance of decentralization, the (sustainable) use of local resources, the interdependence of intellectual and physical experience, the primacy of quality of life over standard of living, and several other issues of equal importance to ecosophy and arcology alike, suggesting that the synthesis of these two portmanteaus could point the way to a possible ecophilosopy of design, or an ecosophy D.

TOOLS OF THE TRADE

Wherever Næss went on his travels and stays in California during this period, the realms of deep ecology and design kept overlapping. Not just on campuses and conferences, but also on climbs. Climbing expeditions with local colleagues took him from the Santa Cruz Mountains to Death Valley, from Mount Baldy to Yosemite,[121] and the latter site is of particular interest in this context. As mentioned above, he and Kvaløy spent much time in Yosemite during their Berkeley sabbatical in 1961, and Næss would return as often as he could. It was also in Yosemite that George Sessions first heard of Næss from a Berkeley student. Sessions had been climbing in Yosemite since the mid-1950s and belonged to a core group of a new generation of "experimentalist" climbers there who made Camp 4, a campground at the north side of Yosemite Valley, a global epicenter of the climbing community.[122] Another key member of that same group of Camp 4 "Beat climbers" was Yvon Chouinard, who laid the foundations for the activewear and outdoor equipment company Patagonia while climbing in Yosemite. Chouinard established Patagonia's precursor, Chouinard Equipment, in 1965 together with a fellow climber, the aeronautical engineer Tom Frost (figure 5.6). They discovered that the rapidly increasing popularity of climbing came at a price. The steel pitons used to climb the steep, sleek walls of Yosemite Valley caused significant damage to the rock surface, and also—when not removed—added to the growing littering problem. Their response was to design a new type of climbing gear which has become known as hexentrics: aluminum chocks to be wedged into cracks and crevices rather than hammered into the surface (figure 5.7). This gear "became the ecologically and morally superior tool,"[123] forming the basis of an expanded portfolio and an overall design philosophy launched in 1972 under the banner of "clean climbing":[124]

Really, the only insurance to guarantee this adventure and the safest insurance to maintain it is exercise of moral restraint and individual responsibility. Thus, it is the style of the climb, not attainment of the summit, which is the measure of personal success. . . . The fewer gadgets between the climber and the climb, the greater is the chance to attain the desired

communication with oneself—and nature. The equipment offered in this catalog attempts to support this ethic.... As we enter this new era of mountaineering, re-examine your motives for climbing. Employ restraint and good judgment in the use of Chouinard equipment. Remember the rock, the other climber—climb clean.[125]

The moralist fault lines over the "aesthetics of adventure" ran deep in Yosemite climbing culture in this period,[126] and Chouinard and his colleagues here expressed an ethos of respect and restraint with regard to the design and use of equipment which is strikingly similar to the concerns Næss had voiced on the same topic in

5.6

The Chouinard Equipment Company crew in front of their first headquarters in Ventura, California in 1969. Left to right: Tom and Dorene Frost, Tony Jessen, Dennis Henneck, Terry King, Yvon Chouinard, Merle, and Davey Agnew. Photo: Tom Frost.

5.7

"Make the rock happy—use a nut." Page from the 1972 Chouinard Equipment "clean climbing" catalog featuring a hexentric nut. Photo courtesy of R. A. Hutchins.

MAKE THE ROCK HAPPY — USE A NUT

To place a nut you must begin by thinking about the shape of cracks. Right from the start clean climbing demands increased awareness of the rock environment. Consider the taper of a crack. Is it converging, that is, flared in reverse, wider inside than at the lip? Or it may be parallel-sided with an even width. Or at the other extreme, flared.

Converging cracks are easiest to fit; find a wide spot up high and drop the nut in behind. Beware of the nut falling out the bottom, however, or breaking through a thin-lipped crack. Flared cracks are easy too, usually unfittable. But important exceptions have been known, chiefly in the form of knobs or bulges in the crack which will take a nut behind or above. Also, don't overlook the possibility of fitting a much smaller nut far back in the dark recesses of the crack.

The usual nut placement is in a vertical crack. Find a section of the crack that closes downward; that is, where the crack is wide above, narrower below. Select the right size nut, place it into the wide section of the crack, and carefully locate it where the crack narrows. Then give the sling a stout downward jerk to wedge the nut securely in place. Inspect the placement for adequate constriction of the crack and test the nut's security (the degree to which it can resist being accidentally dislodged by the climbing rope) by giving an appropriately light outward jerk on the sling. Nuts have the advantage over pitons in that they are more naturally at home in vertical placements. This is their normal environment as it is for the chockstones from which they derive.

But the crack may not have any obvious wide-to-narrow placements. Often the difference between sliding and setting is so subtle that it can hardly be seen and is easier felt.

This is especially true in granite where cracks are quite uniform and nuts were first thought relatively useless. For these trickier fittings it is helpful to have a good selection of nuts within a given size range; a small variation can be crucial. Pick the largest nut that will just fit in the crack (for Hexentrics remember that a change of attitude will slightly change the size) and work

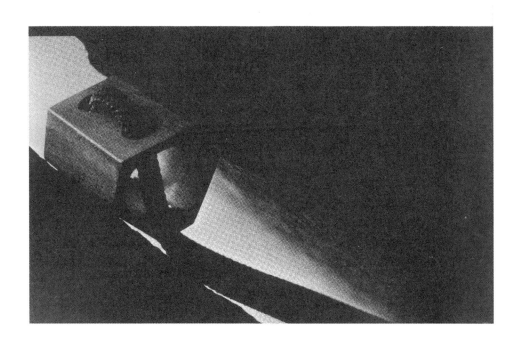

British mountaineering magazines a few years earlier, as discussed at the outset of this chapter. In his 1968 essay on the ethics of mountaineering, Næss had pleaded that climbers "should limit as much as possible the amount of gear and rubbish left behind during climbs and while camping, and . . . minimise scars made on the rock surfaces" by "minimising the use of 'artificial aid'."[127] But Næss had already written about the environmental ethics of bolt climbing 20 years earlier, describing it as a necessary evil, arguing that excessive bolting "reduced the aesthetic experience" by making the mountain "tamer" and appear "used and subdued."[128] No wonder, then, that Næss spent much time talking to the Camp 4 crew on his trips to Yosemite,[129] or that the new equipment and practice he experienced there had a profound impact on climbing culture also in Norway, both in terms of "technology and style."[130] So when Chouinard Equipment offered designs for "clean climbing," it was entirely in line with the ideals of Næss and his Californian colleagues, as well as a verbatim example of Terry Winograd and Fernando Flores's later observation that "in designing tools we are designing ways of being."[131]

The design ethos underpinning "clean climbing" extended well beyond the (literal) nuts and bolts of aided ascents, of course. Devall and Sessions, for instance, also championed "minimum impact camping," a practice seen as exemplifying a broader "attitude of watchful attentiveness to one's recreation and one's responses to the environment."[132] If undertaken with such a "proper attitude" toward their material culture, all outdoor sports activities, from mountain climbing and fishing to kayaking and running, could help their practitioners in "developing a sense of place and intuitive understanding of connections between humans and nonhumans together with a respect for the principle of biocentric equality."[133] Back home in Norway, Nils Faarlund cultivated a distinctly traditionalist view on the design culture of the great outdoors. In 1967, following the Stetind expedition which by and large prompted the new ecophilosophy, Faarlund walked away from his job as a researcher at the Norwegian College of Agriculture in Ås to found a mountaineering school in Hemsedal (Norges Høgfjellsskole) together with his landscape architect wife Helga. He, too, was an eager supporter of "clean climbing," and even served as the regional representative of Chouinard Equipment in Scandinavia from 1967 to 1972.[134] And here the Scandinavian-Californian connection over ecologically informed design of mountaineering equipment becomes particularly close. In 1970, the Swedish engineer and climber Tomas Carlström moved to Hemsedal to join Faarlund's mountaineering school as an instructor. The two shared a penchant for innovative and environmentally friendly equipment, and in 1972 Carlström took it

upon himself to refine the design of Chouinard Equipment's hexentrics by making the cross section asymmetrical and thus more versatile—an improvement Yvon Chouinard and Tom Frost acquired and incorporated in their patent application for the product, granted in 1974.[135] Carlström and Faarlund soon parted ways, however, and Carlström—taking over the agency for Chouinard Equipment—cofounded Skandinavisk Høyfjellsutstyr, an Oslo-based shop devoted to climbing and mountain sports. From this position, he was recruited as a design consultant for Norwegian outdoor equipment company Norrøna, for whom he designed clothing lines as well as equipment, including the world's first tunnel tent with front and rear openings, Ravneskar, introduced in 1972 (figure 5.8).[136]

5.8

Norrøna Ravneskar, the world's first tunnel tent with front and rear openings. Designed by Tomas Carlström and introduced in 1972. Photo courtesy of Norrøna.

Whereas novel gear such as Chouinard's aluminum chocks could be said to have embraced the potential of modern materials and technological advances, Faarlund increasingly favored the tried and tested over new and fancy, claiming that natural fibers such as wool and cotton were both ecologically and functionally superior to fluorine-ridden Gore-Tex (which his former colleague Carlström introduced to the European market in 1977 in the Trollveggen jacket designed for Norrøna), and the flexibility of wooden skis superior to the brittleness of the new fiberglass designs: "We can choose materials that do not destroy nature. And we can get clothing and equipment that is related to free nature and not barriers to it like that astronaut equipment from the modern sporting goods industry. Do not block our roots to the soil with plastics, fiberglass, and aluminum!"[137] To remedy the situation, he demanded a new approach to "product development that strives to utilize recyclable resources."[138] Faarlund's critique of the industry was relentless: "Current equipment catalogues are a poor guide for the perplexed. Tradition is much better. On a practical level, this implies a de-emphasis on clothing and equipment that are designed to *isolate* one as much as possible from the surroundings."[139] Næss, too, decried the "*outfitting pressure*" in the design culture of outdoor life as a commercialized leisure activity.[140] But equipment, and thus design, remained essential to their mountaineering. So much so that they even contributed to the design process. Preparing for the 1964 expedition resulting in the first ascent of the eastern peak of Tirich Mir in Pakistan, they collaborated with the Norwegian sporting goods manufacturer Helsport in developing new tents and lightweight down sleeping bags.[141] For their 1971 Nepal expedition—which was so seminal for the development of ecophilosophy—Faarlund's design efforts resulted in what was allegedly the world's first tunnel tent, manufactured by Helsport, as well as the modular, multifunctional Alpinist backpacks from Bergans (figures 5.9 and 5.10).[142] All of these products were recognized with the Norwegian Design Centre's Mark of Design Excellence and/or the Norwegian Design Award.[143] Thus, the ecophilosopher-climbers were by no means opposed to innovation in design; quite the contrary—it

5.9

The Bergans Alpinist modular backpack designed in collaboration with Nils Faarlund in 1966. Photo courtesy of Nils Faarlund.

NORGE ATTER PÅ LEDERPLASS MED

Bergans ALPINIST 700

Be om demonstrasjon av fire-i-ett bæresystemet som kan brukes som:

★ *pakkramme* for bæring av kasser, vilt, hyttebagasje, osv.

★ *pakkramme-kjempesekk* for bæring frem til hytte eller leir og ellers når tunge og voluminøse laster skal bæres.

★ *meisløs klatresekk/dagstursekk* med bivuakkforlengelse til dags- og bivuakkturer ved vandring, jakt, klatring, ski- og breturer.

★ *pakksekk* under transport eller heising på store klatreturer.

NÅ

★ med forsterkede remfester.
★ innvendig fiksering av innsnøring.

★ med brede ryggbånd på pakkrammen.
★ uten løse remmer.
★ med hurtiginnsnøring uten treing.
★ med vanntett stoff i sekken.

BERGANS ALPINIST 700 er *tilpasningsdyktig* og *robust*, samtidig som den er *enkel* og *lett*.

A/S BERGANS MEIS OG RYGGSEKK — Ø. SLOTTSGT. 7 — OSLO 1

was its entanglements with profit-driven free market capitalism they took issue with. This, of course, is where deep ecology and modernist design ideology overlapped entirely: fashion was bad; tools were good.

The countercultural connections and credentials of this new ecodesign ethics professed by deep ecologists and Yosemite climber-entrepreneurs alike were impeccable, and the notion of tools was at the heart of it all. If the high-altitude outcasts were obsessed by tools, so were their lowland brethren. From the *Whole Earth Catalog*'s insistence on "access to tools," via J. Baldwin's "tool truck," "custom-made for ecological design work,"[144] and Sim Van der Ryn's labeling of his UC Berkeley architecture students as tool-wielding "Outlaw Builders," to San Francisco's technological tool-brimming commune Project One, the Bay Area counterculture was profoundly invested in the liberating and creative potential of tools.[145] In light of this shared devotion to tools, localizing a mountaineering outfitters' enterprise in the midst of the hippie heartland makes more sense than it might first seem to. Chouinard's friend Doug Tompkins also founded an activewear and outdoor equipment company in 1965, The North Face, which became the exclusive wholesaler for Chouinard Equipment. When the company established its first store, in San Francisco's North Beach neighborhood in October 1966, local hippies mingled with Yosemite "dirtbags" at the opening party where Joan Baez worked the crowd while The Grateful Dead played, with Hells Angels in charge of security (figure 5.11). Two years later, in 1968, The North Face moved across the Bay to Berkeley, and expanded from retail to design and manufacturing.[146] That same year, Chouinard and Tompkins embarked on an epic six-month adventure, driving to Patagonia in the southern tip of South America in a VW bus to climb Cerro Fitz Roy—the peak that would appear in the logo of Chouinard's company, which he renamed for the region five years later.[147] Still, the pinnacle of countercultural cachet arguable came with Stewart Brand's inclusion of Chouinard's tools for "clean climbing" in his 1972 *The Last Whole Earth Catalog*.[148] Conversely, hippies began visiting Yosemite, fascinated by the majestic nature and the "dirtbag" lifestyle of the locals alike—an influx not

5.10

"Norway again in the lead with Bergans Alpinist 700." Advertisement published in the mountaineering magazine *Mestre fjellet*, no. 2 (1968). Photo courtesy of Nils Faarlund.

DEEP GREEN

unanimously applauded by the Camp 4 climbers.[149] Meanwhile, The North Face joined Berkeley's bustling countercultural ecodesign scene, developing innovative products like the 1975 Oval Intention "geodesic" tent designed by Bruce Hamilton and Mark Erickson, inspired by Buckminster Fuller, especially his recently published work on "synergetics"—a design which Fuller in turn was so excited about that he included it in his exhibition *The Now House* shown in Vancouver, Canada in May 1976 as a part of Habitat I, the first United Nations Conference on Human Settlements—a follow-up to the UN Conference on the Human Environment in Stockholm four years earlier (Paolo Soleri contributed to both events).[150] A decade later, in a rare example of ecophilosophy's direct impact on commercial design

5.11

Hells Angels security guards at the opening of The North Face's first store in San Francisco's North Beach neighborhood in October 1966. Suki Hill Photography, © 2021.

culture, The North Face founder Tompkins decided to leave the business and devote himself to environmentalism full time upon reading Devall and Session's *Deep Ecology*.[151] Coming full circle, Tompkins then created the Sausalito-based Foundation for Deep Ecology in 1990, which in turn funded the publication of the ten-volume *Selected Works of Arne Naess*.[152]

Patagonia and The North Face were not the only companies to emerge from California's countercultural climbing scene. Other examples of the entrepreneurial spirit and keen interest in equipment design include the equally aptly named Sierra Designs and Alpine Designs.[153] There is of course a certain paradox to this success. Chouinard and his peers turned entrepreneurs partly out of sheer ingenuity and ideology, but also because even climbers had to eat.[154] The design ethos behind "clean climbing" may have been genuinely in line with key tenets of deep ecology, but its business end also generated ever more objects of desire with ensuing environmental ramifications. At the same time, commodities also communicate ideas, and as Michelle Labrague argues, "However fraught and ambiguous its attempts to reconcile slow thinking and environmental concerns with commercial ends, the Patagonia catalogues can be seen as promoting change by spreading deep ecological philosophies across dispersed networks of people."[155] As such, these early ecodesign enterprises are paradigmatic examples of the double bind of "green consumerism." As Matthew Klingle has noted: "At the foundation of Patagonia's entire existence is an environmental history of consumerism full of contradictions and ironies."[156] And the more practical and applied ecophilosophy got, the closer deep ecology got to the realm of design practice—to becoming an ecosophy of design—the more exposed it became to the same contradictions and ironies.

DEEP DESIGN

The many paradoxes, contradictions, and ironies involved in trying to move ecodesign from ideology to action, from theory to practice, are nothing new, of course. Take William Morris, for instance, who dreamt of a world where design was freed of the economic inequalities and environmental destructions imposed on it by industrial capitalism, but ended up manufacturing luxury goods and wallpapers containing highly toxic arsenic.[157] Similarly, as Peder Anker has shown, the compelling link between the environmental philosophies of nature writers like Henry David Thoreau, Aldo Leopold, and Arne Næss, and the designs of their cabins hinges on the paradox that their spartan lives in search of unity with nature were made possible in part by modern technologies and infrastructures.[158] Such incongruities do not imply, though, that ecodesign was or is an inherently impossible concept. As argued elsewhere, "The world is constantly falling apart, but it is also constantly being repaired, reinvented, reconfigured, and reassembled," and environmental histories of design can provide, if not a reconciliation, then at least a way of understanding and living with these discrepancies.[159]

As I hope to have shown by now, there is no dearth of affinities, convergences, links, and nodes connecting deep ecology and design. But these have largely been inconspicuous, and often indirect. Any ready-made, fully articulated ecosophy D is hard to identify. What amounts to the closest contender appeared only in 1996: David Wann's *Deep Design: Pathways to a Livable Future*. Curiously, though, despite its title and the countless reverberations of key deep ecology principles throughout the book, neither Næss nor any of his fellow ecophilosophers are mentioned. A consultant with the US Environmental Protection Agency and teacher of environmental studies at the University of Denver, Wann was neither a philosopher nor a designer. Nevertheless, he drew heavily on Næss's concept of deep ecology, combining it with ideas culled from a new generation of ecodesigners including Peter Calthorpe and William McDonough. The key distinction between shallow and deep ecology which Næss had introduced in Bucharest in 1972 is at the core of Wann's argument, paraphrased in the equivalent distinction between shallow and deep design.[160] Deep ecology's rejection of the "man-in-environment image" and insistence on systemic, relational thinking are easily recognized in Wann's translation into deep design: "No design is an island. Every design is a system that is part of a larger system."[161] Similarly, Wann echoed Næss's paramount principles of diversity and symbiosis, specifying that these apply to design, too. If nature has taught us that monocultures result in ecological calamity, this is as true of design as of agriculture and forestry, he argued. And just like Næss, Wann related the virtues of flexibility and diversity to the need to preserve local variations and thus to the strategy of decentralization. Deep design both requires and promotes "cultural flexibility rather than rigidity, diversity rather than homogeneity, decentralization rather than centralization."[162]

In explaining the neologism "ecosophy," Næss emphasized his preference for the suffix - *sophy* over the logos-derived portmanteaus used to denote so many scholarly disciplines, ecology included. To Næss, the former's root meaning as insight or wisdom implied a much more profound and embodied understanding than did the latter's connotations of reason and knowledge.[163] Wann believed that the same distinction was essential also in design, as a sustainable future depended on making designs "not only 'smarter,' but wiser, that is, more responsive to environmental as well as social needs."[164] Wann is here citing Hungarian architect György Doczi: "Wisdom is a pulling together, knowledge a taking apart. Wisdom synthesizes and integrates, knowledge analyses and differentiates."[165] When Næss distinguished between wisdom and knowledge, between the normative and the (purportedly) objective, it was in large part because he conceived of deep ecology as uniting intellectual insight and practical action.[166] It is the exact same reasoning that made Wann, by way of Doczi, conclude that, like deep ecology, "deep design is active, practical wisdom," not theoretical knowledge.[167] The normative dimension also dovetails deep ecology and deep design in their common criticism of how and which values are habitually measured. Næss devoted considerable attention to faulting the models of mainstream economics (because of their massive influence on governance and policy) for being impervious to all but monetary value, for systematically neglecting qualitative assessments, and for the blind faith in growth as an indisputable aim.[168] Wann wholeheartedly subscribed to all of these critiques, diligently demonstrating the confluence of deep ecology and deep design in such matters: "Deep design acknowledges biological and cultural wealth as well as material wealth."[169] And where Næss unequivocally condemned "the cult of the GNP" and the growth imperative,[170] Wann chimed in, explaining how design had to be based on a much more comprehensive and qualitative understanding of value: "GNP is a quantitative, one-dimensional measure, while total value is qualitative and multidimensional. Total value is not content with growth, but asks, 'Growth of what? For whom? For how long? At what cost? Paid by whom?' . . . Deep design aims for total value."[171]

Neither deep ecology nor deep design harbored luddite tendencies or any inherent antagonisms to technology per se, but advocated for its cautious application duly considering local context and ecological consequences. The appropriate technology movement thus appealed to Næss and Wann both. Comparing deep design to the Taoist approach to mountain climbing, where the ambition is to seek unity with the mountain rather than conquering it—still, remarkably, without any explicit mention of Næss or deep ecology—Wann rhetorically asked: "Do our designs and technologies strive to become one with nature? Not often enough. I'm not making an antitechnology pitch here, but rather a pragmatic pitch for appropriate technologies that meet our needs and nature's."[172] For Wann, appropriate technology was also evidence of the continued relevance of countercultural ecodesign: "Twenty-five years ago, the covers of alternative magazines like *Co-Evolution Quarterly* pictured a future complete with wind generators, organic gardens, and smiling pedestrians. At the time, these visions were dismissed by the American mainstream as the unrealistic dreams of a wild and woolly counterculture. But they're beginning to make a little more sense now."[173] By comparison, Næss—assisted by his former student and colleague from the Ecophilosophy Group, Paul Hofseth—had been planning to design a windmill for supplying electricity at Tvergastein already in 1960,[174] 14 years before the first issue of *Co-Evolution Quarterly*.[175] Even if Wann might be accused of simply being late to the party, and/or of representing a mainstream, "shallow" institution (the EPA), these musings might nonetheless go some way in explaining the belated marriage of deep ecology and countercultural ecodesign in the new union of deep design.

Other actors and venues in the design community, both in Scandinavia and in the United States, made the connections between deep design and deep ecology explicit. When the Scandinavian Design Council in June 1990 organized an international conference in Malmö, Sweden—endorsed by both the International Council of Societies of Industrial Design and the International Council of Graphic Design Associations—on the challenges of design in a rapidly changing world, the list of speakers featured Arne Næss alongside more usual suspects including Victor Papanek and Ezio Manzini. Here, even the designers insisted on the social and cultural contingencies of their activities, acknowledging that ecodesign is not a question of technofixes. Manzini, for instance, argued that "our task is not only a problem of positive action but also a deep cultural problem." To find the path toward a more ecologically sustainable future, he elaborated, "we have to propose a new culture of design that is able to encompass this new evidence of the environmental problems."[176] Spoken like a true deep ecologist.

In his lecture, "Lies and Consequences: Industrial Design and Ecology," Papanek revisited several arguments he had first formulated 20 years earlier, also in Sweden, with the publication of *Miljön och miljonerna*—internationally better known as the subsequent English edition, *Design for the Real World* (see chapter 1). On this return visit, he emphasized how design has, throughout the entire life cycle of a product—from the sourcing of materials, via manufacturing processes, to distribution, use, and discarding—"a profound and direct influence on ecology." Of utmost consequence, therefore, was "to make Designers realize that they face choices and dilemmas in their work that can have long-range ecological consequences" and that therefore "*all* design education must be based on ecological methods and ideas."[177]

If, according to Papanek, ecology in this manner was entirely integral to design, the reverse was equally true. Modern ecodesign had been part and parcel of the modern environmental movement ever since it went mainstream: "When René Dubos and I celebrated the first 'Earth Day' in Minneapolis in 1970, we amended his quote to read: 'THINK GLOBALLY, ACT LOCALLY, PLAN MODESTLY.'"[178] (Dubos, a biologist and celebrated environmentalist, had served as an advisor to the 1972 United Nations Conference on the Human Environment in Stockholm.) Whatever the accuracy of this memoir,[179] or the contested attribution of the quote,[180] Papanek's anecdote represents a narrative in which design and ecology are interwoven. More interestingly, by latching ecodesign ("plan modestly") onto the imperative to seek local responses to global problems, Papanek expressed a design philosophy very similar to deep ecology's emphasis on decentralization and local context.

Intriguingly, in the current context, Papanek had opened his lecture with an epigraph culled from Gary Snyder, the poet-philosopher so dear to Næss and his Californian deep ecology brethren. Fittingly, then, last on the lectern, Næss addressed the audience of (predominantly Scandinavian) design professionals by reiterating key tenets of the deep ecology movement, relating them to the role of design and the place of Scandinavia in the global ecological crisis. The philosopher saw design as a potentially positive force capable of mitigating environmentalism's unhelpful reputation for moralizing by creatively envisioning more sustainable alternatives to the industrial society. Promoting his slogan "simple in means, rich in goals" and the ethos of "universalisability," he held that Scandinavian designers had a "very special responsibility" to design for a "universalisable" lifestyle—that is, a lifestyle which would be ecologically sustainable even if adopted by the global population at large. A tall order, one might say, but Næss, in his characteristically playful and optimistic tone, consoled that it is "a joyful kind of responsibility," albeit one requiring a longer horizon than designers normally consider: "To act today, with the aim to make a lovely 22nd century."[181] Still an outsider to the design community—although probably less so than he had been in California two decades prior—Næss's deliberately practical and action-oriented ecosophy appealed to the organizers and participants of the Malmö conference. As Tapio Periäinen explained, introducing the "unanimously accepted" "Manifesto on Nature, Ecology, Human Needs and Development for the Future" issued at the event, "the theoretical-philosophical level is the basis from which all practical solutions emerge."[182] The fifth and final point of the manifesto, in particular, could have been lifted right off the pages of Næss's *Ecology, Community and Lifestyle*—perhaps with the exception of the word "designers": "We have to establish positive cooperation between designers, industry and users of all categories to ensure the preservation of the richness and variety of our planet and safer and fuller living for everyone."[183] By emphasizing the responsibility of designers (as well as industry and users) in fostering social and ecological diversity, biospherical egalitarianism, and "universalisable" ways of living, the Malmö manifesto translated Ecosophy T into Ecosophy D, showing that the reciprocal relationship between the design community and the deep ecology movement had slowly but surely matured.

At the same time as ecodesign and deep ecology merged at the Malmö conference, a similar meeting took place on the pages of the US craft magazine *The Studio Potter*, whose December 1990 issue was devoted to the theme of "Deep Nature." Studio potters would hardly make it onto Papanek's list of the most environmentally destructive designers,[184] but every kind of design activity has ecological ramifications, something which was not lost on the magazine's editors: "potters are surely part of the problem. We use clay but are ignorant of its true nature; we are dependent on glaze materials that come from Earth's industrial exploiters; we fire our kilns with petrochemical and nuclear energy; we are locked into aesthetics that perpetuate cultural egotism."[185] But, they argued, perhaps there was something about the literally earthbound nature of ceramic design that might help turn the tide: "Can we be among Earth's potential healers through our advocacy of and love for clay's deep nature and the daily blessing of forming with it?"[186] The deep ecologist intervention into the design sphere became even more direct and active when *The Studio Potter* subsequently, via the Norwegian ceramicist Grete Nash, invited Næss himself to write a piece for its twentieth anniversary issue. Næss responded by detheorizing deep ecology and enlisting designers in the struggle: "Potters, like so many others, contribute to the fight against the resulting degradation of life conditions on Earth." Designers, like practitioners of any other occupation, have a part to play in the deep ecology movement, he argued, and need not venerate its theoretical and philosophical debates: "The rank-and-file supporters, the backbone of the movement, need not bother to read the theorists. They need not know the terminology."[187] While the philosopher's view of practitioners' intellectual interests may sound somewhat condescending, it is more significant that by now he counted designers amongst "the backbone of the movement." He elaborated on this point in a lecture delivered the same year, where he emphasized that "since the start of the international ecology movement in the 1960s, architects have been in the forefront, explaining hundreds of small and great ideas about how to make architecture ecologically responsible and progressive."[188] Two decades after Næss first coined the concept of deep ecology, he was publicly addressing design professionals and practitioners, formally acknowledging deep design as integral and key to the broader deep ecology movement, thereby sanctioning an Ecosophy D as a welcome variation on his own Ecosophy T.

The wider legacy of the deep ecology movement is hard to assess, but it has left a lasting impression on environmentalism and anticonsumerism. At home in Norway, the movement gained significant political influence throughout the 1970s, having played a crucial part in the campaign that secured a negative vote in the referendum on Norwegian membership in the European Community—the very embodiment of the capitalism and industrialism the deep ecologists detested.[189] Even if this formal political influence subsequently dwindled, however, it continued to inspire activists at home and abroad. For instance, the radical environmental activist organization Earth First!, emerging in the western United States in 1979, was profoundly inspired by deep ecology in general and the ideas of Næss and Kvaløy in particular.[190] Its founder, Dave Foreman, explicitly considered Earth First! to be "a particular style of deep ecology,"[191] an affiliation Næss acknowledged—even if he appealed to Foreman to moderate his support of ecosabotage as promoted in *Ecodefense: A Field Guide to Monkeywrenching*.[192] Conversely, the title of the festschrift published in the occasion of Kvaløy's fiftieth birthday in 1984 positively exudes monkeywrenching: *Green Pepper in the Turbines* (*Grønn pepper i turbinene*).[193] The deep ecology movement also had a significant influence on Greenpeace in its formative years in the 1970s, and when the organization later established a Norwegian branch, Næss was called upon to serve on its board.[194]

The most immediate and practical impact of Næss's ecosophy T and the deep ecology movement on the material culture of daily life, however, at least on the home front, can probably be found in the organization The Future in Our Hands (Fremtiden i våre hender). Founded in 1974 by advertising apostate Erik Dammann, The Future in Our Hands quickly became an articulate and persistent anticonsumerism advocate, arguably the first of its kind in Scandinavia with an explicitly ecologically motivated basis. The organization was named for Dammann's eponymous best-selling book published two years prior, written in response to his taste for living a materially simple life awoken when he spent half a year with his family at the West Samoan island of Savaii in 1968.[195] Næss considered The Future in Our Hands to be a natural extension of his own work into the popular, practical realm. He wrote the preface for Dammann's book; he was the organization's first chairman of the board; and he immediately began citing both the book and the organization's aims and activities in his texts.[196] He also spoke at the founding meeting, which gathered 3,000 people in an indoor sports arena outside Oslo, alongside Dammann and Georg Borgström.[197]

The Future in Our Hands is mostly recognized for its work to combat consumerism and its ill effects by encouraging people to act more ecologically responsible as citizens and consumers. However, Dammann was trained as a graphic designer at the National College of Applied Art and Craft,[198] and from his career in advertising he knew full well that consumption and design were intrinsically related. In 1971 he wrote about this connection in the design magazine *Nye Bonytt*, reminding designers of their responsibility for the social and ecological ramifications of Western material culture in a manner resembling contemporary critiques such as those by Victor Papanek and Wolfgang Haug.[199] But even the organization's activities reflected this attention to the design side of things. When speaking at the inaugural meeting for a British branch of The Future in Our Hands in 1982, Dammann reported on what had been accomplished in Norway thus far. Examples included a campaign for appropriate/intermediate technology accompanying their efforts to publish a Norwegian edition of E. F. Schumacher's *Small Is Beautiful*;[200] a "Group for Alternative Housing" where architects and others discussed socially and ecologically sustainable housing design; an "Institute for Alternative Production . . . working for the conversion of military and profit-greedy industry into peacefully and socially useful production"; and a "Repair Shop for Bicycles."[201] The work of Dammann and The Future in Our Hands can thus be seen, at least partially, as a pragmatic effort to turn deep ecology into deep design.

CONCLUSION: TOWARD AN ECOSOPHY OF DESIGN

This chapter has charted how a distinctive mode of thinking about the interconnectedness of human and nonhuman nature and of material and nonmaterial culture took form on the mountainsides of Norway, Nepal, and California, and has explored its connections to and consequences for an ecological philosophy of design. Even if rarely explicitly articulated, the connections between deep ecology and deep design are many and multifarious. Scrutinizing foundational texts, especially Arne Næss's early writings on the topic, it becomes clear that key tenets of deep ecology, such as ecological relationalism, biospherical egalitarianism, diversity and symbiosis, complexity over complication, and decentralization and local autonomy, have significant ramifications for any attempt at developing an ecological philosophy of design. But, as shown in this chapter, these connections were not just theoretical. From the very beginning in the late 1960s, the Norwegian ecophilosophers both inspired and were inspired by the work of designers, from the design students and architects they invited into their Ecophilosophy Group to the many countercultural ecodesign initiatives encountered in the Bay Area and the "clean climbing" design philosophy developing in Yosemite.

"Paradoxical as it may seem, it is no accident that Star Wars technology and Deep Ecology both find their fullest expression in that leading sector of Western civilization, California," quipped Ramachandra Guha in a postcolonial critique of the US strand of deep ecology.[202] Even if Næss was a Californian only by (sporadic) adoption, as it were, California and its booming counterculture became very influential both in the formation of his ecophilosophical work as well as in its international recognition and place in the broader deep ecology movement—but also as a site of alignment and exchange for deep ecology and deep design. Næss clearly was no countercultural dropout—even though resigning from his professorship shortly after returning from his 1968–1969 Berkeley sabbaticals could be considered an act of "dropping out," at least for an aging philosophy professor. Trying to explain the allure of ecology to the young generation and their efforts to establish alternative lifestyles, the *New York Times* reported from Berkeley in 1970 that

in a world of machines, they want magic; in a world of frozen foods and TV sets, they want to bake their own bread and make their own music; in a world where there is never enough time, they want to take time; in a world of computers and assembly lines, they want a place and a job that is their own; instead of concrete, they want trees; instead of money, they want joy; instead of status, they want peace. In a world of fragments, they want to be put back together.[203]

This is the constituency that made up Næss's philosophy students as well as the moving forces of the local ecodesign initiatives. What the reporter is describing here is the remarkably fertile ground that deep ecology found in California's counterculture as well as its pertinence to design. In this context, the move from deep ecology to deep design was no leap at all.

As discussed at the outset of this chapter, the controversies over hydropower development were pivotal to the very formation of the deep ecology movement, and both the energy question and the potential of alternative technology were mainstays of its topical repertoire. Arne Næss may have toyed with the idea of building a windmill to supply his cabin with electricity, but as we shall see in the next chapter, it was not in the whitewashed Norwegian mountains but in the Danish fields of green that the windmill—this totem of renewable energy and ecological design—would be transformed from quirky countercultural statement to essential infrastructure.

6

TURBULENT TIMES

Alternative Energy from Experiment to Enterprise

It is almost certain that in a period of transition from the present to the future mode of production in certain countries electricity would not commonly be produced in the backyard. . . . It is a mistake to believe that all large tools and all centralized production would have to be excluded from a convivial society.[1]
—Ivan Illich (1973)

Alternative/renewable energy technologies were an essential element in the emergence of ecological design, and remain so today. The history of Denmark's pioneering windmill industry provides a highly instructive case study to better understand how the discourse on ecological design is not the sole preserve of anticapitalist ideologies, but also comprises commercial considerations and industrial applications. That commercial and ecological concerns converged over alternative energy technologies in the 1970s was no coincidence. As Robert S. Emmet and David E. Nye have recently observed, "Energy long seemed inseparable from progress and economic growth. Since about 1970, however, the understanding of energy has changed fundamentally, and it now is understood to be inseparable from many environmental problems and their solution."[2] And as the ecological ramifications of fossil-fueled power plants and their massive and invasive infrastructure, ranging from strip mines to high-voltage transport corridors, became increasingly apparent, both activists, politicians, professionals, and entrepreneurs began exploring alternative technologies as a way to efficiently and economically tap into renewable energy sources.[3] What started out as design experiments predominantly driven by scarcity or ideology would eventually make their way into the technological mainstream and in some cases—as in the Danish windmill adventure—develop into full-fledged business enterprises. Drawing on insights from business history and the history of technology, this chapter will trace the development of this considerable feat of engineering design and energy policy, from technological experiments, via countercultural initiatives, to commercial enterprise. The windmill industry has taken on such cultural significance in Denmark that when the government (somewhat controversially) launched an official Cultural Canon in 2006, the Gedser Experimental Mill from 1957—with which this chapter begins—was included as one of the twelve works of design which, alongside corresponding selections in other fields, were supposed to provide a broad introduction to Danish cultural heritage.[4] This key category of Danish ecological design has even made its mark on one of the country's other significant export successes, Nordic Noir television, with the windmill industry providing the setting for the first season of the financial crime series *Follow the Money* (*Bedrag*), first aired in 2016.

In terms of energy supply, Denmark is the odd one out of the Scandinavian countries—for obvious geographical-topological reasons. Whereas hydropower generates 95 percent of Norway's electricity and 45 percent of Sweden's, Denmark has had to find other solutions, with wind turbines eventually becoming an essential component. Despite the recent surge in wind power development all across the world, it still only accounts for about 5 percent of global electricity production. But in Denmark, the same share has now reached 47 percent, by far the highest anywhere in the world. A viable home market also spurred a vital export industry, and manufacturers of Danish origin still dominate the global market for windmills. This remarkable success story is the result of a complex process entangling technological, political, economic, ideological, and cultural developments into what has become one of Scandinavia's most significant contributions to the international history of ecological design.

In Denmark, the history of electrical wind power is exactly as long as the history of the power grid: the country's first power plant, or "light station," was opened in 1891, the very same year physicist and educator Poul la Cour constructed the first windmill designed to generate electricity rather than to grind grain or pump water, which is what windmills had been used for up until that point. He reasoned that even if Denmark was poorer than most countries in terms of coal and waterfalls, it was conversely richer than most in terms of wind. If only the vast amounts of energy constantly passing over the flat land could somehow be harnessed, la Cour thought, it might be the key to Denmark's electrification and thus its modernization. He managed to secure governmental funding for the construction of an experimental windmill at Askov College, where he taught. The mill was designed as a simple 8-by-5-meter wooden shed above which rose an 11-meter tower supporting the turbine. One of the main challenges he identified was to control the shifting wind speed, as the direct current (DC) dynamo required steady speed to work properly. Compulsive inventor that he was, la Cour solved this problem by designing an intricate gear mechanism that evened out the varying velocity of the turbine. Another government grant in 1896 allowed him to design and build a second, larger and improved windmill as well as a laboratory with two wind tunnels in which to conduct aerodynamic experiments in search of the ideal blade design (figure 6.1). The architectural structure of this second mill and its adjacent buildings were designed by P. V. Jensen-Klint, who would later design the Grundtvig Church in Copenhagen (1921–1940), built in memory of N. F. S. Grundtvig, the founder of the people's college movement to which Askov College belonged,[5] and a landmark in Danish architectural history. The mill and church architect was also the father of Kaare Klint, widely regarded as the fountainhead of modern Danish furniture design. Anecdotal as they may seem, these personal connections place electricity-generating windmills at the heart of Danish design history from the very beginning. The legacy of la Cour's work would live on in many ways. First and foremost, his principles and patents would inform later technological development. In more practical terms, from 1904 Askov College offered courses training "rural electricians" specializing in windmill technology and construction, and over the coming decades a number of windmills across the country were constructed according to la Cour's design.[6]

Despite these early advances, however, the wind-powered electrification of (rural) Denmark and the decentralized cottage industry la Cour hoped it would bring about were soon cut short by competition from the diesel engine, which in the early twentieth century proved to be a more economic and reliable way to power the dynamos of the still very small electricity plants. But even if it took a long time for wind power to become a significant part of Denmark's energy infrastructure, the seed had been planted and experimentation and technological development continued in fits and starts. The great strides made in aircraft design during World War I were quickly converted into improved blade designs for windmills. As early as 1919, the engineers Johannes Jensen and Poul Vinding presented and patented such a mill with aerodynamic blades inspired by aircraft propellers. Tests showed that their design, marketed as the Agricco Mill, was twice as efficient as la Cour's in terms

of how much of the wind's energy it could capture and convert. More importantly, though, it was designed to run an asynchronous alternating current (AC) generator which could be connected directly to the power grid, greatly expanding the potential impact of wind power. Not surprisingly, aeronautical engineering would continue to be an important source of knowledge and inspiration in the quest for better windmill designs. Another example which achieved at least a nominal commercial application, spurred by the World War II energy shortages, is the F.L.S. Aeromotor from 1941, designed by engineers Helge Claudi Westh and K. G. Zeuthen through

6.1

Poul la Cour's mills at Askov College. The first one, from 1891, is on the right; the second one, built in 1897, is on the left. Photo courtesy of the Poul la Cour Museum.

a collaboration between the cement company F. L. Smith & Co. and the fledgling aircraft manufacturer Skandinavisk Aero Industri A/S. In contrast to earlier versions, these relatively large turbines, with a wingspan of 24 meters, were mounted on top of masts made from cast concrete or steel trusses, giving them a far more modern and industrial appearance.[7] Another decade would pass, however, before the renewable energy rendition of Danish modern appeared in the shape of the Gedser Experimental Mill.

THE MODERN MILL

Denmark's energy supply, which to a large extent relied on imported coal, remained precarious even after the war ended. Coal prices were high, and shipping was in short supply and expensive, challenges which were only exacerbated and protracted by the Korean War. This situation was by no means exclusive to Denmark, but became an international concern and prompted intergovernmental initiatives to explore alternative energy technologies. For instance, the newly established Organisation for European Economic Co-operation (OEEC) convened a series of meetings on wind power, the first held in Paris in April 1950. These meetings led OEEC, which managed the Marshall Plan funds, to push European governments to fund research and development activities in the wind power sector. In response, the Danish Ministry of Public Works granted DKK 300,000 from Marshall Plan funds to wind power experiments in 1954, followed by a similar grant two years later. Even if this support was dwarfed by the DKK 150,000,000 the government allocated to a nuclear energy research center the following year, it created a brief window of opportunity that facilitated the design and construction of what has come to be considered the first modern windmill, the Gedser Experimental Mill.[8]

The Gedser Experimental Mill was designed by Johannes Juul, an electrical engineer with the utility company SEAS. By this time he was an aging man with a long career behind him. Back in 1904, he had attended the first of Poul la Cour's courses for "rural electricians" at Askov College, thus connecting him to the very beginning of wind power experiments in Denmark. His standing in the field also made him the obvious Danish delegate to the OEEC meetings on wind power. When Juul following World War II began thinking in earnest about the possibility of designing windmills which could make substantial contributions to electricity production, the infrastructure of the Danish power grid had become much more centralized and modernized than it had been before the war, and AC generating mills were now the only viable option. He thus picked up where Jensen and Vinding had left off, suggesting that a modern mill must run an asynchronous AC generator in order to become an integral part of the power grid. What really made Juul's concept so influential for the future design of windmills, though, was his recognition of the significance of dimensions and ratios. His set-up was based on the premise that the grid's standard frequency of 50 hertz should be achieved already at a wind speed of 6 meters per second. At this wind speed, the tip of the rotor's blades should move at the speed of 39 meters per second, or 6.5 times the wind speed. This implied a ratio between wingspan, generator size, and speed of rotation which ensured that the mill would become self-regulating, and would set the standard for approaching the design of windmills as a carefully calibrated system in which every component affects every other.[9] Complementing these conceptual deliberations, Juul began practical experiments starting in 1947. One side to this was conducting measurements of wind conditions in order to locate optimal sites for the placement of mills. Another was wind tunnel testing of blades in search of the optimal blade profiles and rotor design. He quickly concluded that airplane wings provided a better model for windmill blades than did propellors, and based on this went on to develop a three-blade configuration which would eventually become the industry standard.[10] Two test mills were built in 1950 and 1952, respectively, which helped identify weaknesses and refine the design concept. The latter, mounted on the concrete tower of a wartime F.L.S. Aeromotor mill in Bogø, proved particularly reliable and remained operative for ten years, producing an annual output of 80,000 kilowatt-hours from a 45-kilowatt generator.[11]

Plans for a much larger mill with a 200-kilowatt generator to be built in Gedser, at the southeastern tip of Denmark, began in 1954. The product of this process, the Gedser Experimental Mill, was inaugurated three years later, in 1957, and would become a landmark both literally and figuratively (figure 6.2). The 25-meter-high reinforced concrete tower with integral supporting gussets was designed by Børge J. Rambøll, professor of structural engineering at the Danish Institute of Technology (Danmarks Tekniske Højskole) and founder of the consultant engineering firm that still carries his name. The rotor design would be a scaled-up version of the concept successfully tested at Bogø, with three fixed blades supported by bracing stags and wires. Constructing the blades required bespoke precision craftwork, executed at the SEAS company's workshop based on Juul's drawings. Each blade was built around a steel beam to which transversal ribs of larch wood were fastened,

6.2

The Gedser Experimental Mill designed by Johannes Juul, operational from 1957 to 1967, and then again from 1977 to 1979. Photo courtesy of Energimuseet.

defining the profile of the blade with a bevel gradually increasing from 3 degrees at the tip to 16 at the hub. This structure was then clad with sheet aluminum. The blade profile was designed to achieve so-called stall regulation, which means that even if the wind speed increases beyond the desired threshold—in this case 15 meters per second—it nevertheless will not make the rotor speed increase any further, as the additional wind force is deflected by the shape of the blades and countered by turbulence.[12] This is arguably the most innovative feature of Juul's design, as it provided a much more reliable solution to the problem of overload than the alternative, so-called pitch regulation, used in most comparable experiments in the US, UK, Germany, and France, which required a considerably more complicated design including mechanically adjustable blades. By the time the Gedser Experimental Mill was up and running, Juul and his design had become something of a phenomenon in the international wind power community, and the mill turned into a site of pilgrimage attracting visits from experts from 23 different nations. Producing a total of 2,242,000 kilowatt-hours of electricity over the course of a decade of continuous operation, Juul's electric rendition of Danish modern made electricity-generating windmills an integral part of Danish cultural identity and helped kickstart a development that would eventually turn Denmark into the undisputed global leader in wind power.[13]

MILLING ABOUT ENERGY POLICY

The Gedser Experimental Mill may have been a remarkable piece of design and a highly rewarding technological experiment, but any industrial-scale development or commercial application was still two decades away. Part of the reason was that following the mill's construction, coal and oil prices dropped considerably, thus removing the immediate economic incentives to invest in wind power. The disincentives were further aggravated by the remarkable growth in the economy from 1957 through the 1960s, as well as by the government's heavy investments in nuclear energy research leading up to and following the opening of the prestigious research facility Risø National Laboratory in 1958. Johannes Juul was not pleased with the waning political support for his life's work. When the Wind Power Commission in 1962 recommended defunding the windmill experiments, he dissented, arguing that his colleagues' conclusion was built on a much too narrow understanding both of the project's value and of the stakes involved. Dismissing its feasibility solely because the electricity produced by the experimental mill proved more expensive than that from conventional coal-fired power plants amounted to a false economy, he reasoned, appealing to a broader societal logic. Connecting the Scandinavian power grids would allow Danish wind power to complement Norwegian and Swedish hydropower in mutually beneficial ways, creating a more stable and resilient energy supply for the entire region. But also for the Danish national economy there was much to gain, according to Juul. Not only would the construction of wind power plants create jobs, but he also saw great potential for export revenue from a specialized Danish engineering industry supplying a global market with windmills and parts.[14] Seen in retrospect, Juul's predictions appear remarkably accurate. He died in 1969, however, on the cusp of the decade that would finally see his vision come to fruition.

Never let a good crisis go to waste, it has been said. That is probably too cynical a framing for the situation at hand, but there is no doubt that the international oil crisis of 1973 provided a welcome opportunity for promoters of alternative energy technologies. And the crisis did hit Denmark particularly hard, because at the time the country's energy supply was composed of 94 percent imported oil and 6 percent imported coal, resulting in some serious soul-searching amongst both politicians and the public (figure 6.3).[15] But the oil crisis was of course an inherently international phenomenon. In the United States also, arguably the epitome of carbon culture, the unexpected and unprecedented scarcity shook things up. Andrew Kirk has vividly described the dual sense of precarity and possibility in this situation: "The energy crisis in particular presented a perfect opportunity for researchers to demonstrate how ecotechnology might offer realistic solutions to pressing environmental issues. Any car-driving adult of the 1970s was aware of how ecological problems of the postwar era were either directly or indirectly linked to the acquisition and distribution of energy."[16] The crisis thus helped generate considerable cultural and political momentum for alternative energy technology. But whereas US initiatives such as California's Office of Appropriate Technology, established by Governor Jerry Brown and directed by ecodesign pioneer Sim Van der Ryn (see chapter 5), and the solar panels President Jimmy Carter had installed on the roof of the White House would be fairly short-lived, shut down as soon as more conservative politicians had the chance,[17] in Denmark the crisis, aided by broader cultural shifts, resulted in more sustained political support for renewable energy technology. Still, US connections would prove central to the eventual success of the Danish wind power adventure in many ways. For instance, when the Association of Danish

Electricity Works (Danske Elværkers Forening) explored the possibility of recommissioning the Gedser Experimental Mill for research purposes a decade after it had ceased operation, it teamed up with the US Energy Research and Development Administration (ERDA). Juul's extraordinary mill was restored and ran again from 1977 to 1979, providing new data and experience which would greatly influence the design and development of new windmills.[18] This collaborative project was met with enthusiasm even from the Californian countercultural ecodesigners we met in chapter 5, who were normally quite skeptical of governmental interference.[19] Little

6.3

The 1973 oil crisis hit Denmark hard. One of the responses was a temporary ban on car driving on Sundays, leaving the country's streets and roads open for other activities. Children playing with their bicycles on Vedbæk Strandvej north of Copenhagen. Photo © John Stæhr/Ritzau Scanpix/NTB.

did they know at this point that, only a few years later, Danish windmills would be popping up all over their home turf.

If the oil crisis, countercultural influences, and the growth of the environmental movement catalyzed the interest in and support for renewable energy technologies, in a converse movement the same forces also bolstered the antinuclear movement. Popular resistance to nuclear energy resulted in political reluctance and delays to the government's initial plan for decarbonizing the Danish power grid. The same dynamic is reflected in the organizational sphere, where the Organization for Information on Nuclear Power (Organisationen for oplysning om atomkraft, OOA) was established in 1973, and two years later contributed, alongside other environmentalist organizations, to the formation of the Organization for Renewable Energy (Organisationen for vedvarende energi, OVE).[20] The latter would quickly become an important arena for fledgling windmill manufacturers to share information, experiences, and knowledge.[21] Notably, environmentally concerned architects and civil engineers were central to these various organizational initiatives, placing design at the heart of the matter. In 1974, architect Flemming Abrahamsen and civil engineer Svend Ganneskov, who both taught at the Copenhagen School of Construction Engineering (Byggeteknisk Højskole), established a unit dubbed Ecological Resource Use (Økologisk ressource anvendelse) which prompted several institutions to become interested in alternative energy technology. At the same time, a band of architecture students and lecturers at the Royal Danish Academy of Fine Arts known collectively as the Freja Group published a handbook of ecological design and taught these principles at a summer school in 1975 which was attended by the founding members of OVE.[22] The following year, the Freja Group contributed to the *ARARAT* exhibition on alternative technology in Stockholm, discussed in chapter 4. Just how current the energy issue was in the design community in this period is exemplified also by the fact that when Industrial Designers Denmark hosted a Nordic conference on industrial design at Røddinge College in October 1980, the program featured a screening of a new Danish documentary film about renewable energy technology.[23]

In terms of both energy policy and environmental concerns, then, the tables had truly turned since the decommissioning of the Gedser Experimental Mill in 1967. Twenty years after its opening in 1958, the Risø National Laboratory—which was built to propel Denmark into the nuclear age—was equipped with a department dedicated to windmill research. Its mandate was explicitly *not* to develop an ideal windmill, but to gather, generate, and share practical knowledge and technical expertise in support of the development of a windmill industry. The same year, 1978, saw the establishment both of the Association of Danish Wind Powerplants (Foreningen af danske vindkraftværker) and the Association of Windmill Manufacturers (Vindmøllefabrikantforeningen). Combined, these various initiatives quickly created a relatively comprehensive institutional framework for the budding industry. Further adding to this trajectory of increased facilitation, the Danish Parliament decreed the following year, in 1979, that windmills sanctioned by the test station at Risø would be eligible for a subsidy equivalent to 30 percent of the acquisition cost—a policy which helped create a viable market for the product and acted as an incentive for the industry.[24] Also in 1979, the government established the Ministry of Energy, which set to work on a comprehensive, long-term energy policy. The resulting *Energiplan 81* was passed in parliament two years later, and included the crucial promise of sustained support for renewable energy technologies, aiming to install up to 10,000 windmills covering 10 percent of the country's electricity supply by the year 2000.[25] This policy and these incentives by and large created the all-important home market and gave entrepreneurs and manufacturers the predictability needed to invest in product development.[26] In the early phase, though, the market was dominated by private enthusiasts and local co-ops. The utility companies were dragging their feet—only when the prospect of nuclear power in Denmark was finally quenched in 1985, followed by considerable political pressure, did they start pulling their weight in creating a substantial home market.[27]

THE COUNTERCULTURAL MILL

While politicians, organizations, utility companies, and the manufacturing industry gradually built a system that would soon make wind energy a commercially viable enterprise, other, independent actors quite literally took matters into their own hands. By far the most spectacular example of this type of DIY ecodesign was the Tvind Mill, built between 1975 and 1978 by a group of over 300 people—teachers, students, activists, enthusiasts, and volunteers—on the grounds of the Tvind School Cooperative in western Jutland. Standing 53 meters tall, featuring rotor blades measuring 27 meters and a 2-megawatt generator, this giant home craft project was the largest windmill in the world at the time. This remarkable feat was the result of a collective, dedicated amateurism cultivated almost *in absurdum* in the Tvind organization as a key principle laid out by its founder, the radical schoolteacher Mogens

Amdi Petersen—but it could not have been realized without essential assistance from technical experts as well. Alternative energy technologies became a crucial concern for the counterculture movement's approach to design—especially in its most famous iterations thriving in the western United States, but also in Scandinavia (see chapters 4 and 5). And even if the Tvind community was a far cry from the stereotypical image of the Californian hippie—the school enforced a strict anti-drugs policy, for instance—the Danish communards shared this fascination with alternative technology and the DIY ethos as a way of challenging mainstream society's rigid infrastructure and material culture.

When the young Amdi Petersen in 1963 together with a group of friends bought a house in Odense, they unwittingly established the first commune of the Danish countercultural movement. The house quickly became a hot spot for leftist political activities, artistic production, and cultural happenings. For instance, they set up an art gallery in the basement, run by sculptor Tom Lindhardt. Here Lindhardt began experimenting with making colorful sculptures designed for children to climb on—which a few years later, in 1970, led him to establish the now world-renowned playground equipment company Kompan.[28] And as Tim Stott has recently shown, playgrounds and play equipment were a favored typology for exploring new approaches to design and the environment at this time in California, too.[29] But this community of cultural radicals would make its mark on the emergence of ecological design in Scandinavia along another trajectory altogether. Following failed plans to sail around the world, in the fall of 1967 Amdi Petersen and his band of motley Maoists sold the house in Odense and bought an old bus which they drove through Continental Europe, Turkey, Afghanistan, Pakistan, and India before ending up in Nepal—a pilgrimage somewhat resembling the ones made by the Norwegian philosopher-climbers discussed in chapter 5, bar the professional philosophizing and advanced mountaineering. Repeating the concept, the following year the Danish merry pranksters drove their bus across North Africa from Morocco to Egypt, adding further to their countercultural clout.[30] These journeys and the period's many student rebellions then led Amdi Petersen in 1970 to found the first component of what would later become better known as the Tvind Schools: the Traveling College (Den rejsende højskole)—a radical take on the traditional Danish system of non-degree-granting colleges (*folkehøjskoler*) to which Askov College (where Poul la Cour conducted his windmill experiments) also belonged. Amdi Petersen's vision for the new school was that it would educate the students—and other citizens of the welfare society—about "Denmark's relation to the fate of developing countries and Danes' relation to millions of subjugated people in Africa, Asia, and Latin America."[31] It is against this backdrop of creative countercultural insurgence and strong commitment to global justice (see chapter 3) that the early phase of the Tvind project and its colossal windmill must be understood (figure 6.4).

The defiant decision to build the world's largest windmill was of course a political statement, intended to draw attention to the project and promote the school's ideology. The tower was cast in reinforced concrete using climbing forms, a process requiring continuous work over a period of 23 days. This method is normally used in large-scale infrastructure projects rather than in amateur builds. The mechanical components were assembled following a certain *bricoleur* logic which better harmonized with the school ethos: the main axle was sourced from a Dutch shipyard, the gearbox was repurposed from a copper mine elevator where it had served as a backup, and the generator was a secondhand find—the latter two both procured from the Swedish company ASEA via acquaintances of the mill builders (figure 6.5).[32] Still, the design of the Tvind Mill relied on cutting-edge technological expertise. Engineers from Risø National Laboratory were consulted throughout the project. The calculations for the blade profiles were culled from research at NASA. The method for constructing the fiberglass blades followed principles developed by Ulrich Hütter, professor of aeronautical engineering at Stuttgart University. Professor Ulrik Krabbe at the Danish Institute of Technology's Laboratory for Electrical Circuits and Machines became deeply involved (on a private, voluntary basis) in the development of the mill's electrotechnical system.[33] It is of course a paradox that an organization which carefully constructed its identity around values of amateurism, manual labor, and self-reliance insisted on building the world's largest windmill, requiring expert assistance from the kind of actors and institutions they so vehemently opposed. But it was the same grandeur and ambition of the project which made it a site of pilgrimage for alternative energy enthusiasts from around the world, attracting 100,000 visitors during the construction period alone.[34] So even if the design solutions at Tvind weren't sufficiently scalable to directly serve as a model for smaller, more mundane projects and its builders were not particularly interested in "giving away our know-how to the first multinational corporation to come knocking,"[35] its status as an icon of alternative energy technology and ecological design made it highly influential nonetheless.

Tvind might have built the largest windmill, but it was far from the only countercultural community or the only "people's college" to experiment with alternative energy technologies in the 1970s. Windmill projects were started at several of these

6.4

The Tvind Mill completed in 1978 towering behind one of the school's characteristic buses crowded with students on the roof. Photo courtesy of Tvindkraft.

schools, including Askov College, where Poul la Cour had pioneered the field 80 years prior. The most advanced and sustained experiments, though, were arguably conducted at Kolding College—established in 1972 by a progressive group of former Askov students and teachers as an offshoot and self-proclaimed radical school. In 1976, architects Carl Herforth and Claus Nybroe published a handbook on solar and wind power which quickly became a much-valued source of information and inspiration for environmentalists and tinkerers within and beyond these schools.[36] Kolding College—which combined a countercultural attitude with a leftist political position, strong environmentalist profile, and design savvy—promptly engaged Herforth and Nybroe themselves: they designed and built a zero-energy building completed in 1977, featuring a solar heating system as well as a grid-connected 22-kilowatt windmill serving as a prototype of a new model from the start-up company Dana Vindkraft, which Nybroe had founded together with engineer Rio Ordell.[37] Simultaneously, a similar project designed by Herforth in collaboration with Friis & Moltke Architects was conducted at another experimental school, the Little College in northern Jutland.[38]

Far beyond these stand-alone didactic experiments at the colleges, the countercultural approach to alternative energy technologies also stimulated the industrial entrepreneurs discussed below. For instance, both Erik Grove-Nielsen, founder of the leading blade manufacturer Økær, and Henrik Stiesdal, who became head of product development first at Vestas and later at Bonus, both cite Herforth and Nybroe's book as a pivotal influence on their early work.[39] Another contemporary initiative of a kindred spirit was the so-called Master Smith Mill (Smedemestermøllen). This was a collaboration between the Northwestern Jutland Institute for Renewable Energy (Nordvestjysk institut for vedvarende energi, NIVA), established in 1974 (and located in Hurup Thy, just a few kilometers from Kristian Vedel's sheep farm and design studio on Thyholm, discussed in chapter 3) and the Danish Society of Master Smiths (Dansk smedemesterforening). The idea behind this project

6.5

The Tvind Mill under construction. The repurposed 18-ton gearbox has arrived and is ready for installation in August 1976. Photo © Ole Lind/Jyllands-Posten/Ritzau Scanpix/NTB.

was that NIVA would develop an "open source" design for a mill which the Society members could then manufacture and market.[40] As it turned out, nothing much came of this scheme in terms of commercial success, but the very idea is indicative of the many connections between the ideal and the real in the design history of Danish wind power.

So, although the Tvind Mill was extreme in terms of its massive size and obsessive collectivism, it was nevertheless representative of a broader bottom-up approach to alternative technology as environmentalism which would prove particularly successful in Denmark. As Ruth Oldenziel and Mikael Hård have argued,

Denmark's do-it-yourself windmill and cargo-bike builders were probably the most successful environmental user groups in Europe. These consumers managed to combine local craft ingenuity and tinkering skills with countercultural transnational concerns for planet Earth. They mobilized grassroots democracy; national legal frameworks; as well as political ideals of community-based self-reliance and social cooperation with global sensibilities.[41]

None of these alternative technologies favored by ecodesign tinkerers "were novel—but their *applications* were novel."[42] And although both the counterculture movement as well as the appropriate technology movement of the 1970s eventually disappeared, the technologies themselves persisted and developed, in many cases becoming integral to mainstream/commercial approaches to ecological design.[43] The Danish windmill industry is a case in point.[44]

SCALING UP: ENTREPRENEURS AND THE EMERGENCE OF AN INDUSTRY

Following the oil crisis, several countries invested significant resources in top-down, large-scale, prestigious windmill projects. Based on the ideal of an economy of scale, both the German and the US governments commissioned advanced research institutes and high-tech aeronautical engineering companies to design, construct, and test mills of unprecedented dimensions: 1- to 3-megawatt generators mounted on 100-meter towers with rotors up to 100 meters in diameter. These all failed spectacularly, despite the involvement of large, leading R&D communities including NASA, Boeing, Lockheed, Westinghouse, MAN, and others—possibly because these projects derived from knowledge communities characterized by compartmentalized expertise and analytic approaches rather than integral processes and gradual learning.[45] Top-down strategies were explored in Denmark as well, starting with the above-mentioned decision in 1976 to run new tests on the Gedser Experimental Mill in collaboration with the US Energy Research and Development Administration (ERDA). The political will to invest in windmill development was bolstered by an examination conducted by the Danish Academy of Technical Sciences which concluded that an investment of DKK 50 million in a 10–15-year perspective would generate the technical knowledge needed to develop and install windmills able to supply 10 percent of the country's electricity consumption. This program facilitated the design and construction from 1979 of two large mills (with 630-kilowatt capacity and 40-meter rotors) in Nibe, west of Aalborg. A heavily subsidized new company called Dansk Vindteknik (Danish Wind Technology) was established to organize the construction of these two experimental mills and the 500–600 commercial mills the program hopefully would bring about. Like the large German and US mills, however, the Nibe mills were riddled with technical problems and would never achieve cost-efficient operation.[46]

Both in the US and in Denmark, then, the top-down strategy failed to release the commercial potential of wind power. In both cases, it would fall to the opposite strategy—bottom-up—to do so. In the early 1980s, approximately 15 US companies had managed to establish themselves in the fledging commercial market for smaller windmills. As in the case of the large US mill experiments, the majority of these companies based their designs on expertise derived from aeronautical engineering. This resulted in very sophisticated products, but they struggled to achieve operational reliability. As it turned out, the technology transfer from aircraft to windmills was less obvious and immediate than expected. When put to the test of real-world conditions, their lightweight constructions proved unable to withstand the constantly shifting and notoriously unpredictable aerodynamic loads and dynamic motions a windmill, as opposed to an airplane, had to endure. This point is illustrated very clearly by the fact that a few years later, U.S. Windpower—one of the very few American companies that did not base its design work on technology transfer from aeronautical engineering—would be the sole surviving US manufacturer left on the market.[47]

In Denmark, two types of bottom-up initiatives contributed to establishing the windmill industry in the latter half of the 1970s. The first, spurred more by the experiences of the oil crisis and by the growing environmental movement, came from independent tinkerers and ideologists. The Tvind Mill discussed above certainly belongs to this category, but it was by no means the only one. Starting from a very different position from the collective, countercultural, educational context at Tvind, and heavily inspired by Johannes Juul's rotor design for the Gedser Experimental Mill, the carpenter Christian Riisager spent three years developing a modest 22-kilowatt (later 30-kilowatt) mill which he started marketing in 1975, making and selling approximately 50 units before his company went bankrupt in 1978.[48] But it was a second type of bottom-up initiative which would eventually succeed in scaling up the production of windmills to a commercially viable enterprise capable of making substantial contributions to the power grid. These came predominantly from small and medium-sized manufacturers of agricultural machinery and mechanical equipment sensing a new business opportunity in a wide-open if still uncertain market catalyzed by increasing popular enthusiasm and political goodwill.[49] By 1980 about a dozen such companies had entered the fledging windmill market, including Vestas, Nordtank, and Bonus, all of which would become key players in the industry. Building well-functioning, commercially viable windmills was largely, at least at this early stage, a process of small-scale, craft-based manufacturing and assembly requiring practical ingenuity and basic mechanical engineering skills. Both in terms of available machinery, tools, know-how, and company culture, these outfits thus proved well placed to develop what was arguably an entirely new product category for an equally new market.[50] Crucial to the success were also the practices of communication and learning amongst the various actors comprising the Danish windmill industry cluster, where insights and experiences were typically shared rather than shielded, as well as the regulatory regimes which facilitated the formation of the cluster.[51]

In his detailed study of knowledge formation in the Danish windmill industry, Peter Karnøe criticizes the notion of technology as applied science and posits that the industry's success runs counter to the widespread view that innovation, technological development, and economic growth are fueled by research-based (scientific) knowledge.[52] Correspondingly, Matthias Heymann has observed that "reliable and successful wind turbine designs have mostly been developed by non-academic engineers, technicians, and artisans in Denmark, while the designs proposed by academic engineers in the 1970s and 1980s mostly failed."[53] When Danish manufacturers managed to stay ahead of the competition, it was not because of top-town strategies, government-funded research programs, or high-tech expertise, but by continuous, cumulative development of an established design configuration and incremental innovation and improvement of their products through practical knowledge and experience-based expertise.[54] Despite the seemingly technological nature of this industry, then, its product development, and by extension its success, were not based on scientific knowledge but on design knowledge.[55] This design knowledge was not only primarily empirically founded but also, as Karnøe points out, cumulative and collaborative in nature. These aspects of designing are routinely underplayed in much design discourse, leading Jan Michl to suggest that design is better understood as *redesign* in order to emphasize precisely the kind of gradual development characterizing design work such as that in the Danish windmill industry.[56]

DESIGNED IN DENMARK, ASSEMBLED IN CALIFORNIA

When a viable home marked emerged in the late 1970s as a result of strategic policy development, economic incentives, and organizational support, it was unique even in a global context. The only other country where there was anything resembling a commercial market for windmills at this point was the United States—or more specifically the state of California, where major tax credits and predictable purchase agreements with the utility companies made wind farms a lucrative investment to the point of earning the moniker the "Great California Wind Rush." The handful of Danish manufacturers who made it through the start-up phase and dominated the growing home market quickly began looking west for expanded opportunities, starting with the export of 40 windmills to California in 1982—a number that rose to approximately 360 already the next year, and further to 1,600 in 1984 and a remarkable 3,000 in 1985. By 1986, Danish manufacturers had captured 70 percent of the booming Californian market.[57] As noted above, the US manufacturers had not succeeded in developing reliable designs, leaving Californian clients more inclined to bet on the Danes with their impressive statistics on operational stability and production figures.[58]

To meet this massive surge in demand, the still young and small Danish manufacturers had to grow (up) fast. Firstly, they needed to expand their production capacity, moving from making one mill at a time to actual serial production (or large batch production). The Vestas V-15 designed by Henrik Stiesdal and Karl Erik Jørgensen and launched in 1981 is considered the industry's very first standardized product, and was the object of the first major export venture when Californian wind farm developer Zond placed an order for 150 of these machines in 1982 (figure 6.6).[59] Vestas responded by building a new factory, and the number of employees grew rapidly from 200 to 1,000.[60] Secondly, the quest for ever-improved efficiency and profitability resulted in a gradual increase in the size and effect of the mills. Whereas the first Danish mills exported to California were equipped with 55-kilowatt generators

and rotors 15 meters in diameter, the industry worked hard and fast to develop mills with 100–130-kilowatt generators and 20-meter rotors, and then larger still. This was no mere question of scaling up existing dimensions and designs, but required comprehensive calculations, careful calibration of components, pushing the limits of the continuous, cumulative, experience-based product development which characterized these companies.

Danish manufacturers led the way not only in terms of reliability, functionality, and standardization, but also in terms of design. As is often the case with new technological products, aesthetics was a low priority in the early phases but became increasingly important as both product and market matured. In the words of one industry

6.6

Rows of Vestas V-15, the first standardized windmill, at a windfarm outside Palm Springs, California. Photo courtesy of Klaus Rockenbauer.

commentator: "Many of the turbines built in California in the early 1980s looked and operated like losing entries in a children's Erector Set competition."[61] Then came Danish design. Vestas and Bonus pioneered the tapered tubular tower design, which gave the mills a much sleeker and more elegant appearance than the three-stage "rocket" tower or the lattice tower which hitherto had dominated. The increasing attention to the visual appearance of windmills became apparent also in the design methods applied. For instance, when the in-house design team at Bonus, consisting of Søren Vinther, Jens Veng, and Henrik Stiesdal, developed the Combi model (figure 6.7), they "produced numerous models in order to visualize the proportions among the tower, nacelle, rotor, and nose cone, all while consulting with the company's staff,

6.7

Bonus Combi B31/300. Photo courtesy of wind-turbine-models.com.

including the technicians, who would service the machine, and the marketing department, who would sell it."[62] This professionalization of the design process is reflected also in that, around 1984–1985, the major manufacturers all established more formalized design departments to better organize the more complex product development processes required to arrive at windmills with five to ten times the capacity of the ones produced only five years prior. Designing windmills thus gradually became less intuitive and more systematic, relying to an increasing degree on sanctioned knowledge, theory, and research, e.g., through the test station at Risø.[63]

The windmill manufacturers' bootstrapping approach to design gradually attracted the attention of what we usually think of as the professional design community, moving the object typology from the generic realm of engineering design into the more self-consciously labeled category of industrial design. In 1984 the Danish Design Council organized an idea competition for new windmill designs, motivated by the ambition that "Denmark should add a design advantage to its technological lead" in this industry.[64] The first prize went to architect Claus Nybroe, coauthor of the 1976 handbook on solar and wind energy discussed above. His design, praised by the jury for its considerate adaptation to the landscape, was for a 60-kilowatt mill with an 18-meter slanting steel tower that would rotate with the direction of the wind. The 16-meter rotor featured blades made from laminated wood with fiberglass tips.[65] Even further afield from the industry standard, one of the runners-up was a small 7.5-kilowatt mill designed by architect Niels Helmer Christensen where both the blades, the nacelle, and the three-legged tower were made from wood. This was a deliberately small-scale, off-grid design intended for individual households rather than windfarms. Arguably the most ecological windmill of all, it remained a prototype.[66] Nybroe's winning entry never became a commercial product either (although he would later do design work for Bonus, including for a very successful 600-kilowatt mill in 1995), but the competition's aim of fostering *Vorsprung durch Design* rang true. As the US wind energy consultant Paul Gipe observed about the design-intensiveness of the wind-powered "Viking invasion" of the Californian landscape:

The Danish design fraternity may quarrel politely among themselves about the merits of the rounded corners on the Danwin nacelle or the "mosquito-like" snout of early Bonus nose cones, but the characteristic most striking to outsiders is that they care, that these concerns are a subject of discussion, that aesthetics takes its place alongside more prosaic design considerations.[67]

The industry's design-cultural recognition at home reached a new threshold when Danwin's model 24/180 received the ID Award (ID prisen) from the Danish Design Council in 1988 (figure 6.8).

Danish windmills eventually would become "design objects" in the more conventional sense of the term as well. In 1993, Nordtank commissioned the esteemed and experienced consultancy Jacob Jensen Design (of Bang & Olufsen fame) to design and develop one of the largest commercial wind turbines in the world. Standing 100 meters tall with a wingspan of 60 meters, this 1.5-megawatt mill could cover the annual electricity consumption of 900 households. The NTK 1500/60 entered

6.8

Danwin 24/180, which received the Danish Design Council's ID Award in 1988. Photo courtesy of wind-turbine-models.com.

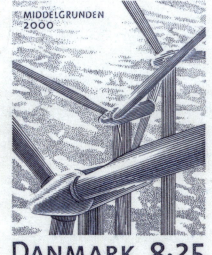

production in August 1995, and subsequently received both the IF Award and the Red Dot Award.[68] The recognition of windmills as objects of design is not restricted to the professional realm. In 1976, at the cusp of the trajectory which would turn the "Danish concept" of windmill design into a product of industrial design, one commentator wrote that "we must hope that the windmills of the future will be designed so as to become worth preserving for posteriority."[69] At the very least, they have gradually become signifiers of Danish identity, cultural heritage, and ecological design. Evocative of this process, in 2007 the Danish postal service issued a series of stamps designed by Bertil Skov Jørgensen featuring four seminal windmill projects (figure 6.9). Commercial canonization was ensured the following year, when Lego launched an 826-piece, 1-meter-high brick model of a contemporary Vestas wind turbine as part of their advanced Creator Expert line (figure 6.10).[70]

CONCLUSION: GOOD-BYE, LENIN?

This chapter has charted the history of wind power in Denmark from early technological experimentation, via an ideologically driven DIY practice, to the emergence of a proper industry. By the mid-1980s, windmills had become a commercial success as an export venture, an accepted (if sometimes contested) part of the official energy policy, and an icon of ecological design. It was only after this phase, though, in the wake of the 1987 Brundtland Commission's report *Our Common Future* that Danish energy policy and environmental policy converged completely on wind power, securing the political foundation and support that propelled wind power's position within Danish energy supply from still quite marginal at the time to its dominant position today.[71] Also on the commercial side much has happened since the initial "Viking invasion" during the Great California Wind Rush. That feverish market

6.9

The Danish postal service's homage to the country's windmill history. The series of stamps featured four iconic windmills (Askov, 1891; Gedser, 1957; Bogø, 1989; Middelgrunden, 2000). Designed by Bertil Skov Jørgensen, engraved by Martin Mörck. Courtesy of PostNord Danmark.

6.10

Lego Vestas Wind Turbine. Photo courtesy of Brickset.

crashed right after it peaked in 1986, when California's very advantageous tax breaks were discontinued. After a few lean years characterized by bankruptcies, restructuring, and consolidation, the Danish windmill manufacturers regained their strength and kept their global lead as international markets emerged and made the industry less vulnerable. In that respect, the more recent history is just as important for the full picture—but it was the pioneering phase discussed in this chapter that saw the rise of "the Danish concept" of windmill design, or "Danish Design,"[72] and the beginning of a world-leading industry built on the backs of enthusiasts and tinkerers in the aftermath of the oil crisis.

Denmark's lead in the industrialization and commercialization of wind power also speaks to a broader tendency in the late 1970s which will be further explored in the coda: the de-ideologization of ecological design. Whereas the countercultural windmill enthusiasts, like their peers populating previous chapters, were primarily driven by a heartfelt personal desire for social change and a strong political-ideological conviction, the entrepreneurs and institutions who eventually brought wind power to the masses operated on a far more pragmatic basis. To them, designing the best windmills possible was more about making money and saving their businesses than about doing good and saving the world. And as seen in the case of "clean climbing" products in chapter 5, the commercialization of ecological design inevitably gives rise to paradoxes and controversies. In the case of windmills, these issues would play out in the form of concerns over noise, visual blight, landscape conservation, and wildlife protection as the mills grew in size and number. Such controversies are closely related to the scale of the technological system, and thus seem inevitable as long as energy policy is geared exclusively or primarily toward the supply side, leaving the consumption side virtually unquestioned.[73] Despite the oil crisis, the rise of the environmental movement, and the increasing public awareness of the climate crisis, the energy culture created in symbiosis with the industrial society "remains intertwined with patterns of consumption and widely accepted economic paradigms."[74] So although the counterculture, activism, and tinkering of the 1970s "paved the way for alternative technology and ecological design to move into the mainstream,"[75] much of its more ideological or even utopian underpinnings were lost along the way.

CODA
Aspen Comes to Scandinavia

Aspen came to Scandinavia in the final week of September 1979.[1] In the history of design, the name of the Colorado town has come to stand for the series of conferences it hosted from 1951 to 2004, the International Design Conference in Aspen (IDCA). Although both the town and the conference are quite place-specific, the latter actually did travel on two occasions—to London in 1978 and to Oslo in 1979. Adding to, rather than standing in for, the annual conferences in Aspen, these two "Transatlantic Shop Talks" brought the IDCA establishment and its agenda into direct dialogue with local design cultures in the UK and Scandinavia, respectively. As we have seen throughout this book, and from studies of earlier periods,[2] transatlantic exchanges in the realm of design were nothing new in the late 1970s—but it bears repeating that a key characteristic of the history of these exchanges is their reciprocal nature, and that they often revolved around shifting understandings of design's social vocation. Even when the social and environmental costs of the consumer society—which in Scandinavia was intimately associated with the United States—became increasingly apparent over the course of the 1960s, with major ramifications also for the self-understanding of designers and their role in society (as seen in chapters 1 and 2), reciprocal US-Scandinavian relations flourished. In the realm of counterculture and design activism, Scandinavian design students and professionals found another America, beyond both Coca-Cola consumerism and MoMA elitism. Conversely, their US counterparts found another Scandinavia, beyond refined teak furniture and "democratic" modernism.[3] James Hennessey, a student at the Institute of Design in Chicago, traveled to Stockholm on a Fulbright scholarship in 1969, where he met compatriot Victor Papanek, beginning a fruitful collaboration resulting, among other things, in their two books on *Nomadic Furniture*. As shown in chapter 4, these countercultural connections could get both complex and contentious, recalling the colliding political worldviews emerging over the United Nations Conference on the Human Environment in Stockholm in June 1972. As the momentum of both counterculture and political activism waned toward the end of the 1970s, though, the dynamics of US-Scandinavian design relations were yet again at a turning point. So, when Aspen came to Scandinavia in 1979, it was part of an effort at realigning interests along vectors of professionalism rather than activism, of problem-solving rather than revolution. The story of how Aspen came to Scandinavia brings together many of the major themes and trajectories running through this book, from the perennial tensions between commercialism and idealism, via the global and ecological entanglements of design, to the faltering responses to the crisis of modernism.

From its foundation in 1951, the International Design Conference in Aspen (IDCA) soon established a reputation as a hotspot for the kingpins of the design world. Backed by industrialist and philanthropist Walter Paepcke and his Aspen Institute, the IDCA was originally intended as a meeting ground for designers and business managers, but gradually evolved into more of an arena for exchanges internal to the design professions. Still, this summer retreat for the well-groomed and well-heeled of the design world was not entirely cut off from the outside world. The twin forces of environmentalism and counterculture hit the IDCA simultaneously, and with considerable force, at the 1970 conference under the heading "Environment by Design." Given the topic, this year's conference drew a very different crowd in addition to the usual senior design professionals. Through its countercultural liaison, Sim Van der Ryn, the IDCA board invited groups such as Ecology Action, Environment Workshop, Farallones Institute, People's Architecture, and Ant Farm (all appearing in chapter 5) to attend the conference. Van der Ryn, a young architect and promoter of ecological design who was on the faculty of UC Berkeley's College of Environmental Design and had acted as liaison in the People's Park controversy in Berkeley the preceding year, most definitely succeeded in drumming up a radical attendance, and the organizers got more than they had bargained for. To the organizers, the conference theme referred to the man-made environment as a site for, and product of, design intervention. The countercultural groups and environmentalist activists, on the other hand, were more concerned with the natural environment as threatened by human activity, including design.[4] The result was a rather chaotic event where the latter groupings ran interference by boycotting the official program and staging a series of alternative happenings and performances, culminating in a set of resolutions developed by the student groups and drafted by Michael Doyle of the Environment Workshop and read aloud during the closing session.[5]

The turmoil at the 1970 conference resulted in some serious soul-searching by the IDCA board. Many felt disillusioned—Eliot Noyes so much so that he resigned as president then and there—and there were discussions about whether the conference, at least in its current format, had run its course.[6] In the end, though, they decided to give it another chance. For the 1971 event, dubbed "Paradox," convener Richard Farson—founding dean of the newly established School of Design at the California Institute of the Arts—attempted to incorporate some of the radical thrust which had nearly toppled the previous edition by addressing critical societal issues such as famines and feminism, as well as the then so topical quest for augmented consciousness. The choice of Buckminster Fuller and Victor Papanek as keynote speakers, with the young, progressive, feminist graphic designer Sheila Levrant de Bretteville also on the program, underlines Farson's effort to accommodate a younger and more radical audience. Papanek's appearance, in particular, speaks to an important Scandinavian influence. As shown in chapter 1, his recent, game-changing book, *Design for the Real World*, was largely a product of his collaborations with Scandinavian design students and was originally published in Swedish in 1970. Papanek thus brought a distinctly Scandinavian flavor to his campaigning for socially and environmentally responsible design, both in his writings and his teaching—first at Purdue University and then at CalArts, where at the time of his Aspen keynote he had just replaced Farson as Dean of the School of Design.[7] Ultimately, though, as Alice Twemlow has argued, the aptly named "Paradox" conference exemplified Jean Baudrillard's critique at the previous event that the establishment, here represented by the IDCA, by any means necessary will assimilate and incorporate dissenting forces to its own ends.[8] The institution and its gatherings thus returned to their former self, an arena for promotion of reformist rather than revolutionary change.[9]

Although the radical sentiment and countercultural activism which characterized the 1970 conference thus waned in subsequent meetings, the IDCA retained its allure to its primary audience of the international design establishment. Scandinavian delegates kept attending, sampling "this intensive way of meeting colleagues, exchanging ideas and experiences" at what one participant described as an "experiment in community."[10] When designer Hedvig Hedqvist of the Swedish

Cooperative Union's textile studio and her husband, film producer Staffan Hedqvist of the Swedish Film Institute, attended the 1971 conference, they felt the thin mountain air was thick with the aftermath of the previous edition. Although they appreciated Farson's efforts at harnessing some of the radical sentiment that had then nearly torn the institution apart, the Swedes were more alienated than impressed: "For a European, the program and the topics and the so-called progressive evaluations presented seemed somewhat naïve. Many of the issues—or, from an American point of view, 'problems'—under debate appear utterly obvious to us." Not even Fuller's marathon lecture on the earth's resources won them over. Drabbed by a feeling of "not being of any use," and perhaps inspired by the declarations and resolutions of the previous year, "the European group" drafted a manifesto offering the IDCA their services. Despite the revolutionary rhetoric, the Hedqvists concluded that "Revolution in the USA is not the same as in Europe; rather it can be equated to liberalism."[11] Such an equation clearly was the biggest paradox of all to the Swedish delegates, at a time when the political climate at home in Scandinavia was perhaps more radical than ever.

Scandinavian delegates in Aspen went on lamenting the apolitical nature of the discussions. Reflecting on his experiences at the 1973 conference, "Performance" (convened by Milton Glaser and Jivan Tabibian), designer and newly elected director of the Swedish Society of Crafts and Design Lennart Lindkvist acknowledged the importance of discussing issues pertaining to "a new global consciousness: environmental destruction, energy crisis and consumption madness, the development of new public transport systems, of new modes of dwelling—of a new quality of life." But with the political dimension ignored or suppressed, these debates tended to become toothless, he believed: "On these matters, everyone is touchingly in agreement and there are no noticeable conflicts of opinion—often due to a lack of political awareness."[12] The depoliticization of design discourse continued apace in Aspen, epitomized in the title of the 1977 conference: "Shop Talk." With tycoons of the big-business design world such as Glaser, George Nelson, and Saul Bass featuring on the agenda, the IDCA was now firmly back in the fold of corporate America and could focus on talking shop rather than saving the world. It was this iteration of the IDCA that came to Scandinavia two years later—not the countercultural/neo-Marxist rebellion of 1970.

Meeting for the first time outside the United States, the IDCA board convened in London in March 1978. The objective was to strengthen ties with British colleagues, and to that aim a joint symposium was organized for mutual exchange of ideas and experiences. Gathering 300 design professionals, this "Transatlantic Shop Talk—Aspen Comes to London" became the conceptual blueprint for a similarly motivated and structured event in Oslo the following year, under the sequel-like title "Transatlantic Shop Talk No. 2—Aspen Comes to Scandinavia." Initiated, planned, and convened by the Norwegian-Swedish duo of Alf Bøe and Ulla Tarras-Wahlberg Bøe—a couple both professionally and privately—this event would be a rare occasion for Scandinavian design professionals to meet with some of their most prominent US counterparts. The American party included names like Saul Bass, Julian Breinart, Ralph Caplan, Ivan Chermayeff, Niels Diffrient, Richard Farson, Milton Glaser, George Nelson, Elizabeth Paepke, Moshe Safdie, and Jane Thompson.[13]

The symposium in Oslo was jointly sponsored by the IDCA and four of the national design organizations in Scandinavia—the Danish Design Council (Dansk designråd); the Finnish Society of Crafts and Design (Konstflitföreningen i Finland); the Norwegian Society of Arts and Crafts and Industrial Design (Landsforbundet norsk brukskunst); and the Swedish Society of Crafts and Design (Föreningen svensk form, formerly Svenska slöjdföreningen)—but it was an entirely private initiative. Immediately following the London event, the Bøes contacted the IDCA with their proposal for a visit to Oslo, which was approved at the organization's board meeting in October 1978.[14] Art historian Alf Bøe had attended the University of Oxford where he specialized in the history of Victorian design theory, followed by postgraduate studies at the University of Oslo. Through subsequent appointments as curator at the Oslo Museum of Decorative Arts (1962–1968), director of the Norwegian Design Centre (1968–1973), senior lecturer in art history at the University of Oslo (1973–1976), and finally director of the City of Oslo Art Collections and the Munch Museum (1976–1995), Bøe established himself as a key player in the organizational life of Norwegian art and design. His already extensive Scandinavian network was strengthened through his second marriage in 1972 to Ulla Tarras-Wahlberg, then director of the Swedish Society of Crafts and Design (1969–1973). Joining forces, the Bøes were highly experienced and well-connected, and few would be better placed to make Aspen come to Scandinavia (figure 7.1).

The Bøes developed a close relationship to the IDCA. When they attended the 1978 Aspen conference, "Making Connections," it was as Eliot Noyes Fellows (Noyes, past president of the IDCA, had died the preceding year) on the invitation of board member Ivan Chermayeff.[15] Shortly after that conference, in July 1978, Chermayeff and his wife Jane Clark Chermayeff—director of education at the Cooper-Hewitt Museum—visited the Bøes in Oslo.[16] The Scandinavian couple were subsequently

7.1

Alf Bøe (right) during his tenure as director of the Norwegian Design Centre, in conversation with H.R.H. Crown Prince Harald at a design exhibition in Antwerp in 1970.

appointed international advisors to the IDCA board of directors,[17] and—inspired by the "Japan in Aspen" heading of the 1979 conference—harbored ambitions of "convincing the board to give their 1982 conference a purely Scandinavian theme."[18] When Aspen came to Scandinavia, then, it should be seen not as a singular incident, but as a key event which formed part of a more sustained, mutual exchange. This is also evident in the Bøes' plans, writing to their corporate sponsors in the wake of the Oslo symposium, to fund a scholarship scheme allowing two young Norwegian industrial designers to attend the 1980 Aspen conference followed by internships at New York design consultancies under the auspices of IDCA directors.[19] "Our people need to see professionalism on a high level, and in business," Alf Bøe explained to US ambassador Louis A. Lerner regarding their plans.[20] Moreover, Bøe explicitly thought of the Oslo symposium as a way of "strengthening our network for the large Scandinavian design exhibition now being planned," alluding to *Scandinavian Modern Design: 1880–1980* opening at the Cooper-Hewitt Museum in New York in 1982.[21]

The symposium took place in Oslo on September 24–25, 1979, but the American delegation arrived in Norway two days prior at the other side of the country, in Bergen—Alf Bøe's hometown—for some acclimatization and sightseeing. Bøe had persuaded the director of the Norwegian State Railways (NSB) to lend them its special conference coach free of charge,[22] allowing the 34 American design dignitaries and their hosts to take the scenic route "across misty and snow-swept mountains to Oslo."[23] Aboard the train, Arild Johansen of the NSB design office presented the company's new and comprehensive design program developed under the leadership of industrial designer Odd Thorsen. The seven-hour journey, routinely touted as one of the world's most scenic train rides, also gave room for an IDCA board meeting. Arriving in Oslo the evening before the symposium, the American guests met up with the Scandinavian delegates at a reception hosted by Ambassador Lerner, who also opened and chaired the proceedings the next morning, thus adding an official luster to the event.[24]

The program was devised following the "shop talk" format of the 1977 conference in Aspen and the 1978 symposium in London (figure 7.2). Alf Bøe, who was more interested in the business of culture and the culture of business than in radical politics and counterculture, wholeheartedly endorsed this approach favoring the practice-centered outlook and its commercial context. To him, "shop talk" entailed an emphasis on "factual information, reciprocal demonstration of work done, or projected. None or very little high-flying theoretical discussions."[25] Though his training and work were steeped in the cultural realm, this emphasis on

TST'2

Transatlantic shop Talk No. 2 - Aspen comes to Scandinavia

a two days' design symposium sponsored by
Dansk Designråd/Danish Design Council
Konstflitföreningen i Finland/Finnish Society of Crafts and
Design
Landsforbundet Norsk Brukskunst/Norwegian Society of
Arts and Crafts and Industrial Design
Föreningen Svensk Form/The Swedish Society for Industrial
Design
International Design Conference in Aspen/IDCA

Monday 24 September & Tuesday 25 September 1979
The Munch Museum, Tøyengaten 53, Oslo

the practice and business end of design fits well with his longstanding efforts to shift the main thrust of both the professional practice and the public perception of design in Scandinavia from the realm of art and culture to that of business and industry. There is thus a clear trajectory running from his main legacy as curator at the Oslo Museum of Decorative Arts, the major 1963 exhibition *Norsk/Norwegian Industrial Design* where he showed lawnmowers, echo sounders, chemical toilets, and motor torpedo boats alongside the more usual furniture and domestic utensils, via his tenure as director of the Norwegian Design Centre—an institution firmly embedded in the political-industrial complex, founded as it was by the Norwegian Export Council and the Federation of Norwegian Industries—to the "Transatlantic Shop Talk" in 1979.[26]

The basic structure of the program was that four representatives of the IDCA would present examples of their own work, matched by corresponding presentations by two representatives of each of the four participating Nordic countries (figure 7.3).[27] To avoid monotonous monologues and ensure a spirited exchange, there were four "discussant facilitators," two American and two Scandinavian: design critic Ralph Caplan and consultant designer George Nelson represented the IDCA, while Per Mollerup, editor of the Danish design magazine *Mobilia*, and the Swedish art historian and design critic Ulf Hård af Segerstad represented the home team. These were chosen for their "quick-witted[ness]," and their brief was "to invigorate the discussion and keep it going."[28] Following an introduction by IDCA president Richard Farson and an "Illustrated History of the Aspen Conference" by past president Jack Roberts, the project presentations commenced. In the program, the presentations by the Americans are deliberately unspecified, referred to only as "Shop Talk," suggesting that the lectures focused on the presenters' own recent projects. First out was Milton Glaser, celebrated graphic designer best known for the "I [heart] NY" campaign (1976). Then followed Niels Diffrient, industrial designer, partner in Henry Dreyfuss Associates, and coauthor of the three-volume ergonomic design

7.2

Program for the symposium "Transatlantic Shop Talk No. 2—Aspen Comes to Scandinavia."

CODA

Monday 24 September

morning

8.30	Registration of participants Main Hall, The Munch Museum
9.00	Welcome. Alf Bøe introduces today's chairman, the U.S. Ambassador to Norway, Mr. Louis A. Lerner
9.20	Introduction. Richard Farson, President, Board of Directors, International Design Conference in Aspen, IDCA
9.40	Illustrated History of the Aspen Conference Jack Roberts, Past President
10.00	Shop Talk Milton Glaser
11.15	The Swedish «10-gruppen» (Group of 10), designing for the textile industry. Inez Svensson, Stockholm
12.00	The Design Programme of the DSB, Danish State Railways. Jens Nielsen, Copenhagen
12.45	Film: «The Powers of Ten» by Charles & Ray Eames
13.00	Lunch in the museum's restaurant
14.00	Shop Talk Niels Diffrient
15.20	Factory and Office buildings in Finland Matti K. Mäkinen, Helsinki
16.00	Living quarters on off-shore platforms Njål R. Eide, Oslo
16.45	Films
17.00	End of day's programme

evening

19.30 (7.30 p. m.)	Supper, dancing, music etc. in the Munch Museum

Tuesday 25 September

morning

9.00	Wave Energy Projects; River & Harbour Laboratory Knut Bönke, Trondheim
9.45	Shop Talk Moshe Safdie
11.15	Study on the Ergonomics of the Hand Maria Benktzon, Stockholm
11.45	Establishing a glass work-shop in Kenya Mikko Merikallio, Helsinki
12.30	Films
13.00	Lunch in the museum's restaurant
14.00	Shop Talk Saul Bass
15.15	Discussion. Summing-up

During the symposium there will be four discussion facilitators,

Ralph Caplan, IDCA	George Nelson, IDCA
Per Mollerup, Denmark	Ulf Hård af Segerstad, Sweden

Biographies of all speakers will be available at the registration on Monday September 24

Please note the invitation for a reception given by the U. S. Ambassador and Mrs Louis A. Lerner at their residence Nobels gate 28, Oslo on Sunday September 23 at 7.30 p. m.

All participants are welcome

---

manual *Humanscale* (1974).[29] The IDCA presenters on day two were Moshe Safdie, architect and urban planner noted for the experimental housing complex Habitat 67 at the Expo 67 world's fair in Montreal and author of *For Everyone a Garden* (1974), and Saul Bass, graphic designer celebrated for his innovative contributions to the making of feature films. Little is known about their lectures, but this star-studded quartet representing the great and the good of American design must have put on an impressive show for their Scandinavian colleagues—approximately 150 of whom attended (figure 7.4).[30]

7.3

Program for the symposium "Transatlantic Shop Talk No. 2—Aspen Comes to Scandinavia."

The Scandinavian projects presented in between the American celebrity shop talks were a disparate assemblage, but all in various ways represented a kind of social responsibility—not the bourgeois "democratic modernism" emblematic of the brand of "Scandinavian design" eagerly and successfully promoted in the US in the 1950s and 1960s, but a new and more radical approach to the social potentialities of design. The first presentation was by Inez Svensson of the Stockholm-based textile design collective 10-gruppen (the 10-group). The collective had been founded

7.4

Singer-songwriter Åse Kleveland performing at the symposium "Transatlantic Shop Talk No. 2—Aspen Comes to Scandinavia" at the Munch Museum. Delegates are seated in front of Munch's monumental crayon sketch for the *Alma Mater* (1910) painting in the University of Oslo's Aula. Photo courtesy of the Munch Museum.

CODA 269

in 1970 in response to cutbacks in the traditionally strong and large Swedish textile industry. Their colorful, brash patterns on mundane textiles stimulated a new DIY/ bricolage design culture, in stark contrast to the refined and harmonious aesthetics of the previous generation. Creating their own workplace, the group also aimed to take greater control over all stages of the process from ideation to market, including opening their own retail outlet.[31] As such, 10-gruppen challenged the social conventions of design both in the sphere of consumption and that of production. Still, they did also collaborate with industry—including IKEA—and this was the topic of Svensson's talk in Oslo.

Next up was Jens Nielsen, head of design and chief architect for the Danish State Railways (DSB), presenting their design program and thus echoing the more intimate presentation of the equivalent Norwegian scheme the IDCA delegation had been given on board the train from Bergen. One of the first of its kind in Europe, the comprehensive and very successful DSB design program introduced in 1971 included everything from typography, wayfinding, and color schemes to uniforms, train sets, and station buildings.[32] These programs are of course examples of corporate design—but the state-owned and public-service nature of these companies gave their design programs very important civic and social functions. Staying with the socially responsible corporate theme, chief architect Matti K. Mäkinen of the Finnish dairy cooperative Valio talked about his experience with the design of factory and office buildings. Throughout the twentieth century, the cooperative movement as a distinct business model driven by ideological and social motivations became a significant political, economic, and cultural force in Scandinavia—as well as a major player in design history (see chapter 1).[33] In this way, co-ops like Valio and state companies such as DSB are highly characteristic of the blurred lines and extensive collaborations between private and public sectors so central to the "Nordic model"—and presumably quite alien to the US delegates in Oslo.

A context more familiar to the Americans was the oil industry—a newcomer to Norway following the discovery of vast quantities of oil on the Norwegian continental shelf from 1969. Architect Njål R. Eide presented his work on "living quarters on offshore platforms," a critical and challenging design task with little to go by in terms of established practice. Interestingly, Eide was already firmly embedded in a quintessentially transatlantic design culture, having worked on the interior design of the Norwegian America Line's ocean liners *Sagafjord* (1965) and *Vistafjord* (1973). The affinities between luxury liners and utilitarian living quarters were probably limited, but the Norwegian-American connections were no less prominent in his more recent commission: US companies were heavily involved in the development of the Norwegian oil industry during the 1970s, providing both financial muscle and essential technical expertise. In a prepared response to Eide's presentation, Bøe had invited the president of the National Association of Norwegian Architects, Ragnvald Bing Lorentzen, to propose a call for governmental aesthetic guidelines for offshore installations. According to Lorentzen, this suggestion did not go down well with the Americans. "This is politics," he recalls them shouting, "We do not involve ourselves in politics!"[34] Other Norwegian delegates recall that the Americans were very reluctant to discuss the environmental and political ramifications of the emerging Norwegian oil industry—or politics in general.[35] This American aversion to engaging with the political dimensions of design reflects the experiences of Scandinavian delegates to the Aspen conferences discussed above, and points to a distinct difference between the two design cultures.

If Eide's presentation of design for offshore oil production represented what has since become the inescapable paradox of Norway's image as an environmentally progressive society (see the introduction), the other Norwegian project presented at the seminar showcased a much more ecologically sustainable energy technology: seawave power. Physicist Knut Bønke of the Norwegian Institute of Technology's River and Harbor Laboratory presented their experiments with power-generating systems made up of a large number of small interacting buoys anchored to the ocean floor and oscillating with the waves. These systems were envisioned for operation along the 1,800-kilometer-long western coast of Norway, where geographic and oceanographic conditions were favorable for this type of experimental energy technology.[36] Both the Norwegian projects presented were thus typologically far off the beaten track of Scandinavian-American design cultural exchanges. The organizers' highly unconventional choice of ambassadors for Norwegian design is reflected also in their successful recruitment of the Norwegian Ministry of Petroleum and Energy as one of the sponsors for the symposium—a body not otherwise associated with the design scene.[37]

The final two Scandinavian projects presented at the event brought the discussions back to dry land. Maria Benktzon, founding partner of Ergonomi Design Gruppen, talked about their "Study on the Ergonomics of the Hand." The Swedish consultancy established in 1969 specialized in ergonomic design, and quickly became noted for their pioneering work on utensils for the physically impaired.[38] With *Humanscale* author Niels Diffrient in the audience, one would think Benktzon's presentation would have found fertile ground—but her own recollection is that her distinctly user-centered approach did not resonate with the US delegation, resulting in the rhetorical question of whether American users existed at all.[39] The very last project to be discussed shared Benktzon's concern for the underprivileged. Supported by the Finnish Society of Crafts and Design, glass artist and scientist Mikko Merikallio had set up the Harrambee Village Glass Industry in Kenya in 1976 with a view to fostering local social and economic growth.[40] Established the same year as ICSID organized the symposium Design for Need in London, and presented in Oslo the same year as ICSID and UNIDO drafted the Ahmedabad Declaration on Industrial Design for Development, Merikallio's project was most decidedly a timely venture and part of a broader Nordic contribution to these efforts at using design expertise as development aid (see chapter 3).

What was the outcome of bringing Aspen to Scandinavia, then? Not surprisingly, the organizers' own official assessment of the symposium was positive: "While the Scandinavian participants were universally impressed by the extremely professional and competent, well-tailored presentations of our US guests, they, on their side, appeared to be impressed by the sense of social responsibility pervading the presentations of many Scandinavian speakers."[41] Not everyone agreed with the Bøes' characterization. Interior architect and design critic Trinelise Dysthe's review of the event was generally supportive, but she felt that, measured against the colorful confidence and polished presentations of the American "big shots," the selected Scandinavian projects were not a good match, and appeared to be left hanging in midair.[42]

The architect Peter Butenschøn, who taught urban planning at the Oslo School of Architecture and served as editor of *Byggekunst*, was not impressed by the symposium. Butenschøn had studied at Georgia Institute of Technology and Harvard University's Graduate School of Design in the late 1960s before joining the Boston architectural firm Kallmann & McKinnell (1970–1972), and thus had a better understanding than most Scandinavians of his generation of the American design world's elite professional culture. He described the IDCA as an institution where "for a week every summer, the stars in the interdisciplinary American design heavens shine their light on visitors and on the grand theme of *design* in today's society."[43] This format did not travel well, at least not to Scandinavia, Butenschøn remarked: "There was jarring music arising in the meeting of the two cultures. In the summer breeze under lofty skies amongst the Aspen mountains, a guru show may provide a dose of enthusiastic inspiration for one's daily work. From the perspective of rigid rows of chairs in a sturdy Norwegian auditorium such a narcissistic elite seems less palatable."[44] To the repatriated Norwegian critic, the visiting American high-rollers had no purchase on the social responsibility of their vocation:

The professional debate amongst the US design establishment is very different from the Norwegian one. There, one seems more concerned with parading Mies chairs into the boardrooms of banks than with the commodity aesthetics of the consumer society. What was marketed at the Munch Museum by Saul Bass, Moshe Safdie and others was the familiar ingredients of an elitist commonness: an irreproachable radical rhetoric as wrapping paper for conventional formalistic exclusiveness. Interesting to behold, skillfully performed, but not particularly inspiring or applicable.[45]

Despite his aversion to the glossy, corporate professionalism he recognized in the US delegation and his underlining of the cultural clash, Butenschøn was not satisfied with the home team either. In his view, the unconventional choice of projects to represent Norwegian design at the symposium—Eide's living quarters on offshore oil platforms and Bønke's wave energy research—were too far removed from the mainstream of the profession and thus "not particularly reassuring and ingenious as a contrast."[46]

The social commitment generally characterizing the Scandinavian designers and projects presented to the IDCA community in Oslo in 1979 may—albeit to varying degrees—have conformed to the resolutions developed by the student groups at the 1970 Aspen conference. Still, they all represented a type of professionally sanctioned design practice, and did not in any way resemble the kind of rebellious antiestablishment design activism imagined by the countercultural protests in Aspen nine years prior (or in Stockholm in 1972) against the detrimental social and environmental effects of mainstream commercial design practice. Even if the Aspen that came to Scandinavia in 1979 by and large had reverted to its pre-1970 self in terms of establishment rather than revolutionary values, and the aim was an amicable exchange of professional experience and future collaboration, the landfall revealed significant cultural discrepancies between American and Scandinavian design cultures. The polished, corporate professionalism displayed by the US delegation provoked suspicion and criticism in their Scandinavian colleagues. Conversely, the nonconsumerist and socially responsible approach to design which characterized the bulk of the Scandinavian projects did not seem to resonate well with IDCA dignitaries deeply connected to corporate America. So, although the highly politicized and ideologically charged discourse entangling design with environmentalism and ecology traced throughout this book was at ebb tide at the turn of the 1980s, the new design culture forged in the wake of modernism still looked rather different from the edge of the earth.

CODA

NOTES

INTRODUCTION

1. Kjetil Fallan, "Nordic Noir: Deadly Design from the Peacemongering Periphery," *Design and Culture* 7, no. 3 (2015): 377–402.

2. Melvin Kranzberg, "Technology and History: 'Kranzberg's Laws,'" *Technology and Culture* 27, no. 3 (1986): 544–560.

3. Kjetil Fallan, "Introduction: The Culture of Nature in the History of Design," in *The Culture of Nature in the History of Design*, ed. Kjetil Fallan (London: Routledge, 2019), 1–15.

4. Brian Eno, "The Big Here and Long Now," The Long Now Foundation, accessed February 2, 2021, https://longnow.org/essays/big-here-long-now/.

5. Kjetil Fallan and Finn Arne Jørgensen, "Environmental Histories of Design: Towards a New Research Agenda," *Journal of Design History* 30, no. 2 (2017): 114.

6. Larry Busbea, *The Responsive Environment: Design, Aesthetics, and the Human in the 1970s* (Minneapolis: University of Minnesota Press, 2020), xvi.

7. Daniel Belgrad, *The Culture of Feedback: Ecological Thinking in Seventies America* (Chicago: University of Chicago Press, 2019), 4.

8. Some of the material in this and the following section first appeared in Kjetil Fallan, "The Object of Design History: Lessons for the Environment," in *A Companion to Contemporary Design since 1945*, ed. Anne Massey (Oxford: Wiley Blackwell, 2019), 260–283.

9. Bruce Mau and the Institute without Boundaries, *Massive Change* (London: Phaidon, 2004).

10. Simon Sadler, "Design's Ecological Operating Environments," in Fallan, *The Culture of Nature in the History of Design*, 19.

11. Jo Guldi and David Armitage, *The History Manifesto* (Cambridge: Cambridge University Press, 2014), 68.

12. Guldi and Armitage, *The History Manifesto*, 68.

13. Fallan and Jørgensen, "Environmental Histories of Design."

14. Anne Massey and Paul Micklethwaite, "Unsustainability: Towards a New Design History with Reference to British Utility," *Design Philosophy Papers* 7, no. 2 (2009): 123.

15. William Morris, *News from Nowhere: or An Epoch of Rest, Being Some Chapters from a Utopian Romance* (1890; London: Routledge, 1970).

16. Sadler, "Design's Ecological Operating Environments," 27.

17. Nicholas Gould, "William Morris," *The Ecologist* 6, no. 4 (1974): 210–212.

18. Ida Kamilla Lie, "'Make Us More Useful to Society!' The Scandinavian Design Students' Organization (SDO) and Socially Responsible Design, 1967–1973," *Design and Culture* 8, no. 3 (2016): 344.

19. Lie, "'Make Us More Useful to Society!,'" 343–344.

20. Sadler, "Design's Ecological Operating Environments," 20.

21. Andrew G. Kirk, *Counterculture Green: The Whole Earth Catalog and American Environmentalism* (Lawrence: University Press of Kansas, 2007).

22. Brian Thill, *Waste* (New York: Bloomsbury Academic, 2015), 8.

23. Ben Highmore, "A Sideboard Manifesto: Design Culture in an Artificial World," in *The Design Culture Reader*, ed. Ben Highmore (London: Routledge, 2009), 1.

24. William McDonough and Michael Braungart, *Cradle to Cradle: Remaking the Way We Make Things* (New York: North Point Press, 2002), 15.

25. Pere Llorach-Massana, Ramon Farreny, and Jordi Oliver-Solà, "Are Cradle to Cradle Certified Products Environmentally Preferable? Analysis from an LCA Approach," *Journal of Cleaner Production* 93 (2015): 243–250.

26. Fallan, "Nordic Noir," 377–402.

27. Clive Dilnot, "History, Design, Futures: Contending with What We Have Made," in Tony Fry, Clive Dilnot, and Susan Stewart, *Design and the Question of History* (London: Bloomsbury Academic, 2015), 131–271.

28. Sabine Höhler, *Spaceship Earth in the Environmental Age, 1960–1990* (London: Pickering & Chatto, 2015), 146.

29. Thomas Hylland Eriksen, *Søppel: Avfall i en verden av bivirkninger* (Oslo: Aschehoug, 2011), 77.

30. David N. Lucsko, *Junkyards, Gearheads, and Rust: Salvaging the Automotive Past* (Baltimore: Johns Hopkins University Press, 2016), 10–11.

31. Viviana Narotzky, "Our Cars in Havana," in *Autopia: Cars and Culture*, ed. Peter Wollen and Joe Kerr (London: Reaktion Books, 2002), 174.

32. Helen Reynolds, "The Utility Garment: Its Design and Effect on the Mass Market 1942–45," in *Utility Reassessed: The Role of Ethics in the Practice of Design*, ed. Judy Attfield (Manchester: Manchester University Press, 1999), 125.

33. Judy Attfield, "Introduction: Utility Reassessed," in Attfield, *Utility Reassessed*, 7.

34. Massey and Micklethwaite, "Unsustainability," 131.

35. Eli Rubin, "The Form of Socialism without Ornament: Consumption, Ideology, and the Fall and Rise of Modernist Design in the German Democratic Republic," *Journal of Design History* 19, no. 2 (2006): 161.

36. Gabriele Oropallo, "Making or Unmaking the Environment: The Role of Envisioning in the History of Sustainable Design," PhD thesis, University of Oslo, 2017, 110–132; Katharina Pfützner, *Designing for Socialist Need: Industrial Design Practice in the German Democratic Republic* (London: Routledge, 2018), 111–138.

37. Jeffrey L. Meikle, *American Plastics: A Cultural History* (New Brunswick: Rutgers University Press, 1997), 242–276; Carl A. Zimring, *Aluminum Upcycled: Sustainable Design in a Historical Perspective* (Baltimore: Johns Hopkins University Press, 2017); Tony Fry and Anne-Marie Willis, *Steel: A Design, Cultural and Ecological History* (London: Bloomsbury Academic, 2015); Jose Martinez-Reyes, "Mahogany Intertwined: Enviromateriality between Mexico, Fiji, and the Gibson Les Paul," *Journal of Material Culture* 20, no. 3 (2015): 313–329.

38. Arindam Dutta, *The Bureaucracy of Beauty: Design in the Age of Its Global Reproducibility* (London: Routledge, 2007).

39. Wolfgang Fritz Haug, *Kritik der Warenästhetik* (Frankfurt am Main: Suhrkamp, 1971).

40. Victor Papanek, *Design for the Real World: Human Ecology and Social Change* (New York: Pantheon Books, 1971).

41. Alfredo Gutiérres, "When Design Goes South: From Decoloniality, through Declassification to *dessobons*," in *Design in Crisis: New Worlds, Philosophies and Practices*, ed. Tony Fry and Adam Nocek (London: Routledge, 2021), 56–73.

42. Marisol de la Cadena, *Earth Beings: Ecologies of Practice across Andean Worlds* (Durham, NC: Duke University Press, 2015), 48.

43. Dipesh Chakrabarty, *Provincializing Europe: Postcolonial Thought and Historical Difference* (Princeton, NJ: Princeton University Press, 2000), 16.

44. Tomás Maldonado, *La speranza progettuale: Ambiente e società* (Turin: Einauldi, 1970).

45. Cindy Kohtala, Yana Boeva, and Peter Troxler, "Introduction: Alternative Histories in DIY Cultures and Maker Utopias," *Digital Culture and Society* 6, no. 1 (2020): 25.

46. Arturo Escobar, *Designs for the Pluriverse: Radical Interdependence, Autonomy, and the Making of Worlds* (Durham, NC: Duke University Press, 2018), 19.

47. Bruno Latour, *We Have Never Been Modern* (Cambridge, MA: Harvard University Press, 1993).

48. Cadena, *Earth Beings*, 93.

49. Rob Nixon, "The Anthropocene: The Promise and Pitfalls of an Epochal Idea," in *Future Remains: A Cabinet of Curiosities for the Anthropocene*, ed. Gregg Mitman, Marco Armiero, and Robert S. Emmett (Chicago: University of Chicago Press, 2018), 8.

50. Tony Fry, *Design Futuring: Sustainability, Ethics and New Practice* (Oxford: Berg, 2009).

51. World Commission on Environment and Development, *Our Common Future* (Oxford: Oxford University Press, 1987), 8.

52. Henrik Pryser Libell and Derrick Bryson Taylor, "Norway's Supreme Court Makes Way for More Arctic Drilling," *New York Times*, December 22, 2020, retrieved April 29, 2021, https://www.nytimes.com/2020/12/22/world/europe/norway-supreme-court-oil-climate-change.html?searchResultPosition=1.

53. Åsne Berre Persen and Nils Hermann Ranum, *Natur og Ungdom: 30 år i veien* (Oslo: Natur og Ungdom, 1997), 45.

54. Janike Kampevold Larsen and Peter Hemmersam, eds., *Future North: The Changing Arctic Landscapes* (London: Routledge, 2018).

55. Margaret Atwood, "It's Not Climate Change—It's Everything Change," *Matter*, July 27, 2015, retrieved April 26, 2021, https://medium.com/matter/it-s-not-climate-change-it-s-everything-change-8fd9aa671804.

56. Donna J. Haraway, *Staying with the Trouble: Making Kin in the Chthulucene* (Durham, NC: Duke University Press, 2016), 1.

57. David Orr, *The Nature of Design: Ecology, Culture, and Human Intention* (Oxford: Oxford University Press, 2002), 5.

CHAPTER 1

1. Gaetano Pesce, "The Period of the Great Contaminations," in *Italy: The New Domestic Landscape: Achievements and Problems of Italian Design*, ed. Emilio Ambasz (New York: Museum of Modern Art, 1972), 212–222; Ingrid Halland, "Error Earth: Displaying Deep Cybernetics in 'The Universitas Projects' and *Italy: The New Domestic Landscape*, 1972," PhD thesis, University of Oslo, 2017, 150–176.

2. These phrases appear in English translations of key texts by Ellen Key (1899) and Gregor Paulsson (1919), respectively, which are included in Lucy Creagh, Helena Kåberg, and Barbara Miller Lane, eds., *Modern Swedish Design: Three Founding Texts* (New York: Museum of Modern Art, 2008).

3. John Kenneth Galbraith, *The Affluent Society* (Boston: Houghton Mifflin, 1958).

4. Monica Boman, "Det absurda konsumtionssamhället," *Form* (1971, no. 3): 136–137; Helena Mattsson, "Designing the 'Consumer in Infinity': The Swedish Co-operative Union's New Consumer Policy, c. 1970," in *Scandinavian Design: Alternative Histories*, ed. Kjetil Fallan (London: Berg Publishers, 2012), 77–78.

5. Sven Thiberg, "80-talet i praktiken," *Form* (1980, no. 1): 2.

6. David Larsson Heidenblad, "Mapping a New History of the Ecological Turn: The Circulation of Environmental Knowledge in Sweden 1967," *Environment and History* 24, no. 2 (2018): 276.

7. Heidenblad, "Mapping a New History of the Ecological Turn," 284.

8. Lena Larsson, "Köp, slit, släng: Några funderingar kring ett slitstarkt ämne," *Form* (1960, no. 7/8): 452.

9. Larsson, "Köp, slit, släng," 450.

10. Larsson, "Köp, slit, släng," 450. Italics in original.

11. Ruth Schwartz Cowan, *More Work for Mother: The Ironies of Household Technology from the Open Hearth to the Microwave* (New York: Basic Books, 1983).

12. Iselin Theien, "Shopping for the 'People's Home': Consumer Planning in Norway and Sweden after the Second World War," in *The Expert Consumer: Associations and Professionals in Consumer Society*, ed. Alain Chatriot, Marie-Emmanuelle Chessel, and Matthew Hilton (Aldershot, UK: Ashgate, 2006), 137–150.

13. Maria Göransdotter and Johan Redström, "Design Methods and Critical Historiography: An Example from Swedish User-Centered Design," *Design Issues* 34, no. 2 (2018): 20–30.

14. Larsson, "Köp, slit, släng," 452.

15. Willy Maria Lundberg, *Ting och tycken* (Stockholm: Rabén & Sjögren, 1960).

16. Ingvar Svennilson, "Varor, produktivitet och konsumtionsval," *Form* (1961, no. 2): 101.

17. Arthur Hald, "Om kvalitet," *Form* (1961, no. 2): 106.

18. Erik Berglund, "Vad kostar skräpet?," *Form* (1961, no. 2): 113.

19. Cilla Robach, *Formens frigörelse: Konsthantverkare och design under debatt i 1960-talets Sverige* (Stockholm: Arvinius, 2010), 287–291.

20. Lena Larsson, "Plast och papp förändrar rummet," *Form* (1967, no. 9): 586–593.

21. Eva von Zweigbergk, "Vem vill bli enhetsmänniska?," *Form* (1961, no. 2): 108.

22. Zweigbergk, "Vem vill bli enhetsmänniska?," 108.

23. Lena Larsson, "Kvalitet som illusion och verklighet," *Form* (1961, no. 2): 110.

24. Orsi Husz, "The Morality of Quality: Assimilating Material Mass Culture in Twentieth-Century Sweden," *Journal of Modern European History* 10, no. 2 (2012): 173–175.

25. Orsi Husz, "Passionate about Things: The Swedish Debate on Throwawayism (1960–61)," *Revue d'Histoire Nordique* 7, no. 1 (2011): 159.

26. Zweigbergk, "Vem vill bli enhetsmänniska?," 108.

27. David Orr, "Conservation and Conservatism," *Conservation Biology* 9, no. 2 (1995): 242–245.

28. Christopher Mount, "Kaj Franck: High Design for Homey Objects," *Scandinavian Review* 81, no. 2 (1993): 52.

29. Kaj Franck, "Material och antimaterial," *Form* (1967, no. 9): 580.

30. Franck, "Material och antimaterial," 580.

31. Superstudio, "Description of the Microevent/Microenvironment," in Ambasz, *Italy: The New Domestic Landscape*, 242.

32. Franck, "Material och antimaterial," 580.

33. Sigfried Giedion, *Mechanization Takes Command: A Contribution to Anonymous History* (New York: Oxford University Press, 1948), 3.

34. Franck, "Material och antimaterial," 580.

35. Franck, "Material och antimaterial," 580.

36. Franck, "Material och antimaterial," 581.

37. Franck, "Material och antimaterial," 581.

38. Sigvard Strandh, ed., *Daedalus 1968: Tekniska Museets årsbok* (Stockholm: Tekniska Museet/ P.A. Norstedt & Söner, 1968), 158.

39. Strandh, *Daedalus 1968*, 158.

40. Dag Romell, "Att förbruka resurser," *Form* (1968, no. 3): 171.

41. Simon Sadler, "Design's Ecological Operating Environments," in *The Culture of Nature in the History of Design*, ed. Kjetil Fallan (London: Routledge, 2019), 19–30.

42. Mårten J. Larsson, "Samhället och formgivaren," *Form* (1968, no. 4): 241.

43. Gunilla Lundahl, "Design: nya signaler," *Form* (1968, no. 7): 417.

44. Ida Kamilla Lie, "'Make Us More Useful to Society!' The Scandinavian Design Students' Organization (SDO) and Socially Responsible Design, 1967–1973," *Design and Culture* 8, no. 3 (2016): 327–361.

45. Marika Hausen, "Papanek—praktisk designideolog," *Form* (1968, no. 2): 94.

46. Husz, "The Morality of Quality," 167.

47. Anon., "Konsumtion—till vilket pris?," *Form* (1968, no. 9): 545.

48. Jan Odhnoff, "Bilden av konsumenten," *Form* (1969, no. 1): 33–35.

49. Per Holmberg, "Valfrihet—en illusion?," *Form* (1969, no. 1): 35.

50. Bruno Latour, *Politics of Nature: How to Bring the Sciences into Democracy* (Cambridge, MA: Harvard University Press, 2004), 131–132.

51. Victor Papanek, *Miljön och miljonerna: Design som tjänst eller förtjänst?* (Stockholm: Bonniers, 1970).

52. Gunilla Lundahl, "Design för verkligheten?," *Form* (1974, no. 6): 249.

53. Gunilla Lundahl, "Bokrecension: Debattbok om design," *Form* (1970, no. 5): 199–200.

54. Victor Papanek, "Design—tjänst eller förtjänst," *Form* (1970, no. 2): 70–73 (quote on p. 73).

55. Brita Åkerman, *Makt åt konsumenten* (Stockholm: Rabén & Sjögren, 1968), 12.

56. Åkerman, *Makt åt konsumenten*, 15–16.

57. Heidenblad, "Mapping a New History of the Ecological Turn," 282.

58. Johan Östling, "Circulation, Arenas, and the Quest for Public Knowledge," *History and Theory* 59, no. 4 (2020): 124.

59. Heidenblad, "Mapping a New History of the Ecological Turn," 271.

60. Paul R. Ehrlich, *The Population Bomb* (New York: Sierra Club/Ballantine Books, 1968).

61. Georg Borgström, *The Hungry Planet: The Modern World at the Edge of Famine* (New York: Macmillan, 1965).

62. Hans Palmstierna, *Plundring, svält, förgiftning* (Stockholm: Rabén & Sjögren, 1967), 74–75.

63. Hans Palmstierna, *Besinning* (Stockholm: Rabén & Sjögren, 1972).

64. Palmstierna, *Besinning*, 104.

65. Hans Palmstiena, Marit Paulsen, Jan Odhnoff, Lena Palmstierna, Sture Andersson, and Gudrun Hjelte, *Framtiden kräver: Energi, arbete, miljö* (Kristianstad: Tidens förlag, 1974), 16.

66. Palmstierna, *Besinning*, 105.

67. Palmstierna, *Besinning*, 116–117.

68. Rolf Blomgren, Johan Dahlberg, Nils H. Edlund, and Stig Gauffin, "Ge pappret evigt liv!," *Form* (1976, no. 2/3): 58.

69. Finn Arne Jørgensen, *Recycling* (Cambridge, MA: MIT Press, 2019), 117.

70. Palmstierna, *Plundring, svält, förgiftning*, 132.

71. Palmstierna, *Plundring, svält, förgiftning*, 80 (emphasis in original).

72. Sten Åke Nilsson, "Dom slänger inte skrotet," *Form* (1971, no. 1): 40.

73. Nathan Shapira, "Design in Developing Countries. Meetings organized by ICSID's Working Group No. 4, 'Developing Countries,' Seventh Congress, International Council of Societies of Industrial Design (ICSID), Ibiza (Spain) October 14–16, 1971," ICSID Archive, University of Brighton Design Archives, GB 1837 DES/ICD/6/4/2.

74. Liv Berg and Krisno Nimpuno, *Recycling: Från skräp till nytta* (Stockholm/Alingsås: L. Berg, 1972).

75. Sten Lundgren, "Strumpskaft och återbruk," *Vi*, June 3, 1972, 7.

76. Anon., "Återbruk," *Vi*, June 3, 1972, 6.

77. Göran Holmberg, "Mer än en pratbubbla," *Vi*, June 3, 1972, 8.

78. Holmberg, "Mer än en pratbubbla," 8.

79. Lena Larsson, "Därför blev slit-och-släng en tvetydig slogan!," *Vi*, June 3, 1972, 29.

80. Larsson, "Därför blev slit-och-släng en tvetydig slogan!," 28.

81. Larsson, "Därför blev slit-och-släng en tvetydig slogan!," 28.

82. Larsson, "Därför blev slit-och-släng en tvetydig slogan!," 29.

83. Larsson, "Därför blev slit-och-släng en tvetydig slogan!," 29.

84. Lena Larsson, "Rummet, tingen och människorna," *Form* (1974, no. 8): 365–366.

85. Lundgren, "Strumpskaft och återbruk," 7.

86. Monica Boman, "Sviket mot brukarna," *Form* (1975, no. 1): 1.

87. Boman, "Sviket mot brukarna," 1.

88. Palmstierna, *Besinning*, 9.

89. Boman, "Sviket mot brukarna," 1 (emphasis in original).

90. Anon., "På vems sida står formgivarne?," *Form* (1975, no. 1): 2.

91. Hans Sjöholm, "Designdebatten: Alltför många designkonsulter sitter idag ensamma," *Form* (1975, no. 6): 211.

92. Hans Wahlforss, "Har designers svikit?," *Form* (1975, no. 1): 4.

93. Sven-Eric Juhlin, "Produktutveckling och miljöansvar," *Form* (1976, no. 2/3): 61–63.

94. Katja Waldén, "Plast och miljö," *Form* (1970, no. 8): 346–347; Katja Waldén, "Plast och design," *Form* (1970, no. 8): 348–349. The notion of "valid" products is taken from Rune Monö, "Ansa när trädet er ungt!," *Form* (1976, no. 5): 202.

95. Marit Paulsen, "Sminkad vardagsvara—för vem och varför?," *Form* (1976, no. 5): 199.

96. Lotta Jonson, "Miljövänligt, resurssnålt, vackert och smaklöst . . . ," *Form* (1976, no. 2/3): 70–72.

97. Monica Boman, "Ekologi i utbildningen," *Form* (1976, no. 2/3): 74–75.

98. Kristina Torsson, "Satsa på bättre, vackrare svenska kläder!," *Form* (1976, no. 8): 296–298.

99. David Orr, *The Nature of Design: Ecology, Culture, and Human Intention* (Oxford: Oxford University Press, 2002), 5.

100. Paulsen, "Sminkad vardagsvara," 201.

101. Palmstiena et al., *Framtiden kräver*, 65, 56.

102. Sven Thiberg, "Ansa miljökosmetikadebatten!," *Form* (1976, no. 6/7): 286.

103. Monica Boman, "Vara och undvara," in *Vara och undvara: Svensk Form på Kulturhuset*, ed. Monica Boman (Stockholm: Föreningen Svensk Form, 1978), 1.

104. Cited in Sven Thiberg, "Dags att undvara," in *Formens rörelse: Svensk form genom 150 år*, ed. Kerstin Wickman (Stockholm: Carlssons, 1995), 275.

105. Boman, "Vara och undvara," 2–3.

106. Gunilla Lundahl, "Återskapa vardagskollektiven!," in Boman, *Vara och undvara*, 38–40.

107. Emin Tengström, "Samskap—ett sätt att leva och producera," in Boman, *Vara och undvara*, 35–37.

108. Tomás Maldonado, *La speranza progettuale: Ambiente e società* (Turin: Einauldi, 1970).

109. Sven Thiberg, "Den nya kvaliteten," in Boman, *Vara och undvara*, n.p.

110. Willy Maria Lundberg, "Känslan för kvalitet," in Boman, *Vara och undvara*, 26–28.

CHAPTER 2

1. Reyner Banham, "Is There a Substitute for Wood Grain Plastic?," in *Design and Aesthetics in Wood*, ed. Eric A. Anderson and George F. Earle (Albany: SUNY Press, 1972), 10.

2. Parts of the material presented in this chapter first appeared as Kjetil Fallan, "Norwegian Wood: Trails to Ecological Design," in *Design Struggles: Intersecting Histories, Pedagogies, and Perspectives*, ed. Claudia Mareis and Nina Paim (Amsterdam: Valiz, 2021), 117–135.

3. Nils Werenskiold, "Den radikale arkitekt-professor," *Aktuell*, February 20, 1971, 28–29; Anon., "Miljøvokteren," *Dagbladet*, May 30, 1970, 5.

4. Robert Esdaile, "Our Environmental Crisis II," *Arkitektnytt* (1966, no. 3): 42.

5. Esdaile, "Our Environmental Crisis II," 42.

6. Robert Esdaile, "Our Environmental Crisis," *Arkitektnytt* (1965, no. 20): 376.

7. Esdaile, "Our Environmental Crisis," 376.

8. R. Buckminster Fuller, *Operating Manual for Spaceship Earth* (Carbondale: Southern Illinois University Press, 1968).

9. Andrew G. Kirk, *Counterculture Green: The Whole Earth Catalog and American Environmentalism* (Lawrence: University Press of Kansas, 2007), 56–64; Simon Sadler, "An Architecture of the Whole," *Journal of Architectural Education* 61, no. 4 (2008): 108–129; Peder Anker, *From Bauhaus to Ecohouse: A History of Ecological Design* (Baton Rouge: Louisiana State University Press, 2010), 68–82.

10. Robert Esdaile, "Evironmental Crisis: Indecision or Enthusiasm?," *Byggekunst* 51, no. 15 (1969): 18.

11. Robert Esdaile, "Our Environmental Crisis III," *Arkitektnytt* (1966, no. 14): 254.

12. Finis Dunaway, *Seeing Green: The Use and Abuse of American Environmental Images* (Chicago: University of Chicago Press, 2016), 66.

13. György Kepes, "Art and Ecological Conciousness," in *The Universitas Project: Solutions for a Post-Technological Society*, ed. Emilio Ambasz (New York: Museum of Modern Art, 2006), 152.

14. Kepes, "Art and Ecological Conciousness," 154.

15. Esdaile, "Our Environmental Crisis III," 254.

16. "Bilag til søknad fra Prof. Robert Esdaile," dated August 21, 1978, Robert Esdailes arkiv, NAM1995:23 Serie D, Nasjonalmuseet for kunst, arkitektur og design (hereafter cited as REA, NAM1995:23).

17. "Protokoll fört vid förberedande samträde mellan interesserade i utställningsprojektet ÄN SEN DÅ . . . den 18 dec. 1968," REA, NAM1995:23 Serie Gc.

18. Anon., ed., *og etter oss . . .* (Oslo: Norges naturvernforbund, 1970).

19. Turid Horgen, Eyvind Kvaale, Heidrun Rising Ness, Dag Norling, Snorre Skaugen, and Gabor Szilvay, "Og etter oss . . . ," *Byggekunst* 51, no. 3 (1969): 84–87.

20. Dunaway, *Seeing Green*, 3.

21. Lars Saabye Christensen, *Beatles* (Oslo: J. W. Cappelens Forlag, 1984), 357.

22. Anon., "Og etter oss . . . ," 5, no. 2 (1969): 34–39.

23. Peder Anker, "Science as a Vacation: A History of Ecology in Norway," *History of Science* 45, no. 4 (2007): 463.

24. Anker, "Science as a Vacation," 463.

25. Robert Esdaile, letters to Sigmund Kvaløy, July 8, 1969, August 31, 1969, and October 1, 1969, REA, NAM1995:23 Serie Gc.

26. Robert Esdaile to Håkon Stenstadvold, June 24, 1966, Statsarkivet i Oslo, A-10583, 02/Da-0170.

27. Robert Esdaile to Håkon Stenstadvold, June 24, 1966, Statsarkivet i Oslo, A-10583, 02/Da-0170.

28. Robert Esdaile to professor Knut Knutsen, undated [1966–1969], REA, NAM1995:23 Serie Gc.

29. Robert Esdaile, memo titled "Til S.A.O.," April 1968, REA, NAM1995:23 Serie D.

30. Robert Esdaile, memo titled "Planlegging ved SAO," undated, REA, NAM1995:23 Serie Ga.

31. Robert Esdaile, memo titled "Planlegging ved SAO," undated, REA, NAM1995:23 Serie Ga.

32. Robert Esdaile to "Tore" [no last name provided], October 24, 1969, REA, NAM1995:23 Serie D.

33. Robert Esdaile, "Perspektives [sic] of architectural education," manuscript dated 1974, REA, NAM1995:23 Serie Gb.

34. Robert Esdaile, "Desentralisering av arkitektutdannelsen," *Arkitektnytt* (1969, no. 9): unpaged.

35. Robert Esdaile, "Undervisningens dilemma," *Arkitektnytt* (1969, no. 9): unpaged.

36. Robert Esdaile to Øystein Dalland, August 22, 1969, REA, NAM1995:23 Serie D.

37. Robert Esdaile to Sigmund Kvaløy, July 8, 1969, REA, NAM1995:23 Serie Gc.

38. Arne Næss to Robert Esdaile, undated [1975], REA, NAM1995:23 Serie D.

39. Minutes from meeting on the decentralization of architecture, March 5, 1970, REA, NAM1995:23 Serie D.

40. Robert Esdaile, "The decentralized school of architecture: A new response to our environmental crisis," unpublished manuscript, January 9, 1975, REA, NAM1995:23 Serie Gc.

41. Robert Esdaile to *Architectural Design* (att: Editorial Assistant Barbara Goldstein), February 10, 1975, REA, NAM1995:23 Serie Gb.

42. Robert Esdaile to the Norwegian Pollution Control Authority, February 17, 1979, REA, NAM1995:23 Serie Gc.

43. Robert Esdaile, "'Jansholet'—Hytte ved Jøssingfjord," *Byggekunst* 58, no. 1 (1976): 6–7.

44. Anker, "Science as a Vacation," 457.

45. Anker, "Science as a Vacation," 455–479.

46. Eilif Dahl, *Økologi for ingeniører og arkitekter* (Oslo: Universitetsforlaget, 1969), n.p. (preface).

47. Dahl, *Økologi for ingeniører og arkitekter*, 28.

48. Sigmund Huse, "Naturforvaltning—Ny ressursvernrettet studieretning ved NLH," *Arkitektnytt* (1974, no. 13): 283–284.

49. Johan Lyche, "Forurensningene—Naturen—Mennesket," *Arkitektnytt* (1968, no. 11): 208.

50. Lyche, "Forurensningene—Naturen—Mennesket," 208.

51. Tormod Alnæs, Bjørn Engø, Håkon Stenstadvold, and Fredrik Wildhagen, "Ressurs-seminar," Statsarkivet i Oslo, A-10583, Statens Håndverks- og Kunstindustriskole, 02/Da—0204.

52. Roar Høyland, "Notat til seminaret for lærere i industriell formgiving ved de nordiske kunstindustriskolene i Oslo 30.10.76," Statsarkivet i Oslo, A-10583, Statens Håndverks- og Kunstindustriskole, 02/Da—0204.

53. Ragnvald Kalleberg, "Lønnsomhet—riktige svar på gale spørsmål?," *Byggekunst* 50 (1968): 157.

54. Kalleberg, "Lønnsomhet," 156.

55. Peder Anker, "Buckminster Fuller as Captain of Spaceship Earth," *Minerva* 45, no. 4 (2007): 426.

56. Fuller, *Operating Manual for Spaceship Earth*.

57. Kalleberg, "Lønnsomhet," 158.

58. Kalleberg, "Lønnsomhet," 156.

59. Kalleberg, "Lønnsomhet," 159.

60. Hsiao-Yun Chu, "Paper Mausoleum: The Archive of R. Buckminster Fuller," in *New Views on R. Buckminster Fuller*, ed. Hsiao-Yun Chu and Roberto G. Trujillo (Stanford: Stanford University Press, 2009), 17.

61. R. Buckminster Fuller, *Earth, Inc.* (Garden City, NY: Anchor, 1973), 173.

62. Edvard Hiorthøy, "Ressurser og metoder," *Byggekunst* 52 (1970): 122.

63. Georg Borgström, *The Hungry Planet: The Modern World at the Edge of Famine* (New York: Macmillan, 1965); Georg Borgström, *Too Many: A Biological Overview of the Earth's Limitations* (New York: Macmillan, 1969).

64. Sunniva Engh, "Georg Borgström and the Population-Food Dilemma: Reception and Consequences in Norwegian Public Debate in the 1950s and 1960s," in *Histories of Knowledge in Postwar Scandinavia: Actors, Arenas, and Aspirations*, ed. Johan Östling, Niklas Olsen, and David Larsson Heidenblad (London: Routledge, 2020), 48.

65. Hiorthøy, "Ressurser og metoder," 122.

66. Hiorthøy, "Ressurser og metoder," 122 (emphasis in original).

67. Hiorthøy, "Ressurser og metoder," 122.

68. Bjørn Simonnæs, "ØKOLOGI med store bokstaver," *Arkitektnytt* (1969, no. 16): 363.

69. Bjørn Simonnæs, "Rovplyndring av energi," *Arkitektnytt* (1974, no. 10): 205.

70. Simonnæs, "Rovplyndring av energi," 205.

71. Carl A. Zimring, *Aluminum Upcycled: Sustainable Design in a Historical Perspective* (Baltimore: Johns Hopkins University Press, 2017).

72. Simonnæs, "Rovplyndring av energi," 205.

73. Simonnæs, "Rovplyndring av energi," 205.

74. Simonnæs, "Rovplyndring av energi," 205.

75. Simonnæs, "Rovplyndring av energi," 205.

76. Erik Dammann, *Fremtiden i våre hender* (Oslo: Gyldendal, 1972).

77. Kjetil Fallan, "'The "Designer"—The 11th Plague': Design Discourse from Consumer Activism to Environmentalism in 1960s Norway," *Design Issues* 27, no. 4 (2011): 40.

78. Simonnæs, "Rovplyndring av energi," 205.

79. Bjørn Simonnæs, "Storbotn gård," *Byggekunst* 58, no. 1 (1976): 8–9.

80. Simonnæs, "Rovplyndring av energi," 205.

81. Jacob Myklebust and Bjørn Simonnæs, "Brekkestranda hotell," *Byggekunst* 53, no. 3 (1971): 108.

82. Elisabeth Seip, "Bjørn Johannes Simonnæs," in *Norsk kunstnerleksikon*, article published November 20, 2014, retrieved December 12, 2016, https://nkl.snl.no/Bj%C3%B8rn_Johannes _Simonn%C3%A6s.

83. Myklebust and Simonnæs, "Brekkestranda hotell," 108.

84. Ida Kamilla Lie, "'Make Us More Useful to Society!' The Scandinavian Design Students' Organization (SDO) and Socially Responsible Design, 1967–1973," *Design and Culture* 8, no. 3 (2016): 327–361.

85. Michelle Labrague, "Patagonia, A Case Study in the Historical Development of Slow Thinking," *Journal of Design History* 30, no. 2 (2017): 175–191.

86. Bergen Kunsthåndverksskole, Årsmelding 1979–81, p. 9, Statsarkivet Bergen, SHKO 007 Da 4.

87. Janina Priebe, "From Siam to Greenland: Danish Economic Imperialism at the Turn of the Twentieth Century," *Journal of World History* 27, no. 4 (2016): 627.

88. Alf Midtbust, "Frem for furua," *Bonytt* (1965, no. 5): 126.

89. Marianne Gullowsen, "Efterlyses . . . ," *Bonytt* (1965, no. 5): 139–140; Arne Remlov, "Det lyktes—så langt," *Bonytt* (1965, no. 7/8): 221–224; Arne Remlov, "Fra det ene til det annet . . . ," *Bonytt* (1966, no. 9): 242.

90. Kjetil Fallan, "Culture by Design: Co-Constructing Material and Meaning," in *Assigning Cultural Values*, ed. Kjerstin Aukrust (Frankfurt am Main: Peter Lang, 2013), 147.

91. Gunnar Sørlie interviewed in Arne Remlov, "Vår mann i Stavanger," *Bonytt* (1965, no. 9): 254.

92. Malin K. Graesse, "The Weaving World of Deep Ecology and Textile Design: Locating Principles of Sustainability at Austvatn Craft Central," MA thesis, University of Oslo, 2017.

93. Robert Friedel, "History, Sustainability, and Choice," in *Cycling and Recycling: Histories of Sustainable Practices*, ed. Ruth Oldenziel and Helmuth Trischler (New York: Berghahn Books, 2015), 219.

94. Harriet Clayhills, "Hytter med system," *Bonytt* (1965, no. 9): 240–243; Liv Schjødt, "Vi trenger hyttemøbler også!," *Bonytt* (1966, no. 1): 12–13.

95. Alf Bøe, *Den norske Designpris de syv første år/The Norwegian Design Award Its First Seven Years* (Oslo: Norsk Designcentrum, 1969), 52.

96. Alf Bøe, "Designed for Leisure Living," *Design*, no. 248 (1969): 32–34.

97. Minutes from meeting on the decentralization of architecture, March 5, 1970, REA, NAM1995:23 Serie D.

CHAPTER 3

1. Sim Van der Ryn and Stuart Cowan, *Ecological Design* (Washington, DC: Island Press, 1996), 57.

2. Marco Armiero and Lise Sedrez, "Introduction," in *A History of Environmentalism: Local Struggles, Global Histories*, ed. Marco Armiero and Lise Sedrez (London: Bloomsbury Academic, 2014), 4.

3. Albert Lewis, "Harambee," *Glass Art* 4, no. 5 (1975): 16.

4. Kjetil Fallan, "'The "Designer"—The 11th Plague': Design Discourse from Consumer Activism to Environmentalism in 1960s Norway," *Design Issues* 27, no. 4 (2011): 36.

5. Saloni Mathur, "Charles and Ray Eames in India," *Art Journal* 70, no. 1 (2011): 34–53; Suchitra Balasubrahmanyan, "Imagining the Indian Nation: The Design of Gandhi's Dandi March and Nehru's Republic Day Parade," in *Designing Worlds: National Design Histories in an Age of Globalization*, ed. Kjetil Fallan and Grace Lees-Maffei (New York: Berghahn Books, 2016), 108–124.

6. Ashoke Chatterjee, "Design in India: The Experience of Transition," *Design Issues* 21, no. 4 (2005): 8–9.

7. Alison J. Clarke, "Design for Development, ICSID and UNIDO: The Anthropological Turn in 1970s Design," *Journal of Design History* 29, no. 1 (2016): 45.

8. Helge Ø. Pharo and Monika Phole Fraser, "Introduction," in *The Aid Rush: Aid Regimes in Northern Europe during the Cold War*, vol. 1, ed. Helge Ø. Pharo and Monika Phole Fraser (Oslo: Unipub, 2008), 10.

9. Christian Friis Bach, Thorsten Borring Olesen, Sune Kaur-Pedersen, and Jan Pedersen, *Idealer og realiteter: Dansk udviklingspolitiks historie 1945–2005* (Copenhagen: Gyldendal, 2008), 196.

10. Mette Strømgaard Dalby, "Kristian Vedel: Industriell designer, pioner og idealist," in *Kristian Vedel*, ed. Lise Schou (Copenhagen: Arkitektens forlag, 2007), 9–14.

11. Jørgen Schou-Christensen, "Kristian Vedel," in *The Lunning Prize*, ed. Helena Dahlbäck Lutteman and Marianne Uggla (Stockholm: Nationalmuseum, 1986), 136–137.

12. Ane Vedel in conversation with the author, August 21, 2019.

13. Jorge F. Rivas Pérez, "Cannibal Homes: Additive Modernity and Design by Absorption in Brazil, Mexico and Venezuela, 1940–1978," in *Moderno: Design for Living in Brazil, Mexico, and Venezuela, 1940–1978*, ed. Gabriela Rangel and Jorge F. Rivas Pérez (New York: Americas Society; Miami: Prisa/Santillana USA, 2015), 15–33.

14. Kristian Vedel to Joe K. Trauerman, April 22, 1965, Kristian Vedel's papers, private collection (hereafter cited as KVP).

15. Vedel to Trauerman, April 22, 1965, KVP.

16. Kristian Vedel to his family, Antwerp, February 25, 1965, Kristian Vedel arkiv Designmuseum Danmark 101 C Rejsebreve og udstillingsplan (hereafter cited as KVA).

17. Vedel to his family, Antwerp, February 26, 1965, KVA.

18. Vedel to his family, Antwerp, February 25, 1965, KVA.

19. Kristian Vedel to his family, Barranquilla harbor, March 21, 1965, KVA; Kristian Vedel to Richard Wagner Hansen at the Ministry of Foreign Affairs of Denmark, April 22, 1965, KVP.

20. Kristian Vedel, manuscript for lecture at Instituto del Diseño Neumann, Caracas, n.d. (March 1965), KVP.

21. Vedel, manuscript for lecture, KVP.

22. Vedel to his family, Barranquilla harbor, March 22, 1965, KVA.

23. Vedel to his family, Escazú, Costa Rica, April 4, 1965, KVA.

24. Vedel to his family, Managua, Nicaragua, April 23, 1965, KVA.

25. Vedel to his family, Escazú, Costa Rica, April 4, 1965, KVA.

26. Vedel to his family, Managua, Nicaragua, April 25, 1965, KVA.

27. Vedel to his family, Peninsula de Nicoya, Costa Rica, April 16, 1965, KVA.

28. Vedel to his family, Peninsula de Nicoya, Costa Rica, April 16, 1965, KVA.

29. Vedel to his family, Guatemala City, May 1, 1965, KVA.

30. Vedel to his family, Guatemala City, May 7, 1965, KVA.

31. Vedel to his family, Guatemala City, May 7, 1965, KVA.

32. Vedel to his family, San Cristóbal de las Casas, Mexico, May 29, 1965, KVA.

33. Vedel to his family, San Cristóbal de las Casas, Mexico, May 29, 1965, KVA.

34. Tore Leifer, Jesper Nielsen, and Toke Sellner Reunert, *Restless Blood: Frans Blom, Explorer and Maya Archaeologist* (San Francisco: Precolumbia Mesoweb Press, 2017).

35. Alex Harris and Margaret Sartor, *Gertrude Blom: Bearing Witness* (Chapel Hill: University of North Carolina Press, 1984).

36. Vedel to his family, San Cristóbal de las Casas, Mexico, May 29, 1965, KVA.

37. Vedel to his family, Mexico City, June 12, 1965, KVA.

38. Vedel to his family, Mexico City, June 12, 1965, KVA.

39. Vedel to his family, Kansas City, June 14, 1965, KVA.

40. Vedel to his family, New York City, June 22, 1965, KVA.

41. Vedel to his family, New York City, June 23, 1965, KVA.

42. Alf Bøe, "Dansk firkløver i Københavns Kunstindustrimuseum," *Dansk Kunsthaandværk* (1966–1967, no. 1): 14–17.

43. Aase Gliemann, "Planlægger u-landsindustri fra Humlebæk gamle smedje," *Jyllands-Posten*, December 27, 1965.

44. Gliemann, "Planlægger u-landsindustri fra Humlebæk gamle smedje."

45. Kristian Vedel, "Foredrag vedr. udviklingslande," manuscript for lecture at Landsforbundet Dansk Kunsthaandværk, n.d. (1965/1966), KVP.

46. Vedel, "Foredrag vedr. Udviklingslande."

47. Vedel, "Foredrag vedr. Udviklingslande."

48. Vedel, "Foredrag vedr. Udviklingslande."

49. Silvia Fernández, "The Origins of Design Education in Latin America: From the hfg in Ulm to Globalization," *Design Issues* 22, no. 1 (2006): 3–19.

50. Danah Abdulla, "The Challenges and Opportunities of Introducing Design Culture in Jordan," in *Design Culture: Objects and Approaches*, ed. Guy Julier, Mads Nygaard Folkmann, Niels Peter Skou, Hans-Christian Jensen, and Anders V. Munch (London: Bloomsbury Academic, 2019), 218.

51. Kristian Vedel, "'Industrial design' i Afrika," *Rapport*, no. 44 (December 1969): 282.

52. Sultan Somjee, "The Arts in Lifelong Education in Kenya," in *The Arts in Life-long Education*, ed. D'Arcy Hayman (Paris: UNESCO; Sofia: Sofia Press, 1977), 57.

53. Daniel Magaziner, "Designing Knowledge in Postcolonial Africa: A South African Abroad," *Kronos: Southern African Histories*, no. 41 (2015): 267.

54. Magaziner, "Designing Knowledge in Postcolonial Africa," 278–280.

55. Selby Mvusi, quoted in Magaziner, "Designing Knowledge in Postcolonial Africa," 281.

56. Daniel Magaziner, "The Foundation: Design, Time, and Possibility in 1960s Nairobi," *Comparative Studies in Society and History* 60, no. 3 (2018): 622–623.

57. Daniel Magaziner, "The Politics of Design in Postcolonial Kenya," in *Flow of Forms / Forms of Flow: Design Histories between Africa and Europe*, ed. Kerstin Pinther and Alexandra Weigand (Bielefeld: Transcript, 2018), 147.

58. Magaziner, "The Foundation," 599–628 (the quote from Mvusi and Morgan's course preparation notes appears on pp. 613–614).

59. Magaziner, "The Foundation," 622–623.

60. Vedel, "'Industrial design' i Afrika," 282.

61. Kristian Vedel to the Ministry of Foreign Affairs, "Interim Report on the Need for Establishment of a Chair of Design at the University College, Nairobi," July 8, 1968, KVP.

62. Vedel, "Interim Report."

63. Vedel, "'Industrial design' i Afrika," 282.

64. Vedel, "Interim Report."

65. Selby Mvusi, "Perspectives on Industrial Design Education in Low-Income Countries" (n.d., c. 1965), in Elza Miles, *Selby Mvusi: To Fly with the North Bird South* (Pretoria: University of South Africa Press, 2015), Companion CD: Academic Papers, 58.

66. Kristian Vedel, "College Development Plan 1970–1973. Faculty of Architecture, Design and Development, Department of Industrial Design," June 26, 1969 / September 24, 1969, KVP.

67. Vedel, "College Development Plan 1970–1973."

68. Dag Rognlien, "Muguga Green (Norse Green)," *Byggekunst* 56, no. 3 (1974): 62.

69. Vedel, "College Development Plan 1970–1973."

70. Amrik Kalsi, "A New Design Education in Kenya," in Schou, *Kristian Vedel*, 83.

71. Kristian Vedel to unidentified family member, Tsavo Gamepark, December 8, 1969, KVP.

72. Personal communication with Sultan Somjee, January 7, 2020; January 20, 2020.

73. Kristian Vedel, manuscript for paper delivered at a symposium on the use of East African timbers in furniture manufacture at Kenya Polytechnic, December 14, 1970, KVP.

74. Vedel, "College Development Plan 1970–1973."

75. E. F. Schumacher, *Small Is Beautiful: A Study of Economics as if People Mattered* (London: Blond & Briggs, 1973).

76. Gabriele Oropallo, "People Have the Power: Appropriate Technology and the Implications of Labour-Intensive Making," in *Craft Economies*, ed. Susan Luckman and Nicola Thomas (London: Bloomsbury Academic, 2018), 83–93.

77. Bach et al., *Idealer og realiteter*, 129.

78. Sultan Firoze H. Somjee Rajan, "Learning to Be Indigenous or Being Taught to Be Kenyan: The Ethnography of Teaching Art and Material Culture in Kenya," PhD thesis, McGill University, 1996, 78–79.

79. J. P. Odoch Pido, "Pedagogical Clashes in East African Art and Design Education," *Critical Interventions: Journal of African Art History and Visual Culture* 8, no. 1 (2014): 128.

80. Kristian Vedel, manuscript for paper delivered at a symposium on the use of East African timbers in furniture manufacture at Kenya Polytechnic, December 14, 1970, KVP.

81. Magaziner, "The Politics of Design in Postcolonial Kenya," 146.

82. Personal communication with J. P. Odoch Pido, November 22, 2019.

83. Magaziner, "The Politics of Design in Postcolonial Kenya," 136, 142–143.

84. Principal Arthur T. Porter to Chancellor Charles E. Young, July 10, 1969, ICSID Archive, University of Brighton Design Archives, GB 1837 DES/ICD/6/4/11 (hereafter cited as ICSID Archive).

85. Magaziner, "The Foundation," 625.

86. Miles, *Selby Mvusi*, 34.

87. Magaziner, "The Politics of Design in Postcolonial Kenya," 137.

88. Nathan Shapira, "Design Education for East Africa," 1970, 25, Nathan Shapira Design Archive at San Francisco State University, University of Nairobi Binder 1, 1.

89. Shapira, "Design Education for East Africa," 8.

90. Pido, "Pedagogical Clashes in East African Art and Design Education," 128.

91. J. P. Odoch Pido quoted in Magaziner, "The Foundation," 624.

92. Kristian Vedel, "Draft Proposal for the Operation of the Design Research and Development Unit," June 22, 1970, KVP.

93. Kristian Vedel, "Draft: Illustration of Recommended Activities of the Unit," March 11–12, 1970, KVP.

94. Vedel, "Draft Proposal for the Operation of the Design Research and Development Unit."

95. Personal communication with Amrik Kalsi, January 7, 2020.

96. Kristian Vedel, "Design Research and Development Unit," August 4, 1970, KVP.

97. Personal communication with Amrik Kalsi, December 11, 2019.

98. Personal communication with Amrik Kalsi, December 11, 2019.

99. Design Research and Development Unit, "Media of Transportation by Use of Human Forces on or by the Body. Report on a Joint Project of 2nd Year Product Design Students and the Design Research and Development Unit, Department of Design, Faculty of Architecture, Design and Development, University of Nairobi," June 1971, KVP.

100. Design Research and Development Unit, "Media of Transportation," 48.

101. Design Research and Development Unit, "Media of Transportation," 10–12.

102. Lorna Schofield, "Design in Kenya for the Tourist Industry and Local People," ICSID Archive, DES/ICD/6/4/1/2.

103. Schofield, "Design in Kenya for the Tourist Industry and Local People."

104. Schofield, "Design in Kenya for the Tourist Industry and Local People."

105. Kristian Vedel to Vice-Chancellor J. N. Karanja, Nairobi, April 29, 1971, KVP.

106. Vedel to Karanja, April 29, 1971.

107. Kristian Vedel to unidentified family member, Tsavo Gamepark, December 8, 1969, KVP.

108. Vedel to Karanja, April 29, 1971.

109. Vedel to Karanja, April 29, 1971.

110. Vedel to Karanja, April 29, 1971.

111. Vedel to his family, Nairobi, May 8, 1971, KVP.

112. Vedel to his family, May 8, 1971.

113. Vedel to his family, May 8, 1971.

114. Vedel to his family, May 8, 1971.

115. Magaziner, "The Politics of Design in Postcolonial Kenya," 149.

116. Magaziner, "The Politics of Design in Postcolonial Kenya," 142.

117. Magaziner, "The Politics of Design in Postcolonial Kenya," 135.

118. Vedel to his family, May 8, 1971.

119. Vedel to his family, May 8, 1971.

120. Kristian Vedel to Sultan Somjee and Gamaliel Mugumbya, Almunécar, Spain, April 9, 1972, KVP.

121. Kristian Vedel, "Udvikling—værdinormer og kreativitet," manuscript for a lecture delivered to the Association for Applied Art and Industrial Design, December 17, 1973, KVP.

122. Vedel, "Udvikling—værdinormer og kreativitet."

123. Vedel, "Udvikling—værdinormer og kreativitet."

124. Vedel to Somjee and Mugumbya, April 9, 1972.

125. Personal communication with Sultan Somjee, January 20, 2020.

126. Sultan Somjee and Gamaliel Mugumbya, "Revised Proposal for the Study Programme," February 18, 1973, KVP.

127. Victor Papanek, "For the Southern Half of the Globe," *Design Studies* 4, no. 1 (1983): 61. The paper was originally written in 1975 as part of his contribution to ICSID's Working Group IV Developing Countries, discussed below.

128. Personal communication with Gamaliel Mugumbya, January 7, 2020; March 9, 2020.

129. Personal communication with Sultan Somjee, January 7, 2020.

130. Personal communication with Sultan Somjee, January 7, 2020. This increased attention to indigenous artifacts is a key feature of what Alison Clarke has labeled the design profession's "anthropological turn" in this period: Clarke, "Design for Development," 43–57.

131. Sultan Somjee, *Material Culture of Kenya* (Nairobi: East African Publishers, 1993).

132. Somjee Rajan, "Learning to Be Indigenous."

133. Kristian Vedel quoted in Ole Bergh, "Er det ikke tåbeligt? Vi indretter os efter god tone for 200 år siden," *Aalborg Stiftstidende*, September 30, 1973.

134. Thomas Ekman Jørgensen, "Utopia and Disillusion: Shattered Hopes of the Copenhagen Counterculture," in *Between Marx and Coca-Cola: Youth Cultures in Changing European Societies, 1960–1980*, ed. Axel Schildt and Detlef Siegfried (Oxford: Berg, 2006), 344.

135. Hans-Christian Jensen and Anders V. Munch, "Environment and Emancipation through Design: Avant-Garde Intervention and Experiments with Social Design in Denmark around 1970," *AIS/Design: Storia e Ricerche* 7, no. 12–13 (2019–2020): 99.

136. Carsten Thau, "Ussing og Hoff—arkitekturen frisatt," in *Susanne Ussing—mellem kunst og arkitektur*, ed. Birgitte Thorsen Vilslev and Carsten Hoff (Copenhagen: Strandberg, 2017), 81–125.

137. Kristian Vedel to his family, southbound, just north of the Azores, March 2, 1965, KVA.

138. Ane Vedel in conversation with the author, August 21, 2019.

139. Kristian Vedel quoted in Ole Bergh, "Fåret er det bedste miljøværn," *Aalborg Stiftstidende*, July 7, 1974.

140. Frede Ladefoged, "12 km uldgarn af et kg uld," *Landsbladet*, September 16, 1977, 51.

141. kate+bodil, "Afrikaneren skal hjælpe indianeren ved at møde på en gård på Thyholm," *Struer Dagblad*, July 18, 1974.

142. Ladefoged, "12 km uldgarn af et kg uld," 51; EN, "Fra universitetet i Kenya til fåreavl på Thyholm," clipping from unidentified newspaper, dated July 5, 1983, KVP.

143. kate+bodil, "Afrikaneren skal hjælpe indianeren."

144. Josine des Cressonières to Gui Bonsiepe, June 30, 1970, ICSID Archive, DES/ICD/6/4/11.

145. Tania Messell, "Contested Development: ICSID's Design Aid and Environmental Policy in the 1970s," in *The Culture of Nature in the History of Design*, ed. Kjetil Fallan (London: Routledge, 2019), 132.

146. Nathan Shapira, "An Outline of Goals for the Design for Developing Countries Commission of the International Council of Industrial Design Societies," May 1970, ICSID Archive, DES/ICD/6/4/5; Josine des Cressonières to Nathan Shapira, February 18, 1971, ICSID Archive, DES/ICD/6/4/11.

147. Fernández, "The Origins of Design Education," 10.

148. Gui Bonsiepe to Josine des Cressonières, November 17, 1970, ICSID Archive, DES/ICD/6/4/11.

149. Josine des Cressonières to Nathan Shapira, June 1, 1971, ICSID Archive, DES/ICD/6/4/11.

150. Des Cressonières to Bonsiepe, June 30, 1970.

151. Nathan Shapira, "Design in Developing Countries. Meetings Organized by ICSID's Working Group No. 4, 'Developing Countries,' Seventh Congress, International Council of Societies of Industrial Design (ICSID), Ibiza (Spain) October 14–16, 1971," ICSID Archive, DES/ICD/6/4/2.

152. Nathan Shapira to Henri Viénot, December 30, 1971, ICSID Archive, DES/ICD/6/4/7.

153. Henri Viénot to Rolf Middelboe, November 24, 1971, ICSID Archive, DES/ICD/6/4/11.

154. Barbro Kulvik-Siltavuori to Henri Viénot, November 6, 1972, ICSID Archive, DES/ICD/6/4/11.

155. The Design Society of Kenya to ICSID, IDSA, ADI, et al., October 19, 1972; Loloshy S. Sagaaf and Amrik S. Kalsi to Nathan Shapira, January 5, 1973, ICSID Archive, DES/ICD/6/4/11.

156. Henri Viénot to Nathan Shapira, November 15, 1972, ICSID Archive, DES/ICD/6/4/11; Josine des Cressonnières to Gui Bonsiepe, January 15, 1973, ICSID Archive, DES/ICD/6/4/3.

157. Henri Viénot to Paul Hogan, February 26, 1973; Carl Auböck to Paul Hogan, October 30, 1973; Paul Hogan to Carl Auböck, November 7, 1973; Carl Auböck to Nathan Shapira, December 17, 1973, ICSID Archive, DES/ICD/6/4/7.

158. Paul Hogan to Nathan Shapira, September 22, 1972, ICSID Archive, DES/ICD/6/4/7.

159. Miles, *Selby Mvusi*, 41.

160. Henri Viénot to Paul Hogan, June 25, 1973, ICSID Archive, DES/ICD/6/4/3.

161. "Minutes of Extraordinary Meeting of ICSID Working Group IV Held at UNIDO Headquarters, Vienna, June 4–6, 1973," ICSID Archive, DES/ICD/6/4/2.

162. Des Cressonnières to Bonsiepe, January 15, 1973.

163. Gui Bonsiepe, "Development through Design. A Working Paper Prepared for UNIDO at the Request of ICSID," April 18, 1973, ICSID Archive, DES/ICD/6/4/1.

164. Gui Bonsiepe, "Design for Industrialization," report of the consensus of opinion of an Expert Group Meeting in Vienna in June 1973 between ICSID's Working Group IV Design in Developing Countries and UNIDO, dated September 29, 1975, ICSID Archive, DES/ICD/6/4/1.

165. "Proposals for UNIDO Midterm Plan Prepared by ICSID Working Group IV (Developing Countries). Meeting of ICSID Board, Brussels—17 November, 1974," ICSID Archive, DES/ICD/6/4/2.

166. "Minutes of ICSID Working Group IV (Developing Countries) Mottram Hall, Mottram St. Andrew, England—June 29–30th, 1974," ICSID Archive, DES/ICD/6/4/2.

167. John Turpin, "The Irish Design Reform Movement of the 1960s," *Design Issues* 3, no. 1 (1986): 16.

168. Underscoring the close bonds within this iteration of Working Group IV, Yran dedicated his professional autobiography to Papanek—"in respectful disagreement": Knut Yran, *A Joy Forever: Knut Yran Talks about Design in Industry* (Melbourne: Industrial Design Institute of Australia, 1980), 14.

169. Victor Papanek to Kristian Vedel, March 21, 1975, KVP.

170. Gui Bonsiepe to Carl Auböck, December 5, 1973, ICSID Archive, DES/ICD/6/4/11.

171. Mark Brutton, "Third World Cautions," *Design*, no. 322 (October 1975): 56.

172. "Minutes of ICSID Working Group IV (Developing Countries), June 29–30th, 1974."

173. The other new members were V. N. Adarkar (India), Eduardo Joselvitch (Argentina), Goroslav Keller (Yugoslavia), and Oscar Mapua (Philippines): "Working Group IV (Developing Countries), Report for Session 1973–1975," ICSID Archive, DES/ICD/6/4/11.

174. Kristian Vedel to Knut Yran, August 3, 1975, KVP.

175. Carl Auböck to Amrik Kalsi, December 16, 1975, ICSID Archive, DES/ICD/6/4/11.

176. "Development and environment" was one of the main themes of the Stockholm conference, and it was a coalition of delegates from the global South who successfully insisted that the new organization's headquarters should be in Nairobi: Peter Stone, *Did We Save the World at Stockholm?* (London: Earth Island, 1973), 143.

177. Amrik Kalsi to Paul Hogan and Working Group IV, June 24, 1975, KVP.

178. Victor Margolin, "Design for Development: Towards a History," *Design Studies* 28, no. 2 (2007): 112.

179. "Minutes of ICSID Working Group IV (Developing Countries), June 29–30th, 1974."

180. Paul Hogan to Sarah Langton-Lockton, November 26, 1975, ICSID Archive, DES/ICD/6/4/11.

181. Paul Hogan to Josine des Cressonnières, August 8, 1975, ICSID Archive, DES/ICD/6/4/11; "Minutes of Meeting of ICSID Working Group IV held at Eindhoven, Netherlands—July 18–19, 1975," ICSID Archive, DES/ICD/6/4/2.

182. "Minutes of ICSID Working Group IV (Developing Countries), June 29–30th, 1974."

183. "Minutes of Meeting of ICSID Working Group IV—July 18–19, 1975."

184. Carl Auböck, "The Role of Industrial Design in the Industrialisation of Developing Countries," paper delivered at the United Nations Conference on Science and Technology for Development, Vienna, 1977, ICSID Archive, DES/ICD/6/4/9.

185. Julian Bicknell and Liz McQuiston, eds., *Design for Need: The Social Contribution of Design* (Oxford: Pergamon Press, 1977).

186. "Working Group IV (Developing Countries), Report for Session 1973–1975," ICSID Archive, DES/ICD/6/4/11.

187. Yran, *A Joy Forever*, 73. The jury included a representative from UNIDO.

188. "Minutes of Meeting of ICSID Working Group IV held at ICSID Secretariat, 45 Avenue Legrand, Brussels, Thursday, 7 April, 1976," ICSID Archive, DES/ICD/6/4/2.

189. "Working Group IV (Developing Countries), Report for Session 1973–1975."

190. Paul Hogan to Carl Auböck, July 27, 1976, ICSID Archive, DES/ICD/6/4/11.

191. "Minutes of Meeting of ICSID Working Group IV—July 18–19, 1975."

192. Auböck, "The Role of Industrial Design in the Industrialisation of Developing Countries."

193. "Ahmedabad Declaration on Industrial Design for Development," January 14–24, 1979, KVP.

194. Carl Auböck, "ICSID Background Paper: The Role of Industrial Design in the Industrialisation of Developing Countries," undated (1978), KVP.

195. "Ahmedabad Declaration on Industrial Design for Development."

196. "Ahmedabad Declaration on Industrial Design for Development."

197. For a relevant critique, see Sulfikar Amir, "Rethinking Design Policy in the Third World," *Design Issues* 20, no. 4 (2004): 72.

198. Chatterjee, "Design in India," 6; Margolin, "Design for Development," 115; Singanapalli Balaram, "Design in India: The Importance of the Ahmedabad Declaration," *Design Issues* 25, no. 4 (2009): 61.

199. Messell, "Contested Development," 131–146.

200. Teresa Hayter, *Aid as Imperialism* (Harmondsworth: Penguin, 1971).

201. Arturo Escobar, *Designs for the Pluriverse: Radical Interdependence, Autonomy, and the Making of Worlds* (Durham, NC: Duke University Press, 2018), 59.

202. Mahmoud Keshavarz, "Violent Compassions: Humanitarian Design and the Politics of Borders," *Design Issues* 36, no. 4 (2020): 27.

203. Thorsten Borring Olesen and Jan Pedersen, "On the Side of the Angels: Altruism in Danish Development Aid 1960–2005," *European Review of History/Revue européenne d'histoire* 17, no. 6 (2010): 890.

204. Kalsi, "A New Design Education in Kenya," 83.

205. Felicity D. Scott, "'Talking Teacher': Radio, Television, and the Oral Channel," in *Victor Papanek: The Politics of Design*, ed. Mateo Kries, Amelie Klein, and Alison J. Clarke (Weil am Rhein: Vitra Design Museum, 2018), 53.

206. Victor Papanek, "Design in Developing Countries 1950–1985: A Summing Up," *Art Libraries Journal* 11, no. 2 (1986): 44.

207. Papanek, "Design in Developing Countries 1950–1985," 45.

208. Victor Papanek, "Reflektioner over Danmark," *BID Danskform* 45, no. 1 (January 1974): 14 (emphasis in original). Papanek himself took this to heart, as he later acknowledged: "While we fought against colonialism and exploitation, I and others failed to appreciate how much we could *learn* in the places we had set out to teach." Victor Papanek, *Design for the Real World: Human Ecology and Social Change*, 2nd ed. (London: Thames and Hudson, 1984), xvii (preface to the second edition).

209. "Meeting of ICSID Working Group IV (Developing Countries), Essen Werden, Germany, October 17 '74," ICSID Archive, DES/ICD/6/4/11.

210. Recently published as Selby Mvusi, "Design Development in Africa Today: Problems and Programming" (1964), in Miles, *Selby Mvusi*, Companion CD: Academic Papers, 6.

211. Cedric G. Johnson, "The Urban Precariat, Neoliberalization, and the Soft Power of Humanitarian Design," *Journal of Developing Societies* 27, no. 3–4 (2011): 448.

212. Knut Yran, interviewed (with the rest of ICSID's Working Group IV) in Brutton, "Third World Cautions," 57.

213. Jamer Hunt, "Very, Very Strange Things: Victor Papanek and the Anxiety of Aesthetics," in Kries, Klein, and Clarke, *Victor Papanek: The Politics of Design*, 190.

214. Mahmoud Keshavarz in Tristan Schultz, Danah Abdulla, Ahmed Ansari, Ece Canli, Mahmoud Keshavarz, Matthew Kiem, Luiza Prado de O. Martins, and Pedro J. S. Vieira de Oliveira, "What Is at Stake with Decolonizing Design? A Roundtable," *Design and Culture* 10, no. 1 (2018): 92.

215. Danah Abdulla in Schultz et al., "What Is at Stake with Decolonizing Design?," 90.

216. Vedel, "Foredrag vedr. Udviklingslande."

217. Kristian Vedel, manuscript for paper delivered at a symposium on the use of East African timbers in furniture manufacture at Kenya Polytechnic, December 14, 1970, KVP.

218. Paul Hogan, "Report of Working Group IV Design for Development," report presented to the General Assembly held in Tokyo in connection with the eighth ICSID congress in Kyoto, October 8, 1973, ICSID Archive, DES/ICD/6/4/5.

219. Hogan, "Report of Working Group IV."

220. Karen Vedel in conversation with the author, August 21, 2019.

221. See, e.g., Elizabeth Tunstall, "Decolonizing Design Innovation: Design Anthropology, Critical Anthropology, and Indigenous Knowledge," in *Design Anthropology: Theory and Practice*, ed. Wendy Gunn, Ton Otto, and Rachel Charlotte Smith (London: Bloomsbury, 2013), 232–250; Amollo Ambole, "Rethinking Design Making and Design Thinking in Africa," *Design and Culture* 12, no. 3 (2020): 331–350.

222. Escobar, *Designs for the Pluriverse*, 62.

223. Arne Næss, *Økologi, samfunn og livsstil: Utkast til en økosofi* (Oslo: Universitetsforlaget, 1974), 143.

224. Hartvig Sætra, "Jamvektssamfunnet er ikkje noko urtete-selskap," *Ny Tid*, August 1, 1979, 10 (emphasis in original).

225. Erik Dammann, *The Future in Our Hands* (Oxford: Pergamon Press, 1979), 108.

226. Sigmund Kvaløy and Liv Møller-Christensen to The Honorable State Minister for Health, His Majesty's Government of Nepal, dated June 12, 1980; Sigmund Kvaløy to NORAD, dated March 16, 1981, Nasjonalbiblioteket. Ubehandlet 185: Arne Næss: Arkiv. 185: 9, Økologi og dypøkologi.

227. Personal communication with Sultan Somjee, February 1, 2020.

CHAPTER 4

1. Barbara Ward and René Dubos, *Only One World: The Care and Maintenance of a Small Planet* (New York: W. W. Norton, 1972), 144.

2. This chapter is in part based on archival research, interviews, and preliminary studies conducted by Ida K. Lie. I am most grateful to Ida for so generously making this material available to me, and for encouraging my development of it.

3. Håkan Agnsäter, *Affischerna från den svenska alternativrörelsen 1967–1979* (Stockholm: Ordalaget Bokförlag, 2013), 96–97.

4. Peter Gwynne, "The World View in Stockholm," *Newsweek*, June 12, 1972, 16.

5. Andrew Jamison, "Greening the City: Urban Environmentalism from Mumford to Malmö," in *Urban Machinery: Inside Modern European Cities*, ed. Mikael Hård and Thomas J. Misa (Cambridge, MA: MIT Press, 2008), 289.

6. "demonstration," in *Oxford Dictionary of English*, 3rd ed. (Oxford: Oxford University Press, 2010), retrieved December 2, 2020, https://www-oxfordreference-com.ezproxy.uio.no/view/10.1093/acref/9780199571123.001.0001/m_en_gb0215720.

7. Alastair Fuad-Luke, *Design Activism: Beautiful Strangeness for a Sustainable World* (London: Earthscan, 2009), xxi.

8. Kjell Östberg, "Sweden and the Long '1968': Break or Continuity?," *Scandinavian Journal of History* 33, no. 4 (2008): 342.

9. Anders V. Munch, Vibeke Riisberg, and Lene Kiærbye Pedersen, "Harmful or Useless? Victor Papanek and the Student Rebellion at Danish Design Schools 1967–1976," in *Lessons to Learn? Past Design Experiences and Contemporary Design Practices: Proceedings of the ICDHS 12th International Conference on Design History and Design Studies*, ed. Fedja Vukić and Iva Kostešić (Zagreb: UPI2M Books, 2020), 137–147.

10. Ida Kamilla Lie, "'Make Us More Useful to Society!' The Scandinavian Design Students' Organization (SDO) and Socially Responsible Design, 1967–1973," *Design and Culture* 8, no. 3 (2016): 327–361.

11. Bo Teglund, "'Vi kommer tillbake i jul.' Alla åldrar gillade alternativet," *Dagens Nyheter*, December 16, 1968.

12. See, e.g., Anna-Maria Hagerfors, "Vallfärd till Kungsans almar," *Dagens Nyheter*, May 13, 1972; "Slaget om almerna blev stor folkfest," *Dagens Nyheter*, May 13, 1971.

13. Thordis Arrhenius, "Preservation and Protest: Counterculture and Heritage in 1970s Sweden," *Future Anterior* 7, no. 2 (2010): 106–123.

14. "Konferensen—teater utan vietnamdebatt," *Dagens Nyheter*, June 3, 1972.

15. "Palmes tal om miljökrig utöser 'djup oro' i USA," *Dagens Nyheter*, June 7, 1972. For a brief discussion of ecocidal warfare as a product of design, see Kjetil Fallan and Finn Arne Jørgensen, "Environmental Histories of Design: Towards a New Research Agenda," *Journal of Design History* 30, no. 2 (2017): 110–111.

16. Felicity D. Scott, *Outlaw Territories: Environments of Insecurity/Architectures of Counterinsurgency* (New York: Zone Books, 2016), 172–175.

17. Russell E. Train, chairman of the United States delegation, cited in Gladwin Hill, "U.S., at U.N. Parley on Environment, Rebukes Sweden for 'Politicizing' Talks," *New York Times*, June 8, 1972.

18. "Palmes tal om miljökrig utöser 'djup oro' i USA"; "USA till motattack: Skarp protest mot Palmes tal," *Dagens Nyheter*, June 8, 1972.

19. *Report of the United Nations Conference on the Human Environment* (New York: United Nations, 1973), 37, accessed October 9, 2020, https://digitallibrary.un.org/record/523249?ln=en.

20. Eric Paglia, "Not a Proper Crisis," *Anthropocene Review* 2, no. 3 (2015): 255.

21. *Report of the United Nations Conference on the Human Environment*, 37; "Två flyglaster USA-aktivister till miljömötet," *Dagens Nyheter*, May 27, 1972.

22. Gabriele Oropallo, "Making or Unmaking the Environment: The Role of Envisioning in the History of Sustainable Design," PhD thesis, University of Oslo, 2017, 86–87.

23. Peter Stone, *Did We Save the World at Stockholm?* (London: Earth Island, 1973), 44.

24. Friedel Ungeheuer, "Environment: Woodstockholm," *Time*, June 19, 1972.

25. "The Tale of the Not So White Bicycles," *Forum: Environment Is Politics*, June 6, 1972.

26. Friends of the Earth (Amory Lovins, Michael Denny, and Graham Searle), *The Stockholm Conference: Only One Earth. An Introduction to the Politics of Survival* (London: Earth Island, 1972), 105.

27. Gary Snyder, "Mother Earth: Her Whales," from *Turtle Island* (New York: New Directions, 1974). Copyright 1974 by Gary Snyder. Reprinted by permission of New Directions Publishing Corp.

28. Björn Berglund, "Miljögrupper misstror FN: Syftet gott—men resultatet?," *Dagens Nyheter*, June 2, 1972.

29. Barry Weisberg, "The Browning of Stockholm: America Takes Its Ecology Show Abroad," *Ramparts*, September 1972, 34.

30. Stone, *Did We Save the World at Stockholm?*, 47.

31. Elisabeth Wettergren interviewed in Erik Centerwall and John Lambert, "A Matter of Words," *Forum: Environment Is Politics*, June 6, 1972.

32. Axel Wannag, "Inntrykk og refleksjoner fra Miljøforum," *Norsk natur* 8, no. 4 (1972): 98.

33. Colophon, *Forum: Environment Is Politics*, June 6, 1972.

34. "Livets Forum räddar oss vid storpublik," *Dagens Nyheter*, June 1, 1972; Björn Berglund, "Stort program i Folkets Forum tar Miljöforums paradnummer," *Dagens Nyheter*, May 19, 1972.

35. Robert J. Bazell, "Human Environment Conference: The Rush for Influence," *Science* 174, no. 4007 (1971): 391.

36. Stone, *Did We Save the World at Stockholm?*, 66.

37. Groups affiliated with the People's Forum included: De förenade FNL-grupperna, Stockholms Afrikagrupp, Vänsterpartiet kommunisterna, Svenska kvinnors vänsterförbund, Palestinagruppen i Stockholm, Eritreagruppen, Antidroggruppen, Alternativ stad, Stadsmiljögruppen, Arbetsgruppen Front mot avfolkningen, Energigruppen i Symbios, Projektgruppen Kapitalism och miljöförstöring, Kommunistiska förbundet marxist-leninisterna, Förbundet kommunist, Revolutionära marxistiska förbundet, Socialistiska läkare, Socialistiska tekniker, Moungruppen i Norge, Svensk-kinesiska vänskapsförbundet, UBV (Latinamerikagrupperna), PowWow, and National Indian Brotherhood. Björn Berglund, "Miljövård är tusen saker. Det gjör splittringen stor," *Dagens Nyheter*, June 4, 1972.

38. "Folkets Forum—ett oberoende alterativ till FNs miljökonferens," press release, retrieved October 12, 2020, http://www.folkrorelser.org/Stockholm1972/dokument/pressmedd-FF-oberoende-alt.PDF (underlining in original).

39. Eva Hernbäck and Rebecka Tarschys, "'Lita inte på FN-konferensen.' Alternativ vecka om försummelserna," *Dagens Nyheter*, June 30, 1972.

40. "FN-konferensen i dag," *Dagens Nyheter*, June 11, 1972.

41. "Folkets Forum—ett oberoende alterativ till FNs miljökonferens."

42. "Två flyglaster USA-aktivister til miljömötet"; Weisberg, "The Browning of Stockholm," 38. The Point Foundation built on Brand's profit from the *Whole Earth Catalog*. The Kaplan Foundation was an educational fund that in the 1960s had been accused of being a conduit for the CIA.

43. Weisberg, "The Browning of Stockholm," 38.

44. Berglund, "Miljövård är tusen saker."

45. Ross Gelbspan and David Gurin, "Woodstockholm '72: The Subject Is Survival," *Village Voice*, May 11, 1972, 29, 34.

46. Åsa Moberg, "Miljövårdskonferensen, Skarpnäck och polisen," *Aftonbladet*, June 1, 1972.

47. Gelbspan and Gurin, "Woodstockholm '72," 29; Ungeheuer, "Environment: Woodstockholm"; Scott, *Outlaw Territories*, 118.

48. Berglund, "Miljövård är tusen saker."

49. "Larmrapport om Skarpnäck: Sexorgier med småflickor i tälten!," *Expressen*, June 9, 1972; "Russinkalas i knarkdebatt," *Dagens Nyheter*, June 11, 1972.

50. Andrew G. Kirk, *Counterculture Green: The Whole Earth Catalog and American Environmentalism* (Lawrence: University Press of Kansas, 2007), 188.

51. Weisberg, "The Browning of Stockholm," 39.

52. Wade Rowland, *The Plot to Save the World: The Life and Times of the Stockholm Conference on the Human Environment* (Toronto: Clarke, Irwin, 1973), 124.

53. Rowland, *The Plot to Save the World*, 124; Scott, *Outlaw Territories*, 120; Weisberg, "The Browning of Stockholm," 39.

54. Berglund, "Miljövård är tusen saker"; Scott, *Outlaw Territories*, 134, 177–178.

55. "Livets Forum räddar oss vid storpublik." *Forum*, the Environment Forum's newspaper, also featured a favorable article on the Hog Farm and their camp at Skarpnäck: "Doing Not Talking," *Forum: Environment Is Politics*, June 6, 1972.

56. "Russinkalas i knarkdebatt."

57. "Kostfackskolan 1971–1972: Årsredogörelse för verksamhetsåret 1971–1972," 8, Konstfacks arkiv, Årsredovisningar 1960–1979, BIB: 2 (hereafter cited as KA).

58. Agnsäter, *Affischerna från den svenska alternativrörelsen*, 99–100.

59. Poster featured in Håkan Agnsäter, *Affischerna 1967–1979*, online exhibition, retrieved October 13, 2020, https://affischerna.se/progg_poster/hall-naturen-ren-doskalle/?order=&y=1972.

60. Poster featured in Agnsäter, *Affischerna 1967–1979*, online exhibition.

61. Eva Trolin cited in Agnsäter, *Affischerna från den svenska alternativrörelsen*, 97.

62. Finis Dunaway, *Seeing Green: The Use and Abuse of American Environmental Images* (Chicago: University of Chicago Press, 2016), 3

63. Agnsäter, *Affischerna från den svenska alternativrörelsen*, 102.

64. "Nystädat varje dag," *Dagens Nyheter*, May 31, 1972.

65. "Det är censur—inte miljövård," *Dagens Nyheter*, June 7, 1972.

66. "Nu har polisen kommit till stan," *Dagens Nyheter*, June 2, 1972; Berglund, "Miljövård är tusen saker"; "Bråkiga miljödemonstranter buras in—på Långholmen!," *Aftonbladet*, June 1, 1972; Gwynne, "The World View in Stockholm," 16.

67. Agnsäter, *Affischerna från den svenska alternativrörelsen*, 101.

68. Östberg, "Sweden and the Long '1968,'" 342–343.

69. Bengt Olvång, *Våga se! Svensk konst 1945–1980* (Göteborg: Författarförlaget, 1983), 99.

70. Kerstin Abram-Nilsson interviewed in "Moment: konstrond bland klotter och affischer på toaletter, T-banestationer och Moderna museet," Sveriges Radio, TV1 (SVT1), November 2, 1971.

71. Östberg, "Sweden and the Long '1968,'" 343.

72. Håkan Nyberg, Alf Linder, Channah Bankier, and Helena Henschen, "Borgerlig bildkonst," *Clarté* 41, no. 1 (1968): 26–30.

73. Olvång, *Våga se!*, 96.

74. Torsten Bergmark, "Affischen visar vägen," *Dagens Nyheter*, April 4, 1968.

75. Personal communication with Eva Trolin, November 12, 2017.

76. "Kostfackskolan 1971–1972," 8–9.

77. Carl Gunnar Edanius, "-Vi vil göra nogot om miljövård också," *Tidsignal*, no. 41 (1968): 5.

78. Tom Hedqvist, "Kläderseminariet," *Modern textil* (1968, no. 10).

79. "Kostfackskolan 1971–1972," 11.

80. "Kostfackskolan 1972–1973: Årsredogörelse för verksamhetsåret 1972–1973," 14, KA, BIB: 2.

81. "Kostfackskolan 1975–1976: Årsredogörelse för verksamhetsåret 1975–1976," 9, KA, BIB: 2.

82. Telephone interview with Varis Bokalders, October 13, 2017. According to Bokalders, the position itself was created as a direct response to the increased interest in environmental issues caused by the UN Conference.

83. *PowWow Newletter*, no. 1 (February 1972), Arbetarrörelsens arkiv och bibliote SE/ARAB/1238/1, retrieved October 22, 2020, https://stockholmskallan.stockholm.se/skblobs/fo/f00a81dc -dc15-4ff1-b550-27734352a5a7.pdf.

84. Gun Leander, "Alternativ buss på stan," *Dagens Nyheter*, June 1, 1972.

85. Berglund, "Stort program i Folkets Forum."

86. "Alternativa sight-seeings," Planning document by Alternative City, May 20, 1972, retrieved October 22, 2020, http://www.folkrorelser.org/Stockholm1972/dokument/sight-seeing-organi sationen.PDF.

87. Like the official UN bicycles, Alternative City's operation was inspired by the white bike stunt organized by the Provo group in Amsterdam in 1965.

88. Alternative City's bike-group, "Love letter to You from Us," unaddressed/open letter to the UN conference organizers, undated (1972), retrieved October 22, 2020, http://www .folkrorelser.org/Stockholm1972/dokument/love-letter-to-un-bikes.PDF.

89. Alternative City's bike-group, "Love letter to You from Us."

90. "Trådbuss visas på Sergels torg," *Dagens Nyheter*, June 3, 1972.

91. Mary Jean Haley, ed., *Open Options: A Guide to Stockholm's Alternative Environmental Conferences* (Sala: Ågren & Holmbergs, 1972), 18; 39.

92. PowWow's choice of name must be understood in light of the sometimes contested infatuation of many environmentalists at the time with Native American culture. This is discussed at length in Daniel Belgrad, *The Culture of Feedback: Ecological Thinking in Seventies America* (Chicago: University of Chicago Press, 2019).

93. Ward and Dubos, *Only One World*, 220.

94. *PowWow Newletter*, no. 1 (February 1972).

95. *PowWow Newletter*, no. 1 (February 1972).

96. Arne Næss, "The Shallow and the Deep, Long-Range Ecology Movement. A Summary," *Inquiry* 16, no. 1–4 (1973): 95–100.

97. "Alternative Forums," *Dagens Nyheter*, June 6, 1972.

98. Kim West, "The Exhibitionary Complex: Exhibition, Apparatus, and Media from Kulturhuset to the Centre Pompidou, 1963–1977," PhD thesis, Södertörn University, 2017, 31, 189.

99. West, "The Exhibitionary Complex," 249; Peter Harper, "Stockholm—POWOW Acts as UN Evades the Issue," *Undercurrents*, no. 2 (Summer 1972): 5–6.

100. Peter Harper in conversation with Simon Sadler, "The Exhibition of People's Technology, 1972," *Digital Culture and Society* 6, no. 1 (2020): 176.

101. Harper in conversation with Sadler, "The Exhibition of People's Technology, 1972," 163.

102. PowWow's exhibition program leaflet cited in Pär Stolpe, "Filialen vid Moderna Museet i Stockholm 1/3 1971–1/7 1973: Rapporten," 81, project report, Moderna Museet, 1974.

103. Stolpe, "Filialen vid Moderna Museet."

104. Scott, *Outlaw Territories*, 210–215.

105. PowWow's exhibition program leaflet cited in Stolpe, "Filialen vid Moderna Museet," 80–81.

106. West, "The Exhibitionary Complex," 250.

107. Scott, *Outlaw Territories*, 215.

108. Peter Harper and Godfrey Boyle, eds., *Radical Technology* (London: Wildwood House, 1976). The same year, Boyle joined the Open University's Department of Design and Innovation and the Energy and Environment Research Unit.

109. Nevertheless, *ARARAT*'s art world credentials were further boosted when a version of the exhibition was shown as Sweden's contribution to the Biennale di Venezia later that year.

110. ARARAT Working Group, "ARARAT: Alternative Research in Architecture, Art and Technology," in *Finlandia, Svezia, Norvegia: Biennale di Venezia '76*, ed. Björn Springfeldt (Venice: Biennale di Venezia, 1976), 13.

111. See, e.g., Marisol de la Cadena and Mario Blaser, eds., *A World of Many Worlds* (Durham, NC: Duke University Press, 2018).

112. Birgitta Nyblom, "USA-satsning på solenergin föder husmode," *Dagens Nyheter*, May 27, 1975.

113. Christina Pech, *Arkitektur och motstånd: Om sökandet efter alternativ i svensk arkitektur 1970–1980* (Göteborg: Makadam, 2011), 100–101.

114. Interview with Bokalders, October 13, 2017.

115. In addition to these, the core group counted photographer Thomas Brandt, engineers Ahti Lemminkäinen and Bertil Jonsson, art historian and cultural heritage officer Bo Lagercrantz, and author Monica Nordenström.

116. Tomas Dalström, "Jan Öqvist: Möten, ekosofi och omtanke," *Meetings*, no. 43 (April 2011).

117. Pech, *Arkitektur och motstånd*, 100–101.

118. Interview with Bokalders, October 13, 2017.

119. Paul Downton, *Ecopolis: Architecture and Cities for a Changing Climate* (Dordrecht: Springer, 2009), 155.

120. Interview with Bokalders, October 13, 2017.

121. Sandy Halliday, *Sustainable Construction* (Oxford: Butterworth-Heinemann, 2008), 13.

122. Birgitta Nyblom, "Tolv Studerar Solhus i USA," *Dagens Nyheter*, March 19, 1975; Nyblom, "USA-satsning på solenergin föder husmode."

123. Hans Nordenström, "Förord," in *Byggande, energi och ekologi: Forskning och projekt. Rapport från en resa i USA*, ed. Monica Nordenström, Egil Öfverholm, and Hans Nordenström (Stockholm: Statens råd för byggnadsforskning, 1975), 9–10.

124. Nordenström, Öfverholm, and Nordenström, *Byggande, energi och ekologi*, 35–36, 48–58, 106–108, 118–122, 288–292.

125. Kirk, *Counterculture Green*, 144–145.

126. Andrew G. Kirk, "Alloyed: Countercultural Bricoleurs and the Design Science Revival," in *Groovy Science: Knowledge, Innovation, and American Counterculture*, ed. David Kaiser and W. Patrick McCray (Chicago: University of Chicago Press, 2016), 313–317.

127. The three buildings are discussed at length in Pech, *Arkitektur och motstånd*, 104–117.

128. Pech, *Arkitektur och motstånd*, 103–104. The Ecothèque opened before the exhibition; after the exhibition closed, Varis Bokalders and his colleagues moved to another location with the ambition that it could document and develop some of the experience *ARARAT* had generated: Birgitta Nyblom, "En fabrik för miljörörelsen," *Dagens Nyheter*, February 6, 1977.

129. Lena Andersson, "Verkstad för Noaks barn (och deras föräldrar)," *Dagens Nyheter*, April 3, 1976.

130. "Vinden driver vårt el-verk," *Dagens Nyheter*, March 28, 1976; "Cykel-bussen drivs med muskel-kraft," *Dagens Nyheter*, March 28, 1976.

131. "Kostfackskolan 1975–1976," 15.

132. "Kostfackskolan 1975–1976," 21.

133. "Kostfackskolan 1975–1976," 9; "Konstnärlig återvänding," *Dagens Nyheter*, March 27, 1976.

134. Interview with Bokalders, October 13, 2017.

135. "Konstnärlig återvänding."

136. "Kostfackskolan 1975–1976," 9.

137. Pia Eldin, Synnöve Mork, and Katja Waldén, "Textil konst och formgivning," in *Tanken och handen: Konstfack 150 år*, ed. Gunilla Widengren (Stockholm: Page One Publishing, 1994), 336.

138. Mah-Jong cited in Salka Hallström Bornold, *Det är rätt att göra uppror: Mah-Jong 1966–1977* (Stockholm: Modernista, 2003), 115.

139. Bornold, *Det är rätt att göra uppror*, 172–183.

140. Kristina Torsson, "Värmeisolerande gardiner på Konstfacks elevutställning," *Dagens Nyheter*, May 17, 1977.

141. Nyblom, "En fabrik för miljörörelsen."

142. Sven Fagerberg, "Araratutställningen öppnad: Mellan posten och byskolan," *Dagens Nyheter*, April 2, 1976.

143. Birgitta Nyholm, "Ararat—avpolitisering i stället for aktivering?," *Dagens Nyheter*, April 30, 1976.

144. Nyholm, "Ararat."

145. James M. Jasper, "The Objects of Political Creativity," in *Design and Political Dissent: Spaces, Visuals, Materialities*, ed. Jilly Traganou (New York: Routledge, 2021), 123.

146. Fuad-Luke, *Design Activism*, 85 (emphasis in original).

147. Catherine Flood and Gavin Grindon, "Introduction," in *Disobedient Objects*, ed. Catherine Flood and Gavin Grindon (London: V&A Publishing, 2014), 20.

148. Flood and Grindon, "Introduction," 8.

149. Jilly Traganou, "Introduction," in Traganou, *Design and Political Dissent*, 10.

150. Oropallo, "Making or Unmaking the Environment," 36.

151. Jamison, "Greening the City," 289.

152. Guy Julier, "From Design Culture to Design Activism," *Design and Culture* 5, no. 2 (2013): 215–236.

153. Stone, *Did We Save the World at Stockholm?*, 134.

154. As such, both the design demonstrators of this chapter and the design philosophers of the next chapter can be said to have promoted the essential transition "from activism to transformative normality," as Ezio Manzini has put it: Ezio Manzini, *Politics of the Everyday* (London: Bloomsbury, 2019), 83.

CHAPTER 5

1. Peter Wessel Zapffe, "Akademisk Fjeldklub" (1955), in Zapffe, *Spøk og alvor: Epistler og leilighetsvers* (Oslo: Gyldendal, 1977), 53.

2. Arne Næss and Inga Bostad, *Inn i filosofien: Arne Næss' ungdomsår* (Oslo: Universitetsforlaget, 2002), 171.

3. Lars Borenius, "Prel schema för Formsemisariet vecka 3–6 1982 (18 jan–12 feb)," December 4, 1981, Konstfacks arkiv, Industridesign—undervisningshandl. och studentarbeten 1981/82, F7DE:6.

4. Personal communication with Selmer's son, Espen R. Collett, July 12, 2019.

5. He would later live briefly in one of the units himself. For a study of Selmer's work, see Elisabeth Tostrup, *Norwegian Wood: The Thoughtful Architecture of Wenche Selmer* (New York: Princeton Architectural Press, 2006).

6. Pauline Madge, "Ecological Design: A New Critique," *Design Issues* 13, no. 2 (1997): 46.

7. Truls Gjefsen, *Arne Næss: Et liv* (Oslo: Cappelen Damm, 2011), 98.

8. Peder Anker, "The Philosopher's Cabin and the Household of Nature," *Ethics, Place and Environment* 6, no. 2 (2003): 138.

9. Arne Næss, *Ecology, Community and Lifestyle: Outline of an Ecosophy*, trans. David Rothenberg (Cambridge: Cambridge University Press, 1989), 93.

10. Arne Næss, "Forord," in Peter Wessel Zapffe, *Barske glæder og andre temaer fra et liv under åpen himmel*, ed. Sigmund Kvaløy (Oslo: Gyldendal, 1969), 7.

11. Peder Anker, *The Power of the Periphery: How Norway Became an Environmental Pioneer for the World* (Cambridge: Cambridge University Press, 2020), 48.

12. Arne Næss, *Tirich Mir: The Norwegian Himalaya Expedition* (London: Hodder and Stoughton, 1950); Arne Næss, *Opp stupet: til østtoppen av Tirich Mir* (Oslo: Gyldendal, 1964).

13. Arne Næss, "Skytsgudinnen Gauri Shankar: Appell om fredning," *Mestre fjellet*, no. 13 (1972): 15; Sigmund Kvaløy, *Økokrise, natur og menneske: En innføring i økofilosofi og økopolitikk* (Oslo: s.n., 1973), 65–88.

14. Andrew Brennan, "Deep Ecology," in *The International Encyclopedia of Ethics*, ed. Hugh Lafollette (Oxford: Wiley-Blackwell, 2013), 1235.

15. Arne Næss, "Some Ethical Considerations with a View to Mountaineering in Norway," *Alpine Journal* 73, no. 317 (1968): 230.

16. Arne Næss, "The Conquest of Mountains: A Contradiction?," *Mountain*, September 1970, 28–29.

17. Arne Næss, "Klatrefilosofiske og biografiske betraktninger," *Mestre fjellet*, no. 22–23 (1976): 15.

18. Næss, "The Conquest of Mountains," 28–29.

19. Nils Faarlund, "A Way Home," in *Wisdom in the Open Air: The Norwegian Roots of Deep Ecology*, ed. Peter Reed and David Rothenberg (Minneapolis: University of Minnesota Press, 1993), 165.

20. Arne Næss, "Modesty and the Conquest of Mountains," in *The Mountain Spirit*, ed. Michael C. Tobias and Harold Drasdo (Woodstock, NY: Overlook Press, 1979), 16.

21. Aldo Leopold, *A Sand County Almanac and Sketches Here and There* (1949; New York: Oxford University Press, 1987), 129; Bill Devall, "The Deep Ecology Movement," *Natural Resources Journal* 20, no. 2 (1980): 309–310.

22. John Seed, Joanna Macy, Pat Fleming, and Arne Naess, *Thinking Like a Mountain: Towards a Council of All Beings* (Philadelphia: New Society Publishers, 1988).

23. Wiebe E. Bijker, *Of Bicycles, Bakelites, and Bulbs: Toward a Theory of Sociotechnical Change* (Cambridge, MA: MIT Press, 1995), 45ff.

24. Nils Faarlund in conversation with the author, September 3, 2020.

25. Nils Faarlund, "Stetind 1966—'tindebestigere' skaper ny giv i naturvernet," in *Arven og gleden—et festskrift til naturen*, ed. Børge Dahle, Finn Wagle, Øystein Dahle, Siri Næss, Nils Faarlund, Aage Jensen, and Sigmund K. Setreng (Trondheim: Tapir akademisk forlag, 2010), 23–25.

26. Satish Kumar, "Sigmund Kvaloy: Let the Rivers Flow," *Resurgence* 13(6/96) (1983): 23–25.

27. Silviya Serafimova, *Ethical Aspects of 20th Century Norwegian Environmental Philosophies* (Sofia: Avangard Prima, 2017), 94.

28. Kvaløy, *Økokrise, natur og menneske*.

29. Erling Amble, Botolv Helleland, Karl G. Høyer, Sigmund Kvaløy, Magne Lindholm, Dag Norling, and Arne Vinje, *Dette bør du vite om EF: Økopolitikk eller EF?* (Oslo: Pax, 1972); Hartvig Sætra, *Den økopolitiske sosialismen* (Oslo: Pax, 1973).

30. Sigmund Kvaløy Setreng, "To økofilosofier i Norge; deres begynnelse og en del til," *Norsk filosofisk tidsskrift* 37, no. 1–2 (2002): 122.

31. Kvaløy, *Økokrise, natur og menneske*, 92, 140–141, 157; Sigmund Kvaløy, "Ecophilosophy and Ecopolitics: Thinking and Acting in Response to the Threats of Ecocatastrophe," *North American Review* 259, no. 2 (1974): 23.

32. Sigmund Kvaløy and Liv Møller-Christensen to The Honorable State Minister for Health, His Majesty's Government of Nepal, dated June 12, 1980; Sigmund Kvaløy to NORAD, dated March 16, 1981; Nasjonalbiblioteket. Ubehandlet 185: Arne Næss: Arkiv. 185: 9 (hereafter cited as NBAN).

33. Turid Horgen, Eyvind Kvaale, Heidrun Rising Ness, Dag Norling, Snorre Skaugen, and Gabor Szilvay, "Og etter oss . . . ," *Byggekunst* 51, no. 3 (1969): 84–87.

34. Peder Anker, "Science as a Vacation: A History of Ecology in Norway," *History of Science* 45, no. 4 (2007): 463; letter from Sigmund Kvaløy, dated June 19, 1969, "to a number of people in the Oslo area, who we believe could be interested in participating in a meeting where new methods of environmental protection, particularly nonviolent protests, will be discussed." Amongst the recipients of the letter were Oslo School of Architecture lecturer Robert Esdaile and his students Snorre Skaugen, Turid Horgen, and Heidrun Rising Ness—all

part of group who organized the exhibition. Horgen, Skaugen, and their fellow student and co-organizer Dag Norling became active members of the *samarbeidsgruppene for natur- og miljøvern* collective. I thank Beata Labuhn for sharing this letter and information.

35. Sigmund Kvaløy, "Mangfold er livsstyrke: Utkast til en økofilosofi," *Byggekunst* 53, no. 4 (1971): 126–127; Sigmund Kvaløy, "Økopolitikk og økofilosofi: Tenkning og handling som svar på trusselen om økososial krise," *Byggekunst* 59, no. 1 (1977): 1–6.

36. Kvaløy, *Økokrise, natur og menneske*.

37. Sigmund Kvaløy, "The Universe Within," *Resurgence*, no. 106 (September/October 1984): 12–21. Testifying to its legacy and continued cultural influence, the Mardøla protest also forms the point of departure for the storyline in Maja Lunde's bestselling novel *The End of the Ocean* (English edition published by Simon & Schuster in 2019).

38. Rune Slagstad, *De nasjonale strateger* (Oslo: Pax, 1998), 467.

39. Anker, "Science as a Vacation," 465.

40. Arne Næss, *Økologi og filosofi: Et økosofisk arbeidsutkast. Tredje preliminære utgave* (Oslo: Universitetsforlaget, 1972).

41. Felicity D. Scott, *Outlaw Territories: Environments of Insecurity/Architectures of Counterinsurgency* (New York: Zone Books, 2016), 188–197.

42. Kristian Bjørkdahl, "Dommedagsdokumentet: *Limits to Growth* og verdens grafiske undergang," in *Kollaps: På randen av fremtiden*, ed. Peter Bjerregaard and Kyrre Kverndokk (Oslo: Dreyer, 2018), 163; 178.

43. Arne Næss, "The Use of Normative Ethical and Political Models in Future Research: Five Methodological Rules Concerning Ecosophical Models," paper read in part at the Third World Future Research Conference, Bucharest, September 3–10, 1972, NBAN 185: 9.

44. Johan Galtung, "Økologi og klassekamp," *Samtiden* (1973, no. 2): 65–83.

45. Peder Anker, "Deep Ecology in Bucharest," *The Trumpeter* 24, no. 1 (2008): 57–58.

46. Arne Næss, "The Shallow and the Deep, Long-Range Ecology Movement. A Summary," *Inquiry* 16, no. 1–4 (1973): 95–100.

47. Næss, "The Shallow and the Deep," 95.

48. Næss, "The Shallow and the Deep," 95–98.

49. Næss, "The Shallow and the Deep," 99.

50. Næss, "The Shallow and the Deep," 96.

51. Kvaløy, *Økokrise, natur og menneske*, 26–38.

52. Næss, "The Shallow and the Deep," 97–98.

53. E. F. Schumacher, *Small Is Beautiful: A Study of Economics as if People Mattered* (London: Blond & Briggs, 1973). The affinity between Schumacher's ideas and the deep ecology movement is evident also from the fact that both Kvaløy and Næss were invited to deliver the Schumacher Lecture in Bristol, in 1983 and 1987 respectively. Their lectures were both published in *Resurgence*: Sigmund Kvaløy, "The Universe Within," *Resurgence*, no. 106 (September/October 1984): 12–21; Arne Næss, "The Basics of Deep Ecology," *Resurgence*, no. 126 (January/February 1988): 4–8.

54. "Økologisk grunnlagsforskning og filosofi," bibliography dated 1971, NBAN 185: 9.

55. Næss, "The Shallow and the Deep," 100; Arne Næss, "Den grønne strømning," unpublished article manuscript, undated (c. 1975), NBAN 185: 10.

56. Næss, "The Shallow and the Deep," 99.

57. Næss, *Økologi og filosofi*, 45.

58. Alan Drengson, "Introduction: The Life and Work of Arne Naess: An Appreciative Overview," in *Ecology of Wisdom: Writings by Arne Naess*, ed. Alan Drengson and Bill Devall (Berkeley: Counterpoint, 2008), 32.

59. Siri Næss, "Self-Realization," in *In Sceptical Wonder: Inquiries into the Philosophy of Arne Naess on the Occasion of his 70th Birthday*, ed. Ingemund Gullvåg and Jon Wetlesen (Oslo: Universitetsforlaget, 1982), 280–281.

60. Not to be confused with what Næss himself once denoted as "'Ecosophy D' (D for Devall)," acknowledging that his Californian colleague Bill Devall formulated views that partially diverged from his own: Arne Næss, "Identification as a Source of Deep Ecological Attitudes," in *Deep Ecology*, ed. Michael Tobias (San Diego: Avant Books, 1984), 269, n. 1.

61. Næss, *Økologi og filosofi*, 1.

62. Arne Næss, *Økologi, samfunn og livsstil: Utkast til en økosofi* (Oslo: Universitetsforlaget, 1974), 51.

63. Næss, *Økologi, samfunn og livsstil*, 107.

64. Næss, *Økologi og filosofi*, 93–94. See also Sigmund Kvaløy, "Sammenhengen mellom økonomisk vekst og økologisk likevekt," in *Økologi og økonomisk vekst*, ed. Mimi Lønnum (Oslo: Elingaard, 1973), 38–55.

65. Arturo Escobar, *Designs for the Pluriverse: Radical Interdependence, Autonomy, and the Making of Worlds* (Durham, NC: Duke University Press, 2018), 142.

66. Trygve Haavelmo, "Forurensningsproblemet fra et samfunnsvitenskapelig synspunkt," *Sosialøkonomen* (1971, no. 4): 5–8.

67. Næss, *Økologi og filosofi*, 101–102.

68. Næss, *Økologi og filosofi*, 175.

69. Næss, *Ecology, Community and Lifestyle*, 26.

70. Næss, *Økologi, samfunn og livsstil*, 142 (emphasis in original).

71. Næss, *Økologi, samfunn og livsstil*, 143 (emphasis in original).

72. Lisa S. Banu, "Defining the Design Deficit in Bangladesh," *Journal of Design History* 22, no. 4 (2009): 309–323; Gabriele Oropallo, "People Have the Power: Appropriate Technology and the Implications of Labour-Intensive Making," in *Craft Economies*, ed. Susan Luckman and Nicola Thomas (London: Bloomsbury Academic, 2018), 83–93.

73. Arne Næss, "The Place of Joy in a World of Fact," *North American Review* 258, no. 2 (1973): 57.

74. Næss, *Økologi, samfunn og livsstil*, 174 (emphasis in original).

75. Arne Næss, "Intrinsic Value: Will the Defenders of Nature Please Rise" (1986), in Reed and Rothenberg, *Wisdom in the Open Air*, 77.

76. Victor Papanek, *Design for the Real World: Human Ecology and Social Change* (New York: Pantheon Books, 1971), 19 (emphasis in original).

77. Næss, *Ecology, Community and Lifestyle*, 30.

78. Næss, *Ecology, Community and Lifestyle*, 175.

79. Næss, *Ecology, Community and Lifestyle*, 175.

80. Herbert Simon, *The Sciences of the Artificial* (Cambridge, MA: MIT Press, 1969), 55.

81. Næss, "Identification as a Source of Deep Ecological Attitudes," 261 (emphasis in original).

82. Næss, *Ecology, Community and Lifestyle*, 85, 168 (emphasis in original).

83. Sigmund Kvaløy, "Man, Nature, and Mechanistic Systems," *North American Review* 264, no. 3 (1979): 35–37.

84. Reed and Rothenberg, *Wisdom in the Open Air*.

85. David Rothenberg, *Is It Painful to Think? Conversations with Arne Naess* (Minneapolis: University of Minnesota Press, 1993), 52–54.

86. Gjefsen, *Arne Næss*, 265–269. Næss and Feyerabend had known each other since the mid-1950s and had several published exchanges on the philosophy of science, e.g., Paul Feyerabend, "'Science': The Myth and Its Role in Society," *Inquiry* 18, no. 2 (1975): 167–181, and Arne Næss, "Why Not Science for Anarchists Too? A Reply to Feyerabend," *Inquiry* 18, no. 2 (1975): 183–194.

87. Bess Williamson, *Accessible America: A History of Disability and Design* (New York: New York University Press, 2019), 105.

88. Design professionals on and off campus seized on the People's Park tumults as a unique opportunity to study participatory design and lobbied hard to save the park: Peter Allen, "The End of Modernism? People's Park, Urban Renewal, and Community Design," *Journal of the Society of Architectural Historians* 70, no. 3 (2011): 354–374.

89. "Økologisk grunnlagsforskning og filosofi"; Arne Næss, "The Case against Science," in *Science between Culture and Counter-Culture*, ed. Catharina I. Dessaur (Nijmegen: Dekker & van de Vegt, 1975), 48; George Sessions, "Ecological Consciousness and Paradigm Change," in Tobias, *Deep Ecology*, 32; Bill Devall and George Sessions, *Deep Ecology: Living as if Nature Mattered* (Salt Lake City: Peregrine Smith Books, 1985), 263; Theodore Roszak, *The Making of a Counter Culture: Reflections on the Technocratic Society and Its Youthful Opposition* (Garden City, N.Y.: Doubleday, 1969); Theodore Roszak, *Where the Wasteland Ends: Politics and Transcendence in Postindustrial Society* (Garden City, NY: Doubleday, 1972).

90. Næss, "The Case Against Science," 32.

91. Timothy Stott, "Ludic Pedagogies at the College of Environmental Design, UC Berkeley, 1966 to 1972," in *The Culture of Nature in the History of Design*, ed. Kjetil Fallan (London: Routledge, 2019), 58–71; Timothy Stott, "Systems in Play: Simon Nicholson's Design 12 Course, University of California, Berkeley, 1966," *Journal of Design History* 32, no. 3 (2019): 223–239.

92. Steven V. Roberts, "The Better Earth," *New York Times*, March 29, 1970, 187.

93. Constance M. Lewallen and Steve Seid, eds., *Ant Farm: 1968–1978* (Berkeley: University of California Press, 2004).

94. Alison Isenberg, *Designing San Francisco: Art, Land, and Urban Renewal in the City by the Bay* (Princeton: Princeton University Press, 2017), 331–332.

95. Andrew G. Kirk, *Counterculture Green: The Whole Earth Catalog and American Environmentalism* (Lawrence: University Press of Kansas, 2007), 47–48.

96. Timothy Gray, *Gary Snyder and the Pacific Rim: Creating Countercultural Community* (Iowa City: University of Iowa Press, 2006), 286. Snyder also spoke during the protests at People's Park in Berkeley in 1969, which Næss joined in: see Daniel Belgrad, *The Culture of Feedback: Ecological Thinking in Seventies America* (Chicago: University of Chicago Press, 2019), 32.

97. Most of these groups were represented at the 1970 edition of the International Design Conference in Aspen, titled "Environment by Design," and dominated the dramatic showdown over ecodesign played out there, discussed in the coda below.

98. Greg Castillo, "Counterculture Terroir: California's Hippie Enterprise Zone," in *Hippie Modernism: The Struggle for Utopia*, ed. Andrew Blauvelt (Minneapolis: Walker Art Center, 2015), 100.

99. Næss, *Økologi og filosofi*, 138–139, 152; Næss, *Økologi, samfunn og livsstil*, 56; 92.

100. Harold Glasser, "George Sessions (1938–2016)," *The Trumpeter* 32, no. 1 (2016): 1–4.

101. George Sessions, "Arne Naess & the Union of Theory & Practice," *The Trumpeter* 9, no. 2 (1991): n.p.

102. Glasser, "George Sessions."

103. Arne Næss and George Sessions, "Basic Principles of Deep Ecology," *Ecophilosophy Newsletter*, no. 6 (May 1984): 3–7; Alan Drengson and Bill Devall, "The Deep Ecology Movement: Origins, Development & Future Prospects," *The Trumpeter* 26, no. 2 (2010): 53–54.

104. Devall and Sessions, *Deep Ecology*.

105. Amy Nerenhausen, "Interview with Bill Devall," *Iowa Journal of Literary Studies* 10, no. 1 (1989): 9–16.

106. See, e.g., George Sessions, "Spinoza and Ecophilosophy," *Ecophilosophy Newsletter*, no. 1 (April 1976): 1–5; Bill Devall, "Currents in the River of Environmentalism," *Econews*, April 1977, 9.

107. Alston Chase, "The Great, Green Deep-Ecology Revolution," *Rolling Stone*, no. 498 (April 23, 1987): 64.

108. Warwick Fox, "The Meanings of 'Deep Ecology,'" *The Trumpeter* 7, no. 1 (1990): 49.

109. Tobias, *Deep Ecology*.

110. Næss, "Modesty and the Conquest of Mountains," 13–16.

111. Michael S. Kaye, *The Teacher Was the Sea: The Story of Pacific High School* (New York: Links Books, 1972), 63, 118–119.

112. Larry Busbea, "Paolo Soleri and the Aesthetics of Irreversibility," *Journal of Architecture* 18, no. 6 (2013): 788, 805, n. 23.

113. Paolo Soleri, Michael Tobias, and Michael Gosney, "Survival or Transcendence—A Dialogue with Paolo Soleri," in Tobias, *Deep Ecology*, 288; George Sessions, "Three Major Events for Ecophilosophy," *Ecophilosophy Newsletter*, no. 2 (May 1979): 2.

114. Scott, *Outlaw Territories*, 206.

115. Paolo Soleri, *Arcosanti: An Urban Laboratory?* (San Diego: Avant Books, 1984).

116. Michael Tobias, "Introduction," in Tobias, *Deep Ecology*, viii.

117. Paolo Soleri, *Arcology: The City in the Image of Man* (Cambridge, MA: MIT Press, 1969), 14.

118. Soleri, Tobias, and Gosney, "Survival or Transcendence," 274 (emphasis in original).

119. Næss, *Ecology, Community and Lifestyle*, 175; Næss, "Identification as a Source of Deep Ecological Attitudes," 261.

120. Soleri, Tobias, and Gosney, "Survival or Transcendence," 286.

121. Arne Næss, "Brev fra Kalifornia-Universitetet i Santa Cruz," *Mestre fjellet*, no. 29 (1980): 2; Dolores LaChapelle, "Our Mutual Love of Mountains," *The Trumpeter* 9, no. 2 (1992): 66–67.

122. Joseph E. Taylor III, *Pilgrims of the Vertical: Yosemite Rock Climbers and Nature at Risk* (Cambridge, MA: Harvard University Press, 2010), 133–137.

123. Taylor, *Pilgrims of the Vertical*, 203.

124. Michelle Labrague, "Patagonia, A Case Study in the Historical Development of Slow Thinking," *Journal of Design History* 30, no. 2 (2017): 175–191.

125. Yvon Chouinard, Tom Frost, and Doug Robinson, "A Word," *Chouinard Equipment*, 1972, 2–3. Catalog copy cited in Labrague, "Patagonia," 186.

126. Taylor, *Pilgrims of the Vertical*, 148ff.

127. Næss, "Some Ethical Considerations," 230.

128. Arne Næss, "Bolteklatring," in *Norsk fjellsport 1948*, ed. C. W. Rubenson and Hans H. Røer (Oslo: Grøndahl & Søns forlag, 1948), 116. An even earlier example can be found in Arne Næss, "Nye klatreruter i Jotunheimen og Nord-Norge," in *Den norske turistforenings årbok 1937*, ed. Rolf Lykken, Erling Hauger, and Andreas Backer (Oslo: Grøndahl & Søn, 1937), 191–192.

129. Gjefsen, *Arne Næss*, 277.

130. Dag Kolsrud, "Hvit ambivalens: Fremveksten av sportsklatring på Kolsås," in *Kolsås: Klatreparadis og naturperle*, ed. Dave Durkan, Jon Gangdal, Geir Grimeland, Gunnar Thon, Tore Nossum, Ola Hanche-Olsen, and Egil Fredriksen (Oslo: Kolsås Klatreklubb, 1992), 115.

131. Terry Winograd and Fernando Flores, *Understanding Computers and Cognition: A New Foundation for Design* (Norwood, NJ: Ablex, 1986), xi.

132. Devall and Sessions, *Deep Ecology*, 187.

133. Devall and Sessions, *Deep Ecology*, 188.

134. Nils Faarlund in conversation with the author, September 3, 2020.

135. US Patent No. 3948485A, retrieved April 3, 2021, https://patentimages.storage.googleapis.com/cc/b8/5d/71be5e580045f2/US3948485.pdf; Hermione Cooper, "Chouinard Hexentrics Set 1–11," The Scottish Mountain Heritage Collection, June 22, 2016, retrieved April 3, 2021, http://www.smhc.co.uk/objects_item.asp?item_id=33127.

136. "Meet one of Norrøna's biggest legends," *Norrøna Blog*, November 16, 2020, retrieved April 3, 2021, https://blog.norrona.com/meet-one-of-norronas-biggest-legends-2/.

137. Nils Faarlund, "Klær og redskap for friluftsliv om vinteren," *Mestre fjellet*, no. 29 (1980): 19–20.

138. Nils Faarlund, "Utstyr for Ferden til Gauri Shankar," *Mestre fjellet*, no. 13 (1972): 24.

139. Faarlund, "A Way Home," 166.

140. Næss, *Ecology, Community and Lifestyle*, 180 (emphasis in original).

141. Nils Faarlund, "Klatrestil, utstyrsutvikling og sikkerhetsfilosofi," in *Tindegruppa ved NTH: Granittballett og bratt beregning*, ed. Nils Faarlund, Ralph Høibakk, Jon Bruskeland, Fridjof Thokle Madssen, and Knut Støren (Asker: TG-kameratene, 2014), 42–50.

142. After this "anti-expedition," however, Faarlund would renounce the use of oil-based materials such as nylon in favor of natural fibers, as discussed above. Nils Faarlund in conversation with the author, September 3, 2020.

143. Nils Faarlund, "Utstyr for Ferden til Gauri Shankar"; "Norsk Designcentrum, årsberetning 1969," Norsk Designråds arkiv. Design og arkitektur Norge.

144. Andrew G. Kirk, "Alloyed: Countercultural Bricoleurs and the Design Science Revival," in *Groovy Science: Knowledge, Innovation, and American Counterculture*, ed. David Kaiser and W. Patrick McCray (Chicago: University of Chicago Press, 2016), 313. Baldwin declared and described his love of tools in the essay "One Highly-Evolved Toolbox," in *Soft-Tech: A Co-Evolution Book*, ed. J. Baldwin and Stewart Brand (New York: Penguin; Menlo Park, CA: Portola Institute, 1978), 8–17.

145. Simon Sadler, "Tools of Oneness: Design for Post-Industrial Communities," in *California: Designing Freedom*, ed. Justin McGuirk and Brendan McGetrick (London: Phaidon, 2017), 157–163.

146. David Browne, "The North Face's Epic 1966 Store Opening, Starring Dirt Bags, Hells Angels and the Grateful Dead," *Men's Journal*, accessed April 16, 2019, https://www.mensjournal.com/gear/north-faces-epic-1966-opening-party-featuring-the-grateful-dead-w446385/.

147. Taylor, *Pilgrims of the Vertical*, 188, 274; Labrague, "Patagonia," 178.

148. Labrague, "Patagonia," 188.

149. Taylor, *Pilgrims of the Vertical*, 199–200.

150. Bruce Hamilton to R. Buckminster Fuller, dated December 4, 1975, published on https://www.outinunder.com/documents/1975-december-correspondence-bruce-hamilton-and-bucky-fuller, accessed April 30, 2019; R. Buckminster Fuller to Hap Klopp, dated March 8, 1976, and Klopp's reply dated March 10, 1976, published on https://www.outinunder.com/documents/1976-north-face-now-house-correspondence, accessed May 10, 2019; R. Buckminster Fuller, *Synergetics: Explorations in the Geometry of Thinking* (New York: Macmillan, 1974).

151. Marisa Meltzer, "Patagonia and The North Face: Saving the World—One Puffer Jacket at a Time," *The Guardian*, March 7, 2019, https://www.theguardian.com/business/2017/mar/07/the-north-face-patagonia-saving-world-one-puffer-jacket-at-a-time (accessed May 13, 2019).

152. Arne Næss, *The Selected Works of Arne Naess*, ed. Harold Glasser and Alan Drengson (Dordrecht: Springer, 2005).

153. Taylor, *Pilgrims of the Vertical*, 188.

154. Taylor, *Pilgrims of the Vertical*, 175.

155. Labrague, "Patagonia," 188.

156. Matthew Klingle, "The Nature of Desire: Consumption in Environmental History," in *The Oxford Handbook of Environmental History*, ed. Andrew C. Isenberg (Oxford: Oxford University Press, 2014), 472.

157. Kjetil Fallan and Finn Arne Jørgensen, "Environmental Histories of Design: Towards a New Research Agenda," *Journal of Design History* 30, no. 2 (2017): 108–110.

158. Anker, "The Philosopher's Cabin and the Household of Nature," 131–141.

NOTES TO CHAPTER 5

159. Fallan and Jørgensen, "Environmental Histories of Design," 117.

160. David Wann, *Deep Design: Pathways to a Livable Future* (Washington, DC: Island Press, 1996), xiv.

161. Wann, *Deep Design*, 5.

162. Wann, *Deep Design*, 43.

163. Næss, *Ecology, Community and Lifestyle*, 37.

164. Wann, *Deep Design*, xiii.

165. György Doczi, *The Power of Limits: Proportional Harmonies in Nature, Art, and Architecture* (Boulder, CO: Shambhala Publications, 1981), 127.

166. Næss, *Økologi, samfunn og livsstil*, 18–21.

167. Wann, *Deep Design*, 31.

168. Næss, *Økologi, samfunn og livsstil*, 87–116.

169. Wann, *Deep Design*, xiv-xv.

170. Næss, *Økologi, samfunn og livsstil*, 107.

171. Wann, *Deep Design*, 40.

172. Wann, *Deep Design*, 195.

173. Wann, *Deep Design*, 196.

174. The plans were abandoned due to battery capacity issues, but revived again 20 years later. Arne Næss to Hanne Gilbo dated August 2, 1980, NBAN 185: 9.

175. Hofseth would later lecture on ecology at the National College of Applied Art and Craft, and eventually go on to serve as Deputy Director-General of the Ministry of the Environment. In that capacity he spoke at a 1987 conference in Oslo on the role of appropriate technology in developing countries: Paul Hofseth, "Ecology and Appropriate Technology," in *Mobilizing Appropriate Technology: Papers on Planning Aid Programmes*, ed. Matthew S. Gamser (London: Intermediate Technology Publications, 1988), 36–39.

176. Ezio Manzini, "The Cultural Tools for an Ecology of the Artificial Environment," in *Scandinavian Design 1990–towards 2000: The Challenge of Internationalization Demands and Needs for a New Millennium*, ed. Ulla Tarras-Wahlberg Bøe (Oslo: Scandinavian Design Council, 1990), 46.

177. Victor Papanek, "Lies and Consequences: Industrial Design and Ecology," in Bøe, *Scandinavian Design 1990–towards 2000*, 52, 54 (emphasis in original).

178. Papanek, "Lies and Consequences," 53.

179. Papanek's self-fashioning practice is riddled with apocryphal accounts associating him with the "right" people: Alison J. Clarke, *Victor Papanek: Designer for the Real World* (Cambridge, MA: MIT Press, 2021).

180. The phrase "think globally, act locally" has also been attributed to David Brower, founder of Friends of the Earth, and was used as that organization's slogan.

181. Arne Næss, "The Future of the Industrialised Society," in Bøe, *Scandinavian Design 1990–towards 2000*, 55–58.

182. Tapio Periäinen, introductory remarks to "A Scandinavian Design Council Manifesto on Nature, Ecology, Human Needs and Development for the Future," in Bøe, *Scandinavian Design 1990–towards 2000*, 63.

183. Jens Bernsen, Tapio Periäinen, Stefán Snæbjørnsson, Ulla Tarras-Wahlberg Bøe, and Lennart Lindkvist, "A Scandinavian Design Council Manifesto on Nature, Ecology, Human Needs and Development for the Future," in Bøe, *Scandinavian Design 1990–towards 2000*, 63.

184. Papanek, *Design for the Real World*, xi.

185. Editorial, *The Studio Potter* 19, no. 1 (1990): n.p.

186. Editorial, *The Studio Potter* 19, no. 1 (1990): n.p.

187. Arne Næss, "Deep Ecology and the Potters in Our Planet," *The Studio Potter* 20, no. 2 (1992): 38–39.

188. Arne Næss, "Architecture and Deep Ecology" (1992), *The Trumpeter* 21, no. 2 (2005): 34.

189. Anker, *The Power of the Periphery*, 79–85; Amble et al., *Dette bør du vite om EF*.

190. Peter Reed and David Rothenberg, "Conclusion: Deep Ecology as a Force for Change," in Reed and Rothenberg, *Wisdom in the Open Air*, 238; Martha F. Lee, *Earth First! Environmental Apocalypse* (Syracuse: Syracuse University Press, 1995), 37–38.

191. "Interview with Dave Foreman. Tucson, Arizona, January 4, 1986. By Bill Devall," Manuscript, 30 pp., NBAN 185: 9.

192. Arne Næss to Dave Foreman dated June 23, 1988, NBAN 185: 9; Dave Foreman, ed., *Ecodefense: A Field Guide to Monkeywrenching* (Tucson: Ned Ludd Books, 1985). Næss later claimed that Foreman "has been a disaster for Deep Ecology": Næss quoted in Peder Anker and Nina Witoszek, "The Dream of the Biocentric Community and the Structure of Utopias," *Worldviews: Global Religions, Culture, and Ecology* 2, no. 3 (1998): 243. For a reflection on the monkey wrench as an anthropocenic tool and on monkeywrenching as an environmentalist strategy, see Daegan Miller, "On Possibility: Or, The Monkey Wrench," in *Future Remains: A Cabinet of Curiosities for the Anthropocene*, ed. Gregg Mitman, Marco Armiero, and Robert S. Emmett (Chicago: University of Chicago Press, 2018), 143–148.

193. Sven Erik Skønberg, ed., *Grønn pepper i turbinene: 16 bidrag om miljøkrisen og veiene ut av den. Til ære for Sigmund Kvaløy Setereng* (Oslo: Universitetsforlaget, 1985).

194. Drengson and Devall, "The Deep Ecology Movement," 51; Frank Zelko, *Make It a Green Peace! The Rise of Countercultural Environmentalism* (Oxford: Oxford University Press, 2013), 48; Gjefsen, *Arne Næss*, 98.

195. Erik Dammann, *Fremtiden i våre hender* (Oslo: Gyldendal, 1972).

196. See, e.g., Næss, *Økologi, samfunn og livsstil*, 74–80.

197. The lectures were published in *Ny livsstil: Om folkeaksjonen Fremtiden i våre hender. Med rapport fra åpningsmøtet* (Oslo: Gyldendal, 1974). Næss's lecture was subsequently included in Arne Næss, *Teknikk, pedagogikk og en ny livsstil: En del artikler og foredrag gjennom 25 år* (Oslo: Universitetsforlaget, 1978), 126–129.

198. Erik Dammann, *Kontraster: Beretning om et mangfoldig liv* (Oslo: Aschehoug, 2005), 50.

199. Erik Dammann, "Omsetningskarusellen," *Nye Bonytt* (1971, no. 1): 16–17; 28.

200. Dammann wrote the preface to the Norwegian edition: E. F. Schumacher, *Smått er godt: Om en økonomi der det er folk som teller* (Oslo: Gyldendal, 1977), 5–7.

201. Erik Dammann, "The Future in Our Hands: Its Conceptions, Aims, and Strategies" (1982), in Reed and Rothenberg, *Wisdom in the Open Air*, 224–226.

202. Ramachandra Guha, "Deep Ecology, or Deep Wilderness? An Eastern Critique of Radical American Environmentalism," manuscript, 10 pp., NBAN 185: 9. The quoted passage is underlined in Næss's copy of the draft. A revised version was subsequently published as Ramachandra Guha, "Radical American Environmentalism and Wilderness Preservation: A Third World Critique," *Environmental Ethics* 11, no. 1 (1989): 71–83. Næss wrote an extensive response to Guha, published as Arne Næss, "Comments on Guha's 'Radical American Environmentalism and Wilderness Preservation: A Third World Critique,'" in *Philosophical Dialogues: Arne Næss and the Progress of Ecophilosophy*, ed. Nina Witoszek and Andrew Brennan (Lanham, MD: Rowman & Littlefield, 1999), 325–333.

203. Roberts, "The Better Earth," 187.

CHAPTER 6

1. Ivan Illich, *Tools for Conviviality* (New York: Harper & Row, 1973), 36–37.

2. Robert S. Emmet and David E. Nye, *The Environmental Humanities: A Critical Introduction* (Cambridge, MA: MIT Press, 2017), 47.

3. See, e.g., Ryan Driskell Tate, "Rural Revolt: Power Line Protests and the Alternative Technology Movement in the United States, 1970s," *Technology and Culture* 62, no. 1 (2021): 1–26.

4. For information about the Cultural Canon and an overview of the selected works, see https://kulturkanon.kum.dk/english/

5. The Danish "people's colleges," or *folkehøjskoler*, are a system of adult education that does not grant degrees but aim to foster personal and cultural development. These schools were based on ideas developed by the writer, poet, philosopher, and pastor N. F. S. Grundtvig (1783–1872), and quickly became a significant feature of Danish culture and society.

6. Flemming Petersen, Bjarning Grøn, Asger N. Kristiansen, and Anette Christensen, *Det danske vindmølleeventyr* (Copenhagen: Fysikforlaget, 2007), 12–18.

7. Petersen et al., *Det danske vindmølleeventyr*, 20–25.

8. Jytte Thorndahl, *Gedsermøllen: Den første moderne vindmølle* (Bjerringbro: Elmuseet, 2005), 55–61.

9. Thorndahl, *Gedsermøllen*, 45.

10. Peter Karnøe, *Dansk vindmølleindustri: En overraskende international succes* (Copenhagen: Samfundslitteratur, 1991), 169.

11. Thorndahl, *Gedsermøllen*, 47–54.

12. Thorndahl, *Gedsermøllen*, 61–64.

13. Thorndahl, *Gedsermøllen*, 74–75.

14. Thorndahl, *Gedsermøllen*, 77–80.

15. Brandon N. Owens, *The Wind Power Story: A Century of Innovation that Reshaped the Global Energy Landscape* (Hoboken, NJ: John Wiley & Son, 2019), 159.

16. Andrew G. Kirk, *Counterculture Green: The Whole Earth Catalog and American Environmentalism* (Lawrence: University Press of Kansas, 2007), 101.

17. Carroll Pursell, "The Rise and Fall of the Appropriate Technology Movement in the United States, 1965–1985," *Technology and Culture* 34, no. 3 (1993): 629–637; Carroll Pursell, "Sim van der Ryn and the Architecture of the Appropriate Technology Movement," *Australasian Journal of American Studies* 28, no. 2 (2009): 17–30.

18. Thorndahl, *Gedsermøllen*, 82–85.

19. J. Baldwin, "Here's an Interesting Bit of News from Our Department of Energy (DOE)," in *Soft-Tech: A Co-Evolution Book*, ed. J. Baldwin and Stewart Brand (New York: Penguin; Menlo Park, CA: Portola Institute, 1978), 71.

20. Benny Christensen, "History of Danish Wind Power," in *The Rise of Modern Wind Energy: Wind Power for the World*, ed. Preben Maegaard, Anna Krenz, and Wolfgang Palz (Boca Raton, FL: CRC Press, 2013), 66.

21. Halfdan Farstad and James Ward, "Wind Energy in Denmark," in *Transitions to Alternative Energy Systems: Entrepreneurs, New Technologies, and Social Change*, ed. Thomas Baumgartner and Tom R. Burns (Boulder, CO: Westview Press, 1984), 93–98.

22. *Freja 74* (Copenhagen: Kunstakademiets arkitektskole, 1974); Ejvin Beuse, "Det folkelige initiativ," in *Vedvarende Energi i Danmark: En krønike om 25 opvækstår 1975–2000*, ed. Ejvin Beuse, Jørgen Boldt, Preben Maegaard, Niels I. Meyer, Jens Windeleff, and Iben Østergaard (Copenhagen: OVEs Forlag, 2000), 13–16.

23. "Teknologi og samfund: Konference for nordiske industridesignere 1980," program leaflet, Konstfacks arkiv, Industridesign—Undervisningshandl. och studentarbeten 1980/81. F7DE:5; Torgny Møller, "Ny film: Dansk Energi," *Naturlig Energi* 1, no. 3 (November 1978): 11.

24. Karnøe, *Dansk vindmølleindustri*, 196–198.

25. Energiministeriet, *Energiplan 81* (Copenhagen: Energiministeriet, 1981).

26. For a detailed discussion of the conglomerate of policies and their effects, see Kristian H. Nielsen, "Danish Wind Power Policies from 1976 to 2004: A Survey of Policy Making and Techno-economic Innovation," in *Switching to Renewable Power: A Framework for the 21st Century*, ed. Volkmar Lauber (Abingdon, UK: Earthscan/Routledge, 2005), 99–121.

27. Flemming Petersen, *Da Danmark fikk vinger: Vindmøllehistorien 1978–2018* (Aarhus: Danmarks Vindmølleforening, 2018), 91–96, 110–111.

28. Jes Fabricius Møller, *På sejrens vej: Historien om Skolesamvirket Tvind og dets skaber Mogens Amdi Petersen* (Copenhagen: Dike, 1999), 19.

29. Timothy Stott, "Ludic Pedagogies at the College of Environmental Design, UC Berkeley, 1966 to 1972," in *The Culture of Nature in the History of Design*, ed. Kjetil Fallan (London: Routledge, 2019), 58–71; Timothy Stott, "Systems in Play: Simon Nicholson's Design 12 Course, University of California, Berkeley, 1966," *Journal of Design History* 32, no. 3 (2019): 223–239.

30. Møller, *På sejrens vej*, 25–27.

31. Mogens Amdi Petersen, "Den rejsende Højskole," *Højskolebladet*, June 26, 1970.

32. Iben Østergaard, "Tvindmøllen—en kollektiv kraftanstrengelse," in Beuse et al., *Vedvarende Energi i Danmark*, 132–139.

33. Jan Krag Jacobsen and Oluf Danielsen, "Tvindmøllen: Græsrodsteknologi eller højudviklet teknologi," *Naturkampen*, no. 5 (1977): 12–23; Peter Sten Andersen et al., "Vindmøllen i Tvind," *Ingeniøren*, June 25, 1976, 16–17.

34. Ruth Oldenziel and Mikael Hård, *Consumers, Tinkerers, Rebels: The People Who Shaped Europe* (Basingstoke, UK: Palgrave Macmillan, 2013), 269.

35. Johannes Grove cited in Vagn Bro, "Møllen bag Tvind-myterne," *Dagens Industri* (1981, no. 5): 17–18.

36. Carl Herforth and Claus Nybroe, *Solenergi, vindkraft: En håndbog* (Copenhagen: Information, 1976).

37. Ejvin Beuse, "Grundtvig køber vindmølleandele," in Beuse et al., *Vedvarende Energi i Danmark*, 41–50; Sanne Wittrup, "Bidt af vindkraft," *Ingeniøren*, September 7, 1984, 10.

38. Aage Johnsen Nielsen, "Et udviklingsforløb," in Beuse et al., *Vedvarende Energi i Danmark*, 51–54.

39. Erik Grove-Nielsen, "Mit liv med vinger," in Beuse et al., *Vedvarende Energi i Danmark*, 140–148; Henrik Stiesdal, "Fra smeden i Herborg til Vestas," in Beuse et al., *Vedvarende Energi i Danmark*, 166–173.

40. Preben Maegaard, "Efterfølgelse af la Cour-traditionen," in Beuse et al., *Vedvarende Energi i Danmark*, 206–213.

41. Oldenziel and Hård, *Consumers, Tinkerers, Rebels*, 270.

42. Oldenziel and Hård, *Consumers, Tinkerers, Rebels*, 270.

43. Carroll Pursell, *The Machine in America: A Social History of Technology* (Baltimore: Johns Hopkins University Press, 1995), 307.

44. Adrian Smith, "Environmental Movements and Innovation: From Alternative Technology to Hollow Technology," *Human Ecology Review* 12, no. 2 (2005): 116.

45. Karnøe, *Dansk vindmølleindustri*, 177–181.

46. Karnøe, *Dansk vindmølleindustri*, 181–183; Owens, *The Wind Power Story*, 168.

47. Karnøe, *Dansk vindmølleindustri*, 184–185.

48. Farstad and Ward, "Wind Energy in Denmark," 93–94.

49. Finn Arler, "Renewables," in *Ethics in Danish Energy Policy*, ed. Finn Arler, Mogens Rüdiger, Karl Sperling, Kristian Høyer Toft, and Bo Poulsen (London: Routledge, 2020), 93–94.

50. Karnøe, *Dansk vindmølleindustri*, 186–196.

51. Kristian H. Nielsen and Matthias Heymann, "Winds of Change: Communication and Wind Power Technology Development in Denmark and Germany from 1973 to ca. 1985," *Engineering Studies* 4, no. 1 (2012): 11–31; Peter Karnøe and Raghu Garud, "Path Creation: Co-creation of Heterogeneous Resources in the Emergence of the Danish Wind Turbine Cluster," *European Planning Studies* 20, no. 5 (2012): 733–752.

52. Karnøe, *Dansk vindmølleindustri*, 47–51.

53. Matthias Heymann, "Signs of Hubris: The Shaping of Wind Technology Styles in Germany, Denmark, and the United States, 1940–1990," *Technology and Culture* 39, no. 4 (1998): 665.

54. Karnøe, *Dansk vindmølleindustri*, 47–51.

55. Karnøe, *Dansk vindmølleindustri*, 113–115.

56. Jan Michl, "On Seeing Design as Redesign: An Exploration of a Neglected Problem in Design Education," *Scandinavian Journal of Design History* 12 (2002): 7–23.

57. Heymann, "Signs of Hubris," 646.

58. Niels I. Meyer, "Vingesus i Wild West," *Ingeniøren*, November 11, 1983, 16–17.

59. Owens, *The Wind Power Story*, 169, 195.

60. Bigitte Dyrekilde and Johan Christensen, *Vestas: Verdensmester for enhver pris* (Copenhagen: Lindhardt og Ringhof, 2017), 25, 36.

61. Owens, *The Wind Power Story*, 197.

62. Paul Gipe, *Wind Energy Comes of Age* (New York: John Wiley & Sons, 1995), 296.

63. Karnøe, *Dansk vindmølleindustri*, 273; Karnøe and Garud, "Path Creation," 743.

64. Sanne Wittrup, "Spændende nyt mølle-design," *Ingeniøren*, June 15, 1984, 3.

65. Wittrup, "Spændende nyt mølle-design."

66. Preben Maegaard, "Dem, der gikk i glemmebogen," in Beuse et al., *Vedvarende Energi i Danmark*, 214–226.

67. Gipe, *Wind Energy Comes of Age*, 296.

68. Information retrieved March 6, 2021, https://jacobjensendesign.com/vestas.

69. Thorkild Schiøler, "Miljøvenlige vindmøller," *Ingeniøren*, May 7, 1976, 27.

70. This illustrates Lego's dual iconicity: it is of course a design-historical icon in itself—but through its own iconicity it also bestows a second-order iconicity upon the modeled products. Kjetil Fallan "LEGO, Denmark (Ole Kirk Christiansen, 1958)," in *Iconic Design: 50 Stories about 50 Things*, ed. Grace Lees-Maffei (London: Bloomsbury Academic, 2014), 176–179.

71. Petersen, *Da Danmark fikk vinger*, 122–126.

72. Nielsen and Heymann, "Winds of Change," 12.

73. Imre Szeman and Dominic Boyer, "Introduction: On the Energy Humanities," in *Energy Humanities: An Anthology*, ed. Imre Szeman and Dominic Boyer (Baltimore: Johns Hopkins University Press, 2017), 3.

74. Emmet and Nye, *The Environmental Humanities*, 55–56.

75. Kirk, *Counterculture Green*, 101.

CODA

1. An earlier version of this coda was originally published as Kjetil Fallan, "Aspen Comes to Scandinavia," in *Scandinavian Design and the United States, 1890–1980*, ed. Bobbye Tigerman and Monica Obniski (Los Angeles: Los Angeles County Museum of Art; Munich and New York: DelMonico Books Prestel, 2020), 289–306.

2. Jeff Werner, *Medelvägens estetik: Sverigebilder i USA* (Hedemora and Möklinta: Gidlunds förlag, 2008); Siv Ringdal, "110 Volts at Home: The American Lista," *Journal of Design History* 27, no. 1 (2014): 79–96; Maggie Taft, "Morphologies and Genealogies: Shaker Furniture and Danish Design," *Design and Culture* 7, no. 3 (2015): 313–334; Per H. Hansen, *Danish Modern Furniture 1930–2016: The Rise, Decline and Re-emergence of a Cultural Market Category* (Odense: University Press of Southern Denmark, 2018); Kjetil Fallan, "Love and Hate in Industrial Design: Europe's Design Professionals and America in the 1950s," in *The Making of*

European Consumption: Facing the American Challenge, ed. Per Lundin and Thomas Kaiserfeld (Basingstoke, UK: Palgrave Macmillan, 2015), 134–156.

3. Ida Kamilla Lie, "'Make Us More Useful to Society!' The Scandinavian Design Students' Organization (SDO) and Socially Responsible Design, 1967–1973," *Design and Culture* 8, no. 3 (2016): 327–361; Elizabeth Guffey, "The Scandinavian Roots of the International Symbol of Access," *Design and Culture* 7, no. 3 (2015): 357–376.

4. Alice Twemlow, "I Can't Talk to You If You Say That: An Ideological Collision at the International Design Conference at Aspen, 1970," *Design and Culture* 1, no. 1 (2009): 23–49.

5. Michael Doyle, "Resolutions by Those Attending the 1970 International Design Conference in Aspen," reprinted in *The Aspen Complex*, ed. Martin Beck (Berlin: Sternberg Press, 2012), 96–97.

6. "Minutes of Meeting of the Board of Directors of the International Design Conference in Aspen, Saturday, June 20, 1970," reprinted in Beck, *The Aspen Complex*, 101–109.

7. Alison J. Clarke, "Buckminster Fuller's Reindeer Abattoir and Other Designs for the Real World," in *Hippie Modernism: The Struggle for Utopia*, ed. Andrew Blauvelt (Minneapolis: Walker Art Center, 2015), 75; Alison J. Clarke, "Victor J. Papanek: Agent Provocateur of Design," in *Victor Papanek: The Politics of Design*, ed. Mateo Kries, Amelie Klein, and Alison J. Clarke (Weil am Rhein: Vitra Design Museum, 2018), 38, 47.

8. Jean Baudrillard, "The Environmental Witch-Hunt: Statement by the French Group, 1970," in *The Aspen Papers: Twenty Years of Design Theory from the International Design Conference in Aspen*, ed. Reyner Banham (New York: Praeger, 1974), 208–210; Alice Twemlow, "'A Guaranteed Communications Failure': Consensus Meets Conflict at the International Design Conference in Aspen, 1970," in Beck, *The Aspen Complex*, 110–135.

9. Alice Twemlow, *Sifting the Trash: A History of Design Criticism* (Cambridge, MA: MIT Press, 2017), 134.

10. Lennart Lindkvist, "Rapport utifrån 1," *Form* (1973, no. 10): 386.

11. Hedvig Hedqvist and Stefan Hedqvist, "Paradox i Aspen," *Form* (1971, no. 7): 298.

12. Lennart Lindkvist, "70-talets designideologi," *Form* (1974, no. 1): 1.

13. As well as Andrea Baynes, Jane Clark Chermayeff, Lou Dorfsman, Helena Hernmarck, Bill N. Lacy, Dottie O'Carroll, Herbert Pinzke, Judith Ramquist, Jack Roberts, Michal Ronnen Safdie, Benjamin Thompson, Jivan Tabibian, and Henry Wolf. "Transatlantic Shop Talk No. 2—Aspen Comes to Scandinavia. List of Participants," document from the private archive of Ulla Tarras-Wahlberg Bøe donated to the author (hereafter cited as UTWB).

14. "Amerikansk/skandinavisk design-symposium, Oslo september 1979," undated and unsigned draft by Ulla Tarras-Wahlberg Bøe and Alf Bøe, UTWB.

15. Telegram from Ivan Chermayeff to Alf Bøe and Ulla Tarras-Wahlberg Bøe dated February 22, 1978, UTWB.

16. Alf Bøe to Jane Clark Chermayeff and Ivan Chermayeff, dated June 30, 1978, UTWB.

17. IDCA President Julian Breinart to Alf Bøe and Ulla Tarras-Wahlberg Bøe dated August 25, 1982, UTWB.

18. Alf Bøe to Byråsjef Chris Prebensen, Kulturkontoret, Det kgl. utenriksdepartement, dated August 29, 1979, UTWB.

19. Alf Bøe and Ulla Tarras-Wahlberg Bøe to various corporate sponsors, "Innbetaling av garantisum—Eventuelt bidrag til stipendier," dated November 12, 1979, UTWB.

20. Alf Bøe to US ambassador Louis A. Lerner, dated October 16, 1979, UTWB.

21. Alf Bøe to Grete Prytz Kittelsen, dated August 8, 1979, UTWB.

22. Einar Schiong, Generaldirektørens kontor, Norges Statsbaner to Alf Bøe, "Skandinavisk/amerikansk designkonferanse 1979—Bruk av NSB's konferansevogn Bergen—Oslo," dated January 17, 1979; Alf Bøe to Jernbanedirektør Knut Skuland, NSB, dated October 1, 1979; UTWB.

23. Ulla Tarras-Wahlberg Bøe and Alf Bøe, "Report from Symposium 'Aspen Comes to Scandinavia—Transatlantic Shop Talk II,'" draft report dated September 1979, UTWB.

24. Bøe and Bøe, "Report from Symposium."

25. Alf Bøe, "Aspen Comes to Oslo: An American/Scandinavian Design Conference," memorandum dated July 17, 1978, UTWB.

26. Alf Bøe, ed., *Norsk/Norwegian Industrial Design* (Oslo: Kunstindustrimuseet i Oslo/Johan Grundt Tanum forlag, 1963); Alf Bøe, *Den norske Designpris de syv første år/The Norwegian Design Award Its First Seven Years* (Oslo: Norsk Designcentrum, 1969); Kjetil Fallan, *Designing Modern Norway: A History of Design Discourse* (London: Routledge, 2017), 135–152.

27. Although in the end the program included only one Danish presentation.

28. Alf Bøe to Niels Diffrient, dated July 4, 1979, UTWB.

29. For a discussion of Diffrient's work on *Humanscale*, with special attention to its inclusion of disability-related measurements, see Bess Williamson, *Accessible America: A History of Disability and Design* (New York: New York University Press, 2019), 158–162.

30. Ulf Hård af Segerstad, "Telefon som äppelmunk," *Svenska Dagbladet*, October 2, 1979.

31. Lasse Brunnström, *Svensk designhistoria* (Stockholm: Raster, 2010), 293–295.

32. Lars Dybdahl, *Dansk design 1945–1975: Produktdesign, Grafisk design, Møbeldesign* (Copenhagen: Borgen, 2006), 312–315.

33. See, e.g., Helena Mattsson, "Designing the 'Consumer in Infinity': The Swedish Cooperative Union's New Consumer Policy, c. 1970," in *Scandinavian Design: Alternative Histories*, ed. Kjetil Fallan (London: Berg Publishers, 2012); Per H. Hansen, *En lys og lykkelig fremtid: Historien om FDB-møbler* (Copenhagen: Strandberg Publishing, 2014).

34. Personal communication with Ragnvald Bing Lorentzen, November 16, 2017.

35. Personal communication with Jan Jeppe Gauguin, November 16, 2017; personal communication with Benedicte Aars-Nicolaysen, November 17, 2017.

36. Charles Simeons, *Hydro-Power: The Use of Water as an Alternative Source of Energy* (Oxford: Pergamon Press, 1980), 68–70.

37. Alf Bøe to Minister of Petroleum and Energy Bjartmar Gjerde, dated August 30, 1979, UTWB.

38. Lasse Brunnström, "Hjälpmedel för ett säkrare och jämlikare liv," in *Svensk industridesign: En 1900-talshistoria*, ed. Lasse Brunnström (Stockholm: Prisma, 2004), 317.

39. Personal communication with Maria Benktzon, November 16, 2017.

40. Albert Lewis, "Harambee," *Glass Art* 4, no. 5 (1975): 16.

41. Bøe and Bøe, "Report from Symposium."

42. Trinelise Dysthe, "Design—en viktig del av miljøet," *Aftenposten*, October 30, 1979, 5.

43. Peter Butenschøn, "Amerikansk design på avveie," *Byggekunst* 61, no. 5 (1979): 369 (italics in original).

44. Butenschøn, "Amerikansk design på avveie," 369.

45. Butenschøn, "Amerikansk design på avveie," 369.

46. Butenschøn, "Amerikansk design på avveie," 369.

BIBLIOGRAPHY

Abdulla, Danah. "The Challenges and Opportunities of Introducing Design Culture in Jordan." In *Design Culture: Objects and Approaches*, ed. Guy Julier, Mads Nygaard Folkmann, Niels Peter Skou, Hans-Christian Jensen, and Anders V. Munch, 214–226. London: Bloomsbury Academic, 2019.

Agnsäter, Håkan. *Affischerna från den svenska alternativrörelsen 1967–1979*. Stockholm: Ordalaget Bokförlag, 2013.

Åkerman, Brita. *Makt åt konsumenten*. Stockholm: Rabén & Sjögren, 1968.

Allen, Peter. "The End of Modernism? People's Park, Urban Renewal, and Community Design." *Journal of the Society of Architectural Historians* 70, no. 3 (2011): 354–374.

Amble, Erling, Botolv Helleland, Karl G. Høyer, Sigmund Kvaløy, Magne Lindholm, Dag Norling, and Arne Vinje. *Dette bør du vite om EF: Økopolitikk eller EF?* Oslo: Pax, 1972.

Ambole, Amollo. "Rethinking Design Making and Design Thinking in Africa." *Design and Culture* 12, no. 3 (2020): 331–350.

Amir, Sulfikar. "Rethinking Design Policy in the Third World." *Design Issues* 20, no. 4 (2004): 68–75.

Anker, Peder. *The Power of the Periphery: How Norway Became an Environmental Pioneer for the World*. Cambridge: Cambridge University Press, 2020.

Anker, Peder. *From Bauhaus to Ecohouse: A History of Ecological Design*. Baton Rouge: Louisiana State University Press, 2010.

Anker, Peder. "Deep Ecology in Bucharest." *The Trumpeter* 24, no. 1 (2008): 56–57.

Anker, Peder. "Science as a Vacation: A History of Ecology in Norway." *History of Science* 45, no. 4 (2007): 463.

Anker, Peder. "Buckminster Fuller as Captain of Spaceship Earth." *Minerva* 45, no. 4 (2007): 426.

Anker, Peder. "The Philosopher's Cabin and the Household of Nature." *Ethics, Place and Environment* 6, no. 2 (2003): 138.

Anker, Peder, and Nina Witoszek, "The Dream of the Biocentric Community and the Structure of Utopias." *Worldviews: Global Religions, Culture, and Ecology* 2, no. 3 (1998): 239–256.

Arler, Finn. "Renewables." In *Ethics in Danish Energy Policy*, ed. Finn Arler, Mogens Rüdiger, Karl Sperling, Kristian Høyer Toft, and Bo Poulsen, 93–121. London: Routledge, 2020.

Armiero, Marco, and Lise Sedrez. "Introduction." In *A History of Environmentalism: Local Struggles, Global Histories*, ed. Marco Armiero and Lise Sedrez, 1–20. London: Bloomsbury Academic, 2014.

Arrhenius, Thordis. "Preservation and Protest: Counterculture and Heritage in 1970s Sweden." *Future Anterior* 7, no. 2 (2010): 106–123.

Attfield, Judy. "Introduction: Utility Reassessed." In *Utility Reassessed: The Role of Ethics in the Practice of Design*, ed. Judy Attfield, 1–10. Manchester: Manchester University Press, 1999.

Bach, Christian Friis, Thorsten Borring Olesen, Sune Kaur-Pedersen, and Jan Pedersen. *Idealer og realiteter: Dansk udviklingspolitiks historie 1945–2005*. Copenhagen: Gyldendal, 2008.

Balaram, Singanapalli. "Design in India: The Importance of the Ahmedabad Declaration." *Design Issues* 25, no. 4 (2009): 54–79.

Balasubrahmanyan, Suchitra. "Imagining the Indian Nation: The Design of Gandhi's Dandi March and Nehru's Republic Day Parade." In *Designing Worlds: National Design Histories in an Age of Globalization*, ed. Kjetil Fallan and Grace Lees-Maffei, 108–124. New York: Berghahn Books, 2016.

Baldwin, J. "One Highly-Evolved Toolbox." In *Soft-Tech: A Co-Evolution Book*, ed. J. Baldwin and Stewart Brand, 8–17. New York/Menlo Park, CA: Penguin/Portola Institute, 1978.

Banham, Reyner. "Is There a Substitute for Wood Grain Plastic?" In *Design and Aesthetics in Wood*, ed. Eric A. Anderson and George F. Earle, 4–11. Albany: SUNY Press, 1972.

Banu, Lisa S. "Defining the Design Deficit in Bangladesh." *Journal of Design History* 22, no. 4 (2009): 309–323.

Baudrillard, Jean. "The Environmental Witch-Hunt: Statement by the French Group, 1970." In *The Aspen Papers: Twenty Years of Design Theory from the International Design Conference in Aspen*, ed. Reyner Banham, 208–210. New York: Praeger, 1974.

Belgrad, Daniel. *The Culture of Feedback: Ecological Thinking in Seventies America*. Chicago: University of Chicago Press, 2019.

Berg, Liv, and Krisno Nimpuno. *Recycling: Från skräp till nytta*. Stockholm/Alingsås: L. Berg, 1972.

Bernsen, Jens, Tapio Periäinen, Stefán Snæbjørnsson, Ulla Tarras-Wahlberg Bøe, and Lennart Lindkvist. "A Scandinavian Design Council Manifesto on Nature, Ecology, Human Needs and Development for the Future." In *Scandinavian Design 1990–towards 2000: The Challenge of Internationalization Demands and Needs for a New Millennium*, ed. Ulla Tarras-Wahlberg Bøe, 63. Oslo: Scandinavian Design Council, 1990.

Beuse, Ejvin, Jørgen Boldt, Preben Maegaard, Niels I. Meyer, Jens Windeleff, and Iben Østergaard, eds. *Vedvarende Energi i Danmark: En krønike om 25 opvækstår 1975–2000*. Copenhagen: OVEs Forlag, 2000.

Bicknell, Julian, and Liz McQuiston, eds. *Design for Need: The Social Contribution of Design*. Oxford: Pergamon Press, 1977.

Bijker, Wiebe E. *Of Bicycles, Bakelites, and Bulbs: Toward a Theory of Sociotechnical Change*. Cambridge, MA: MIT Press, 1995.

Bjørkdahl, Kristian. "Dommedagsdokumentet: *Limits to Growth* og verdens grafiske undergang." In *Kollaps: På randen av fremtiden*, ed. Peter Bjerregaard and Kyrre Kverndokk, 163–180. Oslo: Dreyer, 2018.

Bøe, Alf. *Den norske Designpris de syv første år/The Norwegian Design Award its first seven years*. Oslo: Norsk Designcentrum, 1969.

Bøe, Alf, ed. *Norsk/Norwegian Industrial Design*. Oslo: Kunstindustrimuseet i Oslo/Johan Grundt Tanum forlag, 1963.

Borgström, Georg. *Too Many: A Biological Overview of the Earth's Limitations*. New York: Macmillan, 1969.

Borgström, Georg. *The Hungry Planet: The Modern World at the Edge of Famine*. New York: Macmillan, 1965.

Bornold, Salka Hallström. *Det är rätt att göra uppror: Mah-Jong 1966–1977*. Stockholm: Modernista, 2003.

Brunnström, Lasse. *Svensk designhistoria*. Stockholm: Raster, 2010.

Brunnström, Lasse. "Hjälpmedel för ett säkrare och jämlikare liv." In *Svensk industridesign: En 1900-talshistoria*, ed. Lasse Brunnström, 297–323. Stockholm: Prisma, 2004.

Busbea, Larry. *The Responsive Environment: Design, Aesthetics, and the Human in the 1970s*. Minneapolis: University of Minnesota Press, 2020.

Busbea, Larry. "Paolo Soleri and the Aesthetics of Irreversibility." *Journal of Architecture* 18, no. 6 (2013): 788.

Cadena, Marisol de la. *Earth Beings: Ecologies of Practice across Andean Worlds*. Durham, NC: Duke University Press, 2015.

Cadena, Marisol de la, and Mario Blaser, eds. *A World of Many Worlds*. Durham, NC: Duke University Press, 2018.

Castillo, Greg. "Counterculture Terroir: California's Hippie Enterprise Zone." In *Hippie Modernism: The Struggle for Utopia*, ed. Andrew Blauvelt, 87–101. Minneapolis: Walker Art Center, 2015.

Chakrabarty, Dipesh. *Provincializing Europe: Postcolonial Thought and Historical Difference*. Princeton, NJ: Princeton University Press, 2000.

Chatterjee, Ashoke. "Design in India: The Experience of Transition." *Design Issues* 21, no. 4 (2005): 8–9.

Christensen, Benny. "History of Danish Wind Power." In *The Rise of Modern Wind Energy: Wind Power for the World*, ed. Preben Maegaard, Anna Krenz, and Wolfgang Palz, 33–92. Boca Raton, FL: CRC Press, 2013.

Chu, Hsiao-Yun. "Paper Mausoleum: The Archive of R. Buckminster Fuller." In *New Views on R. Buckminster Fuller*, ed. Hsiao-Yun Chu and Roberto G. Trujillo, 6–22. Stanford: Stanford University Press, 2009.

Clarke, Alison J. *Victor Papanek: Designer for the Real World*. Cambridge, MA: MIT Press, 2021.

Clarke, Alison J. "Victor J. Papanek: Agent Provocateur of Design." In *Victor Papanek: The Politics of Design*, ed. Mateo Kries, Amelie Klein, and Alison J. Clarke, 24–47. Weil am Rhein: Vitra Design Museum, 2018.

Clarke, Alison J. "Design for Development, ICSID and UNIDO: The Anthropological Turn in 1970s Design." *Journal of Design History* 29, no. 1 (2016): 43–57.

Clarke, Alison J. "Buckminster Fuller's Reindeer Abattoir and Other Designs for the Real World." In *Hippie Modernism: The Struggle for Utopia*, ed. Andrew Blauvelt, 68–75. Minneapolis: Walker Art Center, 2015.

Cowan, Ruth Schwartz. *More Work for Mother: The Ironies of Household Technology from the Open Hearth to the Microwave*. New York: Basic Books, 1983.

Dahl, Eilif. *Økologi for ingeniører og arkitekter*. Oslo: Universitetsforlaget, 1969.

Dalby, Mette Strømgaard. "Kristian Vedel: Industriell designer, pioner og idealist." In *Kristian Vedel*, ed. Lise Schou, 9–14. Copenhagen: Arkitektens forlag, 2007.

Dammann, Erik. *Kontraster: Beretning om et mangfoldig liv*. Oslo: Aschehoug, 2005.

Dammann, Erik. "The Future in Our Hands: Its Conceptions, Aims, and Strategies." 1982. In *Wisdom in the Open Air: The Norwegian Roots of Deep Ecology*, ed. Peter Reed and David Rothenberg, 224–226. Minneapolis: University of Minnesota Press, 1993.

Dammann, Erik. *The Future in Our Hands*. Oxford: Pergamon Press, 1979.

Dammann, Erik. *Fremtiden i våre hender*. Oslo: Gyldendal, 1972.

Devall, Bill. "The Deep Ecology Movement." *Natural Resources Journal* 20, no. 2 (1980): 309–310.

Devall, Bill, and George Sessions. *Deep Ecology: Living as if Nature Mattered*. Salt Lake City: Peregrine Smith Books, 1985.

Doczi, György. *The Power of Limits: Proportional Harmonies in Nature, Art, and Architecture*. Boulder, CO: Shambhala Publications, 1981.

Downton, Paul. *Ecopolis: Architecture and Cities for a Changing Climate*. Dordrecht: Springer, 2009.

Doyle, Michael. "Resolutions by Those Attending the 1970 International Design Conference in Aspen." Reprinted in *The Aspen Complex*, ed. Martin Beck, 96–97. Berlin: Sternberg Press, 2012.

Drengson, Alan. "Introduction: The Life and Work of Arne Naess: An Appreciative Overview." In *Ecology of Wisdom: Writings by Arne Naess*, ed. Alan Drengson and Bill Devall, 3–44. Berkeley: Counterpoint, 2008.

Drengson, Alan, and Bill Devall. "The Deep Ecology Movement: Origins, Development & Future Prospects." *The Trumpeter* 26, no. 2 (2010): 53–54.

Dunaway, Finis. *Seeing Green: The Use and Abuse of American Environmental Images*. Chicago: University of Chicago Press, 2016.

Dutta, Arindam. *The Bureaucracy of Beauty: Design in the Age of Its Global Reproducibility*. London: Routledge, 2007.

Dybdahl, Lars. *Dansk design 1945–1975: Produktdesign, Grafisk design, Møbeldesign*. Copenhagen: Borgen, 2006.

Dyrekilde, Bigitte, and Johan Christensen. *Vestas: Verdensmester for enhver pris*. Copenhagen: Lindhardt og Ringhof, 2017.

Ehrlich, Paul R. *The Population Bomb*. New York: Sierra Club/Ballantine Books, 1968.

Eldin, Pia, Synnöve Mork, and Katja Waldén. "Textil konst och formgivning." In *Tanken och handen: Konstfack 150 år*, ed. Gunilla Widengren. Stockholm: Page One Publishing, 1994.

Emmet, Robert S., and David E. Nye. *The Environmental Humanities: A Critical Introduction*. Cambridge, MA: MIT Press, 2017.

Engh, Sunniva. "Georg Borgström and the Population-Food Dilemma: Reception and Consequences in Norwegian Public Debate in the 1950s and 1960s." In *Histories of Knowledge in Postwar Scandinavia: Actors, Arenas, and Aspirations*, ed. Johan Östling, Niklas Olsen, and David Larsson Heidenblad, 39–58. London and New York: Routledge, 2020.

Eriksen, Thomas Hylland. *Søppel: Avfall i en verden av bivirkninger*. Oslo: Aschehoug, 2011.

Escobar, Arturo. *Designs for the Pluriverse: Radical Interdependence, Autonomy, and the Making of Worlds*. Durham, NC: Duke University Press, 2018.

Faarlund, Nils. "Stetind 1966—'tindebestigere' skaper ny giv i naturvernet." In *Arven og gleden—et festskrift til naturen*, ed. Børge Dahle, Finn Wagle, Øystein Dahle, Siri Næss, Nils Faarlund, Aage Jensen, Sigmund K. Setreng, 23–25. Trondheim: Tapir akademisk forlag, 2010.

Faarlund, Nils. "A Way Home." In *Wisdom in the Open Air: The Norwegian Roots of Deep Ecology*, ed. Peter Reed and David Rothenberg, 157–168. Minneapolis: University of Minnesota Press, 1993.

Fallan, Kjetil. "Norwegian Wood: Trails to Ecological Design." In *Design Struggles: Intersecting Histories, Pedagogies, and Perspectives*, ed. Claudia Mareis and Nina Paim, 117–135. Amsterdam: Valiz, 2021.

Fallan, Kjetil. "Aspen Comes to Scandinavia." In *Scandinavian Design and the United States, 1890–1980*, ed. Bobbye Tigerman and Monica Obniski, 289–306. Los Angeles/Munich and New York: Los Angeles County Museum of Art/DelMonico Books Prestel, 2020.

Fallan, Kjetil. "Introduction: The Culture of Nature in the History of Design." In *The Culture of Nature in the History of Design*, ed. Kjetil Fallan, 1–15. London: Routledge, 2019.

Fallan, Kjetil. "The Object of Design History: Lessons for the Environment." In *A Companion to Contemporary Design since 1945*, ed. Anne Massey, 260–283. Oxford: Wiley Blackwell, 2019.

Fallan, Kjetil. *Designing Modern Norway: A History of Design Discourse*. London: Routledge, 2017.

Fallan, Kjetil. "Nordic Noir: Deadly Design from the Peacemongering Periphery." *Design and Culture* 7, no. 3 (2015): 377–402.

Fallan, Kjetil. "Love and Hate in Industrial Design: Europe's Design Professionals and America in the 1950s." In *The Making of European Consumption: Facing the American Challenge*, ed. Per Lundin and Thomas Kaiserfeld, 134–156. Basingstoke, UK: Palgrave Macmillan, 2015.

Fallan Kjetil. "LEGO, Denmark (Ole Kirk Christiansen, 1958)." In *Iconic Design: 50 Stories about 50 Things*, ed. Grace Lees-Maffei, 176–179. London: Bloomsbury Academic, 2014.

Fallan, Kjetil. "Culture by Design: Co-Constructing Material and Meaning." In *Assigning Cultural Values*, ed. Kjerstin Aukrust, 135–163. Frankfurt am Main: Peter Lang, 2013.

Fallan, Kjetil. "'The "Designer"—The 11th Plague': Design Discourse from Consumer Activism to Environmentalism in 1960s Norway." *Design Issues* 27, no. 4 (2011): 30–42.

Fallan, Kjetil, and Finn Arne Jørgensen. "Environmental Histories of Design: Towards a New Research Agenda." *Journal of Design History* 30, no. 2 (2017): 103–121.

Farstad, Halfdan, and James Ward. "Wind Energy in Denmark." In *Transitions to Alternative Energy Systems: Entrepreneurs, New Technologies, and Social Change*, ed. Thomas Baumgartner and Tom R. Burns, 93–98. Boulder, CO: Westview Press, 1984.

Fernández, Silvia. "The Origins of Design Education in Latin America: From the hfg in Ulm to Globalization." *Design Issues* 22, no. 1 (2006): 3–19.

Feyerabend, Paul. "'Science': The Myth and Its Role in Society." *Inquiry* 18, no. 2 (1975): 167–181.

Flood, Catherine, and Gavin Grindon, eds. *Disobedient Objects*. London: V&A Publishing, 2014.

Foreman, Dave, ed. *Ecodefense: A Field Guide to Monkeywrenching*. Tucson: Ned Ludd Books, 1985.

Fox, Warwick. "The Meanings of 'Deep Ecology'." *The Trumpeter* 7, no. 1 (1990): 48–50.

Friedel, Robert. "History, Sustainability, and Choice." In *Cycling and Recycling: Histories of Sustainable Practices*, ed. Ruth Oldenziel and Helmuth Trischler, 219–225. New York: Berghahn Books, 2015.

Friends of the Earth (Amory Lovins, Michael Denny, and Graham Searle). *The Stockholm Conference: Only One Earth. An Introduction to the Politics of Survival*. London: Earth Island, 1972.

Fry, Tony. *Design Futuring: Sustainability, Ethics and New Practice*. Oxford: Berg, 2009.

Fry, Tony, Clive Dilnot, and Susan Stewart. *Design and the Question of History*. London: Bloomsbury Academic, 2015.

Fry, Tony, and Anne-Marie Willis. *Steel: A Design, Cultural and Ecological History*. London: Bloomsbury Academic, 2015.

Fuad-Luke, Alastair. *Design Activism: Beautiful Strangeness for a Sustainable World*. London: Earthscan, 2009.

Fuller, R. Buckminster. *Earth, Inc.* Garden City: Anchor, 1973.

Fuller, R. Buckminster. *Operating Manual for Spaceship Earth*. Carbondale: Southern Illinois University Press, 1968.

Galbraith, John Kenneth. *The Affluent Society*. Boston: Houghton Mifflin, 1958.

Giedion, Sigfried. *Mechanization Takes Command: A Contribution to Anonymous History*. New York: Oxford University Press, 1948.

Gipe, Paul. *Wind Energy Comes of Age*. New York: John Wiley & Sons, 1995.

Gjefsen, Truls. *Arne Næss: Et liv*. Oslo: Cappelen Damm, 2011.

Göransdotter, Maria, and Johan Redström. "Design Methods and Critical Historiography: An Example from Swedish User-Centered Design." *Design Issues* 34, no. 2 (2018): 20–30.

Graesse, Malin K. "The Weaving World of Deep Ecology and Textile Design: Locating Principles of Sustainability at Austvatn Craft Central." MA thesis, University of Oslo, 2017.

Gray, Timothy. *Gary Snyder and the Pacific Rim: Creating Countercultural Community*. Iowa City: University of Iowa Press, 2006.

Guffey, Elizabeth. "The Scandinavian Roots of the International Symbol of Access." *Design and Culture* 7, no. 3 (2015): 357–376.

Guha, Ramachandra. "Radical American Environmentalism and Wilderness Preservation: A Third World Critique." *Environmental Ethics* 11, no. 1 (1989): 71–83.

Guldi, Jo, and David Armitage. *The History Manifesto*. Cambridge: Cambridge University Press, 2014.

Gutiérres, Alfredo. "When Design Goes South: From Decoloniality, through Declassification to *dessobons*." In *Design in Crisis: New Worlds, Philosophies and Practices*, ed. Tony Fry and Adam Nocek, 56–73. London: Routledge, 2021.

Haley, Mary Jean, ed. *Open Options: A Guide to Stockholm's Alternative Environmental Conferences*. Sala: Ågren & Holmbergs, 1972.

Halland, Ingrid. "Error Earth: Displaying Deep Cybernetics in 'The Universitas Projects' and *Italy: The New Domestic Landscape*, 1972." PhD thesis, University of Oslo, 2017.

Halliday, Sandy. *Sustainable Construction*. Oxford: Butterworth-Heinemann, 2008.

Hansen, Per H. *Danish Modern Furniture 1930–2016: The Rise, Decline and Re-emergence of a Cultural Market Category*. Odense: University Press of Southern Denmark, 2018.

Hansen, Per H. *En lys og lykkelig fremtid: Historien om FDB-møbler*. Copenhagen: Strandberg Publishing, 2014.

Haraway, Donna J. *Staying with the Trouble: Making Kin in the Chthulucene*. Durham, NC: Duke University Press, 2016.

Harper, Peter, in conversation with Simon Sadler. "The Exhibition of People's Technology, 1972." *Digital Culture & Society* 6, no. 1 (2020): 153–184.

Harper, Peter, and Godfrey Boyle, eds. *Radical Technology*. London: Wildwood House, 1976.

Harris, Alex, and Margaret Sartor. *Gertrude Blom: Bearing Witness*. Chapel Hill: University of North Carolina Press, 1984.

Haug, Wolfgang Fritz. *Kritik der Warenästhetik*. Frankfurt am Main: Suhrkamp, 1971.

Hayter, Teresa. *Aid as Imperialism*. Harmondsworth: Penguin, 1971.

Heidenblad, David Larsson. "Mapping a New History of the Ecological Turn: The Circulation of Environmental Knowledge in Sweden 1967." *Environment and History* 24, no. 2 (2018): 265–284.

Herforth, Carl, and Claus Nybroe. *Solenergi, vindkraft: En håndbog*. Copenhagen: Information, 1976.

Heymann, Matthias. "Signs of Hubris: The Shaping of Wind Technology Styles in Germany, Denmark, and the United States, 1940–1990." *Technology and Culture* 39, no. 4 (1998): 641–670.

Highmore, Ben. "A Sideboard Manifesto: Design Culture in an Artificial World." In *The Design Culture Reader*, ed. Ben Highmore, 1–11. London: Routledge, 2009.

Hofseth, Paul. "Ecology and Appropriate Technology." In *Mobilizing Appropriate Technology: Papers on Planning Aid Programmes*, ed. Matthew S. Gamser, 36–39. London: Intermediate Technology Publications, 1988.

Höhler, Sabine. *Spaceship Earth in the Environmental Age, 1960–1990*. London: Pickering & Chatto, 2015.

Hunt, Jamer. "Very, Very Strange Things: Victor Papanek and the Anxiety of Aesthetics." In *Victor Papanek: The Politics of Design*, ed. Mateo Kries, Amelie Klein, and Alison J. Clarke, 180–191. Weil am Rhein: Vitra Design Museum, 2018.

Husz, Orsi. "The Morality of Quality. Assimilating Material Mass Culture in Twentieth-Century Sweden." *Journal of Modern European History* 10, no. 2 (2012): 152–181.

Husz, Orsi. "Passionate about Things: The Swedish Debate on Throwawayism (1960–61)." *Revue d'Histoire Nordique* 7, no. 1 (2011): 135–160.

Illich, Ivan. *Tools for Conviviality*. New York: Harper & Row, 1973.

Isenberg, Alison. *Designing San Francisco: Art, Land, and Urban Renewal in the City by the Bay*. Princeton: Princeton University Press, 2017.

Jamison, Andrew. "Greening the City: Urban Environmentalism from Mumford to Malmö." In *Urban Machinery: Inside Modern European Cities*, ed. Mikael Hård and Thomas J. Misa, 281–298. Cambridge, MA: MIT Press, 2008.

Jasper, James M. "The Objects of Political Creativity." In *Design and Political Dissent: Spaces, Visuals, Materialities*, ed. Jilly Traganou, 123–130. New York: Routledge, 2021.

Jensen, Hans-Christian, and Anders V. Munch. "Environment and Emancipation Through Design: Avant-Garde Intervention and Experiments with Social Design in Denmark around 1970." *AIS/Design: Storia e Ricerche* 7, no. 12–13 (2019–2020): 88–109.

Johnson, Cedric G. "The Urban Precariat, Neoliberalization, and the Soft Power of Humanitarian Design." *Journal of Developing Societies* 27, no. 3–4 (2011): 445–475.

Jørgensen, Finn Arne. *Recycling*. Cambridge, MA: MIT Press, 2019.

Jørgensen, Thomas Ekman. "Utopia and Disillusion: Shattered Hopes of the Copenhagen Counterculture." In *Between Marx and Coca-Cola: Youth Cultures in Changing European Societies, 1960–1980*, ed. Axel Schildt and Detlef Siegfried, 333–352. Oxford: Berg Publishers, 2006.

Julier, Guy. "From Design Culture to Design Activism," *Design and Culture* 5, no. 2 (2013): 215–236.

Kalsi, Amrik. "A New Design Education in Kenya." In *Kristian Vedel*, ed. Lise Schou, 81–88. Copenhagen: Arkitektens forlag, 2007.

Karnøe, Peter. *Dansk vindmølleindustri: En overraskende international succes* (Copenhagen: Samfundslitteratur, 1991).

Karnøe, Peter, and Raghu Garud. "Path Creation: Co-creation of Heterogeneous Resources in the Emergence of the Danish Wind Turbine Cluster." *European Planning Studies* 20, no. 5 (2012): 733–752.

Kaye, Michael S. *The Teacher Was the Sea: The Story of Pacific High School*. New York: Links Books, 1972.

Kepes, György. "Art and Ecological Conciousness." In *The Universitas Project: Solutions for a Post-Technological Society*, ed. Emilio Ambasz, 150–159. New York: Museum of Modern Art, 2006.

Keshavarz, Mahmoud. "Violent Compassions: Humanitarian Design and the Politics of Borders." *Design Issues* 36, no. 4 (2020): 20–32.

Kirk, Andrew G. "Alloyed: Countercultural Bricoleurs and the Design Science Revival." In *Groovy Science: Knowledge, Innovation, and American Counterculture*, ed. David Kaiser and W. Patrick McCray, 305–336. Chicago: University of Chicago Press, 2016.

Kirk, Andrew G. *Counterculture Green: The Whole Earth Catalog and American Environmentalism*. Lawrence: University Press of Kansas, 2007.

Klingle, Matthew. "The Nature of Desire: Consumption in Environmental History." In *The Oxford Handbook of Environmental History*, ed. Andrew C. Isenberg, 467–511. Oxford: Oxford University Press, 2014.

Kohtala, Cindy, Yana Boeva, and Peter Troxler. "Introduction: Alternative Histories in DIY Cultures and Maker Utopias." *Digital Culture and Society* 6, no. 1 (2020): 5–34.

Kolsrud, Dag. "Hvit ambivalens: Fremveksten av sportsklatring på Kolsås." In *Kolsås: Klatreparadis og naturperle*, ed. Dave Durkan, Jon Gangdal, Geir Grimeland, Gunnar Thon, Tore Nossum, Ola Hanche-Olsen, and Egil Fredriksen, 113–123. Oslo: Kolsås Klatreklubb, 1992.

Kranzberg, Melvin. "Technology and History: 'Kranzberg's Laws'." *Technology and Culture* 27, no. 3 (1986): 544–560.

Kvaløy Setreng, Sigmund. "To økofilosofier i Norge; deres begynnelse og en del til." *Norsk filosofisk tidsskrift* 37, no. 1–2 (2002): 117–126.

Kvaløy, Sigmund. "Man, Nature, and Mechanistic Systems." *The North American Review* 264, no. 3 (1979): 35–37.

Kvaløy, Sigmund. "Ecophilosophy and Ecopolitics: Thinking and Acting in Response to the Threats of Ecocatastrophe." *The North American Review* 259, no. 2 (1974): 16–28.

Kvaløy, Sigmund. *Økokrise, natur og menneske: En innføring i økofilosofi og økopolitikk*. Oslo: s.n., 1973.

Kvaløy, Sigmund. "Sammenhengen mellom økonomisk vekst og økologisk likevekt." In *Økologi og økonomisk vekst*, ed. Mimi Lønnum, 38–55. Oslo: Elingaard, 1973.

Labrague, Michelle. "Patagonia, A Case Study in the Historical Development of Slow Thinking." *Journal of Design History* 30, no. 2 (2017): 175–191.

LaChapelle, Dolores. "Our Mutual Love of Mountains." *The Trumpeter* 9, no. 2 (1992): 66–67.

Larsen, Janike Kampevold, and Peter Hemmersam, eds. *Future North: The Changing Arctic Landscapes*. London: Routledge, 2018.

Latour, Bruno. *Politics of Nature: How to Bring the Sciences into Democracy*. Cambridge, MA: Harvard University Press, 2004.

Latour, Bruno. *We Have Never Been Modern*. Cambridge, MA: Harvard University Press, 1993.

Lee, Martha F. *Earth First! Environmental Apocalypse*. Syracuse: Syracuse University Press, 1995.

Leifer, Tore, Jesper Nielsen, and Toke Sellner Reunert. *Restless Blood: Frans Blom, Explorer and Maya Archaeologist*. San Francisco: Precolumbia Mesoweb Press, 2017.

Leopold, Aldo. *A Sand County Almanac and Sketches Here and There*. 1949; New York: Oxford University Press, 1987.

Lewallen, Constance M., and Steve Seid, eds. *Ant Farm: 1968–1978*. Berkeley: University of California Press, 2004.

Lie, Ida Kamilla. "'Make Us More Useful to Society!': The Scandinavian Design Students' Organization (SDO) and Socially Responsible Design, 1967–1973." *Design and Culture* 8, no. 3 (2016): 327–361.

Lucsko, David N. *Junkyards, Gearheads, and Rust: Salvaging the Automotive Past*. Baltimore: Johns Hopkins University Press, 2016.

Lundberg, Willy Maria. *Ting och tycken*. Stockholm: Rabén & Sjögren, 1960.

Madge, Pauline. "Ecological Design: A New Critique." *Design Issues* 13, no. 2 (1997): 44–54.

Magaziner, Daniel. "The Foundation: Design, Time, and Possibility in 1960s Nairobi." *Comparative Studies in Society and History* 60, no. 3 (2018): 599–628.

Magaziner, Daniel. "The Politics of Design in Postcolonial Kenya." In *Flow of Forms / Forms of Flow: Design Histories between Africa and Europe*, ed. Kerstin Pinther and Alexandra Weigand, 134–151. Bielefeld: Transcript, 2018.

Magaziner, Daniel. "Designing Knowledge in Postcolonial Africa: A South African Abroad." *Kronos: Southern African Histories*, no. 41 (2015): 265–286.

Maldonado, Tomás. *La speranza progettuale: Ambiente e società*. Turin: Einauldi, 1970.

Manzini, Ezio. "The Cultural Tools for an Ecology of the Artificial Environment." In *Scandinavian Design 1990–towards 2000: The Challenge of Internationalization Demands and Needs for a New Millennium*, ed. Ulla Tarras-Wahlberg Bøe, 46–50. Oslo: Scandinavian Design Council, 1990.

Margolin, Victor. "Design for Development: Towards a History." *Design Studies* 28, no. 2 (2007): 111–115.

Martinez-Reyes, Jose. "Mahogany Intertwined: Enviromateriality between Mexico, Fiji, and the Gibson Les Paul." *Journal of Material Culture* 20, no. 3 (2015): 313–329.

Massey, Anne, and Paul Micklethwaite. "Unsustainability: Towards a New Design History with Reference to British Utility." *Design Philosophy Papers* 7, no. 2 (2009): 123–135.

Mathur, Saloni. "Charles and Ray Eames in India." *Art Journal* 70, no. 1 (2011): 34–53.

Mattsson, Helena. "Designing the 'Consumer in Infinity': The Swedish Co-operative Union's New Consumer Policy, c. 1970." In *Scandinavian Design: Alternative Histories*, ed. Kjetil Fallan, 65–82. London: Berg Publishers, 2012.

Mau, Bruce, and the Institute without Boundaries. *Massive Change*. London: Phaidon, 2004.

McDonough, William, and Michael Braungart. *Cradle to Cradle: Remaking the Way We Make Things*. New York: North Point Press, 2002.

Meikle, Jeffrey L. *American Plastics: A Cultural History*. New Brunswick: Rutgers University Press, 1997.

Messell, Tania. "Contested Development: ICSID's Design Aid and Environmental Policy in the 1970s." In *The Culture of Nature in the History of Design*, ed. Kjetil Fallan, 131–146. London: Routledge, 2019.

Michl, Jan. "On Seeing Design as Redesign: An Exploration of a Neglected Problem in Design Education." *Scandinavian Journal of Design History* 12 (2002): 7–23.

Miles, Elza. *Selby Mvusi: To Fly with the North Bird South*. Pretoria: University of South Africa Press, 2015.

Miller, Daegan. "On Possibility: Or, The Monkey Wrench." In *Future Remains: A Cabinet of Curiosities for the Anthropocene*, ed. Gregg Mitman, Marco Armiero, and Robert S. Emmett, 143–148. Chicago: University of Chicago Press, 2018.

Møller, Jes Fabricius. *På sejrens vej: Historien om Skolesamvirket Tvind og dets skaber Mogens Amdi Petersen*. Copenhagen: Dike, 1999.

Morris, William. *News from Nowhere: or An Epoch of Rest, Being Some Chapters from a Utopian Romance*. 1890; London: Routledge, 1970.

Munch, Anders V., Vibeke Riisberg, and Lene Kiærbye Pedersen. "Harmful or Useless? Victor Papanek and the Student Rebellion at Danish Design Schools 1967–1976." In *Lessons to Learn? Past Design Experiences and Contemporary Design Practices: Proceedings of the ICDHS 12th International Conference on Design History and Design Studies*, ed. Fedja Vukić and Iva Kostešić, 137–147. Zagreb: UPI2M Books, 2020.

Myrvang, Christine. *Forbruksagentene: Slik vekket de kjøpelysten*. Oslo: Pax, 2009.

Næss, Arne. *The Selected Works of Arne Naess*, ed. Harold Glasser and Alan Drengson. Dordrecht: Springer, 2005.

Næss, Arne. "Architecture and Deep Ecology." 1992. *The Trumpeter* 21, no. 2 (2005): 29–34.

Næss, Arne. "Comments on Guha's 'Radical American Environmentalism and Wilderness Preservation: A Third World Critique'." In *Philosophical Dialogues: Arne Næss and the Progress of Ecophilosophy*, ed. Nina Witoszek and Andrew Brennan, 325–333. Lanham, MD: Rowman & Littlefield, 1999.

Næss, Arne. "Intrinsic Value: Will the Defenders of Nature Please Rise." 1986. In *Wisdom in the Open Air: The Norwegian Roots of Deep Ecology*, ed. Peter Reed and David Rothenberg, 70–81. Minneapolis: University of Minnesota Press, 1993.

Næss, Arne. "The Future of the Industrialised Society." In *Scandinavian Design 1990–towards 2000: The Challenge of Internationalization Demands and Needs for a New Millennium*, ed. Ulla Tarras-Wahlberg Bøe, 55–58. Oslo: Scandinavian Design Council, 1990.

Næss, Arne. *Ecology, Community and Lifestyle: Outline of an Ecosophy*, trans. David Rothenberg. Cambridge: Cambridge University Press, 1989.

Næss, Arne. "Identification as a Source of Deep Ecological Attitudes." In *Deep Ecology*, ed. Michael Tobias, 256–270. San Diego: Avant Books, 1984.

Næss, Arne. "Modesty and the Conquest of Mountains." In *The Mountain Spirit*, ed. Michael C. Tobias and Harold Drasdo, 13–16. Woodstock, N.Y.: Overlook Press, 1979.

Næss, Arne. *Teknikk, pedagogikk og en ny livsstil: En del artikler og foredrag gjennom 25 år.* Oslo: Universitetsforlaget, 1978.

Næss, Arne. "Why Not Science for Anarchists Too? A Reply to Feyerabend." *Inquiry* 18, no. 2 (1975): 183–194.

Næss, Arne. "The Case Against Science." In *Science Between Culture and Counter-Culture*, ed. Catharina I. Dessaur, 25–48. Nijmegen: Dekker & van de Vegt, 1975.

Næss, Arne. *Økologi, samfunn og livsstil: Utkast til en økosofi.* Oslo: Universitetsforlaget, 1974.

Næss, Arne. "The Shallow and the Deep, Long-Range Ecology Movement. A Summary." *Inquiry* 16, no. 1–4 (1973): 95–100.

Næss, Arne. "The Place of Joy in a World of Fact." *The North American Review* 258, no. 2 (1973): 53–57.

Næss, Arne. *Økologi og filosofi: Et økosofisk arbeidsutkast. Tredje preliminære utgave.* Oslo: Universitetsforlaget, 1972.

Næss, Arne. *Opp stupet: til østtoppen av Tirich Mir.* Oslo: Gyldendal, 1964.

Næss, Arne. *Tirich Mir: The Norwegian Himalaya Expedition.* London: Hodder and Stoughton, 1950.

Næss, Arne. "Bolteklatring." In *Norsk fjellsport 1948*, ed. C. W. Rubenson and Hans H. Røer, 100–120. Oslo: Grøndahl & Søns forlag, 1948.

Næss, Arne. "Nye klatreruter i Jotunheimen og Nord-Norge." In *Den norske turistforenings årbok 1937*, ed. Rolf Lykken, Erling Hauger, and Andreas Backer, 179–193. Oslo: Grøndahl & Søn, 1937.

Næss, Arne, and Inga Bostad. *Inn i filosofien: Arne Næss' ungdomsår.* Oslo: Universitetsforlaget, 2002.

Næss, Siri. "Self-Realization." In *In Sceptical Wonder: Inquiries into the Philosophy of Arne Naess on the Occasion of his 70th Birthday, ed.* Ingemund Gullvåg and Jon Wetlesen, 270–281. Oslo: Universitetsforlaget, 1982.

Narotzky, Viviana. "Our Cars in Havana." In *Autopia: Cars and Culture*, ed. Peter Wollen and Joe Kerr, 169–176. London: Reaktion Books, 2002.

Nielsen, Kristian H. "Danish Wind Power Policies from 1976 to 2004: A Survey of Policy Making and Techno-economic Innovation." In *Switching to Renewable Power: A Framework for the 21st Century*, ed. Volkmar Lauber, 99–121. Abingdon: Earthscan/Routledge, 2005.

Nielsen, Kristian H., and Matthias Heymann. "Winds of Change: Communication and Wind Power Technology Development in Denmark and Germany from 1973 to ca. 1985." *Engineering Studies* 4, no. 1 (2012): 11–31.

Nixon, Rob. "The Anthropocene: The Promise and Pitfalls of an Epochal Idea." In *Future Remains: A Cabinet of Curiosities for the Anthropocene*, ed. Gregg Mitman, Marco Armiero, and Robert S. Emmett, 1–18. Chicago: University of Chicago Press, 2018.

Nordenström, Monica, Egil Öfverholm, and Hans Nordenström, eds. *Byggande, energi och ekologi: Forskning och projekt. Rapport från en resa i USA*. Stockholm: Statens råd för byggnadsforskning, 1975.

Oldenziel, Ruth, and Mikael Hård. *Consumers, Tinkerers, Rebels: The People Who Shaped Europe*. Basingstoke, UK: Palgrave Macmillan, 2013.

Olesen, Thorsten Borring, and Jan Pedersen. "On the Side of the Angels: Altruism in Danish Development Aid 1960–2005." *European Review of History/Revue européenne d'histoire* 17, no. 6 (2010): 881–903.

Olvång, Bengt. *Våga se! Svensk konst 1945–1980*. Göteborg: Författarförlaget, 1983.

Oropallo, Gabriele. "People Have the Power: Appropriate Technology and the Implications of Labour-Intensive Making." In *Craft Economies*, ed. Susan Luckman and Nicola Thomas, 83–93. London: Bloomsbury Academic, 2018.

Oropallo, Gabriele. "Making or Unmaking the Environment: The Role of Envisioning in the History of Sustainable Design." PhD thesis, University of Oslo, 2017.

Orr, David. *The Nature of Design: Ecology, Culture, and Human Intention*. Oxford: Oxford University Press, 2002.

Orr, David. "Conservation and Conservatism." *Conservation Biology* 9, no. 2 (1995): 242–245.

Östberg, Kjell. "Sweden and the Long '1968:' Break or Continuity?" *Scandinavian Journal of History* 33, no. 4 (2008): 339–352.

Östling, Johan. "Circulation, Arenas, and the Quest for Public Knowledge." *History and Theory* 59, no. 4 (2020): 111–126.

Owens, Brandon N. *The Wind Power Story: A Century of Innovation that Reshaped the Global Energy Landscape*. Hoboken, NJ: John Wiley & Son, 2019.

Paglia, Eric. "Not a Proper Crisis." *The Anthropocene Review* 2, no. 3 (2015): 247–261.

Palmstierna, Hans. *Besinning*. Stockholm: Rabén & Sjögren, 1972.

Palmstierna, Hans. *Plundring, svält, förgiftning*. Stockholm: Rabén & Sjögren, 1967.

Palmstiena, Hans, Marit Paulsen, Jan Odhnoff, Lena Palmstierna, Sture Andersson, and Gudrun Hjelte. *Framtiden kräver: Energi, arbete, miljö*. Kristianstad: Tidens förlag, 1974.

Papanek, Victor. "Lies and Consequences: Industrial Design and Ecology." In *Scandinavian Design 1990–towards 2000: The Challenge of Internationalization Demands and Needs for a New Millennium*, ed. Ulla Tarras-Wahlberg Bøe, 51–54. Oslo: Scandinavian Design Council, 1990.

Papanek, Victor. "Design in Developing Countries 1950–1985: A Summing Up." *Art Libraries Journal* 11, no. 2 (1986): 44–51.

Papanek, Victor. "For the Southern Half of the Globe." *Design Studies* 4, no. 1 (1983): 61–64.

Papanek, Victor. *Design for the Real World: Human Ecology and Social Change*. New York: Pantheon Books, 1971.

Papanek, Victor. *Miljön och miljonerna: Design som tjänst eller förtjänst?* Stockholm: Bonniers, 1970.

Pech, Christina. *Arkitektur och motstånd: Om sökandet efter alternativ i svensk arkitektur 1970–1980.* Göteborg: Makadam, 2011.

Pérez, Jorge F. Rivas. "Cannibal Homes: Additive Modernity and Design by Absorption in Brazil, Mexico and Venezuela, 1940–1978." In *Moderno: Design for Living in Brazil, Mexico, and Venezuela, 1940–1978,* ed. Gabriela Rangel and Jorge F. Rivas Pérez, 15–33. New York: Americas Society; Miami: Prisa/Santillana USA, 2015.

Persen, Åsne Berre, and Nils Hermann Ranum. *Natur og Ungdom: 30 år i veien.* Oslo: Natur og Ungdom, 1997.

Pesce, Gaetano. "The Period of the Great Contaminations." In *Italy: The New Domestic Landscape: Achievements and Problems of Italian Design,* ed. Emilio Ambasz, 212–222. New York: Museum of Modern Art, 1972.

Petersen, Flemming. *Da Danmark fikk vinger: Vindmøllehistorien 1978–2018.* Aarhus: Danmarks Vindmølleforening, 2018.

Petersen, Flemming, Bjarning Grøn, Asger N. Kristiansen, and Anette Christensen. *Det danske vindmølleeventyr.* Copenhagen: Fysikforlaget, 2007.

Pfützner, Katharina. *Designing for Socialist Need: Industrial Design Practice in the German Democratic Republic.* London: Routledge, 2018.

Pharo, Helge Ø., and Monika Phole Fraser. "Introduction." In *The Aid Rush: Aid regimes in Northern Europe during the Cold War,* Volume 1, ed. Helge Ø. Pharo and Monika Phole Fraser. Oslo: Unipub, 2008.

Pido, J.P. Odoch. "Pedagogical Clashes in East African Art and Design Education." *Critical Interventions: Journal of African Art History and Visual Culture* 8, no. 1 (2014): 119–132.

Priebe, Janina. "From Siam to Greenland: Danish Economic Imperialism at the Turn of the Twentieth Century." *Journal of World History* 27, no. 4 (2016): 619–640.

Pursell, Carroll. "Sim van der Ryn and the Architecture of the Appropriate Technology Movement." *Australasian Journal of American Studies* 28, no. 2 (2009): 17–30.

Pursell, Carroll. *The Machine in America: A Social History of Technology.* Baltimore: Johns Hopkins University Press, 1995.

Pursell, Carroll. "The Rise and Fall of the Appropriate Technology Movement in the United States, 1965–1985." *Technology and Culture* 34, no. 3 (1993): 629–637.

Reed, Peter, and David Rothenberg, eds. *Wisdom in the Open Air: The Norwegian Roots of Deep Ecology.* Minneapolis: University of Minnesota Press, 1993.

Reynolds, Helen. "The Utility Garment: Its Design and Effect on the Mass Market 1942–45." In *Utility Reassessed: The Role of Ethics in the Practice of Design,* ed. Judy Attfield, 125–143. Manchester: Manchester University Press, 1999.

Ringdal, Siv. "110 Volts at Home: the American Lista." *Journal of Design History* 27, no. 1 (2014): 79–96.

Robach, Cilla. *Formens frigörelse: Konsthantverkare och design under debatt i 1960-talets Sverige.* Stockholm: Arvinius, 2010.

Roszak, Theodore. *Where the Wasteland Ends: Politics and Transcendence in Postindustrial Society*. Garden City, N.Y.: Doubleday, 1972.

Roszak, Theodore. *The Making of a Counter Culture: Reflections on the Technocratic Society and Its Youthful Opposition*. Garden City, N.Y.: Doubleday, 1969.

Rothenberg, David. *Is It Painful to Think? Conversations With Arne Naess*. Minneapolis: University of Minnesota Press, 1993.

Rubin, Eli. "The Form of Socialism without Ornament: Consumption, Ideology, and the Fall and Rise of Modernist Design in the German Democratic Republic." *Journal of Design History* 19(2) (2006): 155–168.

Sadler, Simon. "Design's Ecological Operating Environments." In *The Culture of Nature in the History of Design*, ed. Kjetil Fallan, 19–30. London: Routledge, 2019.

Sadler, Simon. "Tools of Oneness: Design for Post-Industrial Communities." In *California: Designing Freedom*, ed. Justin McGuirk and Brendan McGetrick, 157–163. London: Phaidon, 2017.

Sadler, Simon. "An Architecture of the Whole." *Journal of Architectural Education* 61, no. 4 (2008): 108–129.

Sætra, Hartvig. *Den økopolitiske sosialismen*. Oslo: Pax, 1973.

Schou-Christensen, Jørgen. "Kristian Vedel." In *The Lunning Prize*, ed. Helena Dahlbäck Lutteman and Marianne Uggla, 136–137. Stockholm: Nationalmuseum, 1986.

Schultz, Tristan, Danah Abdulla, Ahmed Ansari, Ece Canli, Mahmoud Keshavarz, Matthew Kiem, Luiza Prado de O. Martins, and Pedro J. S. Vieira de Oliveira. "What Is at Stake with Decolonizing Design? A Roundtable." *Design and Culture* 10, no. 1 (2018): 81–101.

Schumacher, E. F. *Small Is Beautiful: A Study of Economics as if People Mattered*. London: Blond & Briggs, 1973.

Scott, Felicity D. "'Talking Teacher:' Radio, Television, and the Oral Channel." In *Victor Papanek: The Politics of Design*, ed. Mateo Kries, Amelie Klein, and Alison J. Clarke, 48–63. Weil am Rhein: Vitra Design Museum, 2018.

Scott, Felicity D. *Outlaw Territories: Environments of Insecurity/Architectures of Counterinsurgency*. New York: Zone Books, 2016.

Seed, John, Joanna Macy, Pat Fleming, and Arne Naess. *Thinking Like a Mountain: Towards a Council of All Beings*. Philadelphia: New Society Publishers, 1988.

Serafimova, Silviya. *Ethical Aspects of 20th Century Norwegian Environmental Philosophies*. Sofia: Avangard Prima, 2017.

Sessions, George. "Arne Naess & the Union of Theory & Practice." *The Trumpeter* 9, no. 2 (1991): n.p.

Sessions, George. "Ecological Consciousness and Paradigm Change." In *Deep Ecology*, ed. Michael Tobias, 28–58. San Diego: Avant Books, 1984.

Simeons, Charles. *Hydro-Power: The Use of Water as an Alternative Source of Energy*. Oxford: Pergamon Press, 1980.

Simon, Herbert. *The Sciences of the Artificial*. Cambridge, MA: MIT Press, 1969.

Skønberg, Sven Erik, ed. *Grønn pepper i turbinene: 16 bidrag om miljøkrisen og veiene ut av den. Til ære for Sigmund Kvaløy Setereng*. Oslo: Universitetsforlaget, 1985.

Slagstad, Rune. *De nasjonale strateger*. Oslo: Pax, 1998.

Smith, Adrian. "Environmental Movements and Innovation: From Alternative Technology to Hollow Technology." *Human Ecology Review* 12, no. 2 (2005): 113–119.

Snyder, Gary. *Turtle Island*. New York: New Directions, 1974.

Soleri, Paolo. *Arcosanti: An Urban Laboratory?* San Diego: Avant Books, 1984.

Soleri, Paolo. *Arcology: The City in the Image of Man*. Cambridge, MA: MIT Press, 1969.

Somjee Rajan, Sultan Firoze H. "Learning to Be Indigenous or Being Taught to Be Kenyan: The Ethnography of Teaching Art and Material Culture in Kenya." PhD thesis, McGill University, 1996.

Somjee, Sultan. *Material Culture of Kenya*. Nairobi: East African Publishers, 1993.

Somjee, Sultan. "The Arts in Lifelong Education in Kenya." In *The Arts in Life-long Education*, ed. D'Arcy Hayman, 55–60. Paris: UNESCO; Sofia: Sofia Press, 1977.

Springfeldt, Björn, ed. *Finlandia, Svezia, Norvegia: Biennale di Venezia '76* (Venice: Biennale di Venezia, 1976).

Stone, Peter. *Did We Save the World at Stockholm?* London: Earth Island, 1973.

Stott, Timothy. "Ludic Pedagogies at the College of Environmental Design, UC Berkeley, 1966 to 1972." In *The Culture of Nature in the History of Design*, ed. Kjetil Fallan, 58–71. London: Routledge, 2019.

Stott, Timothy. "Systems in Play: Simon Nicholson's Design 12 Course, University of California, Berkeley, 1966." *Journal of Design History* 32, no. 3 (2019): 223–239.

Strandh, Sigvard, ed. *Daedalus 1968: Tekniska Museets årsbok*. Stockholm: Tekniska Museet/P.A. Norstedt & Söner, 1968.

Szeman, Imre, and Dominic Boyer. "Introduction: On the Energy Humanities." In *Energy Humanities: An Anthology*, ed. Imre Szeman and Dominic Boyer, 1–13. Baltimore: Johns Hopkins University Press, 2017.

Taft, Maggie. "Morphologies and Genealogies: Shaker Furniture and Danish Design." *Design and Culture* 7, no. 3 (2015): 313–334.

Tate, Ryan Driskell. "Rural Revolt: Power Line Protests and the Alternative Technology Movement in the United States, 1970s." *Technology and Culture* 62, no. 1 (2021): 1–26.

Taylor, Joseph E. III. *Pilgrims of the Vertical: Yosemite Rock Climbers and Nature at Risk*. Cambridge, MA: Harvard University Press, 2010.

Thau, Carsten. "Ussing og Hoff—arkitekturen frisatt." In *Susanne Ussing—mellem kunst og arkitektur*, ed. Birgitte Thorsen Vilslev and Carsten Hoff, 81–125. Copenhagen: Strandberg, 2017.

Theien, Iselin. "Shopping for the 'People's Home': Consumer Planning in Norway and Sweden after the Second World War." In *The Expert Consumer: Associations and Professionals in Consumer Society*, ed. Alain Chatriot, Marie-Emmanuelle Chessel, and Matthew Hilton, 137–150. Aldershot, UK: Ashgate, 2006.

Thiberg, Sven. "Dags att undvara." In *Formens rörelse: Svensk form genom 150 år*, ed. Kerstin Wickman, 268–283. Stockholm: Carlssons, 1995.

Thill, Brian. *Waste*. New York: Bloomsbury Academic, 2015.

Thorndahl, Jytte. *Gedsermøllen: Den første moderne vindmølle*. Bjerringbro: Elmuseet, 2005.

Tobias, Michael, ed. *Deep Ecology*. San Diego: Avant Books, 1984.

Tostrup, Elisabeth. *Norwegian Wood: The Thoughtful Architecture of Wenche Selmer*. New York: Princeton Architectural Press, 2006.

Traganou, Jilly, ed. *Design and Political Dissent: Spaces, Visuals, Materialities*. New York: Routledge, 2021.

Tunstall, Elizabeth. "Decolonizing Design Innovation: Design Anthropology, Critical Anthropology, and Indigenous Knowledge." In *Design Anthropology: Theory and Practice*, ed. Wendy Gunn, Ton Otto, and Rachel Charlotte Smith, 232–250. London: Bloomsbury, 2013.

Turpin, John. "The Irish Design Reform Movement of the 1960s." *Design Issues* 3, no. 1 (1986): 3–21.

Twemlow, Alice. *Sifting the Trash: A History of Design Criticism*. Cambridge, MA: MIT Press, 2017.

Twemlow, Alice. "'A Guaranteed Communications Failure': Consensus Meets Conflict at the International Design Conference in Aspen, 1970." In *The Aspen Complex*, ed. Martin Beck, 110–135. Berlin: Sternberg Press, 2012.

Twemlow, Alice. "I Can't Talk to You if You Say That: An Ideological Collision at the International Design Conference at Aspen, 1970." *Design and Culture* 1, no. 1 (2009): 23–49.

Van der Ryn, Sim, and Stuart Cowan. *Ecological Design*. Washington, DC: Island Press, 1996.

Wann, David. *Deep Design: Pathways to a Livable Future*. Washington, D.C.: Island Press, 1996.

Ward, Barbara. *Spaceship Earth*. New York: Columbia University Press, 1966.

Ward, Barbara, and René Dubos. *Only One World: The Care and Maintenance of a Small Planet*. New York: W. W. Norton, 1972.

West, Kim. "The Exhibitionary Complex: Exhibition, Apparatus, and Media from Kulturhuset to the Centre Pompidou, 1963–1977." PhD thesis, Södertörn University, 2017.

Williamson, Bess. *Accessible America: A History of Disability and Design*. New York: New York University Press, 2019.

Werner, Jeff. *Medelvägens estetik: Sverigebilder i USA*. Hedemora/Möklinta: Gidlunds förlag, 2008.

Winograd, Terry, and Fernando Flores. *Understanding Computers and Cognition: A New Foundation for Design*. Norwood, NJ: Ablex, 1986.

World Commission on Environment and Development. *Our Common Future*. Oxford: Oxford University Press, 1987.

Yran, Knut. *A Joy Forever: Knut Yran Talks About Design in Industry*. Melbourne: Industrial Design Institute of Australia, 1980.

Zapffe, Peter Wessel. *Spøk og alvor: Epistler og leilighetsvers*. Oslo: Gyldendal, 1977.

Zapffe, Peter Wessel. *Barske glæder og andre temaer fra et liv under åpen himmel*. Ed. Sigmund Kvaløy. Oslo: Gyldendal, 1969.

Zelko, Frank. *Make It a Green Peace! The Rise of Countercultural Environmentalism*. Oxford: Oxford University Press, 2013.

Zimring, Carl A. *Aluminum Upcycled: Sustainable Design in a Historical Perspective*. Baltimore: Johns Hopkins University Press, 2017.

INDEX

Page numbers in italics indicate illustrations.

A&E Design, 55
Abdulla, Danah, 111–112, 140
Abrahamsen, Flemming, 239
Abram-Nilsson, Kerstin, 157, 161–163, 171, 178, 179
ABS (thermoplastic), 55
Activism, among students in higher
    education, 147
Afdal, Torbjørn, 91
Affluent Society, The (Galbraith), 78–79
African design, 112–113
AGA stove, 175
Ahlström, Tom, 55
Ahmedabad Declaration on Industrial Design
    for Development, 136–137, 272
Åkerman, Brita, 43–44
Alexander, Christopher, 40, 47
Alpine Designs, 219
Alternative Christmas, 148
Alternative City (United Nations Conference
    on the Human Environment), 163–165
Alternative Oil Debate, 17
Alternative technology, 21–22, 77
   and Department of Industrial Design at
     University of Nairobi, 114–118
   exhibitions at United Nations Conference
     on the Human Environment, 146
   and Tvind windmill, 240–246
American Butterflies (Kleiva), 6, 7, 8
American West, 202. *See also* California
"Amused to Death" (Water), 25
And after Us . . . (traveling exhibition), 47–48,
    66–71, 72, 81, 194
   exhibition catalog, *68–71*
Anker, Peder, 76, 219
Anshelm, Klas, 173
Antell, Olof, 171
Ant Farm, 205, 260

Anthropocene, 15, 36
Appropriate technology, 77. *See also*
    Alternative technology
ARARAT (Alternative Research in Architecture,
    Resources, Art and Technology), 146, 170–
    172, 179–180, 239
   criticisms of, 180–183
   exhibition (1976), 173–177
   and Konstfack, 177–179
   and PowWow, 170
   textiles at, 178–179
   and United Nations Conference on the
     Human Environment, 170, 171
   visit to the United States (1975), 172–173
Archer, Bruce, 40
Architects, and specialization, 79–80
Architecture Museum (Stockholm), 165
Arcosanti, 172, 207. *See also* Soleri, Paolo
Arkitektnytt (magazine), 63, 77
Arkitim, Hans Østerhaug, 94
Armiero, Marco, 97
Armitage, David, 3–4
Arnfred, Birgit, 103
Arnfred, Tyge, 103
ASEA, 242
Askov College, 231, 233
   and Traveling College, 241–242
Aspen Design Conference. *See* International
    Design Conference in Aspen;
    Transatlantic Shop Talk No. 2—Aspen
    Comes to Scandinavia
Association for Applied Art and Industrial
    Design, 125
Association for Rational Application of
    Electricity (FERA), 38, 40
Association of Danish Electricity
    Works, 237–238

Association of Danish Wind Powerplants, 240
Association of Norwegian Landscape
    Architects, 77
Association of Windmill Manufacturers, 240
Asynchronous AC windmill generator, 232, 234
Atelier Populaire, 162
Atwood, Margaret, 17
Auböck, Carl, 134, 136–137
Austin, Mary, 207

Back-to-the-land movement, 199
Baer, Steve, 172, 173
Baez, Joan, 217
Baldwin, J., 207, 217
Bass, Saul, 262, 263, 268, 273
Battle of the Elms (Alternative City), 148, *149*
Baudrillard, Jean, 261
Beatles (Christensen), 67
Bekken, Torbjørn, 91
Belgrad, Daniel, 3
Benktzon, Maria, 271–272
Berg, Liv, 49
Bergans, 214–217
Bergen School of Architecture, 87
Bergen School of Craft and Design, 87
Berglund, Erik, 31
Bergström, Arne, 163
Berkeley (California), Næss in, 202–205
Bernadotte, Sigvard, 151
Besinning (Palmstierna), 45
"Big Here" (Eno), 2
Bike restoration and distribution scheme
    (Alternative City), 164
Biodiversity, 17
Biomimical processes, 40–41
Bionics, 40
Birch, 88
Björnstjerna, Mikael, 31
Blom, Frans, 105–106, 108
Blom, Gertrude Duby, 105–106, 108
Bøe, Alf, 263, 265, 267
Bøe, Ulla Tarras-Wahlberg, 263, 265
Boeing, 246
Bogø, 234
Bokalders, Varis, 163, 164, 169, 171, 177–178

Boman, Monica, 54, 57, 58
Bønke, Knut, 271, 273
Bonsiepe, Gui, 130, 132, 133, 135, 136
Bonus, 248, 251
Borgström, Georg, 45, 67, 72, 81, 226
Boyle, Godfrey, 169–170
Boyntt, 88, *89*, 90–91
Brånby, Ann-Britt, 179
Brand, Stewart, 6, 8, 155–156, 180, 205, 217
Braungart, Michael, 10
Breinart, Julian, 263
Brekkestranda Fjordhotell, 85–86
Brennan, Andrew, 188–189
Bricolage, 11
British Alpine Club journal, 189
British Council of Industrial Design, 94
Brochmann, Odd, 63
Brower, David, 207
Brown, Jerry, 237
Bruksbo, 91
Brundtland Report, 11, 16
Bucharest, third World Future Studies
    Federation conference in, 195, 196
    Næss's lecture at, 196–198, 220
Butenschøn, Peter, 272, 273
Butler, Andy, 205
Byggekunst (magazine), 74, 78, 80, 194
    front cover, *75*

Cabins, leisure, 88
    Næss's Tvergastein, 185, 187, *188*, 199, 222
    Trysik cabin, 94
Cadena, Marisol de la, 15
Caine, Graham, 172
California
    clear-felling of forests in, 205
    climbing in, 209–212
    counterculture, 203, 217–218
    and deep ecology, 202–209
    Office of Appropriate Technology, 237
    and windmill technology, 249–252
California hippie, caricature of, 6, 241
Calthorpe, Peter, 220
Caplan, Ralph, 263, 267
Carling, Bengt, 176

Carlsson, Åke, 157
Carlström, Tomas, 212–213
Cars
    electric Saab 96, *39*
    Esdaile on, 63–64
    Mars II, *39*
    recycling, 11–12
Carson, Rachel, 35, 67
Carter, Jimmy, 237
Casa Na Bolom, 106
Castillo, Greg, 205
Castro, Fidel, 63
Celloplast, 51
Central Institute of Design (German
    Democratic Republic), 13
Cerro Fitz Roy, 217
Chakrabarty, Dipesh, 14
Chalmers Institute of Technology, 47–48,
    49, 66–67
Change, and design, 3–6, 8
Chatterjee, Ashoke, 99
Chermayeff, Ivan, 263
Choice, freedom of, 42
Chouinard, Yvon, 209–210, 213, 214, 217, 219
Chouinard Equipment, 193, 209–212, 213
Christensen, Lars Saabye, 67
Christensen, Niels Helmer, 252
Christie, Niels, 180
Clarke, Alison, 99
Clarté (magazine), 162
Clean Air Pod (Ant Farm), 205
Clean climbing technologies, 22, 209–212,
    217, 227
Climate change, as consequence of
    design, 10, 15–16
Climate Lawsuit, 16
Climbing and climbers, 187–191
    clean (low-impact) climbing, 22, 86,
    187–188, 209–213
    gear, 209–219
Club of Rome, 81, 83, 195
Code of ethics, Boman's instigation of
    debate about, 55
Co-Evolution Quarterly, 222
Cold War, and ecology, 65

Colliver, George, 206
Colonialism, and justice, 15, 142
Combi windmill model (Bonus), 251–252
Commoner, Barry, 154
"Comprehensive thinking," 80
Conservatism, and conservationism, 35–36
Consumer in Infinity, 26
Consumer research and advice, in
    Scandinavia, 28
Consumption, 20, 26. *See also*
    Recycling and reuse
    appeal to convenience and leisure, 28
    contested nature of, 27
    cost of, 41–44
    design as metabolism, 81–82
    disposability vs. durability, 26–27, 28, 30
    as empowering, 30
    environmental ramifications, 27, 35–41
    and freedom of choice, 42
    and Fuller's *Operating Manual for Spaceship
    Earth*, 79–80
    and Galbraith's *The Affluent Society*,
    78–79
    and household sciences, 42–43
    and planned obsolescence, 28
    and plastics, 55–57
    by producers, 20
    and taste, 33–34
Convenience, appeal to, 28
Cooperative Union (KF), 26
    Rabén & Sjögren publishing house, 45
    and reuse, 51–53
Copenhagen Cabinetmakers' Guild, 100
Copenhagen School of Construction
    Engineering, Ecological Resource
    Use unit, 239
Costa Rica, Vedels in, 102, 104, 108
Counterculture, California, 203, 217–218
Cowan, Ruth Schwartz, 28
Co-working Group for the Protection of
    Nature and the Environment (University
    of Oslo), 73
Cradle to Cradle (C2C) framework, 10
Craft-intensive manufacturing, 31
Crisp, Michael, 176

Cuba
  and Esdaile, 63
  US cars recycled in, 11–12
Cuban missile crisis, 65

Dahl, Eilif, 76
Dalén, Gustaf, 175
Dammann, Erik, 84, 142, 225–226
Danish Academy of Technical Sciences, 247
Danish Center for Development
    Research, 125, 126
Danish Design Council, 252, 253, 263
Danish East Asiatic Company, 87
Danish Institute of Technology, 234
Danish International Development Agency
    (DANIDA), 21, 99, 113, 126, 141
Danish modern, 236
Danish Museum of Decorative Art, 108, 110
Danish National Bank, Jubilee Fund, 127–128
Danish Society of Arts and Crafts and
    Industrial Design, 111
Danish Society of Master Smiths, 245–246
Danish State Railways (DSB), 270
Dansk Vindteknik, 247
Danwin, windmill model 24/180, 253
Death and Life of Great American Cities, The
    (Jacobs), 198
Death Valley, 206, 209
de Bretteville, Sheila Levrant, 261
Decolonial critique of design for
    development, 138–141
Deep design, 219–226
Deep Design: Pathways to a Livable Future
    (Wann), 220
Deep ecology, 22, 185–186, 226–229. *See also*
    Næss, Arne
  and arcology, 207–209
  and California culture and
    counterculture, 202–206
  and clean climbing technologies, 22, 209–
    212, 217, 227
  deep design, 219–226
  Deep Ecology (ed. Tobias), 207, 208
  Deep Ecology: Living as if Nature Mattered
    (Devall and Sessions), 206–207, 219

  and ecosophy, 191–198
  and ecosophy D, 198–202, 226–229
  mountains and alpine climbing,
    187–191
  and social justice, 142
Deep Ecology (ed. Tobias), 207, 208
Deep Ecology: Living as if Nature Mattered
    (Devall and Sessions), 206–207, 219
Dencik, Lars, 180
Denmark
  Cultural Canon (2006), 230
  electrical wind power, history, 230–233
  energy supply, 230
  Ministry of Energy, 240
  Ministry of Environmental Protection, 2
  Ministry of Foreign Affairs, 112
  power grid, 233–234, 237, 239
  Wind Power Commission, 236
des Cressonières, Josine, 131
Design and designers, 1–3. *See also*
    Development, design for
  African, 112–113
  and change, 3–6, 8
  design knowledge, and windmills, 249
  ecosophy D (*see* Ecosophy)
  furniture (*see* Furniture design and
    manufacture)
  as garbage, 8–14
  and justice, 14–19
  as management of material flows,
    36–37
  as metabolism, 82
  participatory, 86
  as redesign, 249
  and resources, 8–14
  and specialization, 79–80
Design and the United Nations Conference on
    the Human Environment, 145, 207
  activist attitude, 147
  Alternative City, 164–165
  alternative technology, exhibitions, 146
  contested legacy of, 145
  counterconferences and alternative
    platforms at, 151, 153–156
  Environmental Forum, 153–154, 173

graphic language of protest, 156–163
intergovernmental and nongovernmental
    organizations at, 151, 182–183
Life Forum, 155–156
People's Forum, 154–155, 156, 166
poster, 143, *144*, 145
and PowWow, 153, 154, 165–170
protest environment, 147–150 (*see
    also* Design and the United Nations
    Conference on the Human Environment:
    graphic language of protest)
Design for Disassembly, 47
Design for Need (exhibition and
    symposium), 135–136
Design for the Real World (Papanek), 43,
    261
"Design for Tourism" (workshop), 123
Design history, 1–4
"Design in Kenya for the Tourist Industry and
    Local People" (Schofield), 122–123
Design (magazine), 94, 139–140
Design Research and Development Unit
    (University of Nairobi), 118–123
    causes behind Vedel's departure, 123–126
    and decolonial critique of design for
        development, 139
Design Society of Kenya, 131
Design with Nature (McHarg), 198
Design without Borders, 98
Devall, Bill, 206–207, 212
Development, design for, 21, 97–98. *See also*
    Vedel, Kristian
    decolonial critique of, 138–141
    and East Africa, 99
    and ICSID Working Group IV, 130–137
    interest in and intervention into non-
        Western societies and cultures, 98–99
Dictatorship of the material, 37
Diffrient, Niels, 263, 267–268, 271
Dirtbag lifestyle, 217–218
Dirty design, 10
Disposability and disposable design, 30, 31,
    33, 37, 54
    Papanek on, 43
    and throwawayism debate, 20, 26–27, 35

DIY/bricolage design culture
    at Oslo IDCA conference, 270
    Tvind windmill, 240–246
Doczi, György, 221
Domebook (Kahn), 207
Dome Cookbook (Baer), 173
Doyle, Michael, 205, 261
Drop City (commune), 173
Dubos, René, 166, 223
Dunaway, Finis, 67, 157
Durability and durable design, 26, 28
    Larsson's diatribe against, 30, 31, 33, 34
    Lundberg's praise for, 30, 31
    Papanek on, 43
    and quality, 31
Dysthe, Trinelise, 272

Eames, Charles, 98
Eames, Ray, 98
Eames Report (Eames and Eames), 98–99
Earth as spaceship metaphor, 82
Earth Day (1970), 59, 65
Earth First!, 225
East Africa, 49
    design education in and by, 112–118
    prioritized by Scandinavian development
        aid agencies, 99
    "upcycling" in, 49
Ecocide, 150, 156
Eco-defense: A Field Guide to Monkeywrenching
    (Foreman), 225
Ecological design, 1. *See also* Ecosophy: and
    ecosophy D
    Danish, 230
    Vedels' sheep farm as an experiment
        in, 128–129
Ecologist, The, 5
Ecology
    Esdaile and, 65
    and landscape architecture, 74, 76–77
    Simonnæs's early distrust of, 82–83,
        86–87
Ecology Action, 203, 205, 260
Ecology Center (Berkeley), 205
Ecology, Community and Lifestyle (Næss), 223–224

Ecophilosophy, 22. *See also* Deep ecology; Ecosophy
and *ARARAT*, 171
Ecophilosophy Group, 71, 194, 222, 227
Ecophilosophy Newsletter, 206
Ecosophy, 22, 76, 191–198
and ecosophy D, 198–202, 226–229
Edberg, Boï, 161
Ehrich, Hans, 55
Ehrlich, Paul, 45, 154
Eide, Njål R., 270–271, 273
Eidsvoll Rivefabrikk, 92
Ekecrantz, Jan, 180
Electric vehicles, experimental, 39
Electrolux gas absorption refrigerator, 175
El Salvador, Vedels in, 105
Emmet, Robert S., 229
Energiplan 81, 240
Energy
and economic growth, 229
and environmental concerns, 37–38
nuclear, 239
oil crisis, 1970s, 237–240
and progress, 229
Engman, Lars, 174
Eno, Brian, 2
"Environmental Crisis, The" (Esdaile), 63–67
Environmental Forum (United Nations Conference on the Human Environment), 153–154
Environmentalism
and disposability, 35–41
intellectual landscape of, 74, 76–77
local and global at the same time, 97–98
Environmental justice, 16–17
Environmental problems, global, 21–22
Environment and the Millions: Design as Service or Profit?, The (Papanek), 42–43
Environment by Design (IDCA), 23
Environment Centre (Sweden), 163
Environment Tomorrow (exhibition), 37–40
Environment Workshop (San Francisco), 205, 260, 261
Ergonomi Design, 55, 271

Erickson, Mark, 218
Eriksen, Tore Linné, 67
Eriksson, Birgitta, 179
Eriksson, Björn, 169
Escobar, Arturo, 15, 138, 141
Escuela de Diseño y Artesanías (Mexico City), 108
Esdaile, Robert, 62, 80, 81, 94
And after Us . . . , 47–48, 66–71
DIY cabin, 74, *75*
"The Environmental Crisis," 63–66
and local context and environment, 71–74
European Conservation Year, 59

Faarlund, Helga, 212
Faarlund, Nils, 188, 190, 191, 193, 212–214
Farallones Institute, 205, 260
and *ARARAT*, 172
Farson, Richard, 261, 262, 263, 267
Federation of Norwegian Industries, 267
Fehn, Sverre, 63
Fernández, Silvia, 111
Fernández-Shaw, Daniel, 103
Fernemo, Ivar, 67
Feyerabend, Paul, 203
50' X 50' Pillow (Ant Farm), 205
Filialen (Moderna Museet), 167
Finnish Society of Crafts and Design, 98, 263, 272
Fiskeby, 51
5-15 modular storage system, *93*
5000 poliser har dragits saman för att skydda dej från FN-konferensens delegater (protest poster), *160*, 161
Flores, Fernando, 212
F. L. Smith & Co., 233
Flygare, Barbro, 157
Follow the Money (Bedrag), 230
For a Technology in the Service of the People! (exhibition), 146, 166–167, 169, 170, 171–172, 180, 181–182
Ford Foundation, 98
Foreman, Dave, 225

Form (magazine), 27, 30–31, *32*, 34
  Boman editorial favoring restraint, 54–55
  and environmental sustainability, 36, 40, 41–42
  review of Papanek's *The Environment and the Millions*, 442–443
Forun: Environment Is Politics (newsletter), 153–154
Fossil fuels, Simonnæs on, 83
Fox, Warwick, 207
Framtiden kräver: Energi, arbete, miljö (Palmstierna et al.), *46*, 47, 57
Franck, Kaj, 36–37, 53
Freedom of choice, 42
Free speech movement, 203
Freja Group (Royal Danish Academy of Fine Arts), 239
Friends of the Earth, 72, 207
Friis & Moltke Architects, 245
Frödin, Ulf, 157, 159
From Plant to Garment (slideshow), 179
Frost, Tom, 209, 213
Fuad-Luke, Alastair, 147, 181
Fuller, R. Buckminster, 10–11, 40, 47, 55, 65, 218, 261, 262
  on specialization and "comprehensive thinking," 79–81
Furniture design and manufacture
  and disposable design, 31
  indigenous materials for, 87, 88–91
  tropical materials for, 87–88
  use of pine for, 88, 90–94
  and whole-system thinking, 94
Furniture Industry Trade Council, 90
Future in Our Hands, The (Dammann) 84, 142, 225–226
Futurum AS, 91
Futurum line, Rastad & Relling, 91

Gabrielsen, Rolf, 91
Gadget society, 26, 54, 59
Galbraith, John Kenneth, 26, 78
Galtung, Johan, 195–196, 203
Gandhi, Mohandas K., 98, 194
Gandhi Institute (Varanasi, India), 203

Ganneskov, Svend, 239
Garbage, design as, 8–14
Gedser Experimental Mill, 168, 230, 233–236, 239, 247, 248
Geodesic domes, 173, 207
German Democratic Republic (East Germany), Central Institute of Design, 13
Giedion, Sigfried, 37
Gillberg, Björn, 163
Gip, Stephan, 31
Gipe, Paul, 252
Glasenapp, Jörg, 133, 137
Glaser, Milton, 262, 263, 267
Göransdotter, Maria, 28
Gore-Tex, 214
Gould, Nicholas, 5
GRAS, 6
Grassroots activism, 84
Grateful Dead, The, 217
Great California Wind Rush, 249, 255
Green Party (Miljöpartiet) (Sweden), 40
Greenpeace, 16
Green Pepper in the Turbines (Kvaløy), 225
Grigoriev, N. K., 131
Group for Alternative Housing, 226
Grove-Nielsen, Erik, 245
Grundtvig, N. F. S., 231
Grundtvig Church, 231
Guatemala, Vedels in, 105, 108
Guevara, Ernesto "Che," 63
Guha, Ramachandra, 227
Guldi, Jo, 3–4
Gustavsberg, 55

Haavelmo, Trygve, 199
Habitat I, 218
Haggert, Bruce, 172
Hald, Arthur, 30, 31
Håll naturen ren (poster), *158*, 159
Hamilton, Bruce, 218
Hannover Principles, 10
Hansson, Ritva, 179
Haraway, Donna J., 19
Hård, Mikael, 246
Hård, Ulf, 151, 267

Hardin, Garret, 207
Harper, Douglas, 11
Harper, Peter, 168, 169–170
Harrambee Village Glass Industry, 98, 272
Haug, Jon, 90
Haug, Wolfgang, 226
Hausen, Marika, 40–41
Hayter, Teresa, 138
Hedqvist, Hedvig, 261–262
Hedqvist, Staffan, 262
Heidenblad, David Larsson, 27
Height, Frank, 135–136
Hells Angels, 217, *218*
Helseth, Edvin, 92, 94, *95*
Helsport, 214
Hemesdal, mountaineering school in, 212–213
Hennessey, James, 259–260
Henschen, Helena, 178–179
Herforth, Carl, 245
Herløw, Erik, 126
Hesland, Rolf, 91
Heymann, Matthias, 248
Highmore, Ben, 10
Hiorthøy, Edvard, 80, 81–82
Hitler, Adolf, 74
Hoff, Carsten, 127–128
Hofseth, Paul, 222
Hogan, Ian, 169
Hogan, Paul, 132, 133–134, 135, 140–141
Hog Farm collective, 6
    at United Nations Conference on the
        Human Environment, 155, 169, 180
Holmberg, Per, 42
Home Research Institute (HFI), 28–30, 43
Homo economicus, 42
Horgen, Turid, 71
Høst, Elin, 63
House of Culture (Stockholm), exhibition on
    ethics of consumption, 57
Høyland, Roar, 77
"Humans and the Environment" (seminar), 40
Humanscale (Diffrient), 271
Humboldt State University, 205–206
Humphrey, Cliff, 205
Hungry Planet, The (Borgström), 81

Hunt, Jamer, 140
Husz, Orsi, 34
Hütter, Ulrich, 242
Hveding, Vidkunn, 83
Hydropower, Norwegian and Swedish, 237

IF Award, 255
IKEA, 31, 94, 270
Images in the City—Alternatives to
    Advertising, 161
India Report (Eames and Eames), 98–99
Indochina, war in. *See* Vietnam war
    and protest
Indonesia, 49
Industrial Designers in Denmark, 108, 110, 239
"Industry—Environment—Product Design"
    (seminar), 40, 47
Intentions in Architecture (Norberg-Schultz), 80
Intermediate technology, 115. *See also*
    Alternative technology
Intermediate Technology Development Group
    (ITDG), 115–116
International College (Los Angeles), New
    Natural Philosophy program, 207, 208
International Commission of Enquiry into US
    War Crimes in Indochina, 150
International Council of Graphic Design
    Associations, 222
International Council of Societies of
    Industrial Design (ICSID), 48, 49
    Ahmedabad Declaration on Industrial
        Design for Development, 136–137, 272
    "Design for Industrialization" policy
        paper, 132–133
    Design for Need (exhibition and
        symposium), 135–136
    Developing Countries/Design Information
        Group (DC/DIG), 136
    eighth congress, 140
    Interdesign '78, 137
    and Malmö conference, 222–224
    and Mvusi, 112
    Philips Award, 136
    seventh congress, 131
    and UNIDO, 131, 132, 133, 135, 136–137

and United Nations Conference on the
Human Environment, 151
and Vedel, 130, 131, 133–134, 137, 138, 139, 140
Working Group IV (design in developing
countries), 130–137, 141–142
International Design Conference in Aspen
(IDCA), 23, 259–260
Aspen 1970 conference, 260–261, 273
Aspen 1971 and 1973 conferences, 261–262
Japan in Aspen theme, 265
London conference (1978), 259, 262–263
Oslo conference (*see* Transatlantic Shop
Talk No. 2—Aspen Comes to Scandinavia)
shop talk format, 265, 267
International Union of Architects (IUA), 63
Italian Global Tools, 5
Italy: The New Domestic Landscape
(exhibition), 25
I-Thou, and ecology, 66

Jacob Jensen Design, 253, 254
Jacobs, Jane, 198
Jamison, Andrew, 182
Janse, Per, 163, 169
Jasper, James, 181
Jeffers, Robinson, 206, 207
Jensen, Johannes, 231, 234
Jensen-Klint, P. V., 231
Johansen, Arild, 265
Jonasson, Christer, 26
Jørgensen, Bertil Skov, 255
Jørgensen, Finn Arne, 2, 47
Jørgensen, Karl Erik, 249
Jøssingfjord, Esdaile's DIY cabin at, 74
Juhlin, Sven-Eric, 55
Justice, and design, 14–19
Juul, Johannes, 233–234, 236–237, 248

Kahn, Lloyd, 207
Kalleberg, Ragnvald, 78–80, 81, 82
Kalsi, Amrik, 119, 126, 131, 134–135, 137, 138
Karlholmsbruk, 51
Karl Sørlie & Sønner, 91
Karnøe, Peter, 248
Karolinska Institutet, 44

Kaufmann, Edgar, Jr., 108
Kenya Industrial Estate, 126
Kenyatta International Convention Center, 134
Kepes, György, 65–66, 81
Keshavarz, Mahmoud, 140
Kikuyu people (Kenya), 119, 122
Kilkenny Design Workshops, 133
Kirk, Andrew, 8, 155, 172
Kitchens, and "rational" consumption, *29*
Kjærholm, Poul, 100, 113
Kleiva, Per, 6, 8
Klingle, Matthew, 219
Klint, Kaare, 100, 231
Knutsen, Knut, 72
Kolding College, 245
Kompan, 241
Konrad Steinstads Snekkerverksted, 91
Konstfack College of Arts, Crafts and Design,
38, 40, 153–154, 186
Abram-Nilsson's coordination of protest
posters project, 161–163
and *ARARAT* exhibition, 171, 177–179
ceramics studio, *38*
Department of Ceramics and Glass with
Industrial Design, 163
Department of Decorative Painting,
156, 162–163
Department of Furniture and Interiors,
163
Department of Graphic Design, 163
Department of Textile Design, 163
and Mah-Jong, 179
posters for United Nations Conference
on the Human Environment, 143, *144,*
145, 156–161
Koppel, Henning, 100
Krabbem Ulrik, 242
Kranzberg, Melvin, 2
Kungsträdgården park (Stockholm), and
Battle of the Elms, 148, *149*
Kvaløy, Sigmund, 73
on *And after Us . . .* , 71
climbing with Næss, 188–189, 209
and deep ecology, 193–194, 198, 208, 225
and ecosophy D, 202

INDEX

345

Kvaløy, Sigmund (cont.)
on environmental protection or aid to
developing countries, 142
New Natural Philosophy at International
College, 207
pilgrimage to Gandhi Institute, 203

Labrague, Michelle, 86, 219
LaChapelle, Dolores, 207
la Cour, Poul, 230–232, 233, 241, 245
Landscape architecture, and environmental
issues, 74, 76–77
*Language of the Revolution—Communist
Posters from All over the World, The*
(exhibition), 162
Larsen, Bjørn A., 98
Larsson, Lena, 26, 30, 31, 34, 36, 41, 45, 54–55, 59
against durability, 27–28
on recycling and reuse, 53–54
Larsson, Mårten J., 40
Last Whole Earth Catalog, The, 217. *See also
Whole Earth Catalog, The*
Latour, Bruno, 15, 42
Le Corbusier, 63
Lego, model of Vestas wind turbine, 255, 256
Leisure, appeal to, 28
Lennon, John, 36
Leopold, Aldo, 191, 219
Lerner, Louis A., 265
Lerup, Lars, 172
Lie, Ida Kamilla, 40, 86
"Lies and Consequences: Industrial Design
and Ecology" (lecture), 222–223
Life Forum (United Nations Conference on the
Human Environment), 155–156, 163
Limits to Growth (Club of Rome), 81, 83, 195
Lindhardt, Tom, 241
Lindkvist, Lennart, 262
Lindström, Eva, 157
Local context and architecture, Esdaile's
interests in, 71–74
Lockheed, 136
Løken, Bibben, 91
"Long Now" (Eno), 2
Lorentzen, Ragnvald Bing, 271

Lövin, Björn, 26
LSD, 203
Lucsko, David, 11
Lundahl, Gunilla, 40, 42–43, 58–59, 171
Lundberg, Willy Maria, 26, 30, 34, 36, 59
Lunning Prize, 100–102
Lyche, Johan, 77

Madge, Pauline, 186
Magaziner, Daniel, 117, 125
Mah-Jong (clothing brand), 178–179
Mahogany, 87
Mäkinen, Matti K., 270
Makt åt konsumenten (Åkerman), 43–44
Maldonado, Tomás, 15, 59
Malmkvist, Siw, 26
Malmö, Sweden, international conference
in, 222–224
MAN, 246
"Manifesto on Nature, Ecology, Human Needs
and Development for the Future" (Malmö
conference), 223–224
Manzini, Ezio, 222
Marcus, Claire Cooper, 203
Mardøla River
hydroelectrical power development of, 83
protests, 194, *195*
Marshall Plan, 233
Mars II car, 39
Massey, Anne, 4, 13
Material power of things, 34
Materials
and materials research, 37
morality of, 91
Maya, Lacandón, 106
McDonough, William, 10, 220
McHale, John, 80, 81
McHarg, Ian, 198
McLaughlin, Donal, 151
Mead, Margaret, 154
"Media of Transportation by Use of Human
Forces on or by the Body" (Design
Research and Development Unit,
University of Nairobi), 119, 121
Meeker, Joseph, 206, 207

Merikallio, Mikko, 98, 271

Messell, Tania, 130

Metropolitan Museum of Art (New York), 100

Mexico, Vedels in, 102, 105–108

Michl, Jan, 249

Micklethwaite, Paul, 4, 13

Midtbust, Alf, 87–88

Mies van der Rohe, Ludwig, 273

Miles, Elza, 117

Miljön och miljonerna: Design som tjänst eller förtjänst? (Papanek), 42–43

Minimum impact camping, 212

Mobilia (magazine), 267

Moderna Museet (Stockholm), 26, 146, 162

   ARARAT exhibition (1976), 173–177

   project space, Filialen, 167

"Modesty and the Conquest of Mountains" (Næss), 207

Moen, Harry, 91

Møller-Jensen, Viggo, 103

Mollerup, Per, 267

Monark Petit bicycles, 151, *152*

Morgan, Derek, 113, 114

Mörk, Lennart, 171

Morris, William, 4–5, 91, 219

"Mother Earth: Her Whales" (Snyder), 153

Mountain (magazine), 189

Mountain Spirit (Tobias), 207

Mount Baldy (California), 209

Muguga Green (Nairobi), 114

Mugumbya, Gamaliel, 126

Muir, John, 207

Munters, Carl, 175

Murakami, Haruki, 61

Museum of Modern Art (MoMA, New York), 25

Mvusi, Selby, 114

  design expertise as a decolonial project, 112–113

  foundation course on "man/environ interaction," 113

  and ICSID, 132, 134

on "industrial," 117

  and Shapira, 117–118, 124–125, 134

  Vedel and, 114, 124–125, 139

Myklebust, Jacob, 85

Mysen Møbelindustri, 91

Nadkarni, Sudhakar, 136

Næss, Arne, 22, 71, 83, 91, *190*

  and climbing, 187–191

  on colonialism and social justice, 142

  and deep design, 219–226

  and deep ecology in the American West, 202–208

  ecosophy, 76, 185, 191, 193–198

  ecosophy D (ecosophy of design), 198–202, 226–228

  gear for climbing, 209–219

  Tvergastein, 185, 187, *188*

Næss, Siri, 193, 199

Narotzky, Viviana, 11–12

NASA, 242, 246

Nash, Grete, 224

National College of Applied Art and Craft (Copenhagen), 6, 66, 67, 186, 194

  and Oslo School of Architecture, 71

  Resource Seminar on environmental issues (1973), 77

National Consumer Council (Sweden), 28, 43

National Council of Swedish Youth, 153

National Defense Research Institute, 44

National Federation of Furniture Manufacturers, 87, 90

National Museum of Science and Technology, 37–38

Native American hunting practices, 205–206

Nature management and preservation, intellectual landscape of, 76

Negative complexity, 208

Nehru, Jawaharlal, 98

Nelson, George, 262, 263, 267

Neo-Malthusian discourse, 81, 83

New Alchemy Institute, 172–173

  and *ARARAT*, 172

New Natural Philosophy (International College, Los Angeles), 207, 208
News from Nowhere (Morris), 4–5
Newsweek (magazine), 143, 145
Nicaragua, Vedels in, 105
Nicholson, Simon, 203
Nielsen, Jens, 270
Nilsson, Sten Åke, 49
Nimpuno, Krisno, 49
Nixon, Rob, 15
Nomadic Furniture (Papanek and Hennessey), 260
Norberg-Schulz, Christian, 63, 72, 78, 80, 194
Nordenström, Hans, 171
Nordic design, 62
Nordic Noir, 230
Nordtank, 248, 253
Norling, Dag, 71
Norrøna, 213, 214
Norsk/Norwegian Industrial Design (1963), 267
North Face, The (clothing company), 217, 218, 219
Northwestern Jutland Institute for Renewable Energy (NIVA), 245–246
Norway
    discovery of offshore oil, 16–17
    and European Community, 225
    foundations of ecological design in, 61–62
    Ministry of Environmental Protection, 2
    Ministry of Petroleum and Energy, 271
Norwegian Agency for Development Cooperation (NORAD), 98, 113, 134
Norwegian Alpine Club, 187
Norwegian America Line, 270–271
Norwegian College of Agriculture, 74, 76, 77, 84
Norwegian Design Centre, 267
Norwegian Export Council, 267
Norwegian Foundation for Design and Architecture, 98
Norwegian Home Craft Association, 90
Norwegian Institute of Technology, 73–74
    alpine club, 190–191, 193
    River and Harbor Laboratory, 271
Norwegian Pollution Control Authority, 74

Norwegian Society for the Conservation of Nature, 67, 84
Norwegian Society of Arts and Crafts and Industrial Design, 263
Norwegian State Railways (NSB), 265
Norwegian wood, as metaphor for ecological design, 61, 63, 96
Nøstvik, Karl Henrik, 114–115, 134
Now House, The (exhibition), 218
Noyes, Eliot, 261
NTK windmill, 253, 255
Nuclear power, 239
Nuts. *See* Clean climbing technologies
Nybroe, Claus, 245, 252
Nye, David E., 229
Nye Bonytt (magazine), 226
Nygren, Veronica, 178–179

Objects, in durability and disposability debate, 36–37
Ocean liners, design for, 270–271
Odhnoff, Jan, 42, 57
Odum, Eugene P., 76
Office for Measurement and Product Testing (Germany), 13
Offshore North Sea (ONS) meeting, 17
Oil crisis, 1970s, 237–240
Oil industry, at Oslo meeting of IDCA, 270, 271
Oil or Fish? (Roalkvam), 8, 17, *18*
Økologi for ingeniører og arkitekter (Dahl), 76
Oldenziel, Ruth, 246
"Only One Earth," 151
Operating Manual for Spaceship Earth (Fuller), 65, 79–80
Opsvik, Peter, 98
Öqvist, Jan, 171
Organization for European Economic Co-operation (OEEC), 233
Organization for Information on Nuclear Power (OOA), 239
Organization for Renewable Energy (OVE), 239
Oropallo, Gabriele, 182
Orr, David, 19, 57

Oslo Museum of Decorative Arts, 267
Oslo School of Architecture, 48, 66, 67, 94, 186, 194
  and ecology, 76
  and National College of Applied Art and Craft, 71
Östberg, Kjell, 147
Østbye, Eivind, 76
Østerhaug, Hans, 94
Östling, Johan, 45
Our Common Future (Brundtland Commission), 11, 16, 255
Outlaw Builders, 217
Outpost, Esdaile's conception of an, 73
Oval Intention geodesic tent, 218

Paepcke, Elizabeth, 263
Paepcke, Walter, 260
Palme, Olof, 8, 150
Palmstierna, Hans, *48*, 55, 67
  And after Us . . . , 47–48, 72
  Besinning, 45, 54
  Framtiden kräver: Energi, arbete, miljö, *46*, 47, 57
  "Industry—Environment—Product Design" (lecture at seminar), 47
  Plundring, svält, förgiftning, 45, 48–49
  and Swedish environmentalism, 44–45
  and United Nations Conference on the Human Environment, 150
Palmstierna, Lena, 57
Papanek, Victor, 6, *48*, 142, 201, 226
  and biomimical processes and learning from nature, 40–41, 123
  Design for the Real World, 222
  on geopolitics, 138–139
  and Hennessey, 260–261
  and ICSID, 133, 135, 136, 137
  at IDCA (1971), 261
  at "Industry—Environment—Product Design" seminar, 47, *48*
  "Lies and Consequences: Industrial Design and Ecology" (lecture), 222–223
  Nomadic Furniture, 260
  relationship to Scandinavia, 42

  on students from developing countries, 126
  at Suomenlinna seminar (1968), 55
  and wastefulness of design practice, 43
Participatory design, 86
Patagonia (clothing company), 209, 219
Paulsen, Marit, 56, 57
p'Bitek, Okot, 125
Peccei, Aurelio, 195
"People and the Environment II," 6
People's Architecture, 205, 260
People's Atelier, 162
People's Forum (United Nations Conference on the Human Environment), 154–155, 156, 166
  and PowWow, 169
People's Park (Berkeley), 203, *204*, 260
Periäinen, Tapio, 223
"Period of the Great Contaminations, The" (Pesce), 25
Perrot, Roy, 151
Pesce, Gaetano, 25
Petersen, Mogens Amdi, 240–242
Pido, J. P. Odoch, 117, 118
Pine, 88, 91–95
Pitons, 209. *See also* Clean climbing technologies
Plastics, 55–56
  recycling, 55, 56
Plundring, svält, förgiftning (Palmstierna), 45, 48–49
Point Foundation, 155
"Pollutions—Nature—Human" (conference), 77
Polystyrene (thermoplastic), 55
Population Bomb, The (Ehrlich), 45
Portola Institute, and *ARARAT*, 172
Posters, protest, 143, *144*, 145, 156–163
Poul Kjærgaard & Partners, 113
PowWow, 153, 163, 165–169
  and *ARARAT*, 170
Price elasticity, 31
Primitivism, 112–113
Project One (commune), 217

Protest and protest artifacts, 181
  at *ARARAT* (*see ARARAT*)
  For a Technology in the Service of the People!
    (exhibition), 146, 166–167, 169, 170, 171–172,
    180, 181–182
  graphic language of, 156–163
  Mardøla River, 194, *195*
  People's Park (Berkeley), 203
  posters, 143, *144*, 145, 156–163
Provo anarchist group, 151
PVC (plastic), 55, 56

Quality, of consumer products, 30, 31

Rabén & Sjögren (Cooperative Union), 45
Radical Technology (Harper and Boyle), 170
Rag rug technique, demonstrated at *ARARAT*
  exhibition, 178
Rambøll, Børge J., 234
Randers, Jørgen, 83
Rastad & Relling, 91
  Futurum line, 92
Ravneskar (tent), 213
Reagan, Ronald, 203
Recycling and reuse, 11–12, 37, 49–51, 58, 59
  Larsson on, 53–54
  of plastics, 55
  Vi issue on, 51–53
Recycling: Från skräp till nytta (Berg and
  Nimpuno), 49, *51*
Recycling House (*ARARAT* exhibition), 173, 174
Red Dot Award, 255
Redström, Johan, 28
Relling, Adolf, 91
Remlov, Arne, 90–91
Reuse. *See* Recycling and reuse
Richard, Cliff, 26
Riisager, Christian, 248
Risø National Laboratory, 236, 240, 242
Roalkvam, Terje, 6, 17
Roberts, Jack, 267
Rockefeller Foundation, 112, 117, 202
Røddinge College, 239
Rognlein, Dag, 63
Rolling Stone (magazine), 207

Rolwaling Valley (Nepal), 142, 193–194
Romell, Dag, 40
Rosewood, 87
Royal Danish Academy of Fine Arts, 126
Royal Institute of Technology,
  students from, 174
Royal Waterfall Board, 40
Ruskin, John, 4
Ryan, Chris, 169

Saab 96, electrified, *39*
Sadler, Simon, 3, 8, 40
Sætra, Hartvig, 142
Safdie, Moshe, 263, 273
Sagafjord (ocean liner), 270
SAN (thermoplastic), 55
Santa Barbara, oil spill, 205
Santa Cruz Mountains, 209
Scandinavia, 1
  power grid, 237
Scandinavian design, 1–2, 62
  and change, 3–6
Scandinavian Design Council, 222
Scandinavian Design Students' Organization
  (SDO), 6, 40, 147
Scandinavian Modern Design: 1880–1980
  (exhibition), 265
Schofield, Lorna, 122–123
School of Art and Design (Helsinki), 37
School of Arts and Crafts (Copenhagen), 6, 100
School of Design (California Institute of the
  Arts), 261
School of Design and Crafts (Gothenburg), 171
Schumacher, E. F., 115, 198, 226
Science (magazine), 154
Scott, Felicity, 169
SEAS, 233, 234
Sedrez, Lise, 97
Self-realization, 201–202, 208
Selmer, Wenche, 186
Semb-Johansson, Arne, 74, 76
"Seminar on Tourism and Vocational
  Training" (Nairobi), 123
Sergels torg (Stockholm), 164
Sessions, George, 206–207, 209, 212

"Shallow and the Deep Ecology Movement, The" (Næss lecture), 196–198
Shapira, Nathan, 117–118, 124–125, 130–132, 134
Shepard, Paul, 207
Shopping, psychology of, 30
Sierra Club, 206
Sierra College, 206
Sierra Designs, 219
Silent Spring (Carson), 17, 35
Silkscreen, and protest posters, 156
Simon, Herbert, 201
Simonnæs, Bjørn, 62, 82–87
Sjödahl, Anna, 161
Sjöholm, Hans, 55
Skandinavisk Aero Industri A/S, 233
Skandinavisk Høufjellsutstyr, 213
Skaugen, Snorre, 71
"Slit och släng" (song), 26
Small Is Beautiful (Schumacher), 115–116, 198, 226
Snyder, Gary, 153, 205, 207, 223
Social Democratic Party (Sweden), 44
Solar panels, on roof of White House, 237
Soleri, Paolo, 154, 172, 173, 207–209, 218
Solheim, Elsa, 91
Solheim, Nordahl, 91
Somjee, Sultan, 126, 131, 142
Song of Lawino (p'Bitek), 125
Sørlie, Gunnar, 90–91
Spaceship, earth as, 82, 200–201
Spaceship Earth (Ward), 79
Specialization, 79–80
and "comprehensive thinking," 80–81
Stange Bruk, 94
Stetind (mountain), 191–193
Stetind in Fog (painting), *192*
Stiesdal, Henrik, 245, 249, 251
Stolpe, Pär, 167, 175
Stone, Peter, 153, 182–183
Støren, Knut, 191
Stott, Tim, 241
Strasser, Susan, 11
Straw Bale House (*ARARAT* exhibition), 173
Street Farmers, 172
Street Farm House, 172

Strömdahl, Jan, 180
Strong, Maurice, 145, 151
Studio Potter, The (magazine), 224–225
"Study of the Ergonomics of the Hand" (Ergonomi Design), 271–272
Sundby, Ragnhild, 67
Sun Wing (*ARARAT* exhibition), 173–174, 179
Suomenlinna seminar (1968), 55
Sustainability and sustainable development, 27
and environmental histories of design, 2
Svartdal, Gunleik, 91
Svedberg, Eva Karin, 164
Svennilson, Ingvar, 30–31
Svensson, Inez, 269–270
Sveriges Television, 30
Sweden
Environmental Protection Agency, 1–2, 26, 44, 145, 150
proposal for United Nations Conference on the Human Environment, 145
Royal Waterfall Board, 40
throwawayism debate, 20, 26–27 (*see also* Throwawayism debate)
Swedish Council for Building Research, 171
Swedish Society of Crafts and Design, 27, 30, 31, 40, 43
"Consumption—at what cost?" (1968 annual conference theme), 41–42
debate on environmental cosmetics, 55–56
Swedish UN Association, 153
Synergetics, 218
Systems Design (Nairobi), 119
Systemtre A/L, 92

Tabibian, Jivan, 262
Tarras-Wahlberg, Ulla, 263, 265
Teak, 87
Teknorama, 37
Thiberg, Sven, 27, 57
Thompson, Jane, 263
Thoreau, Henry David, 219
Thorsen, Odd, 265
Thrift, and throwawayism, 33

Throwawayism debate, 20, 26–27, 35
   and consumer durables, 27–34
   environmental ramifications, 35–41
   Palmstierna on, 45, 47
   and planned obsolescence, 28
   in reuse issue of *Vi*, 53
Thy Camp, 127–128
Thyholm, 127–130
Time (magazine), 151
Ting och tycken (Lundberg), 59
Tirich Mir (mountain in Pakistan), 187, 214
Titania mines, 74
Tobias, Michael, 207, 208
Tollin, Claes, 163
Tompkins, Doug, 217, 219
Tools for Progress (ITDG), 116
Too Many (Borgström), 81
Torsson, Kristina, 178–179
Traganou, Jilly, 182
Tramway Society, 164
Transatlantic Shop Talk—Aspen Comes to London, 262–263
Transatlantic Shop Talk No. 2—Aspen Comes to Scandinavia, 259, 260, 262–263, 272–273
   Butenschøn's impressions of, 272–273
   program, 265–268
   Scandinavian projects presented, 269–272, 273
Trauerman, Joe K., 102
Trolin, Eva, 143, 145, 157, 162
Trollveggen jacket, 214
Trysil cabin, 94
Trysil Municipal Forest District, 94
Tseringma/Gauri Shankar (mountain in Nepal), 188–189
Tvergastein (Næss's mountain cabin), 185, 187, *188*, 199, 222
Tvind School Cooperative, 240–241
   Traveling College, 241–242
Tvind windmill, 240–246, 248
Twemlow, Alice, 261
Tyrbo furniture series, 94, *95*

Undercurrents (magazine), 169, 172
United Kingdom, Utility Scheme, 12–13

United Nations, Economic and Social Council, 150
United Nations Association of Norway, 67
United Nations Conference on Human Settlements, 218
United Nations Conference on the Human Environment, 6, 21, 26, 44, 49, 59, 205, 223, 260. *See also* Design and the United Nations Conference on the Human Environment
   "an American show," 153
   and *ARARAT*, 170
   criticisms and contested legacy, 145, 152, 153, 181
   Declaration on the Human Environment, 145
   Distinguished Lecture Series, 195
   Monark Petit bicycles at, 151, *152*
   "Only One Earth" slogan, 151
   and recycling and reuse, 51
United Nations Environment Programme (UNEP), 145
   and ICSID, 134–135
   and IPCC, 145
   Rio Earth Summit (1992), 145
United Nations Industrial Development Organization (UNIDO), 131, 132, 133, 135, 136–137, 142
United States, Energy Research and Development Administration (ERDA), 238, 247
Universitas Project (Museum of Modern Art), 65
University of California, Berkeley
   and *ARARAT*, 172
   College of Environmental Design, 203
   and Næss, 202–205
University of California, Davis, 205
University of California, Santa Cruz, 206, 207
University of Nairobi, 99, 112. *See also* Design Research and Development Unit
   Department of Industrial Design, 114–118
   design education at, 112
   Faculty of Architecture, Design and Development building, 113

and Mvusi, 112
Vedel's report to Danish Ministry of Foreign
Affairs concerning, 113–114
University of Oslo
course in ecology, 76
Department of Zoology, 193
University of the Pacific, 206
Upcycling, 49, 178
Ussing, Susanne, 127–128
U.S. Windpower, 247
Utility Scheme (UK), 12–13

Valdemar, Axel, 171
Valio, 270
Van der Ryn, Sim, 172, 203, 217, 237, 260
Vara och undvara (exhibition), 57–59
Vår Gård, 41
Vedel, Ane, 101–102, 104, 105, 108, 114, 128
Vedel, Kristian, 21, 99, *101, 110, 116,* 140–142, 245
and appropriate technology in Kenya,
116–117, 139
causes behind departure from
Nairobi, 123–126
in Central America and Mexico, 103–108,
110–111, 139
and Department of Industrial Design at
University of Nairobi, 114–118
and Design Research and Development
Unit, 118–123, 139
early career, 100–102
in Humlebæk, 110
and International Council of Societies of
Industrial Design, 130, 131, 133–134, 137,
138, 139, 140
Lunning Prize, 100–102
media interest in, 111–112, 127
and Mugumbua (student), 126
and Mvusi, 124–125
plan for a new department at University of
Nairobi, 114–115
reflections on time in Nairobi, 125
report to Danish Ministry of Foreign
Affairs, 113–114
and Shapira, 124–125
sheep farm on Thyholm, 127–130, 139

and Somjee (student), 126
in Venezuela, 103–104
Venezuela, Vedels in, 103–104
Veng, Jens, 251
Vestas, 248
Lego model of wind turbine, 255, *256*
V-15, 249
Vesterlid, Are, 94
Vi (magazine), 51
Viénot, Henri, 131, 132
Vietnam war and protest, 148, 150, 154,
155–156, 179
Vik, Rolf, 67, 72
Vinding, Poul, 231, 234
Vindkraft, Dana, 245
Vinther, Søren, 251
Vistafjord (ocean liner), 270
Voll, Jon, 191
von Platen, Baltzar, 175
von Zweigbergk, Eva, 31, 33–34, 35–36
Vorsprung durch Design, 252

Wahlforss, Henrik, 55
Wallender, Jan, 30
Wann, David, 220–222
Ward, Barbara, 79, 166
Washing machine, Larsson on, 28
Waste, and design, 8–14
Water, Roger, 25
Weaving, in Central America and Mexico,
105, 106, *107*
Wegener, Hans J., 100
Westh, Helge Claudi, 232
Westinghouse, 246
"White Sea" (Konstfack main hall), 154
Whole Earth Catalog, The, 6, 8, 65, 205, 217
Whole Earth Festival (UC Davis), 205
Whole systems thinking, 20, 40, 41, 65, 80
Wind farms, in California, 249–250
Windmill design, 255, 257
aerodynamic blades, 231–232
assembled in California, 249–252
and asynchronous AC generator, 232, 234
at experimental school and
colleges, 242, 245

Windmill design (cont.)
  F.L.S. Aeromotor, 232–233
  Gedser Experimental Mill, 230, 233–236,
    239, 247, 248
  la Cour's designs, 230–231
  Master Smith Mill, 245
  stamp series in homage to, *254, 255*
  Tvind mill, 240–246, 248
  and variable wind speeds, 231
  windmills as design objects, 253
Windmills and the windmill industry, Danish,
    229, 255, 257
  assembled in California, 249–252
  bottom-up initiatives (1970s), 247–248
  and countercultural ecodesign, 240–246
  Danish manufacturers (1980s), 250–251
  early history, 230–233, 255
  and energy crises of the 1970s, 237–240
  and environmental concerns, 239–240
  top-down, large-scale projects, 246–247
  after World War II, 233–236
Winograd, Terry, 212
Workers' Education Association, 154
World Design Science Decade 1965–75
    (Fuller), 80
World Future Studies Federation, 195
Wright, Frank Lloyd, 73

Yosemite Valley, 202
  Camp 4, 209, 212, 218
  climbing and clean climbing in, 209–
    212, 217, 227
  dirtbag lifestyle, 217–218
Young Friends of the Earth Norway, 16, 17
Yran, Knut, 133, 136, 139–140

Zapffe, Peter Wessel, 187
Zeuthen, K. G., 232–233
Zome Primer (Baer), 173
Zomeworks, 172
Zond, 249